THE
GREAT
OUTDOORS
CATALOG

THE GREAT OUTDOORS CATALOG

KENN and **PAT OBERRECHT**

WINCHESTER PRESS

Library of Congress Cataloging in Publication Data
Main entry under title:
The Great outdoors catalog.
1. Camping—Outfits, supplies, etc.—Catalogs.
2. Outdoor recreation—Equipment and supplies—Catalogs.
I. Oberrecht, Kenn. II. Oberrecht, Pat.
GV191.76.G73   688.7'6'5   77-22842
ISBN 0–87691–241–2
ISBN 0–87691–240–4 pbk.

Published by Winchester Press
205 East 42nd Street
New York, N.Y. 10017

WINCHESTER is a Trademark of Olin Corporation used by Winchester Press, Inc.
under authority and control of the Trademark Proprietor.

Printed in the United States of America

Dedication

Since this book is the product of a loving partnership, we wish to dedicate it to four other partnerships very near and dear to us: to Charlie and Barb, Gary and Kathy, Phil and Jan, Sam and Nancy—our love and friendship.

CONTENTS

Introduction

In order for this book to be published with the most up-to-date information available, we had to work against a tight deadline, and we emphasized this point when we sent letters to more than 2,200 manufacturers and suppliers of outdoor products. If a company or product line is not included in this book it could be for one or several reasons. First, since our space was limited, we had to select some products to the exclusion of others. This exclusion in no way reflects on the quality of a product, although that may have been one reason for disqualifying a product or company. If we felt a product did not fit within our editorial framework, we excluded it. If a company failed to send sufficient materials and illustrations, we either scratched it off our list or sent a follow-up letter requesting more information or illustrations, depending on how important we considered the product line to be.

Some companies did not respond at all. A few responded unfavorably. Some missed the deadline, and others just didn't do much to help get their products into our book.

During the first four weeks after we sent out our initial inquiries, the catalogs, brochures, letters, and illustrations poured in at a rate of more than 100 a week. We kept abreast of this material daily by reviewing literature, filing, cross-referencing, sending follow-up letters, making phone calls, and sighing a lot.

Six weeks into the project we had compiled more than enough material and we began roughing out the first draft. Within four months we had several rooms filled with files of catalogs and illustrations, but we also had this book finished and on its way to the publisher.

How This Book Can Save You Time and Money

If you wanted to compile an extensive list of manufacturers and suppliers of outdoor products, you could buy all the outdoor magazines you could lay your hands on and go through them methodically, reading all the ads and jotting down addresses. The cost of the magazines alone would be far greater than the price of this book. Yet, your list would only be a partial one.

You could then head for your local bookstore to buy all the various books that contain indexes of manufacturers and suppliers, any one of which might cost you as much or more than this book. Then you could try to get addresses from manufacturing associations, but you would probably fail here, since this information is tough to get unless you can convince the associations that releasing the addresses will benefit their members.

Already, you would have spent a tidy sum just to get the addresses. You still have the catalogs to order. Some of them are free; others cost anywhere from 25¢ to $10. Some will prove extremely valuable, while others will be totally useless for your purposes. And don't forget the postage, stationery, and envelopes. All of this will cost you, and for some literature you will have to send a self-addressed and stamped envelope.

We've already done most of this for you by compiling this book. And we have culled out those companies that would be of no interest or would be unable to serve you. Sure, you still have to send for your own catalogs and brochures, but you won't have to send for as many, and when you do write for literature you will know that it is material that will be of value to you. Furthermore, all the addresses are listed for you in alphabetical order in our "Index of Companies" at the back of the book.

In this book, though, we give you more than names and addresses. We tell you a bit about the companies and their product lines. Best of all, we describe representative products offered by these companies, which should help you determine whether or not you need to send for their literature.

How to Use This Book

The simplest way to use this book is to browse through it at your leisure and enjoy it. When you find a product that interests you, mark it. Then, if you want to know more about any item or if you want a copy of the company's latest catalog, use our handy listing to find the mailing address and to learn whether or not there is a charge for the material you're interested in.

The book is divided into chapters by category. In each chapter, companies are listed in alphabetical order. The most specialized companies will appear only in their respective chapters and in the listing, while more diversified companies will show up throughout the book. In the case of the latter, we have directed you to the other chapters where a given company's products can be found. This cross-referencing is located in the introductory material about the company's product line.

We have also tried to tell you a bit about the companies whenever possible, but we have done this only once for each company to avoid needless repetition. Such background material will be found in the first chapter where the company is listed. So you might have to back track in a few instances to find the background material.

About the Products and Companies

We are outdoor folks. We hunt, fish, canoe, boat, camp, backpack, and travel extensively. We feel that this kind of experience has helped us to pick the kind of products you want to read about. While we have used many of the products and have dealt with many of the companies represented in this book, we haven't tried them all. Thus, the material in this book is not meant as an endorsement of any product or company. We make no guarantees on any products, companies, or services. We have mentioned some of the favorable experiences we have had with particular products and companies, but, again, we cannot guarantee that you will feel the same way about them. After all, people's tastes and judgments vary greatly.

The product descriptions are largely the words of the manufacturers or suppliers. Some are transcribed nearly word for word from catalogs, brochures, news releases, and specification sheets. We have edited them for clarity and conciseness, and we have tried to omit most of the superlatives that might be objectionable, while leaving intact those that shouldn't bother anybody. For example, if a manufacturer claimed his backpack to be the best in the world, we could not very well use that statement without offending other manufacturers of fine backpacks. On the other hand, if a manufacturer said that his super new lure has a vibrating, darting, wiggling action that drives bass wild, we included it as part of the description. We doubt that anybody can object to such statements.

On Prices

There was a time when prices changed very little from year to year, and many catalogs stayed virtually the same for several years at a time. It wasn't too long ago that practically all name-brand fishing lures were in the same price range and sold for that price everywhere. And gas was 23¢ a gallon; coffee was 89¢ a pound . . .

Well, all that has changed. Not only are prices changing from year to year, but from month to month. Consequently, it is impossible to give you guaranteed, firm, current prices. Few manufacturers' catalogs carry such guarantees. And many companies have ceased putting prices in their catalogs altogether. Instead, they supply a supplementary price sheet that they can update as often as needed.

So the prices in this book are *for reference purposes only*. They are included for your convenience and to give you an idea of what you might expect to pay. But we urge you to check current prices at a nearby dealer, or to write for catalogs if you will be ordering by mail.

There was a time also when the only discount prices were to be found in discount catalogs. Local dealers and department stores charged the suggested retail prices. This is still the case for some products, but many product lines are now sold through the discount department stores as well as the discount mail-order companies, and in such great volume that the discounted price has become the rule rather than the exception. And since the Federal Trade Commission frowns upon suggested list prices that do not reflect the actual selling prices, some companies no longer suggest retail prices. For this reason, you will find some products described in our book with no prices. We suggest that you shop around to find the best price, through a local dealer, discount store, or one of the mail-order companies in this book.

We cannot guarantee to answer letters from readers, but we would like to hear from you if you have been extremely pleased or dismally disappointed with any of the products and companies in this book. And if you have suggestions on how the book can be improved, or if you know of products and companies that ought to be considered for possible inclusion, let us know. We promise to read all letters, and we will certainly put your praises, complaints, and suggestions to use in any future edition of *The Great Outdoors Catalog*.

Please address your letters to:
Kenn & Pat Oberrecht
THE GREAT OUTDOORS CATALOG
P.O. Box 1253
Coos Bay, Oregon 97420

CHAPTER ONE

SHOPPING FOR OUTDOOR PRODUCTS

How to Shop Wisely

Whether you are shopping by mail or at a local shopping center, it pays to do so systematically, purposefully, and with forethought. Impulse buying can be extremely costly and sometimes fruitless.

The best way to be a prepared shopper is to keep lists of your needs. That may sound terribly elementary—especially to you seasoned shoppers—but there are really few outdoors people who could provide you with a shopping list at any given time, because they just don't take the time to note supplies that are running low until it comes time to buy. That is usually during the beginning of the season when local demand runs high and supply runs low.

When we don't keep track of needs we are forced to buy sporadically and, consequently, we shop too often, thus wasting time and money. And we're unable to take advantage of off-season and end-of-season bargains because we've blown the budget on emergency needs.

We keep a notebook with lists of our needs. As fly-tying materials, decoy paints, wads, primers, freeze-dried foods, outboard motor oil, cleaning solvents, lubricants, film, and sundry items begin to run low, we list them. Then every few months we send off orders to replenish our stocks. Meanwhile, if we learn of a local sale on one or several of our listed items, we can take advantage of that, too.

We also time our buying to keep from coming up short during any season. We'll order worm hooks and plastic worms during our winter steelhead season, and decoy rope and anchors in the spring.

By keeping ahead of our needs we are able to shop with less frequency and to buy in greater quantity. This not only saves time, but it saves money in several ways. First, quantity buying is almost always cheaper. You get much more for your money if you buy bulk spools of monofilament line than if you buy enough to fill a reel. And this holds for shotshell wads, film, hooks, and countless other supplies.

Furthermore, quantity buying enables you to deal with companies that won't otherwise accept your orders—manufacturers and distributors that set a minimum dollar value on each order and, sometimes, a minimum quantity on particular items. These are companies that normally sell only to dealers, not necessarily because they don't like to sell directly to consumers, but because it isn't economical for them. They deal in volume, and they set the minimums so they can continue to do business that way. If you can meet the minimums, you can take advantage of some dandy prices.

We will caution you here to read carefully the catalogs of manufacturers, distributors, and importers to determine these minimum order restrictions. As far as we're concerned, a $50 minimum order is not nearly as restrictive as it used to be, especially if you shop as we have suggested. Some minimum quantities, however, can be quite troublesome. While a minimum allowable quantity of a dozen lures of one size and color, or 100 hooks of the same size and style, might not pose any problem for the moderately serious fisherman, a minimum of a dozen fillet knives or fishing hats might.

This is one case when shopping with friends can help immensely. Many companies will offer dealer's prices to clubs. So you can either get together with the members of your local rod and gun club, or you can get your hunting and fishing buddies together to form a club. It won't be long before you will be buying in bulk quantities and case lots and finding that your dollar will go twice as far.

Some mail-order companies offer breaks in shipping costs for quantity purchases and even ship orders over a certain value with no charge for shipping.

How to Shop by Mail

Shopping by mail does not necessarily mean buying by mail. After all, when we go shopping from store to store, we don't always walk in with the intention of buying something. We often go to look, to investigate, to compare prices and quality, to ask questions, to find out what is available from a particular store and what is not. There are times, however, when we go out in pursuit of some particular piece of merchandise, and it certainly helps to know where to find it. If we have done some shopping around beforehand, we can save time and trouble by going to the right store first time out.

There are times when we have no idea where to find locally some product we have seen advertised nationally. So we turn to the Yellow Pages of the phone directory and start calling dealers. If we find several dealers handling the same product, we check for prices and we ask questions about the product. If it is a major item, perhaps we will be concerned about guarantees, service, repairs, and replacement parts.

All of this falls under the heading of shopping, and it is no different if conducted by mail, except that instead of touching and physically examining an item, we must rely upon written descriptions and specifications, photographs, drawings, and diagrams.

Sometimes catalog descriptions are far more informative than what a shop owner can tell us. And, often, a dealer will refer us to the manufacturer's literature to answer our questions about materials, specifications, and the like. While we are always pleased to find a dealer who is an expert on the products he sells, in this day of mass merchandising and giant discount department stores, few sales clerks know any more about their products than which shelf it can be found on.

So even when we plan to buy from a local source, we attempt to learn as much as we can about a product or line of products before we buy, and more often than not this means writing to the manufacturer for his descriptive material. In the case of a major item, such as a boat or recreational vehicle, usually the only way to find the nearest dealer is to write to the manufacturer.

In the pages of this book you will find not only the mail-order suppliers of outdoor products, but manufacturers and distributors as well, which may or may not sell by direct mail. There are several reasons for including the manufacturers. One is that they are able to provide a great wealth of technical information, much of which we have included in our product descriptions. Additionally, they can answer questions that might baffle a local dealer or sales clerk. They can steer potential buyers to nearby outlets, and if there is no dealer within a reasonable distance, the sensible manufacturer is going to agree to sell his product directly to you. Those companies that indicated that they were not interested in reader inquiries have been excluded from this book.

We don't mean to imply that we do all our shopping for outdoor products by mail. Certainly, we take advantage of local sales and specials. We buy at sports shops, and we frequent local marinas, RV dealers, and camping-supply outlets. But, on the whole, we admit to a strong preference for mail-order purchasing, and we often shop by mail before buying locally.

A major reason for our preference for mail-order sources is reliability. We can depend upon the prominent mail-order firms to keep a fairly consistent stock. Their catalogs are readily at hand, on file for whenever we need them. We can shop in the comfort of our home and can plan our purchases intelligently and at our leisure. There are no crowds, no parking problems or traffic congestion to put up with, and we can generally depend on finding what we're after.

There is no overt pressure to buy a particular item. If we have doubts or questions, we can send letters to manufacturers for descriptive literature that allows us to compare advantages of various makes and models.

It's still a joy to go to a fly shop where the proprietor is a virtual storehouse of information on his products and on the local fishing, or the gun shop where the dealer seems to know all there is to know about his firearms, both new and used. And we sincerely hope such shops are going to be with us forever, though we have noticed (and lamented) their decline in recent years. So until there is a resurgence of the personal little sport shop staffed by experts, or until the big discount department stores start hiring people who know that there are, indeed, differences between DT6F and H-4831, or between a fast taper and a modified choke, or brush buttons and brush pants, we'll continue to shop by mail for most of our needs.

Ordering Catalogs and Descriptive Literature

There is no magic formula for ordering catalogs and literature from the companies listed in this book. Once you have determined which companies you wish to write, simply turn to the back of the book where you will find names and addresses in alphabetical order.

We have also indicated whether or not there is a charge for the literature. The price of the material is found in parentheses after the zip code. If (SASE) appears after the zip, send a self-addressed, stamped envelope—large, business size—along with your request.

If no price appears, you can assume that the literature is free. We checked all catalogs and brochures for prices and asked each company to let us know if they charged for their materials. If we found no prices on their catalogs or in their correspondence, we have to assume that there was no charge. You may find that some companies have since decided to charge for their catalogs or that some catalog prices have increased. We're sorry for that, but we have no control over such changes.

For catalogs and brochures with a fee of less than $1 you can simply tape coins to your letter, although there is some risk in this practice. For any literature costing a dollar or more, we suggest that you send a personal check. We send checks for all catalogs, regardless of price.

When you write for free catalogs, here's a tip that won't cost you much and will really help to speed things up. To the top of your letter attach with a paper clip one or two first class postage stamps and a gummed mailing label with your name and address on it. Smaller companies will use the stamps and the mailing label and will appreciate your consideration. Larger companies might prefer to use their own mailing label and postage machines. But in either case, the stamps and label will make your letter a real attention-getter, and you will usually get quick service.

It also helps to send a SASE when you are writing to a company with specific questions about their products. There's something about an uncancelled stamp affixed to an addressed envelope that sort of nags the recipient to respond. It's a trick that works, and often the company will return your SASE to you unused when they reply.

Buying by Mail

Many mail-order companies are set up for credit card orders and will allow you to buy with your BankAmericard, Master Charge, or other major credit card. Some companies have restrictions on the amount that can be paid by personal check. Others will accept personal checks in any amount, but will not ship your order until the check has been cleared by your bank, which will normally delay shipment of your order by as much as ten days.

We recommend that you use one of the credit cards that the company honors or pay by certified personal check, cashier's check, or personal money order. These methods of payment will eliminate needless delays. Many banks now offer special accounts to their customers that include a number of benefits, such as no charge on money orders and cashier's checks. If you do much buying by mail, such an account could save you money. So check with your bank.

While hundreds of products in this book can be ordered and delivered by mail, some cannot or should not be. Some can be ordered by mail but must be shipped by private carrier. Federal law prohibits the mail-order sale of some firearms, ammunition, and most components. These restrictions and the exceptions are summarized in the introduction to Chapter 4.

Many companies now ship their products via United Parcel Service. UPS is generally cheaper and almost always faster than parcel post. And we have found that UPS handles parcels much more carefully than the U.S. Postal Service does. We have shipped and received hundreds of packages over the years, both by UPS and parcel post. Dozens of them that went by parcel post have been damaged in transit, while we have never received a damaged package from UPS.

A note of caution, though: UPS cannot deliver to a post office box. So be sure to give your residence address when ordering anything that is to be shipped by United Parcel Service. And don't order UPS shipment if you are going to be away from your home for an extended period. UPS will make three attempts to deliver, after which they will return the package to the sender.

When You Have a Gripe

Today, consumers have more protection under the law than they've had at any time in history, and this includes mail-order consumers. Mail-order businesses are bound by law to live up to their advertised services and to fill orders promptly. Most mail-order companies are legitimate businesses with fine reputations. In fact, in all our mail-order dealings over the years, we have had problems with only two companies, one of which is now out of business. When this company was on the verge of bankruptcy, we were among the few customers who got a refund check. In fact, when the company finally folded, more than 65 percent of its outstanding orders went unfilled and no refunds were made.

How did we luck out? Well, it was more than luck. When the company refused to ship a product that had been backordered for three months and ignored our follow-up letters, we sent one more letter to them, with carbon copies to the Better Business Bureau and the Office of Consumer Affairs in Washington, D.C. Within ten days we had a refund check.

The other company that gave us problems is still in business, and although we dealt with them for several years, we never were satisfied with their service, which seemed to deteriorate from year to year. Finally, when we sent them an order for sixty-four items, only to have thirty-one of them backordered and yet another arrive in damaged condition, we wrote to the president of the company, telling him unpolitely what he could do with the balance of our order and demanding an immediate refund. This company, incidentally, is not included in our book.

If you run into a problem with any company, there are several steps you should take. First, give the company the benefit of the doubt. There could be a legitimate reason or explanation for the problem. Write a letter of complaint, and address it to the Customer Service Department of the company. Allow ten days for a response.

If you hear nothing, address your second letter to the president of the company and tell that person that if you get no response within ten days you will send copies of all correspondence regarding this matter to his local Better Business Bureau and to the Office of Consumer Affairs in Washington. And if you still get no response, do precisely that.

This should take care of your problem, but if it doesn't, and if the money involved is significant, you can seek assistance through the courts, through the U.S. Postal Service (possible mail fraud), or you can get more help from the Office of Consumer Affairs. Many states now have consumer affairs agencies, too. So be sure to check out that avenue.

There is really no reason for anyone to get gypped by any company that intends to stay in business. And even a company that is teetering on the brink of bankruptcy is likely to meet your demands if you show them the clout you have as a consumer. But chances are you will never have to use any of these measures. Deal with reputable firms and you should enjoy trouble-free mail-order purchasing for as long as you wish.

By the way, here's an address you will want to keep handy just in case:

Director of the Office of Consumer Affairs
Department of Health, Education, and Welfare
Washington, D.C. 20201

For a free copy of the booklet, *Shopping By Mail? You're Protected!*, order publication No. 319D from the Consumer Information Center, Pueblo, Colorado 81009.

CHAPTER TWO

FISHING TACKLE, ACCESSORIES, AND SUPPLIES

Hundreds of companies specializing in the manufacture, distribution, and sale of fishing tackle exist in this country. Brand names and registered trademarks surely number in the tens of thousands and might seem excessive and confusing to some. But when you consider the increasing demands of millions of American fishermen, you might begin to wonder how these companies can crank out enough gear to keep all of us satisfied.

Some of these firms are huge corporations that make vast quantities of tackle each year and employ hundreds of people. Others are basement or garage operations, run by an individual, a family, or a couple of fishing buddies. But no matter what their size or output capabilities, they all have one thing in common: they manufacture and sell products that help us have fun. Here's an introduction to some of these companies and a sampling of what they have to offer to the fisherman.

ACTION LURE CO.

Plastic worms that breathe? Well, not really, but the Breathing Worm (Pat. Pend.) from Action Lure Co. has thirty-six air chambers molded into it that are designed to trap air and release tiny bubbles at every twitch of the lure. The thin ribs of the worm function as sound chambers to attract bass, and at the aft end is a twist-type tail.

Little brother to the Breathing Worm is the Breathing Grub. Other lures in ALC's catalog include plugs and spinner baits that should interest bass fishermen and bass as well.

Breathing Worm—Tested by pros for three years. Sizes: 4¾ and 6 inches. Available in nineteen colors, including multicolors.

Breathing Worm

Breathing Grub—Scented with strike oil. Colors: smoke, mean green, brown, pearl, chartreuse, black, and silver.

Breathing Grub

Humper Shallow Runner—Plastic body, stainless steel weight and rattle. Chipproof, lacquer paint, guaranteed not to leak. Bronze hooks. Runs 2 to 5 feet. Available in eleven colors. Price: $2.60.

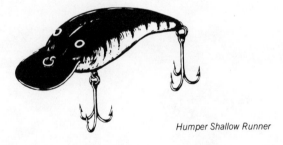

Humper Shallow Runner

Humper Deep Runner—Same as Shallow Runner, except with larger lip that allows lure to run from 6 to 8 feet deep. Price: $2.60.

Humper Deep Runner

Spinner Baits—Chipproof, super-tough four-coat paint job, extra-long wire to make lures more weedless, rubber skirts. Choice of orange, char-

treuse, hammered nickel, or hammered copper blades. Available in nine colors. Sizes: ½, ⅜, ¼, and ⅛ ounce. Price: $2.

Spinner Bait

S. S. ADAMS CO.

The Adams Outrigger Planer and Drone Release is the only fishing item that this company manufactures and should be of interest to those who enjoy trolling. The release holds fishing lines with preset pressure, and tension is adjustable. As an outrigger release, lines will be held at any boat speed.

As a planer release, all drag on the planer is eliminated.'. The planer, tied to the stern of the boat with a hand line, disengages when the bait is struck and can then be pulled in by hand. With the fishing line free, the fisherman can enjoy playing his fish.

As a drone release, the sinker is allowed to slide back to the swivel attached to the leader or lure when a fish strikes.

Adams Outrigger Planer and Drone Release—Made of Delrin plastic and stainless steel. Diameter: 1½ inches. Weight: 1¼ ounces. Price: $3.98/pair.

SNAP LINE UNDER ONE BUTTON

ADJUST TENSION

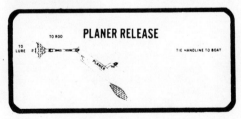

PLANER RELEASE

DRONE OR TROLLING SINKER RELEASE

Adams Outrigger Planer and Drone Release Instructions

ALADDIN LABORATORIES, INC.

This company manufactures Perrine automatic fly reels, both horizontal and vertical mount, as well as a line of Perrine ventilated aluminum fly and spin boxes. Their entire line of reels is guaranteed for life.

Another product from Aladdin includes Jon-E Warmers (see Chapter 12).

Perrine No. 50 Reel—Horizontal mount, free-stripping automatic with snubbing brake. Line capacity: adequately holds all line weights up to and including L6F, DT5F, and WF9F. Weight: 8⅞ ounces. Color: gold and autumn brown.

Perrine No. 87 Reel—Vertical mount, free-stripping automatic. Line capacity: adequately holds all line weights up to and including L8F, DT8F, and WF10F. Weight: 9⅛ ounces. Color: gold and Colorado green.

Perrine No. 98 Box
Perrine No. 99 Box
Perrine No. 101 Box

Perrine No. 98 Box—Lined with a special polypropylene mold to tenderly and securely hold 100 wet or dry flies upright. Dimensions: 3¾ inches wide by 6 inches deep by 1⅜ inches thick.

Perrine No. 99 Box—Has six coil clips for sixty eyed flies, one large coil clip, five plastic lined compartments for lures that are covered by a locking inner lid. Dimensions: 3¾ inches wide by 6 inches deep by 1¼ inches thick.

Perrine No. 101 Box—One side has powerful magnetic insert. Other side has four coil clips and three ten-point clips. Dimensions: 3¾ inches wide by 6 inches deep by 1¼ inches thick.

ALEXANDRIA DRAFTING CO.

What can a drafting company possibly provide for fishermen? This one produces some of the finest fishing atlases and structure maps that we've seen anywhere. Our only disappointment with their line is that it doesn't cover the entire country.

The company was organized in 1956 as a cartographic drafting operation, and in 1969 produced the first of its outdoor atlases, the *Virginia Outdoor Recreation Atlas*. ADC currently offers seven fishing and boating atlases and fourteen fishing maps and charts of Southern freshwater and saltwater areas.

Salt Water Sport Fishing and Boating in Virginia—A large format, 10½×14-inch, 33-page atlas covering the lower Potomac, James River, Chesapeake Bay, and the Atlantic Ocean from Virginia Beach north to Assateague Island. Includes index to fishing areas as well as information on charter boats, marinas, and other facilities, and contains fishing tips and full-color illustrations of marine game fishes. Price: $7.44 postpaid.

Salt Water Sport Fishing and Boating in Virginia—A full 50 pages and a Cape Hatteras area center spread were required to completely cover the North Carolina coast, including all rivers emptying into the Atlantic. The large format atlas also includes an index of fishing areas and directory of marinas, as well as fishing tips and full-color illustrations of area marine game fishes. Price: $8.62 postpaid.

Bass Structure Fishing—*Santee-Cooper Lakes*—This 48-page atlas contains 26 pages of bottom contour maps and covers the productive waters of Lakes Marion and Moultrie, beginning approximately 45 miles north of Charleston, South Carolina. Each map page gives compass reference, water depth, underwater structures, and marina, ramp, and campground facility locations. Included also are articles on structure fishing, largemouth bass, striped bass, crappie fishing, boat selection, and more. Price: $5.93 postpaid.

Outer Banks North Carolina Fishing Map—Price: $2.47 postpaid.

Hatteras Offshore Fishing Chart—Price: $2.47 postpaid.

Bass Structure Fishing Map—*Lake Gaston*—Price $2.47 postpaid.

Atlases and Maps

Note: All sheet maps can be plastic laminated and furnished flat for $8.80, which includes postage and handling.

AL'S GOLDFISH LURE CO.

Here's a company that manufactures a large line of fishing lures, beginning, of course, with Al's Goldfish lure and ranging through spoons, spinners, jigs, plugs, flies, poppers, and plastic worms. Additionally, their catalog lists a fairly large line of terminal tackle and some interesting accessories, such as Kwik-Klip snaps and Hook Bonnets.

Al's Goldfish—Available in gold, copper, nickel, neon blue, fluorescent orange, and Jack Frost finish. Sizes: 3/16 and ¼ ounce.

Al's Big Flash—Behaves like a school of bait fish. Rig it between the sinker and your lure or bait to get the best darting action. Works perfectly with spoons and plugs as well as natural baits. Made of genuine spring brass, hand polished. Finish: brass, nickel, or prism scale on nickel. Sizes: 4½ and 6 inches.

FoamEgs—Shoeleather tough, soft as down, and as appealing as nature, these baits are fish oil impregnated for milking action. This unusual material stays on the hook for reuse even after catching a fish and immediately regains its shape. Available in large, medium, and small sizes, packed ten, twelve, and fifteen to a bag.

Hook Bonnets—Keep hooks sharp, make lures safe to carry, and prevent tackle box tangles. Just snap on and pop off. Small Hook Bonnets fit treble hook sizes 8 through 12; medium fits sizes 2 through 6; large fits 1 through 2/0. Price: 49¢ per bag of ten.

| Small for Trout | Medium for Spinning | Large for large hooks |

FoamEgs

Kwik-Klip Snaps

Al's Goldfish

Al's Big Flash

AMERICAN IMPORT CO.

The fishing tackle line from AIC includes L. M. Dickson rods, reels, lures, and terminal tackle and accessories, and most items are economically priced.

Other product lines from AIC appear in Chapters 4, 5, 8, 9, and 12.

L. M. Dickson Telescopic Casting Rod #3609—Chromed stainless steel bridge guides, composition cork handle, anodized reel seat, and plastic tip protector are featured on this rod. Length closed: 15½ inches. Length extended: 6 feet. Color: dark brown. Price: $10.95.

L. M. Dickson Rod/Reel Combo #35—A new item from AIC, this compact outfit can be tucked into a suitcase or car trunk. Incorporates a spinning reel in the handle, complete with star drag and belt clip. Price: $18.95.

Samson #999 H.D. Spin-Casting Reel—Stainless steel rotor, brass pinion gear, ceramic pin pickup, level-wind spool, and star drag are features in this reel. Weight: 12.5 ounces. Gear ratio: 3.5:1. Capacity: 200 yards. 16# line. Price: $15.95.

L. M. Dickson Heavyweight Fly Reel #399—Chromed ring and line guard, adjustable drag, 4-inch spool diameter. Weight: 10.5 ounces. Color: metallic brown/bronze. Price: $17.95.

L. M. Dickson Kentfield Automatic Fly Reel #686—Free-stripping reel with folding trigger. Weight: 9.5 ounces. Finish: green anodized. Price: $12.95.

L. M. Dickson H.D. Level Wind Reel #9559/C—This reel has solid Bakelite sideplates and important internal components are stainless steel. Reinforced brass spool is chrome plated, as is brass star drag. Weight: 18.5 ounces. Gear ratio: 2.8:1. Capacity: 250 yards. 27# monofilament. Price: $25.95.

L. M. Dickson Telescopic Casting Rod #3609

Samson #999 H. D. Spin-Casting Reel

L. M. Dickson Heavyweight Fly Reel #399

L. M. Dickson Kentfield Automatic Fly Reel #686

L. M. Dickson H.D. Level Wind Reel #9559/C

APPLIED OCEANOGRAPHIC TECHNOLOGY CORP.

Since overwhelming scientific evidence has shown that olfaction plays a major role in most fishes' search for food, Applied Oceanographic's research group has developed a line of lures that dispense a fish-attracting odor.

Chumin Lures, as they're called, are used in conjunction with Chumin Pellets that are compounded to produce a highly concentrated fish-attracting odor. The pellets are inserted into the lure where they mix with water and dissolve over a period of about thirty minutes, while continuously emitting powerful olfactants that draw fish to the lure.

Four different types of saltwater Chumin Lures are available in colors Glo, clear, pink, green, amber, and smoke. All lures come with a supply of pellets, but additional pellets may be purchased, too. You'll have to buy through a dealer, unless you want to place a minimum order of $250.

6-inch Chumin Squid—Rigged for trolling with 80-pound-test Steelon (see Berkley) and Mustad 7/0 cadmium-plated and tinned hook. Price: $4.98.

Chumin Squid Jig—Available in three lengths, all packed with flexible white jig weights. Sizes and weights: 3 inches with 4/0 hook, ¾ ounce or 1½ ounces; 4 inches with 6/0 hook, 1½ or 3 ounces; 6 inches with 8/0 hook, 3 or 5 ounces. Prices: $3.49 (3 inches), $3.98 (4 inches), and $4.49 (6 inches).

Chumin Shrimp—Designed to be fished like natural shrimp. Three shrimp and bag of pellets in each package. Price: $1.98.

Chumin Grub—Packaged with lead heads in white, black, red, or yellow. Grub colors are same as other Chumin Lures. Sizes and weights: 3 inches with 4/0 hook, ⅜ or ⅝ ounce; 6 inches with 6/0 hook, ½, 1½, or 3 ounces. Prices: $1.98 (3 inches) and $2.98 (6 inches).

Chumin Pellets—Prices: 89¢ for package of ten, $3.50 for package of fifty.

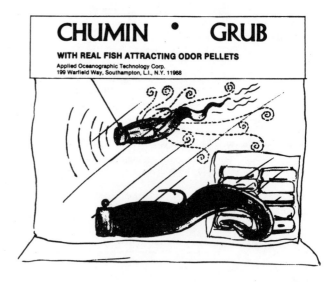

Chumin Lures

AQUASONIC LURES, INC.

"The Hole Idea" is what Aquasonic is laying claim to with a line of lures now available after more than eight years of designing and field testing. While the five different styles of Aquasonic lures appear outwardly similar to a number of other lures that have been around for a while, each Aquasonic lure is equipped with a maze of channels, designed to produce a measured flow of water through the lure.

As the lure is retrieved, water enters through holes in the mouth or lip and exits through holes in the belly at a controlled rate, generating hydrosonic compression waves.

Aquasonic researchers have determined that a bass is attuned to sound frequencies within the range of 10 to 30 cycles per second and have designed their lures to generate pulsating waves inside that range.

There are twelve color combinations available for all lures. For $8, Aquasonic will send you their latest catalog, a decal, and two lures.

Chatterbox—Sinks slowly with a vibrating action. Underwater, the lure's swimming motions force water through the fluid chambers, generating bass-attracting sounds. Weight: ½ ounce.

Chatterbox Too—Can be buzzed across the surface or fished with a jigging or pumping action. Weight: ½ ounce.

Lil' Noisy—Floats or dives to middepths. Unlike the Chatterbox, retrieve speed will vary the number of compression waves emitted per second, though remaining well within the 10- to 30-cycle range. Weight: ½ ounce.

Deep Baby Noisy—A small, deep-running lure. Varying retrieve will change the emission rate of hydrosonic compression waves. Weight: ¼ ounce.

Chatterbox Too

Deep Baby Noisy

ARNOLD TACKLE CORP.

If ice fishing is your kind of sport, Arnold makes your kind of tackle. While the Arnold catalog does list some bugs and poppers, most of their line is hand-crafted for the cold-feet set. Included are tools for digging holes in the ice, and tackle for fishing through the holes.

Model VJ-65 Ice Drill—Two-piece jointed drill, cuts a 6½-inch hole through 36 inches of ice with high-carbon, aircraft steel bit. Plastic handle grip. Protective bit guard. Price: $20.

Blue Streak Ice Spud—A three-piece jointed spud for convenient carrying, precision crafted of the finest materials. Weight is in the blade. Welded construction, hardened tool steel blade, hollow ground cutting edge, and nylon safety handle cord are features of this tool. Price: $13.

Tiger Claw Ice Creeper—Heavy, 12-gauge steel ice creepers. Cleat is zinc plated. Has web strap with nickel-plated buckle and tip. Price: $1.85 pair.

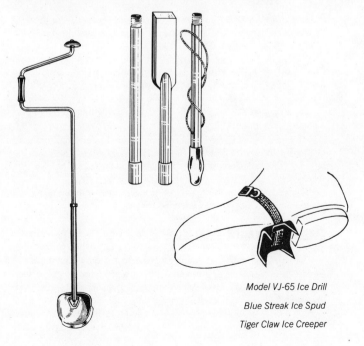

Model VJ-65 Ice Drill

Blue Streak Ice Spud

Tiger Claw Ice Creeper

Magnum Tip-Up—Oversize red fluorescent flag, nonrusting metal parts and aluminum spool with handle are features of this new item with feather-light tripoff. Capacity: 375 feet. 72# line. Price: $5.50.

Saturn All-Metal Tip-Up—Adjustable line guide prevents tangles. Three selective trip settings. Tripod construction—folds to 20×2×2 inches. Plastic filled oversize fluorescent flag. All metal construction. Leakproof, windproof, freezeproof. Catches the light hitters. Price: $7.25.

Ice Rods—Equipped with 11-inch turned hardwood handles and glass blades. Available with 14-inch 22-inch, and 33-inch blades. Price: $1.50 (14-inch blade), $1.75 (22-inch blade), $2 (33-inch blade).

No. 50-S Ice Skimmer—Arnold's most popular ice skimmer. All steel, heavily zinc plated, welded construction. Cup is 5 inches in diameter and 2 inches deep with rimmed edge to retain ice. Heavy 10-inch wire handle. Price: $1.

No. 70-SB Ice Skimmer—Skimmer plus gaff for the game fisherman. Handle is 24 inches long. Cup is 5 inches in diameter and 2 inches deep. Rugged all-steel construction with heavy zinc plating. Price: $1.75.

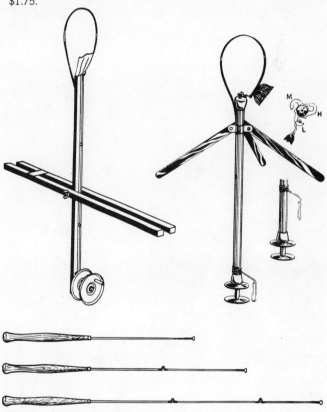

Magnum Tip-Up

Saturn All-Metal Tip-Up

Ice Rods

AUTO-GAFF, INC.

Gaffs galore! That's what's available from this company—dozens of different gaffs and kits for making your own. Their hooks are made of tempered stainless steel or aluminum, and the three-sided, diamond-shaped Shark's Tooth Point is a patented design. In addition to gaffs to fit any fisherman's needs, Auto-Gaff also offers salmon tailers and flounder gigs.

Of particular interest to those who have lost fish during the crucial gaffing process is the patented spring-loaded line of gaffs and tailers. You simply cock the mechanism, ease the gaff under the fish, and release the trigger with a flick of the thumb. The hook then recoils 4 inches and gaffs your fish automatically. Quick and simple.

All gaffs are equipped with point guards—clear tubes that slip over the gaff hooks to protect points and fishermen.

Automatic Gaffs—Available in lengths from 32 to 61 inches, with either 3- or 4-inch hooks. Hooks are made of ¼-inch-square tempered stainless steel. Handles are 1-inch diameter aluminum. Prices: from $12.55 to $22.90.

Salmon Tailer—Automatic, spring-loaded tailer with stainless steel snare and 4-inch aluminum handle. Price: $30.

Tackle Box Gaff—This lightweight gaff was designed for all fishermen casting in surf, lake, or river. Its retractable tempered aluminum hook with the Shark's Tooth makes it possible to carry in your tackle box, hip pocket, boot, etc. Weight: 8 ounces. Length closed: 15 inches. Length extended: 24 inches. Price: $7.

Flying Gaff #FG8—Approximately 96 inches overall length, with 1¼-inch diameter aluminum handle. Barbed 8-inch hook is ½ inch in diameter. Price: $59.65.

Bridge Gaff #BG2—A must for bridge or pier fishermen. Attach a heavy handline to the gaff, then lower it on your fishing line through snap and swivel attached to the gaff, and gaff fish with handline. Four ¼-inch round tempered stainless steel hooks in one sleeve. Hook size: 2½ inches. Price: $16.35.

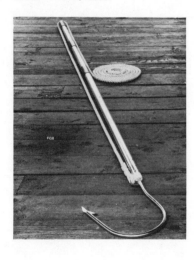

Flying Gaff #FG8
Bridge Gaff #BG2

BASS ATTACKER

A broad line of top-quality rod-building materials is featured by Bass Attacker. For those who would rather buy a finished rod than build their own, everything from fly rods to surf rods is available. Such brand names as Fenwick, Featherweight, Lew Childre, Fuji, Browning Silaflex, Gudebrod, and Mildrum can be found in the 22-page catalog. Satisfaction is guaranteed to all customers, by allowing any item to be returned, unused, within ten days for a full refund.

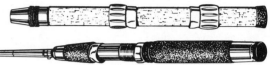

Featherweight Spinning Rod Handles
Featherweight Casting Rod Handles

Fenwick HMG Graphite Fly Rod Blanks—A total of fifteen different two-piece blanks available, ranging in length from 6 feet 3 inches to 10½ feet, for AFTMA line sizes 4 to 11. Prices: from $44.95 to $82.95.

Fenwick HMG Graphite Spinning Rod Blanks—Available in one piece and two piece in sizes from ultralight to steelhead. Ten models range in length from 4½ feet to 8 feet 9 inches. Prices: from $29.95 to $73.95.

Fenwick HMG Graphite Casting Rod Blanks—All six blanks available are one piece, ranging in length from 54½ inches to 60½ inches. Prices: from $36.95 to $37.95 (from $3.80 to $4 more for blanks with butt ferrules).

Browning Silaflex Fiberglass Fly Rod Blanks—Eleven one-piece and two-piece blanks available, ranging in length from 6 feet 11 inches to 8 feet 11 inches, for AFTMA line sizes 5 to 11. Prices: from $8.50 to $20.

Browning Silaflex Fiberglass Spinning Rod Blanks—Ten models available in one piece and two piece in ratings from ultralight to light salt water. Lengths range from 5 feet 5½ inches to 7 feet 1 inch. Prices: from $9.50 to $13.50.

Browning Silaflex Fiberglass Casting Rod Blanks—Five medium- and heavy-action blanks available, all one piece. Lengths are from 4½ feet to 6½ feet. Prices: from $8.50 to $9.50.

Featherweight #6KR Pistol-Grip Handle—Regular, black casting rod handle, featuring cushiony, nonslip Kraton grip. Price: $6.50.

Featherweight #6A-30 Casting Rod Handle—Straight handle with 5½-inch cork grip. Price: $5.50.

Featherweight #AK-1 Spinning Rod Handle—Brown and gold, 7/16-inch to 11/16-inch bore, with fixed seat easily cemented to blank. Price: $6.90.

Featherweight #22AMG Spinning Rod Handle—Features sliding Magnu-Grip on cork handle. Price: $4.50.

BEAD CHAIN TACKLE CO.

Probably best known for their rugged and rustproof chain swivels, Bead Chain also offers assortments of flexible spinners, weighted spinners, stainless steel snaps, casting and trolling leads, keel leads, leaders, and stainless steel spoons.

"Every bead a swivel" is what they say about their uniquely designed terminal tackle. End rings are one-piece construction. Beads are made of Monel and are guaranteed not to rust. Snaps are stainless steel and equipped with safety hooks for positive locking.

Bead Chain Plain Swivels—Four sizes available. Prices: from $1.59 to $2.86 per dozen.

Bead Chain Single Snap Swivels—Six sizes available. Prices: from $2.29 to $3.82 per dozen.

Bead Chain Lock Type Snap Swivels—Three sizes available. Prices: $2.54, $3.18, and $3.82 per dozen.

Bead Chain Double Snap Swivel—Three sizes available. Prices: $3.18, $3.82, and $4.71 per dozen.

Bead Chain Flexible Spinners—Available in single- and double-blade models, in nine sizes and styles. Blade finishes: nickel, silver, or gold. Prices: from $3.18 to $10.18 per dozen.

Bead Chain Casting and Trolling Leads—Available in thirteen weights from ¼ ounce to 16 ounces. Prices: from $4.45 to $28.62 per dozen.

Bead Chain Keel Leads—Eight sizes available from ¹/₁₆ ounce to 4 ounces. Prices: from $3.82 to $12.72 per dozen.

Bead Chain Swivel

Plain Swivel

Single Snap Swivel

Double Snap Swivel

Lock Type Snap Swivel

Flexible Spinners

Casting and Trolling Lead

Keel Lead

BERKLEY AND CO.

Located in the northwest corner of Iowa, in the heart of the Iowa Great Lakes country, Berkley has become one of the major manufacturers of quality fishing tackle. Their line includes a considerable offering of fishing lines, as well as rods, reels, and terminal tackle.

Berkley also manufactures marine and cordage products that are covered in Chapter 3.

Berkley Trilene and Trilene XL—These lines are best suited to long-distance casting, where distance means more than super abrasion resistance. These lines offer superb handling, small diameter, low wind resistance, minimum set, good knot strength and controlled stretch. Test weights: from 2# to 80#. Colors: Trilene—blue or smoke; XL—high visibility clear.

Berkley Trilene Tensimatic and Dura Tuff—These lines are designed for heavy-duty fishing of all kinds—bass fishing in heavy structure, fishing in rocky areas, on tough coastal shores, or anywhere where abrasion resistance is more important than distance casting. Test weights: from 4# to 80#. Colors: Tensimatic—high visibility green; Dura Tuff—copper or sea mist green.

Berkley Spin Chief and Dew Flex—Economical prices, limpness, and surface uniformity make these Berkley monofilament lines strong favorites among anglers everywhere. Test weights: from 4# to 150#. Color: mist blue.

Berkley Depth-O-Matic—This is a special nylon line designed to tell you line depth at a glance. It changes color every 10 feet. Test weights: from 15# to 40#.

Berkley Specialist Fly Lines—Floating lines, sinking lines, floating/sinking lines with 10 feet of sinking tip. Double-taper and weight-forward lines, blunt-tipped weight-forward lines for salt water and bass, level lines and shooting tapers. Colors: white, yellow, and brown. An assortment of shapes, weights, and densities available to cover every possible fly-casting situation.

Berkley Knotless Tapered Leaders—Patented fly-casting leaders that incorporate unique design and material features. Standard trout tapers for normal stream fishing. Heavy tapers for bass, salmon, steelhead, and saltwater use. You'll also find Quik Sink leaders, chemically treated to sink rapidly and get the fly down. Lengths: from 6 to 9 feet. Tip sizes: from 6X to 0X.

Berkley Steelon Leaders—Known by anglers everywhere as the "nylon leader with the heart of steel," Steelon leaders are made for virtually every kind of fish, every type of fishing—fresh water and salt.

Berkley Steelon Trolling Line—Seven strands of stainless steel, twisted for strength and coated with tough durable nylon. Color: dark brown.

Berkley Catfish and Bullhead Rig—12-inch leader with 6-inch dropper.

Berkley Lightweight Saltwater Rig—24-inch leader with two 6-inch droppers.

Berkley Saltwater Rigs—Each consists of a leader and two 6-inch droppers. Materials: nylon or stainless steel wire. Lengths: 15 or 24 inches. Test weights: 40# to 210#.

Berkley Crappie, Perch, Panfish Rigs—Lightweight rigs equipped with hooks ranging in size from 8 to 3/0.

Berkley Para/Metric Rods—A fisherman's rod, made for the man who takes his fishing seriously. Color: mahogany with dark brown wraps, gold trim. Features: matched actions, specie cork grips, detachable pistol grip on bait-casting models, live-action ferrule for one-piece feel, top-quality guides, aluminum reel seats.

Berkley Cherrywood Rods—The fast taper actions most fishermen like and a value price tag. Color: rich cherrywood, accented with translucent nylon monofilament wraps over brilliant chrome foil. Features: live-action ferrules, anodized aluminum reel seats, specie cork grips, molded pistol grips on bait-casting models.

Berkley Buccaneer Rods—Freshwater rods priced within every angler's budget. Color: walnut epoxy finish with color-coordinated wraps and trim. Features: specie cork grips, brown anodized aluminum reel seats, live-action ferrules.

Berkley Buccaneer Saltwater Rods—Designed for rugged freshwater and saltwater action. Color: same as Buccaneer series. Features: chrome-plated stainless steel guides and tip tops, brown anodized reel seats, specie cork grips, live-action ferrules.

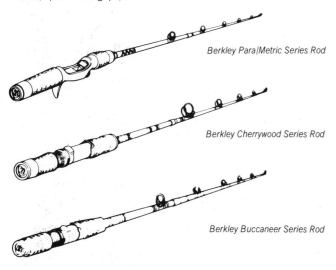

Berkley Para/Metric Series Rod

Berkley Cherrywood Series Rod

Berkley Buccaneer Series Rod

Berkley Model 725 Spinning Reel—Berkley's top-of-the-line open-face reel. Ball-bearing action. Machine cut helical pinion. Left/right handle. Stainless steel bail. Retrieve: 4.2:1. Comes spooled with 330 yards of 8# Trilene XL.

Berkley Model 604 Spinning Reel—First-rate ultralight reel. Features exclusive cam-operated bail system. Handle folds down for easy storage. Side plate removable with the twist of a coin. Antifoul drag knob. Hard chromed line pickup. Retrieve: 3.6:1..Comes spooled with 200 yards of 4# Trilene XL.

Berkley Model 690 Spinning Reel—First-class saltwater reel with magnum spool. Features patented cam-operated bail. Has large antifoul drag knob and hard chromed line pickup. Fold-down handle. Retrieve: 3.6:1. Comes spooled with 300 yards of 20# Trilene Tensimatic.

Berkley Model 300 Spin-Casting Reel—Rugged all-metal construction. Smooth die-cast gear system, star drag, and aluminum shroud with hardened ring. Retrieve: 3:1. Comes spooled with 125 yards of 8# Trilene XL.

Berkley Model 1056 Fly Reel—One-piece cast-aluminum frame. Exclusive lever bar drag system and three-position check give you positive control of a fish on the run. Press-out spool makes line replacement easy. Comes with tool kit. Capacity: 45 yards of Berkley Specialist 18# Dacron backing, 30 yards of Berkley WF7F Specialist fly line.

Berkley Reels

BILL'S WHOLESALE BAIT

Bill Boychuck's catalog isn't what we would call visually exciting, but the extensive line of custom-made lures is certainly impressive, and the prices are some of the lowest we've seen.

While the word "custom" seems to be used with considerable license these days, Bill's lures are indeed hand made, one at a time, to the customer's specifications. When you order lures, you tell Bill the size, color, blade design and finish, whether the hooks should be dressed or not, and he and his staff make them to your specifications. All brass is hand polished, and hooks are presharpened. And if you're not satisfied, you can return merchandise for a full refund.

According to the catalog, there are more than twenty-five million changes that can be made for you on their line of lures. Additionally, they stock rod blanks and accessories, but these are not included in the catalog. If you want to build a rod, you simply write and tell them what you have in mind. They will send you a list of materials you will need and a price for everything. If the price suits you, they will send you a kit containing everything you need to build that rod.

In addition to the already low prices in the catalog, several items in their most recent listing were marked down by 50 percent. The catalog also includes some hooks, sinkers, and materials for making your own lures.

Spinner Bait—Tail color and bait body color are your choice. Blade: polished brass. Hook: 1/0 bronze. Length: 3 inches. Price: 45¢.

Silver Minnow Spinner—All parts nickel-plated. Length: 2¾ inches. Hook: #8 treble. Price: 30¢.

Fat Spoon—Polished brass, with bronzed treble hook and attractor. Price: 15¢.

Bass Master Spinner—Solid polished brass body with embossed brass blade and yellow beads before and after body. Length: 2 inches. Price: 45¢.

Trouter Spinner—Nickel-plated body with front blade spinner and rear propeller. Length: 2 inches. Hook: #12 nickel treble. Price: 35¢.

Spoon—Nickel-plated with #12 nickel treble hook and attractor. Length: 1½ inches. Price: 15¢.

Shad Dart Heads—Lead dart heads molded on gold hooks. Sizes: ⅛ and ¼ ounce. Prices: 6¢ and 8¢.

BOMBER BAIT CO.

Here's a company that has been around for a long time, producing one of the all-time favorite lures—the Bomber. While the Bomber, in all its various sizes and colors, is surely the most well known in the Bomber

Bait line, their catalog includes a variety of other top-quality plugs, jigs, and spinner baits. Bomber offers surface lures, deep divers, shallow runners, poppers, spoons, and alphabet lures.

Bomber—Designed as a deep-diving, fast-wiggling lure. Even though all but the 200 series are floating lures, Bombers will run deep on retrieve. The broad diving bill drives the lure to depths and acts as a snag guard. Pulling link on all lures is adjustable. Available in thirty-three colors and five sizes.

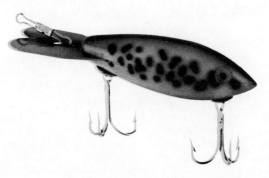

Bomber

Pinfish—A fast-vibrating, slow-sinking lure that sends out high-frequency underwater sounds at the slightest movement. A slow sinker, it can be fished shallow over underwater grass, weed beds, stumps, and logs, even at fairly slow retrieves, by holding the rod tip high. To fish deep, let lure sink, at the rate of about 1 foot per second. Available in twenty-seven colors. Sizes: ¼, ⅜, and ½ ounce.

Water Dog—An extra-deep running lure with a fast-vibrating motion. Broad diving bill sends this lizardlike bait to depths never before attained on a lure of this type. Tail spinner, attached with a snap swivel, can be replaced with a trailer fly, skirt, bucktail, or pork rind, without impairing lure's action. Available in thirty-three colors. Sizes: ¼, ½, and ⅝ ounce.

Bushwacker—Spinner baits available with single, tandem, or twin spinners. Semiweedless and semisnagless. Available in sixteen colors. Replacement skirts and replacement blades in nine different finishes can be purchased too. Sizes: ¼, ½, and ¾ ounce.

Bushwhacker Spinner Baits

Bomber Jig—Nylon tail molded into the lead case makes it virtually impossible to tear the nylon out. Available in twelve colors. Hook is cadmium-plated for saltwater use. Sizes: 2¾, 3, 3¼, and 3½ inches. Weights: ¼, ½, ¾, and 1 ounce.

BRIDGEPORT SILVERWARE MANUFACTURING CO.

A subsidiary of Bead Chain Tackle Company, Bridgeport manufactures a line of lures and weights mainly for saltwater fishing, including the popular Diamond Jigs and Squids, VI-KE lures, and stainless steel spoons.

Their smaller spoons are designed for freshwater or saltwater use.

"Snag-Less" Diamond Jig—This new jig has been introduced as a result of tests indicating that a single hook attached by a swivel has less tendency to snag bottom than a treble hook. Finish is highly polished nickel. Equipped with single Mustad O'Shaughnessy hook. Weights: from 1 to 8 ounces. Prices: from $1.29 to $1.85.

Heave & Haul Jig—For cod and pollack fishing. Bright polished nickel finish. Heavy-duty, clogproof, free-running brass swivel. Length: 6½ inches. Weights: 1 and 1½ pounds. Prices: $4.73, $5.45.

Heave & Haul Jig

Eel Skin Jig—Equipped with swiveled safety chain and O'Shaughnessy hook. Bright nickel finished head. Length: 10¼ inches. Hook size: 8/0. Weight: 3 ounces. Price: $3.11.

Drail—Weight used in trolling for all kinds of fish. Keeps lure down to desired depth, while preventing snagging on bottom. Equipped with free-running heavy-duty brass swivel at each end. Weights: from ½ to 4 pounds. Prices: from $1.79 to $6.29.

Drail

BURKE FISHING LURES

Under the leadership of Bing McClellan, Burke continues to produce a fine line of favorite fishing lures while bringing out new and exciting products each year. The 1976 catalog introduced the new Burke Wig-Wag Minno that has proven deadly for all game fish in fresh and salt water. The cover of the 1977 catalog pictures fish caught from the Arctic Circle to Costa Rica on the same lure. So they have now introduced a Magnum Minno that has caught striped bass, lake trout, tarpon, and many other game fish.

Also new is a nifty "Better Buzzer" Dedly Dudly spinner bait and the Wiglworm—a marriage between their Wig-Wag Worm and their Erthworm series.

Rigged Erthworms—Ready-to-go worms in sizes for panfish to bass. Quality harnesses, gold hooks, and flashing spinners. Sizes: 2½, 3½, 6, and 8 inches. Available in a variety of colors. Prices: from 95¢ to $1.40.

Rigged Erthworm

Buckshot Worms—Body segments reflect and magnify light. Worm can be cut back to smaller size if worn. Available in thirteen colors. "Hottail" Buckshot available in nine color combinations. Sizes: 6, 7½, and 9 inches. Prices: $2.25/dozen, $2.75/dozen, $3.50/dozen.

Buckshot Worms

Wig-Wag Worms—The blade-thin feather tail makes this lure work best at slow speeds. Rigged Texas style or on a weedless hook, this worm will put fish on the stringer. Available in seventeen colors. Sizes: 7 and 9 inches. Prices: $2.50/dozen, $3.50/dozen.

Wig-Wag Worms

Wiglworm—A brand-new "Action Erthworm," this lure is a combination of the Burke lifelike crawlers with the great tail-swimming action of the Wig-Wag Worm. Double trouble for bass. Available in ten colors. Sizes: 4, 6, and 8 inches. Prices: $1.80/dozen, $2.25/dozen, $2.75/dozen. Rigged Wiglworms are higher.

Wiglworms

"Skimmer" Dedly Dudly—A better buzzer, this spinner bait will pop to the surface and stay there, even at slow speeds. Flat head makes it supersnagless in pads, timber, or grass. And it's heavy enough to throw in the wind. Available in seventeen colors with silver blades. Sizes: ⅜ and ⅝ ounce. Prices: $2.50, $2.75.

Wig-Wag Minno—For more than a year this new lure has been proving to both experts and the average fisherman that it catches fish. The true minnow profile and incredible swimming action are enticing to all varieties of game fish and panfish, fresh and salt water. Available in thirteen colors. Sizes: ⅛ ounce on #6 gold jig hook (four spare bodies), ⅜ ounce on 2/0 forged jig hook (three spare bodies), ⅝ ounce on 4/0 forged jig hook (two spare bodies), 1¼ ounces on 6/0 forged jig hook (one spare body). Prices: $1, $1.25, $1.35, $1.75.

Wig-Wag Minno

Minno-Spin—Burke added an elbow spinner to the Wig-Wag Minno to make a great spinner bait. Colors: same as Wig-Wag Minno. Sizes: ⅛ ounce (three spare bodies), ⅜ ounce (two spare bodies), ⅝ ounce (one spare body). Prices: $1.25, $1.35, $1.40.

Mino-Spin

Jig-A-Do-Eel—An old favorite for striped bass, and deadly on other large game fish in fresh and salt water. Available in nine colors. Length: 8½ inches. Weights: ½ and 1 ounce. Prices: $1.95, $2.50.

Jig-A-Doo Eel

CISCO KID TACKLE, INC.

Another manufacturer that has been around for a long time, Cisco Kid Tackle offers a line of time-proven lures. In addition to listing specifications on their lures, the Cisco Kid catalog offers an abundance of fishing know-how.

Art Wellsten, designer and manufacturer of Cisco Kid lures, is a member of the Fishing Hall of Fame who has fished all over the United States and Canada, taking practically every variety of freshwater and many saltwater fish on his lures.

All Cisco Kid lures are available in eleven different colors.

Spin Cisco Kid #100—Designed for the spinning and spin-casting fisherman, this medium-deep runner can either be trolled or cast. It imitates a small minnow and is deadly on a slow retrieve. Tops for bass, trout, walleye, and other game fish. Length: 1⅝ inches. Weight: ¼ ounce. Price: $2.25.

Midget Cisco Kid #300—A medium-deep runner that is suitable for spinning, spin-casting, or bait-casting tackle. A terrific bass bait when retrieved at medium speed. Walleyes like it retrieved slowly. Length: 2¼ inches. Weight: ⅜ ounce. Price: $2.25.

Cisco Kid Diver #1300—An extra-deep runner that sinks fast and digs deep. No extra weight required. Fish in 20-foot depths by letting lure sink. Retrieve after the cast and the Diver will run about 14 feet deep. Length: 2¼ inches. Weight: 7/16 ounce. Price: $2.25.

Spin Jointed Cisco Kid #1000—A shallow to medium runner. It is streamlined and looks like a small minnow. Can be retrieved at any speed. Length: 1¾ inches. Weight: ¼ ounce. Price: $2.50.

Jointed Cisco Kid #500—A middepth runner that can be cast or trolled. One of the few jointed lures that can be retrieved effectively at slow speeds. Tops for all game fish. Length: 2½ inches. Weight: ⅜ ounce. Price: $2.50.

#500 Jointed Cisco Kid

Husky Cisco Kid #600—A great lure for muskies, northern pike, and saltwater game fish, this one runs deep and is a top choice for trolling. Has enticing live-bait action. Lightweight for all-day casting. Length: 6¼ inches. Weight: 1⅓ ounces. Price: $4.

#600 Husky Cisco Kid

DALE CLEMENS CUSTOM TACKLE

If you're into rod building, or want to be, you should know about this company and the man who runs it. Dale is the author of the book, *Fiberglass Rod Making* (Winchester Press, 1974), which is must reading for anyone interested in this craft. He is also the president of an organization for custom rod builders called Rod Crafters. For information on the organization you can drop him a note.

The Clemens line is extensive and includes many of the familiar name brands of fishing rod components and rod-building supplies and tools, as well as quite a few exclusive items available only from Clemens.

Dale wrote to tell us about an unbelievable discovery he made recently when he uncovered a supply of about 3,000 American-made Tonkin cane blanks, built about thirty years ago. As we go to press, prices have not yet been determined on these split-cane blanks, but you should be able to get prices by the time you read about it. The line will include blanks for fly and spinning rods.

Clemens Dual Versatility Pack Rod Blanks—Available in 6- or 7-foot combination fly/spin models. Precision-ground hollow glass ferrules and two butt sections for separate handle assemblies. Sections are 19 inches long. Price: $13.95.

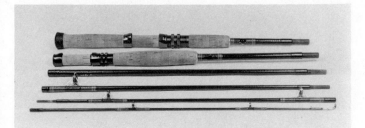

Clemens Dual Versatility Pack Rod Blanks

Clemens Fly Reel Seat—Made of 6061-T832 aluminum for strength and durability with jamproof, precision-machined threads (not rolled). Machined hood. Full-length milled slot reduces side pressure on hoods, and seats reel positively. Separate end cap has knurled edge for quick removal and is equipped with rubber O-rings. Finishes: black or high polished. I.D.: .625 inch. O.D.: .8125 inch. Price: $6.50.

Clemens Detachable Fly Butt—A necessity for playing any large fish on a fly rod. Carry in your pocket while casting, then easily insert it. Precision machined from same quality material as the Clemens Fly Seat. The plunger has two rubber O-rings. The round rubber cap is pure comfort. All parts are threaded for disassembly, so you can glue on cork rings and shape as desired. Price: $6.50.

Walnut Fly Reel Seat—Milled slot, machined hood, and beautiful impregnated walnut that is completely waterproof. Made from Clemens' finest components. I.D.: .690 inch. Price: $10.50.

Clemens Customgrip—Exclusive, shapable, lightweight cushion grip that is revolutionizing custom rod building. Same weight as cork, with excellent nonslip texture, wet or dry. Developed by Clemens to be cut and shaped just like cork. Available shaped or unshaped. Shaped lengths: 6, 7, 8 inches. Shapes: Cigar, Straight Taper. Unshaped lengths: 9, 18 inches. Prices: $2, $2.35, $2.70 (shaped); $2.30, $4.35 (unshaped).

Rod Lathe—Use to shape cork or customgrip and turn hosels and caps right on the blank. Make underwraps quickly and easily. It is impractical to use a regular lathe because of the short bed and lack of any "whip" control in the midsection. Complete rod lathe includes head assembly

with Super Chuck, motor, pulleys, belt, and variable speed foot control. Order rod roller or ball bearing rod supports separately. Price: $129.95.

Ball Bearing Rod Lathe Supports—Use Rod Lathe on any power head and these rollers for the most perfect rod-building machine. Completely eliminates whipping and vibration. Blanks run true, even at the highest speeds, by clamping between three, friction-free, 1-inch ball bearings. Use without power for hand wrapping guides. Lower section quickly adjusts to height at any point of taper along any size blank. Top section lowers to clamp on top of blank. Best control obtained with two units, but one will work on many applications. Prices: $19.95 each, $37/pair.

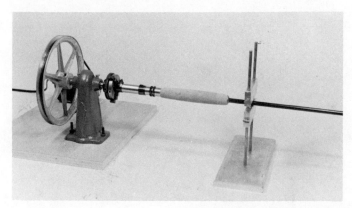

Rod Lathe and Ball Bearing Lathe Supports

CREATIVE SPORTS ENTERPRISES

According to Sarah Puyans, this business "is owned by two characters—Dave Inks and Andre Puyans (husband) who are experts in their field. Andy is known internationally for his tying (the Loopwing and the A.P. Nymph to mention only two) as well as his reputation as a fisherman. Dave is equally well known, teaches for Fenwick, and is sought after for his knowledge of fly-tying materials. Our business has grown tremendously each year. We do two schools each summer in Montana, with such guest instructors as Ernest Schwiebert and Steve Rajeff. We have a travel service, handling trips to Costa Rica, Alaska, and Baja.

"If anyone needs to know anything about fly-fishing, come see us—the coffee pot is always on. Or give us a call. If we don't know the answer, we'll get it for you."

Sarah told us that they don't yet have a catalog, but are struggling to get one put together. Meanwhile, they are using a retail price list of their fly-tying materials and tools.

Here's a sampling from that list.

Golden Pheasant—Head and neck. Price: $2.85.

Ostrich Herl—Available in black, brown, gray, green, orange, red, white, and yellow. Price: 50¢.

Dubbing Fur—Badger, beaver, gray and red fox, coyote, mink, muskrat, otter, opossum, raccoon, black rabbit, brown rabbit, gray rabbit, olive rabbit, and white rabbit. Price: 50¢.

Chenille—Available in seventeen colors. Packaged 3 yards, carded. Price: 35¢.

Tinsel—Available in silver or gold; flat, oval, or embossed. Price: 40¢/spool.

Supreme Vise—Price: $15.

Bobbins—No. 4 or No. 5. Price: $3.25.

Hackle Pliers—Three models available—English, Custom, and Trout Fly. Prices: $2.25, $1.40, $1.20.

CREEK CHUB BAITS

Grandpa was a youngster when the first Creek Chub plugs started catching fish, and since its founding in 1906, this company has produced plugs that have become favorites throughout the world. The Pikie Minnow is one of the best musky and pike plugs around today and has been for years. And the Striper Strike is a favorite among striped bass fishermen everywhere.

Creek Chub's trophy-producing baits are credited with four world records:

Largemouth Bass—22 pounds 4 ounces, taken on a Creek Chub Jointed Wag-Tail by George Perry in 1932, Montgomery Lake, Georgia.

Muskellunge—69 pounds 15 ounces, taken on a Creek Chub Jointed Pikie by Arthur Lawton in 1957, St. Lawrence River, New York.

Striped Bass—66 pounds (largest striper ever taken on a popping-type plug), taken by Harold Slater in 1964 on a Creek Chub Striper Strike off the Connecticut coast.

Snook—36 pounds (largest snook ever taken on 12# line), taken by Don Dobbins in 1970 on a Creek Chub Wiggle Diver on the Colorado River, Costa Rica.

The entire line of Creek Chub Baits includes sixteen different lures.

Jointed Pikie—Jointed body floater. Runs medium deep on retrieve. Weights: from ⅛ to 4 ounces. Lengths: from 1⅝ to 14 inches. Prices: from $2.55 to $7.25.

Striper Strike—Deadly topwater bait for striped bass and bluefish. Available in five colors. Weights: ½, ¾, 1, 1½, and 2¼ ounces. Prices: from $3.15 to $4.60.

Streeker—Underwater minnow with twin sonic propellers. Has the natural look and action that attract prowling game fish. Available in seven colors. Lengths: 3 and 4½ inches. Weights: ⅜ and 1 ounce. Prices: $2.65, $3.90.

*Injured Minnow*1—Perennial topwater favorite. Floats on its side like an actual injured minnow. Works with varying rod tip action. Available in eight colors. Lengths: from 1⅝ to 2¾ inches. Weights: ⅛ to ½ ounce. Prices: from $2.55 to $2.90.

Creek Chub Jointed Pikie, Striper Strike, Streeker, Injured Minnow

CREME LURE CO.

The number of serious bass fishermen who have never used plastic worms at some time probably wouldn't fill an average-size bass boat. Certainly, the plastic worm is the most used, the most abundant, the most written about, and the most successful of bass lures. And the guy to blame is Nick Creme, who developed the plastic worm in his wife's kitchen in Akron, Ohio, more than a quarter-century ago.

Creme Lures continue to be turned out in great quantities, but no longer from a kitchen stove. The facilities are now in Tyler, Texas, where a large line of soft plastic baits is manufactured.

Creme's 6-Inch Scoundrel—The world's first plastic worm. Available in thirteen colors. Also available in slip-sinker kits that include three 4/0 hooks and three ¼-ounce slip sinkers.

Creme's 4-Inch Scoundrel—The original plastic worm now in 4-inch size, perfect for light tackle and short strikers. Comes in nine colors.

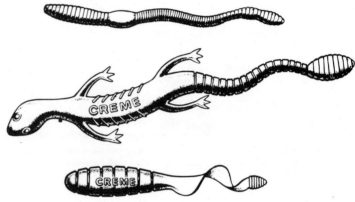

Creme Baits

Creme's 6-Inch Shimmy Lizard—Imitates roe-eating salamanders, hated by bass. Special lazy action of shimmy tail is dynamite in winter and spring. Available in ten colors.

Creme's 4-Inch Scally Wag—Superaction bait, ideal for jig fishing. Great as a trailer on spinner baits. Available in eleven colors.

JACK DICKERSON'S, INC.

Jack sends out a hefty mail-order catalog that is full of familiar brands of fishing tackle at competitive prices. While his line includes some boating and hunting items, fishermen should find it most interesting and useful.

Everything is represented in the 70-page catalog—rods, reels, lines, leaders, lures, and terminal tackle. A good one for browsing and shopping.

See Chapter 3 for other Dickerson products.

Heddon Sonar—Need a lure that casts easily and gives you the right action at any retrieve speed? Sonar is the lure for you. Designed with three magic holes to secure your line in, each hole gives you a different depth and action. Colors: silver, gray shad, gold, hot orange, and red head. Lengths: 1⅞ and 2⅜ inches. Weights: ¼ and ½ ounce. Dickerson's price: $1.55.

Heddon Chugger—Lily pad chugger for big bass. Ideal for pockets or around lily pads. When line is jerked a chugging noise is produced. Colors: perch; red head; silver, yellow, red and white, and black and white shore minnows. Weights: ¼, ⅜, and ⅝ ounce. Dickerson's prices: $1.65 (¼ ounce), $1.75 (⅜ and ⅝ ounce).

Uncle Josh Bait Frog—The green pork frog with a purpose. Use with any weedless hook or spoon and you have one of the most versatile weedless lures possible. You can fish it anywhere, anytime, in any water. For all panfish, trout, walleye, bass, and pike. Colors: frog and chartreuse. Weight: ¼ ounce. Size: 1×2½ inches. Dickerson's price: 85¢ each, $9.15/dozen.

Uncle Josh Bait Frog

Berkley Steelon Casting Leaders—Sizes: 6, 9, and 12 inches. Dickerson's price: $2.40/dozen.

Zebco De-Liar—The storyteller's friend. Combination scale and tape measure. Preset compression spring assures precision accuracy. Rustproof finish. Sizes: 8 pounds and 24 inches, 28 pounds and 42 inches. Dickerson's prices: $1.19, $1.75.

DICKEY TACKLE CO.

This company specializes in ice fishing and has a complete line of hard-to-find items for the ice fisherman. The company has been in business for twenty years and offers quality tackle at good prices.

All-purpose Ice Rod—Equipped with a foolproof nonfouling combination handle and reel. Adjustable drag. Cork hook holder. Completely rigged with Dickey sponge rubber bobber, monofilament line and lure. Ready to catch fish. Lengths and actions: 28 inches overall with light-action shaft, 38 inches light action, 38 inches heavy action. Price: $4.95.

Ice Rod Stand—Did you ever turn around while ice fishing and have your rod disappear through the hole? This unique rod-saver and rod-stand combination can prevent such mishaps. Body molded of tough light plastic. Light, strong legs of fiberglass, stands 5 inches at triggered position and measures 14 inches wide when sprung. Price: $1.50.

"Ice-Off" Bobber—At last, an ice float made of soft cellular rubber that floats indefinitely. Any bobber will ice up when used in freezing temperatures, but the Dickey Ice-Off Bobber can be squeezed or even stepped on to remove the ice coating. Six shapes and sizes available. Colors: yellow, red, black, and green. Prices: from 15¢ to 50¢.

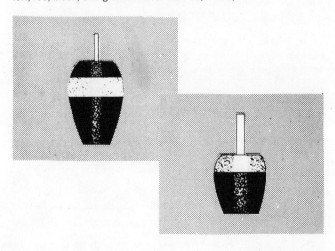

"Ice-Off" Bobbers

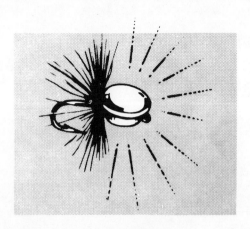

Dickey Pearl

Dickey Pearl—A sensational new ice-fishing lure. Nothing seems to be more natural in the water. There are times when bluegills, sunfish, perch, and crappies go crazy over this lure. Dickey recommends the large size with cornborer, wood grub, mousee, or wax worm. Great for trout. Patterns: natural pearl body with yellow, black, and red feather hackle, or rubber hackle. Sizes: #10 and #12. Price: 45¢.

Double Martini—You'll never guess how this lure got its name, but it has meant double trouble for many a fish. Especially effective on bluegills, crappies, and bass. Price: 40¢.

DOLL TACKLE, INC.

Not long ago, Zebco, Inc. sold out their entire line of Doll lures to Cotten Cordell. So the famous Doll products are now manufactured in Hot Springs, Arkansas—an area that is fast becoming a lure capital of sorts.

"The New Doll," as the line of lures is now being promoted, but which includes all the old favorites as well, includes the Doll Fly (actually a jig) and all its cousins, as well as spinner baits, grubs, and plugs for freshwater and saltwater fishing.

Doll Fly with Hair—Favorite of the "old favorites," this is the original jig that made Doll Fly a tackle box name among fishermen everywhere. It's made with extra bushy bucktail hair nestled around the shank so the hook won't show. The head is finished with high-gloss, chip-resistant epoxy paint. It's hand dressed with nylon thread. Hook: O'Shaughnessy cadmium-plated, heavy wire. Weights: from 1/64 to 2 ounces. Comes in nine colors and color combinations.

Crappie-Go-Crazy—When the crappie action gets hot, you'll be happy to have a handful of Crappie-Go-Crazy jigs along. This little lure creates a sensation that drives crappie critters wild. Use it with a bobber or without. Jig it at any depth. Hand tied with nylon thread.

Bitty Bite—Cast this one close to cover and let it sink slowly, then twitch the tip of the rod lightly. Even the wariest of game fish will be lured out of hiding, and a strike is sure to follow. Comes in multicolors and various sizes.

Doll Lures

EDMUND SCIENTIFIC CO.

A fat, 162-page catalog crammed with interesting and hard-to-find items is yours for 50¢ mailed to Edmund. There are more than 4,500 items described, many of which are useful to the outdoorsman—especially the tinkerers and do-it-yourselfers. Several products are of particular value to fishermen and are described below. Other Edmund products can be found in Chapters 3, 4, 5, 7, 11, and 12.

Electroplating Kit—Now, in minutes, you can restore scratched, worn, or rusted areas on thousands of things. Ideal for refinishing fishing reels where chrome plating is damaged. Seven different kits available for various finishes. Chromelike kit price: $13.95. Metal polish: $1.50/4-ounce jar.

Throw-Away Razor Blade Knives—So inexpensive you can discard them when they get dull. Countless uses for tackle tinkerers, rod builders, fly-tyers, and lure makers. Price: $6.95/50 postpaid, $12.90/100 postpaid.

Hemostat Surgical Pliers—Here's another tool that tackle tinkerers and fly-tyers will find useful. Hemostats are also great hook disgorgers. Jaws lock closed. Sizes: 5 inches with Tip A, 5½ inches with Tip B. (Tip A is for extra small work.) Prices: $3.95 postpaid (5 inches, Tip A), $4.25 postpaid (5½ inches, Tip B).

Diffraction Skin Jewels—They break up light into rainbow colors. Great for adding fish appeal to spoons and spinners. Pressure-sensitive adhesive backing. Can be cut and shaped with scissors. Price: $3/dozen postpaid.

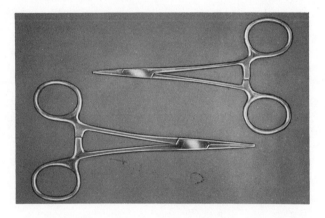

Hemostat Surgical Pliers

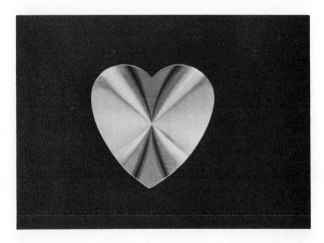

Diffraction Skin Jewels

LOU J. EPPINGER MANUFACTURING CO.

The name Eppinger might not immediately ring a bell with everyone, but if the Dardevle brand is unfamiliar to you, you're new to the sport of fishing. Some of the finest casting spoons available are manufactured with the highest quality materials by Eppinger and branded with the familiar sign of the Devil's head. They've been catching all sorts of freshwater and saltwater game fish since the turn of the century, and Dardevle has become a byword among fishermen everywhere.

In addition to enlarging the line of Dardevle spoons over the years and adding new finishes, Eppinger has revived some of the old proven fish-catching designs of J. T. Buel who invented and patented the first metal trolling lure back in the 1830s.

Dardevle—Still the outstanding choice of discriminating sportsmen everywhere because of its famous wiggle and wobble that tantalize all game fish. Available in a wide choice of colors and color combinations. Size: 3⅝ × 1¼ inches. Weight: 1 ounce. Price: $2.40.

Dardevle

Fluted Spinners

Notangle Spinner

Fluted Spinner—America's first metal trolling lure, invented by J. T. Buel, the Baitmaker of Whitehall, New York, once again made available to sportsmen. Still manufactured in the tradition of the nation's earliest craftsmen. Available with feathered or bucktail treble. Sizes: 1/0, 2/0, and 3/0. Prices: $2.50, $2.75, $3.

Notangle Spinner—A lure with the unique bend in the wire that prevents line twist, the newly designed Notangle Spinner is now available in three sizes that provide worry-free trolling. Sizes: ⅛, ¼, and ½ ounce. Prices: from $1.40 to $2.30.

FACTORY DISTRIBUTORS

Another Fort Smith, Arkansas, company, Factory Distributors offers a line of Rabble Rouser lures and Yum-Yum worms—proven bass getters.

There are nine sizes and styles of Rabble Rouser lures designed by Doug Parker. These lures have taken honors in numerous bass-fishing tournaments. Dennis Rogers, in fact, won the world's largest fishing trophy by using a crawdad-colored deep-diving Rabble Rouser Roo-Tur on Tenkiller Lake in Oklahoma.

Half-ounce Rabble Rouser Topwater—The casting-size topwater lure with hollow mouth and large eyes creates pops and gurgles and rolling darts and dives. Has new Clatter Rattle. Available in fifteen colors. Length: 3¼ inches. Hooks: two trebles. Available with or without rear propeller.

Rabble Rouser Roo-Tur—A deep-diving lure designed to go down after the "hawgs." This lure has great swimming action and a loud Clatter Rattle. Fantastic for trolling. Sizes: ¼ and ½ ounce. Available in sixteen colors.

Rabble Rouser RabbleR—All-purpose lure that combines the fish-catching qualities of the spinner bait and the crank bait into one to make the only true swimming spinner bait. Head pivots to allow fantastic, almost weedless swimming action. Can be fished without the spinner wire, with or without the skirt, with grub, worm, eel, frog, or pork rind.

Yum-Yum Worms—High floaters available in twenty-five colors and color combinations. Super soft and strong. Come 12, 20, or 100 to a package. Length: 6 inches.

Rabble Rouser Lures and Yum-Yum Worms

FEATHERWEIGHT PRODUCTS

Another name that is widely known and respected among rod builders is Featherweight. The product line includes rod blanks, guides, ferrules, handles and other components, as well as tools and materials for building fine rods. If you write for a catalog, be sure to send two bucks for their booklet, "How To Build Custom Quality Casting, Spinning and Fly Rods," by Ralph Brinkerhoff.

Paddle Rod Wrapper—An economical time saver for the fisherman who wraps his own rods. Base of each rod holder is weighted for excellent stability, and is covered with felt to protect desk or table top. Adjustable spring on thread holder allows you to select the best tension for the job. Accommodates rods of virtually any length and diameter. Price: $39.20.

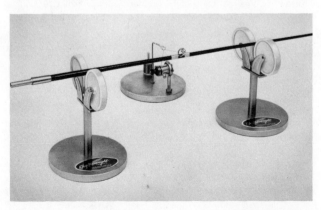

Paddle Rod Wrapper

Portable Electric Rod Wrapper—Helps you achieve professional results quickly and easily. Sturdy sewing machine motor with speed control on foot switch. Features grinding wheel to feather guides to a thin edge. Stanchion moves to accommodate rods of various lengths. Jacob's ½-inch chuck, oil fittings for shaft lubrication. Tucks away into a box 15×10×13 inches. Price: $95.20.

FENWICK

A big name among fishing-tackle manufacturers, Fenwick offers an extensive line of top-quality rods and rod-building components for all types of fishing, as well as a number of saltwater lures and various wire products.

Their 40-page general catalog describes the complete line of Fenwick HMG Graphite and Fenwick fiberglass fishing rods. It also contains charts on how to balance fly-fishing outfits, recommendations for various types of rods for different fishing situations, and sections on wire leaders and deep-water lures. The cost of their catalog is normally 25¢, but if you mention *The Great Outdoors Catalog* when you write, Fenwick will send their catalog free of charge. The same offer applies to Fenwick's "Rod Builder's Guide and Rod Blank Catalog" which normally sells for 25¢. So don't forget to mention our book.

Fenwick also conducts fly-fishing schools and has a booklet available that describes the curriculum and tells about various school locations. This one is free to interested persons.

HMG Graphite Fly Rods

HMG Graphite Spinning Rods

HMG Graphite Casting Rods

HMG Graphite Big Game Trolling Rods

Fly/Spin Combo Rods

Multi-piece Feralite ®

Fenwick Rods

HMG Graphite Fly Rods—Small in diameter, tough, and durable, these rods make distance casting much more relaxing. HMG will easily handle the next heavier line weight than that for which it is rated. Models up to #8 come with cork body reel seat; #9 to #12 line rods have anodized aluminum reel seats. All have ceramic stripping guides and chrome-plated snake guides. All are packed in nylon bags within durable hard cases. Lengths: from 6½ to 10½ feet. Weights: 1⅞ to 5¼ ounces. For AFTMA line sizes #4 through #12.

HMG Graphite Spinning Rods—Extremely small in diameter—from 25 to 40 percent smaller than their fiberglass counterparts—these rods will amaze you with their casting ability. Lengths: from 4½ feet (ultralight) to 9 feet (mooching). All conventional actions available.

HMG Graphite Casting Rods—These are the HMG equivalent of the Lunkerstiks. They are fitted with the new stronger, lightweight, detachable handle in choice of pistol or conventional grip, and with the revolutionary Grip-lok joiner that connects to the handle without a butt ferrule. All are one piece with ceramic guides and tip-tops. Lengths: 5 feet 5 inches to 6 feet. Shaft weights: from ⅞ to 1⅝ ounces.

HMG Big-Game Trolling Rods—Built to the same exacting standards and with the same components as the equivalent line class rods in the deluxe series fiberglass. Overall lengths: 6 feet 9 inches, 6 feet 10 inches. Butt lengths: from 19 to 20½ inches. Line classes: 12#, 20#, 30#, 50#, 80#, and 130#.

Voyageur Fly/Spin Combo Rods—Change from fly rod to spinning rod in a matter of moments. The reversible-handle Fly/Spin Combos let the traveling angler enjoy Fenwick performance in a versatile travel rod. Both handle wet, dry, streamer flies and nymphs as well as spinning lures. The SF74-4 is designed primarily for the spin fisherman who wants the fly-rod option. The SF75-5 is primarily for the fly-rod man who wants the spin option. Lengths: 7 and 7½ feet. Spinning line test: 2# to 6#. AFTMA fly line size: 6.

Flippin' Stik—Another first from Fenwick in bass rods. Flippin' is the delicate new technique of offering a lure to bass lying in shallows. The Flippin' Stik has unusual sensitivity with an extra stiff tip to set the hook faster. Guides and tip-tops are ceramic; handle is cork with 4-inch foregrip and 7-inch reargrip, and double-locking anodized aluminum reel seat. Length: 7½ feet. Weight: 8⅜ ounces. Line test: 15# to 30#.

The Long Ones—Fenwick's Long Ones are for steelhead and salmon, plus an ultradelicate 9-footer that's great for sea trout and bonefish as well as steelhead. They give you sensitivity without being fragile—strength and power without wobble or bounce. Available in a variety of lengths and actions, from 7½ to 9 feet. All rods in this series are two piece and use the Feralite ferrule, thus offering one-piece action and performance, while giving you the transportation convenience of a sectional rod.

Lunkerstik 2000—New for 1977, the Lunkerstik 2000 is a totally new type of casting rod, with an innovative handle that completely eliminates the need for a butt ferrule, and with an exciting new higher modulus fiberglass material in rod blank. To this Fenglass rod Fenwick has added a lighter, stronger handle. Guides are aluminum oxide for low line wear.

A. J. GALLAGER

From this company comes a complete line of "Common Sense" fly and spinning lure books (carriers). A wide assortment of designs is available in imitation leather, cowhide, and pigskin.

Common Sense Envelope Type Fly Book—These fly books have envelopes instead of springs and can be used for carrying flies, leaders,

etc., all of which can be clearly seen and easily removed. Envelopes are of white tag cloth with transparent celluloid front and each book is equipped with a felt drying pad. Size: 6½×3½ inches. Prices: $3.25 (imitation leather), $5.00 (chrome cowhide).

Common Sense Envelope Type Fly Book

Folder Type Fly Book—Imitation leather folder with springs attached to the inside cover. Also has two waterproofed parchment envelopes for leaders, etc. Will carry four dozen flies. Size: 7×3½ inches. Price: $3.25.

Streamer Fly Book—A practical book for carrying all types of streamer flies. Has four heavy felt pads with bound edges. Each pad has small leather pockets sewn to each end, back, and front, and ringed eye of streamer fly is inserted into these pockets. Capacity is at least forty-eight flies. Cover has extra pocket for leaders. Prices: $5.75 (imitation leather), $6.25 (chrome cowhide).

GANDER MOUNTAIN, INC.

In addition to offering a large line of top-quality products for outdoorsmen, Gander Mountain is a company that offers excellent discount prices and superb service. Every item in their catalog is guaranteed to meet your approval, and their return policy is hassle-free. No need to write for authorization to return any item. Simply ship it back with a note telling them whether to replace the item or refund your money. We might add, though, that we have never had to return anything to them, and we have dealt with them for about twelve of their eighteen years in the business.

Gander Mountain issues two catalogs a year—the Spring-Summer, which is heavy in fishing tackle, and the Fall-Winter with a beefed-up hunting line.

Below is a small sampling of the Gander Mountain fishing-tackle line. Other items offered by this company can be found in Chapters 3, 4, 5, 6, 7, 8, and 9.

Fenwick HMG 7½-Foot Graphite Fly Rod—Light action for medium-size streams—small dry flies. Weight: 2⅝ ounces. AFTMA line: #5. G.M. price: $94.47.

Fenwick Fenglass 2061 6-Foot Lunkerstik Casting Rod—Medium-action, one-piece rod. Weight: 2¼ ounces. For 12# to 25# line and lures to 1¼ ounces. G.M. price: $28.67.

Eagle Claw 8-Piece All-Purpose Travel Rod—The one rod for all your fishing. New eight-piece "Trailmaster" sets up five different ways to give you five great rods in one—6-foot 9-inch spinning rod, 6-foot 9-inch fly rod, 5½-foot spin-casting rod, 5½-foot bait-casting rod, 5-foot trolling rod. Made from highest-grade glass with exclusive "Uni-Fit" ferrules.

Built to fit any popular size 15-inch tackle box with room to spare for other tackle. Vinyl case included. G.M. price: $29.97.

Berkley Para-Metric P30 7-Foot Spinning Rod—Medium-light action, for 6# to 17# line and lures to ¾ ounce. Weight: 5½ ounces. G.M. price: $16.97.

Garcia Avocado #8200 4½-Foot One-Piece Spinning Rod—Ultralight action, for 1# to 6# lines and ¹⁄₁₆- to ¼-ounce lures. G.M. price: $11.97.

Garcia Ambassadeur #8324 6½-Foot Two-Piece Casting Rod—Medium-soft action rod for lines from 8# to 20# and lures from ½ to 1 ounce. G.M. price: $24.97.

Eagle Claw Blue Pacific #1425 Spinning Reel—Medium freshwater reel. Gear ratio: 4.2:1. Line capacity: 275 yards of 15# line. Weight: 22 ounces. G.M. price: $19.47.

Heddon #3200 Casting Reel—An extremely fine quality free-spool casting reel at a budget price. Features unique clutch that totally disengages wind and gears during cast, an exclusive automatic centrifugal drag system, calibrated spool tension, precision steel ball bearings and helical gears, man-sized power handle, antibacklash control, and star drag. Gear ratio: 4.1:1. Capacity: 120 yards 15# line. Complete with plastic storage case, wrench, oil, spare parts, and reel case. G.M. price: $29.97.

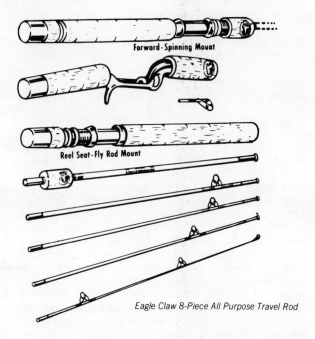

Forward-Spinning Mount

Reel Seat-Fly Rod Mount

Eagle Claw 8-Piece All Purpose Travel Rod

Garcia ABU-Matic 170 Spin-Casting Reel—Sophisticated reel features adjustable star drag and Syncro drag—instantly adjusts automatically to your needs. No-twist oscillating spool. Positive antireverse. Self-lubricating bushings. Gear ratio: 3:1. Comes fully loaded with 15# Royal Bonnyl line. G.M. price: $18.97.

Martin Tuffy 63 Fly Reel—Pushbutton spool is fine etched and ventilated for maximum performance. On/off click-type drag. Two hardened, plated line guides for right- or left-hand use. Capacity: 35 yards of #8 line. Weight: 3¾ ounces. G.M. price: $5.47.

Eppinger's Original Dardevle Lure Kit—Contains one each of the following red and white lures: 3/16, ¼, ²⁄₅, ³⁄₅, and 1 ounce. G.M. price: $6.85.

GAPEN'S WORLD OF FISHIN', INC.

Dan Gapen has a dandy catalog, chock-full of time-proven, fish-catching lures, as well as tips on fishing various baits in different fishing situations. Newest in the Gapen line are "Slip" lures and the Bait Walking Sinker. Other Gapen products include jigs, grubs, spinner baits, plastic worms, and flies.

Slips—Here's a line of lures designed to cast well and dig deep on the retrieve. They can be used on spinning or casting rods and can be cast, trolled, or jigged. They vibrate hard, creating fish-attracting turbulence. They are available in six different designs and two weights. The ⅜-ounce Slip is for use in depths of less than 15 feet. The ⅝-ounce Slip is for depths of 30 feet and will dive to 24 feet on a normal retrieve. Designs: Shad, Sea Horse, Ripple Fish, De Minnow, Shoveler, Digger. Colors: black, purple scale, blue scale, orange scale, perch, dark shiner, fluorescent orange, and fluorescent red. Prices: $1.25 (⅜ ounce), $1.45 (⅝ ounce).

Bait Walker Sinker—A great new idea for live bait and still fishing, as well as for working floating artificial baits near the bottom. Sizes: ⅝, 1, 1½, 2 ounces. Prices: 75¢, 85¢, $1, $1.50.

Eel-Jig—Available in yellow, black, purple, and blue. Weights: ⅜ and ⅝ ounce. Prices: $1.10, $1.25.

Weedless Eel-Jig—Same colors and weights as Eel-Jig. Prices: $1.35, $1.50.

Weedless Eel-Jig

Ugly Bug—Great jig-lure for walleye, bass, pike, musky, and panfish. Colors: white, yellow, black, purple, brown, orange, and chartreuse. Weights: 1/16 to ½ ounce. Prices: from 85¢ to $1.10.

Ugly Bug Plus—Same as above, but with spinner bait wire and blade attached. Prices: from $1.35 to $1.65.

GARCIA CORP.

A long respected name in fishing tackle, Garcia needs no introduction. A complete line of rods and reels for spinning, spin-casting, bait-casting, fly-fishing, and trolling is available from Garcia. Additionally, the company produces fishing lines, lures, and accessories.

The *Garcia Fishing Annual* is distributed nationally and is available at newsstands, supermarkets, and sports shops. It sells for $1.50. The first half of the annual is packed with fishing articles and photographs by some of the top fishing writers in the country. The aft half of the book is a catalog of current Garcia tackle.

The company conducts a fishing awards program for freshwater and saltwater game fish. Description of the program and a registration form are found in the *Garcia Fishing Annual*. In addition to fishing tackle, Garcia also offers a line of fish-finders and an oxygen probe (Chapter 3), as well as firearms (Chapter 4).

Mitchell Rods—The actions of each of these new spinning rods are superb, combining light weight with outstanding power and response. This is especially true of the new Power Taper (PT) action rods. Their large diameter butt areas give them tremendous muscle, yet they remain light, comfortable, and well balanced in use. Fiberglass blanks are indi-

Garcia Rods

wonderfully comfortable Foam Light grips that feel great and telegraph every tiny signal your line sends up. All guides and tip-tops are of ceramic Conoglide. All two-piece rods use special flexible glass ferrules. Lengths: from 5 to 7½ feet. Actions: light to medium-stiff.

Garcia Brown Rods—This line offers the angler a complete range from which to choose. They include spin-casting, bait-casting, boat, popping, and trolling rods. It's in the area of spinning, though, that the wide span of Brown rods really stands out. They range from little 5-foot ultralight wands, capable of flicking out lures as light as 1/16 ounce, to big 11-foot 4-inch surf rods with the power and backbone to hurl a 5-ounce lure farther out than you'll probably ever need. There are thirty-six different rods in this series, with every kind of action to fit nearly any type of fishing situation, including such special-purpose rods as the #2572 with a special extra-soft action for casting salmon-egg clusters without tearing them, and the #B526, with its very heavy, very powerful action that can handle up to a 50# line and 6-ounce lure—a perfect heavy-duty spinning rod for musky or chinook salmon.

Mitchell 300/300C Reels—Superior performance has made these reels superstars in the freshwater fishing world. Garcia gave the 300 a superlative system of eight precision-made gears to deliver its power in a velvet hush, a one-piece bail that couldn't pinch your line if it wanted to, and a line guide made of tungsten carbide. The 300 is equipped with a pushbutton spool for quick and easy switching of spools. Other features include Teflon drag, oilite bushings, one-spot lubrication, thermo-baked corrosion-resistant finish, convenient antireverse, and folding handle with comfort-formed grip. The 300C has a hardened roller line guide and tempered steel roller bearings.

Mitchell 402 Reel—Saltwater fishing is a tough test of men and tackle, and the Garcia Mitchell 402, with its 4.5:1 retrieve ratio and big power, is the reel that experienced anglers reach for when the fish are running big. It and the standard-retrieve #302 carry all the power you need, with polished stainless steel ball bearings and self-lubricating oilite bushings to deliver all that power with unbelievable smoothness. Other features include a new anti-inertia brake, hard-chromed line guide, folding handle, Teflon drag, and helical-cut gears.

Kingfisher GK-24 Spinning Reel—One of the reels from the economy family, the GK-24 is a fine choice for all-around freshwater spinning. It has a line capacity of 200 yards of 10# standard-diameter mono, protected by a fully adjustable drag. The axle shaft rides in SKS carbon steel ball bearings, and the retrieve ratio is a fast 4:1.

Ambassadeur Standard-Retrieve Bait-Casting Reels—Each of the standard-retrieve reels shares a retrieve ratio of 3.6:1, but that's the only thing that's standard about them. After all, there's nothing standard about features like two braking systems—one centrifugal and one mechanical—that work together to form a virtually perfect antibacklash control. Nor is there anything standard about a powerful, velvet-smooth multidisk star drag, enclosed silent level wind with stainless steel pawl, free spool with automatic reengagement, anodized corrosion-resistant finish and quick, no-tool takedown. The group includes the classic Ambassadeur 5000, the great 5000D with the extra power of direct drive, and the 5000C with the addition of stainless steel ball bearings.

HARBEN MANUFACTURING CO.

No more flying scales. No fuss. No muss. Those are Harben's claims about their new fish scaler, which is the only fishing product we know of that is offered by this company.

Harben Fish Scaler—A precision engineered fish scaler with seventy-two scalpel edges that will cleanly remove all scales. One-piece design of aluminum alloy. It is bright for lifetime use—noncorroding, nonrusting. Weight: 1½ ounces. Price: $1.49.

vidually cut, rolled, and cured, and each blank is completely hand made as a single unit. All wrappings are protected by Conoguard, an exclusive finish that actually penetrates the wrappings and bonds directly to the shaft. Ferrules are made of structural fiberglass, thus eliminating the dead spot found in many two-piece rods. Grips are select-grade specie cork. Lengths: from 5 to 7½ feet. Actions: ultralight to medium-heavy (PT).

Ambassadeur Rods—These casting rods are rapidly achieving recognition as bass rods of excellence comparable to that of the Ambassadeur bait-casting reels. The actions of each of these rods vary, of course. But all of them share a feeling of crisp muscular power combined with outstanding sensitivity. The grips on all Ambassadeur bait-casting rods are

JAMES HEDDON'S SONS

When I was a young boy, growing up in southwestern Ohio, there were four constants in my life—the joy of fishing, A. J. McClane's articles in *Field & Stream,* the Heddon catalog, and low grades in arithmetic. As I've grown older, I've noticed that some things change and some things stay the same. I'm still no good at math, and fishing is just as exciting to me as it ever was. But McClane is retired now, and Heddon's catalog is a far cry from that great volume I used to mail off for every year. It cost a quarter then—which was a lot for a catalog in those days—but it was jammed with descriptions of great fishing lures, rods, and reels. In the back were sections on fresh and salt water game fish, including the current world records, which I had committed to memory shortly after I learned to read.

Make no mistake; Heddon still manufactures top-quality tackle, and has added new gear to its line of time-tested equipment for the angler. In fact, a fair share of the tackle that Patty and I use has the Heddon brand on it, and the first artificial bait I ever owned was a Heddon River Runt Spook—a plug that caught my first largemouth bass and many more in the years that followed, has had the hooks replaced on it a half-dozen times, and is now retired.

Heddon offers a lot of good tackle, and their catalog is worth having. It's just too bad that they don't produce that wonderful volume they put out twenty years or so ago. Certainly, printing costs have gone up drastically, but I, for one, would be willing to send them a buck or two for something like the old Heddon catalog.

—K.O.

Mark Legacy Rods—The quality starts with carefully made rod blanks. After they are formed they are precisely cured at 290° to give uniform action, great strength, and fine sensitivity. The fly rods deliver fine, smooth, small loops. The pewter look is deep and lustrous. It's then protected by the finest finish available. The guides are the finest aluminum oxide—hard, smooth. The low-profile handle is sleek and comfortable, with special Gatorhide pattern and finish that says the best.

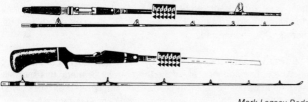

Mark Legacy Rods

Mark Galaxy Rods—Deep, rich, earthy, lustrous. Rod and handle colors are matched. So much beauty and all married to tried and true tradition. Carbide guides for long line life; a fine offset handle, complete with specie cork, super Heddon actions—strong, consistent, sensitive. One of the finest rods Heddon has ever built.

Slipstick Rods—Modern styling and actions—traditional Heddon quality. This jet black beauty sports a modern, comfortable handle; hard, smooth, long-lasting aluminum oxide guides; hard-hitting actions with just the right sensitivity and flex. The fly rods deliver a smooth "small loop" line.

Mark Graphite Rods—Light, strong, sensitive, consistent, and married to a sleek, light, modern handle—beautiful. The guides are the best aluminum oxide made. And Heddon brings it to you at an affordable price.

Model 282 Spinning Reel—Top-of-the-line standout with outstanding features, like a super-smooth disk drag system, silky smooth, three-race ball-bearing system on crank and main shaft, helical gears, forced and machine cut to really stand up when cranking in the fish. A high-speed

retrieve, convertible right-left handle. Super quality and color coordination to give you years of smooth, dependable fishing. Rated for freshwater use. Capacity: 200 yards of 8# line. Gear ratio: 4.5:1. Weight: 13.5 ounces.

Model 409 Trolling Reel—Smooth-acting star drag. All metal spool, 2⅛-inch wide with full, free-spool action. Level wind. Plate diameter: 3 inches. Gear ratio: 3:1. Capacity: 300 yards of 20# mono. Weight: 20 ounces.

Model 340 Fly Reel—Single-action, large-capacity fly reel. Handles up to and including AFTMA #10 line. Weight: 5¾ ounces.

Big Bud—For good fun and good fishing. It has been extensively tested in Florida, Missouri, Texas, Michigan, and Minnesota on bass, northerns, and muskies. Weight: ⅝ ounce.

Crazy Crawler—A consistent catcher of large game fish. When cast, metal side baffles cause noisy crawling action that infuriates fish. Particularly effective on bass, pike, and pickerel. Available in six colors. Lengths: 1¾ and 2⅜ inches. Weights: ¼ and ⅝ ounce.

BIG BUD®

CRAZY CRAWLER®

HEFNER PLASTICS, INC.

One category of fishing tackle that has undergone a rather silent revolution is tackle boxes, and Hefner has a revolutionary new design to offer anglers. Their line of Tackle Tamer boxes incorporates a system of "lazy Susan" drawers, and should be of particular interest to boat fishermen.

Model 108 Tackle Tamer—Arranged for the fisherman who needs many lures at his fingertips, this new box has more compartments per pound of box than is believable. Constructed of tough, durable ABS plastic. Eight big shallow trays, 1⅝ inches deep each, with eleven compartments; two big deep trays with sixteen movable dividers for up to twenty compartments. A total of 108 compartments. Price: $39.95.

Model 76 Tackle Tamer—Six shallow trays and one deep tray with eight movable dividers for a total of seventy-six compartments. Price: $27.95.

Model 32 Tackle Tamer—The deluxe economy model with two big shallow trays and one deep tray for a total of thirty-two compartments. Price: $16.95.

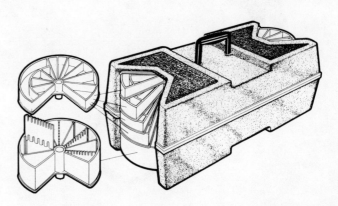

Model 108 Tackle Tamer

HYPARK SPECIALTY CO.

From this company come several products of possible interest to fishermen.

Tac-L Keeper—A 10½-inch Ethafoam rod with plastic caps on each end for holding snelled hooks, live minnow rigs, spinner baits, live bait harnesses, flies, etc. Tac-L Keeper is easy and quick to use. It floats, and there are no springs for hooks and line to get caught in. Holds all size lures, even up to 6-inch minnow rigs. Price: $1.89.

Mino-Mizer—Aerates and cools water to keep bait alive and alert for days in a standard minnow bucket, or in tanks up to thirty gallons. Mino-Mizer floats and atomizes the water into a fine spray for maximum oxygenation. Great for freshwater and saltwater bait. Operates on a 6V lantern battery, and with a special 12V converter can be hooked up to a boat or car battery. Price: $12.95. Converter: $2.15.

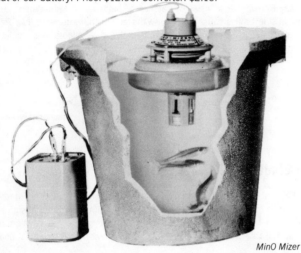

MinO Mizer

JET-AER CORP.

G-96 is the familiar brand name marketed by this company, and it is far more extensive than we realized. While we have used a number of G-96 products over the years, we found in reviewing their catalog that we had only sampled a tiny portion of what they have to offer to the outdoorsman.

Other G-96 products will be found in Chapters 4, 8, 9, and 11.

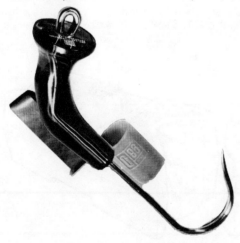

Model 2090 Surf Gaff

G-96 Jet Aerator—Pumps bubbles of fresh air into water to keep bait alive. Works in fresh or salt water. Sealed motor is unaffected by rain or damp weather. Rigid foam dispensing head won't clog or collapse. High-impact case is maintenance-free. Special clamp fits even the thickest plastic minnow bucket. Price: $5.95.

Model 2090 G-96 Surf Gaff—Combines unique sure-grip handle with tempered stainless steel hook in specially designed plastic holster, which enables you to wear the Surf Gaff on your belt. It remains within easy reach for immediate use. Price: $10.95.

G-96 Pure Silicone Fishing Reel Lube—Specially formulated to lubricate and protect both freshwater and saltwater reels. Use on metal, plastic, and rubber parts. Protects against saltwater corrosion, weather, wear, and rust. Price: 98¢/1-ounce can.

G-96 Spray Dry Fly—Waterproofs and protects dry flies. Pocket-size aerosol spray waterproofs flies or feathers without changing their shape. Dries quickly so that fly is ready for immediate use. Price: $1.75/3-ounce can.

G-96 Old Fashioned Anise Scented Fish Lure—Contains a blend of ingredients, including anise scent, which attracts fish through their sense of smell, a sense that is extremely acute in most game fish. Spray it on regular bait, fly, or lure. It attracts more fish, ensures more strikes. Use for both freshwater and saltwater fish. Pocket-size aerosol can— convenient to carry, won't break, spill, or spoil. Price: $1.98/3-ounce can.

G-96 Rod Finish—Refinishes glass fishing rods and makes them look factory new. Easy to use spray produces a hard, scratch-resistant finish that resists saltwater and sand abrasion. Remains flexible without cracking, chipping, or peeling. Price: $1.89/7-ounce can.

G-96 Clear Epoxy Rod Finish—Easy to use, one-step epoxy rod finish in aerosol spray (contains no fluorocarbons). It will produce a hard, high-gloss, scratch-resistant, professional finish that will resist weathering and will not chip, crack, or peel. For use on all types of fishing rods. Price: $1.98/6-ounce can.

G-96 Rod Winding Color Preservative—This quick-drying preservative locks in the hue and intensity of the thread color pigment. It is specially designed to be compatible and provide an ideal base for all types of rod finishes. Dries in fifteen to twenty minutes. Price: $1/1-ounce jar.

LOUIS JOHNSON CO.

If you have ever tossed a weedless spoon and pork rind into the weeds or lily pads, there's a good chance that the spoon was a Johnson Silver Minnow. In addition to that famous bait, Johnson offers a number of other spoons for casting, trolling, or jigging. And the Silver Minnow is no longer just silver.

Johnson Silver Minnow—The weedless Silver Minnow is famous for working in tanglesome weeds and stumpage. While this is the hardest area in which to catch a fish, it is also where the best catch is often made. The Silver Minnow, forged for accurate, pinpoint casting, greater distance and better wobble, will help bring the big ones in every time. Colors: silver, gold, black nickel, fluorescent orange, and chartreuse. Lengths: 1¼, 2, 2¼, 2¾, 3, and 4 inches. Weights: 1/24, ⅛, ¼, ½, ¾, and 1⅛ ounces.

Johnson Bucktail Spoon—Add a bucktail trailer to Johnson's exclusive forged spoon and you have an unbeatable combination. Pinpoint casting, flashing 35° side-to-side wobbling retrieve—great catches. Color:

silver with yellow bucktail. Lengths: 2, 2¼, 2¾, and 3 inches. Weights: ⅛, ¼, ½, and ¾ ounce.

Lucky Lujon—Catch what you want, where you want with this versatile forged brass lure that lets you cast a "country mile." Designed in the true Nordic tradition, the Lujon has irresistible action, whether it's trolled or retrieved normally. When jiggled up and down, its weighted head makes it look like a feeding minnow. Also available in weedless model. Colors: chrome, brass, fluorescent orange, and chartreuse. Lengths: 1½, 2½, 3½, and 4½ inches. Weights: ⅛, ⅜, 1, and 2½ ounces.

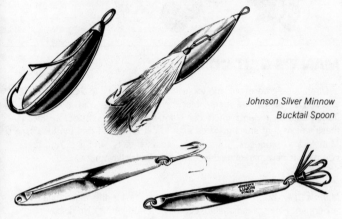

Johnson Silver Minnow
Bucktail Spoon

Lucky Lujon and Weedless Lujon

LAZY IKE CORP.

Lazy Ike is another lure that has been around for a long time and is a proven favorite among fishermen everywhere. But the company also offers an assortment of other lures, including plugs, jigs, spinner baits, and plastic worms. Additionally, Lazy Ike manufactures catfish baits and accessories for anglers.

Lazy Ike—The world-famous lure is now available in a wide variety of sizes and colors to fit any fishing situation and to take all game fish and panfish. These are subsurface lures with a tantalizing wiggle. Size range is from the tiny 1¹⁄₁₆-inch, ¹⁄₃₂-ounce fly rod lure to the hefty 3½-inch, ⅝-ounce bruiser for bass, muskies, and northern pike.

Lazy Ike

Do-Bait Hooks—These Lazy Ike originals hold soft doughy baits many times longer than ordinary hooks. Single and treble types available.

Lazy Ike Appetite—This forty-year favorite was the first dough bait ever placed on the market, and is the best-known bait in catfish territory. Comes in 1-pound buckets.

Lazy Ike Bloody Bait—A new tested and proven blood-thickened, blood-rich bait. It has produced record-size catches. For all catfish. Comes in 1-pound buckets.

LIMIT MANUFACTURING CORP.

The 62-page catalog from Limit is full of rod-building and lure-making components and is a browser's delight. Rod components include most of the top name brands. For the tackle tinkerer, plastic worm molds and materials are available, as are assorted hardware items, lure bodies, jig molds, and spinner bait parts.

Colorado Spinner Blades—All blades are of finest quality materials. Finishes are bright and durable. Brass and copper finishes are lacquer coated to prevent tarnishing. Finishes: nickel, brass, hammered nickel, hammered brass, hammered copper. Painted blades also available. Sizes #1 through #8. Prices: start at 40¢/dozen.

Jig-Spinner Wire Form—Form to make a jig-spinner bait. Wire diameter: .028 inch. Sizes: 1¼×1½ inches (#1), 1½×1¾ inches (#2). Prices: $1.20/25, $1.30/25.

Split Rings—Finest quality nickel-plated steel. Sizes: #1, #3, and #5. Prices: 40¢/50, 75¢/100, $3/500.

Formed Spinner Heads—Spinner bait heads in tapered shape. Sizes: ¼ and ⅜ ounce. Prices: 30¢ each, $2.75/dozen.

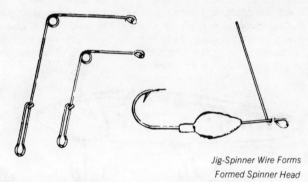

Jig-Spinner Wire Forms
Formed Spinner Head

Banana Head Jigs—Banana head molded on fine wire gold hook. Weights: ¼ and ⅜ ounce. Price: $1.25/dozen.

Plug Screw Eyes—Available in small, medium, and large. Prices: 39¢/25, $1.19/100.

LISK-FLY MANUFACTURING CO.

While Lisk offers a line of lures that includes spinners, jigs, flies, nymphs, plastic worms, and their new Miracle Plug, one of their greatest fish producers has to be their famous Little Skunk. It is one of the best crappie and bluegill lures we have ever used, and we've taken a number of other game fish with it, too.

A new wrinkle on panfishing is a modification of the Little Skunk called the Skunk Nymph, which employs the little jig body used on the Little Skunk, along with a tiny piece of plastic worm.

Little Skunk—Fast-sinking body on finest gold hook. Trailer hook is tied with fluffy white hackle. Very effective when used as a trailer lure. Hook size: #8. Trailer size: #12. Available in seven colors. Price: 85¢.

Skunk Nymph—Small lead-bodied bug, molded on #8 hook. Comes with four 2-inch plastic worms. Cut small piece of worm about the length of the body of the nymph and then hook as close to the end of the worm as possible. Weighted body sinks fast. Pull slowly across bottom of lake for best results. Available in assorted colors. Price: 75¢.

Skunk Nymph

Lisk Miracle Plug—For use in all types of fishing, this lure is built hollow with a transparent body. Bait inserted through removable head is magnified. Besides live bait, various objects such as colored beads can be used inside the lure. Metal balls can be used to cause a rattle. Baking soda placed inside will cause lure to fizz. Lengths: 1½ and 4 inches. Prices: $1.25, $1.35.

LOOP A LINE, INC.

"Your deadly double eye is the greatest improvement to the great sport of fishing since the hook."

—Tom Hollatz, Author
The Guides of the North Woods

"Be a quick-change artist and stop wasting line and time."

—Gadabout Gaddis
The Flying Fisherman

What these experts are talking about is an ingenious device that makes lure changing quick and easy and eliminates the need for tying another knot every time a lure is changed. It is called the DDE (deadly double eye) and is standard equipment on Loop A Line lures. It can be purchased also in kit form for converting other lures. Look for many new Loop A Line products in the future, too.

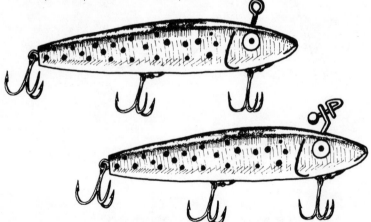

Lure before and after Loop A Line Conversion

M-F MANUFACTURING CO., INC.

This must be the year for nifty new products, because in addition to a line of molds and materials for making plastic worms, M-F is offering a new item we think will find much interest among outdoors people. It is described below.

Tooth Saver Line and Knot Cutter—Stop biting your line and searching for your cutters. Put a Tooth Saver on your reel. Simple to install and use. Made of heat-treated stainless steel for sharpness and durability. Cuts mono and braided line. Fits the following reels: Ambassadeur 5000, 5500C, 6000, 6500C series; Diawa Millionaire V/3H/5H/6H/6B series; Quick 600 and 800 series; Lew's Speed Spool BB-1. Price: $2.98/pair.

Tooth Saver

MANN'S BAIT CO.

Open our big worm box and you'll think you walked into a candy store, as such smells as strawberry, blackberry, pineapple, and grape drift from the compartments where our Mann's Jelly Worms reside. Besides these worms that smell good enough to eat (and isn't that the idea?), Mann's also produces grubs, plugs, spinner baits, and jigs. And the company is now marketing the Jelly Worm Oil for flavoring any soft plastic baits.

Mann's Jelly Worm—This super-soft worm is for the discriminating fisherman. Fine craftsmanship, combined with Mann's own discoveries in the formulating and the use of soft plastics has made possible the naturallike appearance and action of the Jelly Worm. It has all the fish-catching qualities. Available in fifteen different flavors. Sizes: 4, 6, 7, 8, and 9 inches. Prices per twenty-count bag: $2.40, $4, $5, $6. Also available in $1-Pak.

Fat Albert—This bait has all the fish-catching qualities that have ever been built into a lure. Two built-in sound chambers counterbalance the weights. Available in ten popular colors. Weights: ⅜ and ½ ounce. Prices: $2.50, $2.75.

Frog Mann—A superb surface bait. This lure is excellent for early morning or late evening bassin'. A BB shot inside throws off fine sound waves that big bass just can't resist. Available in six colors. Weights: ¼ and ⅜ ounce. Prices: $2.25, $2.50.

Woolly Bully Spinner Baits—Perfect for fishing in weeds and around grass beds, this spinner bait has a long shaft that makes it virtually weedless. Matched blades for maximum vibration and performance. Use with skirt or grub. Available in single and tandem spins. Weights: ¼, ⅜, and ⅝ ounce. Colors: white, yellow, black, chartreuse, fire red, white/black, and chartreuse/black. Prices: $1.85 (single), $1.95 (tandem).

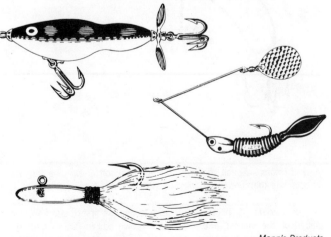

Mann's Products

MARTIN REEL CO.

We have all lost fish, and most of us have tales about the "big one that got away." But when a fish is lost, about all most of us ever do is maybe cuss a little when it happens, and repeat the story time and again, allowing the fish to grow properly between tellings.

Not so with Herman W. Martin. When he lost a trophy fish because of fly line that had become tangled in the bottom of his boat, he decided to do something about it. He designed the first Martin automatic fly reel to keep the same thing from happening again, and had it patented in 1884.

Since those days the Martin Reel Company has become established as a highly respected manufacturer of fine fly reels. Today their line includes spinning and spin-casting reels as well as rods and other tackle.

They will send you their catalog free of charge, and if you write, be sure to ask for their pamphlets, "Fly Fishing is Easy" and "Fly Fishing for Bass."

Martin Model 72 Fly Reel—This is a fast-retrieve, multiple-action fly reel with exclusive one-way 360° floating Teflon disk drag. Wind line on three times faster than with a single-action reel, then play the fish off the smooth drag—an unbeatable combination. On/Off click. Twin hardened plated line guides. Changes easily to right- or left-handed use. Capacity: 35 yards. WF9F, plus 150 yards backing. Ratio: 3:1.

Martin Blue Chip Fly Reel—An automatic fly reel so carefully crafted that only a limited number are made each year. So well engineered that each reel is guaranteed for five years against defects—even wear. Pushbutton tension release. Adjustable trigger. Silent wind. Quick-acting brake. Complete with soft deerskin pouch. Weight: 9¼ ounces. Capacity: 30 yards DT8F, 35 yards WF8F. Finished in light bronze with silver trim.

Martin Model 220 Spin-Casting Reel—A new reel carefully designed and tooled to provide the youngster with a reel that's easy to handle. Comes complete with 80 yards of 6# mono. Star drag. Stationary spool prevents line twist. Multipoint pickup. Permanent antireverse click. Aluminum front cover. Weight: 6 ounces. Color: two-tone black and gold.

Model 220 Spin-Casting Reel

Martin Breeton Model 804SRM Spinning Reel—High-speed reel with extra corrosion proofing. Noiseless helical gears. Stainless steel shaft with quiet ball-bearing mounting. Belted spool. Tough, seven-plate drag system. Stainless bail. Carbide line roller. Folding stainless handle. On/Off antireverse click. Ratio: 4.75:1. Weight: 11 ounces. Made in France.

Sovereign Travel Set—Freshwater and saltwater gear in one compact Naugahyde travel case, includes ball-bearing mounted, helically geared

U.L. spinning reel Model 104 with 5:1 retrieve and Teflon drag; 804SRM saltwater spinning reel; Model 66 single-action fly reel with pushbutton release spool and click drag. Tubular rods include #31-666, 6½-foot spin-fly and 6½-foot #1-666 saltwater spinning. Model 641 fly box and 99002 lure box also included. Naugahyde case measures 16½× 7½×4½ inches, has interior case with room for all reels, lure boxes, plus space for extra spool and other gear.

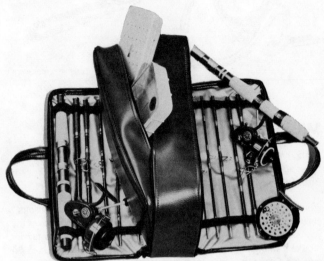

Sovereign Travel Set

MILDRUM MANUFACTURING CO.

This company manufactures quality fishing rod mountings that are carried by a number of rod-building suppliers listed in this chapter. Their line includes guides and tip-tops for casting, spinning, fly, trolling, and big-game rods. They also offer stainless steel roller guides and tip-tops.

Casting and Trolling Mountings—These mountings incorporate either stainless steel or Mildarbide (Carboloy) rings. All stainless steel mountings are chrome-plated for additional wear resistance. Mildarbide offers the greatest wear resistance. SSE series guides are heavy-duty, with extra-heavy chrome, stainless steel rings. ME series guides are heavy-duty, frame extra-heavy chrome, Mildarbide rings. SSEL series guides are lightweight, stainless steel rings. SFSSE series are stamped frame guides, stainless steel rings. SSWT is an all-purpose, economical wire-supported top, rugged enough for casting and trolling, but light enough for spinning. SSDL are lightweight supported tops, stainless steel rings. SSD are heavy-duty supported tops with extra-heavy chrome, stainless steel rings. MD are heavy-duty supported tops, Mildarbide rings.

Casting and Trolling Mountings

Mildrum Ceramic "Linesavers"—These rings are the hardest, most wear-resistant rings currently used for guides and tops. Material is the purest aluminum oxide currently available (over 99 percent). They have achieved a high polish and reduce line abrasion to a minimum. The shock ring and the ceramic ring are locked in by rolling over the stainless steel band. They are not solely a force fit. The bands and frames are both of 18-8 stainless steel, the best for corrosion resistance. The frames have feet long enough to ensure secure fastening to the blank. Series MAC guides and MATS supported tops.

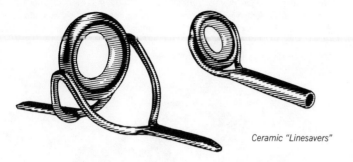

Ceramic "Linesavers"

MILLER FISHING TACKLE

The name of the game at Miller's is bass. And to win the game they have developed several new baits—two spinner baits and the new Buzz-Tail Worm (Pat. Pend.).

White Tornado—A spinner bait that comes with "deadly instructions," showing six different ways the lure can be fished at various times of the year. Also special tips on where to find bass. Serrated lizard tail for fabulous swimming legs. Fish-attracting sound from combination of #4 and #5 Colorado blades. Arm design directly over hook makes lure virtually snagless. Colors: shad white, licorice, raspberry purple, lemon, chartreuse, royal blue. Price: $1.79.

White Tornado

Buzz-Tail Worm—A new worm with a thin, small double tail that quivers with the slightest movement and moves in a throbbing, swimming motion with a sweep of the rod or turn of the reel. The outer body is made of soft wedge-shaped segments that trap and release air bubbles and give the body a soft alive feel. Colors: black, blue, brown, purple, grape, green, strawberry, and smoke. For murky waters, two glow-in-dark colors: purple and orange. Length: 6 inches. Field Tester Special: five $1.29 packs of Buzz Tail Worms for only $5, includes free color patch.

O. MUSTAD & SON, INC.

If you want to know the truth, Mustad operates Norway's largest zipper factory. They also manufacture nails and woodscrews at their Oslo facilities. Another part of the Mustad group produces coffee and margarine. And all this time you thought they made hooks. Well, indeed they do. They've been in business since 1832, and they are one of the oldest and largest manufacturers of sport and commercial fish hooks in the world.

They produce tens of thousands of different finishes and patterns of hooks and export them to more than 130 countries around the world. In some primitive countries, Mustad hooks are even used for barter and exchange. The Mustad line is extensive, and their catalog contains a wealth of hook-learning.

Mustad-Carlisle Hooks—Superior hooks for many uses. An excellent live-bait hook. Finishes: gold-plated, black, bronzed, blued, tinned, bright, nickel-plated, red. Sizes: 10/0 to 20.

Hollow-Point Mustad-Beak Hooks—Another favorite among bait fishermen. This hook is available in a one-slice or two-slice shank to hold bait on the hook. Finishes: bronzed, gold-plated, nickel-plated, cadmium-plated, tinned. Sizes: 10/0 to 16.

Mustad-O'Shaughnessy Hooks—A favorite design among saltwater fishermen, this hook is forged and ringed. Finishes: black, bronzed, nickel-plated, gold-plated, copper-plated, tinned, bright. Sizes: 14/0 to 16.

Mustad-Treble Hooks—Excellent as a bait hook or for use in lure making and replacing defective hooks on lures. Finishes: bronzed, gold-plated, nickel-plated, cadmium-plated, tinned, bright. Sizes: 14/0 to 26.

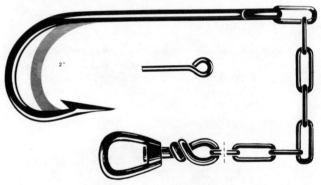

Shark Hook

Mustad-Shark Hooks—Going after Jaws? Here's the hook for you. This brute is big and tough and comes equipped with a ¾-meter chain and swivel. Finish: tinned. Gap sizes: 1 to 6 inches.

Mustad Baiting Needles—Here's something that's not always easy to find everywhere. And if you want to do a neat job of sewing bait fish onto a hook, you need baiting needles. Finishes: black, bronzed, red. Sizes: 6 to 12 inches, 8 to 18 centimeters.

NETCRAFT CO.

For most fishermen, any year is divided into two parts—the fishing season and that other horrible period. It's tough enough for most of us to get through the off-season, but those blustery winter days would be unbearable without the Netcraft catalog.

As the Netcraft folks say, it is truly a fisherman's dream book, with more than 5,000 items in its 172 pages. Besides a long list of brand-name tackle, there are many hard-to-find items and some things you can only buy from Netcraft. There are rods, reels, lures, terminal tackle, line, kits, and supplies for just about any do-it-yourself project you could have in mind.

We go way back with Netcraft, and over the years they have kept their prices low and their level of service high. Their catalog is free. So be sure to send for it if you haven't already.

Oilette—Automatically delivers just a fraction of a drop of oil exactly where you want it. No drip, no smear. Fits in pocket like a pen. Netcraft price: 65¢.

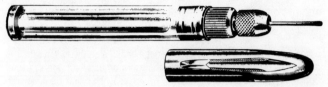

Oilette

Net Making Kit No. 100—Here's everything you need to start making your own nets. The kit includes Netcraft's finest clamp-on fixtures as well as four shuttles, four gauges, numerous rings, miscellaneous hardware, and a 72-page instruction manual, "Make Nets—Here's How." Learn to make your own landing nets, live nets, turtle traps, South Seas cast nets, carry bags, camping hammocks, and learn to repair nets, too. Netcraft price: $8.95.

36-Inch Floating Nylon Live Net—Made of ¼-inch oval knitted nylon with five Styrene floats. Has two 12-inch rings. Mesh is small enough that fish can't gill or hurt themselves and can't get away. Netcraft price: $4.50.

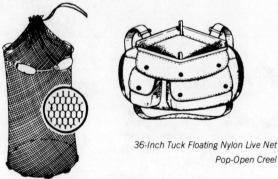

36-Inch Tuck Floating Nylon Live Net
Pop-Open Creel

Pop-Open Creel—Fine-mesh canvas drill—rubberized inside. Look at the tackle and lunch pockets. Instantly pops open—pops tightly closed. Ventilated ends. Netcraft price: $3.50.

Plastic Scaler—Has fifty-two sharp and hard teeth, pointed half to the left and half to the right. Whisk the scales off fast in either direction. Netcraft price: 25¢ each or 39¢/pair.

Fuzzy Yarn—For jigs, flies, lures. Also a must for every steelheader's tackle box. Colors: fire red, chartreuse, and white. Netcraft price: 60¢.

Economy Sinker Molds—Very well built—a real buy at this low price. No wires required. Casts perfect bank-type sinkers. Has handy clamps for quick, positive holding. One mold makes four sizes from ⅜ to 1 ounce, and casts eight sinkers at a time. Another mold makes five sizes from 1 to 4 ounces. Netcraft price: $4.15 each. Special offer: both molds for $7.35.

Denmaster Wall Rod Rack—Handsome and practical. Holds twelve rods, each nested in rubber cup support. Attractive hardwood back strip. Length: 24 inches. Netcraft price: $4.95.

Split Ring Pliers—No more broken thumb nails when you have this tool that opens all sizes of split rings and holds them firmly while you slip on hooks, blades, screw eyes, etc. Netcraft price: 85¢.

Fish Holder—Hold those wicked jaws wide open for easy hook removal with this handy item. Netcraft price: 70¢ each, $1.25/pair.

Netcraft Lacquer Kit—Renew old lures and make them look like new. Finest quality DuPont lacquer. Brush in every bottle. Ideal for plugs, bass bugs, spinning lures, spoons, floats, etc. Dries instantly with brilliant gloss. Colors: red, yellow, green, black, white, orange, and clear. Netcraft price: $2.50.

Netcraft Speed-Wrap Kit—Eight-piece set for rods, jigs, and flies. Using Netcraft's new techniques and special tools you can now speed-wrap a guide leg in three minutes, tie off locking wraps in five seconds, do a rod in less than an hour. You'll enjoy the ease of wrapping jigs and tying flies. You get two bobbins, Speed-Wrap Rod Thread Holder and Clamp, three spools of thread, No. 33 Lock-Wrap Tie-Off Tool, plus illustrated instructions. Netcraft price: $3.95.

Netcraft Hairjig Kit—First you make a Hairjig Insert (A). This insert of Dynel Fishair plus jig hook and collar has its hair ends sealed by an electric heat gun, supplied with kit. Drop insert into mold, pour lead, and in a jiffy out comes a real beauty. Hair is sealed permanently. No thread wraps required. Kit includes four precision die-cast molds, 110V electric heat seal gun, Dynel Fishair in five colors, 100 eyelets, generous supply of jig hooks, wire former, beads, tubing, and miscellaneous parts, plus a 36-page, well-illustrated instruction manual. Netcraft price: $11.95.

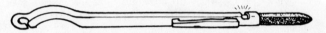

Angler's 3 in 1 Fishing Tool

Angler's 3 in 1 Fishing Tool—Quick-acting disgorger slips over the line. Follow it down to fish and give a quick twist—fish drops off. Has hook hone, blade for cutting line, and handy pocket clip. Netcraft price: 59¢.

Spinoff Electric Fish Scaler—It's a breeze to scale fish this new electric way. While brisking off the scales with amazing ease, you do it with perfect safety. Very ruggedly made. Handsomely packaged in screw-lid container. Netcraft price: $18.45.

NORMARK CORP.

From this company comes the famous Rapala wood lure, as well as variations of the original model and some new lures and accessories for your fishing pleasure. In the tradition of the late Lauri Rapala, each Original Floating Rapala represents more than thirty tested manufacturing steps. They're high-quality lures and proven fish-getters.

Normark knives are found in Chapter 9.

Original Rapala Floating Model—The most advanced materials have only improved the inventor's revolutionary concept: stainless steel wire encircles the select balsa wood and secures the razor-sharp hooks. Plastic lip material, metal foils, and coating films combine to complete a lure that has become a worldwide standard for all fishing. Colors: silver, gold, perch, blue, and fluorescent red. Lengths: 2, 2¾, 3½, 4⅜, 5¼, and 7 inches.

Original Balsa Fat Rap Model—Casts like a charm, rides as light as a feather over obstructions and then responds as quick as a cat to work strong and deep upon retrieve. With a long nose to fend off underwater obstacles, the Fat Rap rides up quickly during any pause, and its needle-sharp hooks will hold the most determined bass. Colors: perch, fluorescent red, shad, and crawdad. Lengths: 2 and 2¾ inches. Weights: ⅜ and ½ ounce.

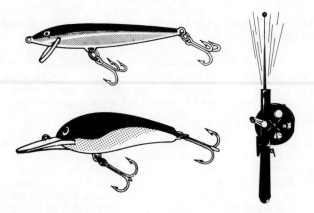

Rapala Lures and Thrumming Rod

Thrumming Rod and Reel—From pike to panfish and even lake trout—the Finnish secret of Thrumming is deadly. The new Normark Thrumming vertical fishing rod/reel combination puts the lure straight down deep. Lets you vibrate lure by squeezing button on handle (tip vibrates and in turn makes the lure pulsate and quiver). Complete with unique depth meter in reel, storage space in handle, and new larger capacity reel with adjustable drag washer. Overall length: 19 inches.

Skinning Board—An ingenious new board designed for cleaning catfish. Length: 24 inches. Width: 6 inches. Board material: sealed, select hardwood. Clamp is made of plate-tempered steel with stainless steel spring.

NYLON NET CO.

Here's a company that we just happened onto a few years back, and are we glad that we did. They're good folks, they have a nifty catalog, their prices are low, and their service is fast. Don't be fooled by the name, though. While they do sell every kind of net imaginable, their line includes quite a bit more.

Common Sense Minnow Seines—Inexpensive, lightweight minnow seines, fitted with all necessary leads and floats, complete and ready to fish. Available in ⅛- and ¼-inch polyester mesh. Tarred nets are slightly higher in price, but are recommended for longer wear and easier handling. They have greater resistance to dirt, abrasion, entanglement on sticks, weeds, etc. Tarred seines are treated with black net bond (Texaco Net Coat). All seines listed are 4 feet deep. Lengths: from 4 to 50 feet. Prices: ⅛-inch mesh—$1.52 to $15.94 (regular), $2.29 to $20.08 (tarred); ¼-inch mesh—$1.66 to $17.39 (regular), $2.44 to $21.78 (tarred).

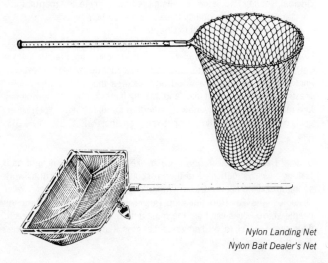

Nylon Landing Net
Nylon Bait Dealer's Net

Nylon Cast Nets—Complete and ready to use for catching shrimp, minnows, and all types of bait fish. Fully tapered nets are expertly crafted from the finest grade nylon webbing. These nets will give long, trouble-free service, catch after catch. Mesh sizes: ¼, ⅜, ½, ¾, and 1½ inches. Radii: 3 to 12 feet. Prices: from $16.19 to $112.45.

Nylon Landing Nets—Aluminum hoop and handle will float. Handle lengths: 1½, 2, 2½, and 3 feet. Hoop diameters/net depths: 15/18, 16/30, 20/30, and 22/36 inches. Mesh size: 1 inch. Prices: $2.25, $3.02, $4.15, $4.98.

Nylon Bait Dealer's Nets—So you're not a bait dealer. If you fish with live minnows and seine them yourself, there are times when one of these nets really does a slick job—when wind waves wash bait fish into shore, when minnows are tightly schooled in small pools near bridges, rapids, dams, etc. Mesh size: ⅛ and ³⁄₁₆ inch. Handle lengths: 20 to 42 inches. Prices: from $4.96 to $6.70.

Dipsey Swivel Sinkers—Sold only by the box. Sinker weights: ⅛, 3/16, ¼, ⅜, ¾, 1, 2¼, and 3 ounces. Price per box of 36: 90¢, $1.09, $1.23, $1.44, $2.09, $2.95, $5.57; $2.13 (box of 12—3 oz. only).

Bank Sinker
Egg Sinker

Bank Sinkers—The most universally used style of sinker. Complete range of sizes for freshwater casting up to deep-sea bottom fishing. Sold only in 5-pound bags. Sizes: ½, 1, 2, 3, 4, 6, and 8 ounces. Price: $4.31/bag.

Egg Sinkers—Smooth, oval shape with hole through the center for line. Popular sinker for freshwater and saltwater fishing and fishfinder rigs. Sold only in 5-pound bags. Weights: ⅛, ¼, ½, ¾, 1, 1½, 2, 3, 4, and 6 ounces. Price: $5.16/bag.

ORVIS CO., INC.

Some of the finest fly rods in the world are made at the Orvis Rod Shop in Manchester, Vermont. They have been building rods since 1856, and today they have more expert rodmakers working for them than at any time in their history. They build all their rods, from start to finish, of the best materials available. Whether it's an exquisite Tonkin bamboo rod, one of graphite, or the more economical fiberglass, you can count on superior craftsmanship and rigid quality control if the Orvis name is on it.

But it doesn't stop with rods. Orvis offers a broad line of top-quality fishing tackle, including reels, flies, fly-tying tools, and a number of hard-to-find items. They issue catalogs in the spring and fall, and they send out a special Christmas catalog, too. Orvis also offers classes at their Fly Fishing School, and they will send you a booklet on these if you write them.

If you've been in a quandary over the differences (advantages and disadvantages) among different rod blank materials, be sure to write for the free Orvis booklet, "Comparison of Bamboo, Graphite and Glass Rods." In addition to fine fishing tackle, Orvis also offers custom-made shotguns, outdoor apparel, and specialty items that can be found in Chapters 4, 8, and 12.

Orvis Battenkill Fly Rods—These impregnated bamboo fly rods have been the standard of excellence for many generations. They are exquisite in appearance and flawless in action. They are available in many

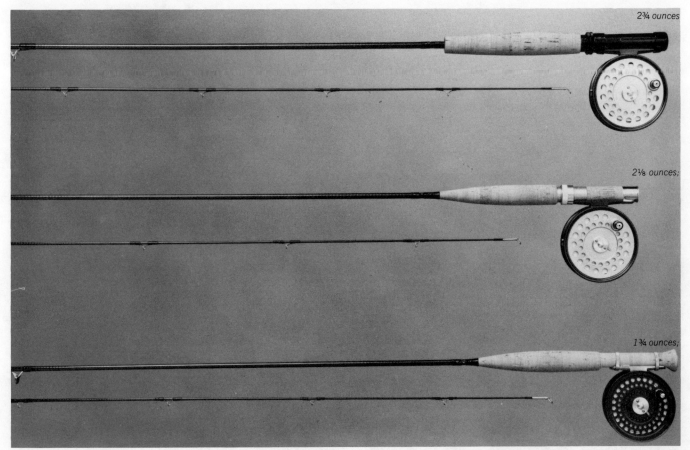

2¾ ounces

2⅛ ounces;

1¾ ounces;

7½-Foot Graphite Rod

models to cover the tastes and casting styles of individual fishermen. They come in the widely popular two-piece models and the classic traditional three piece. Because these are Orvis impregnated bamboo, the finish is in the rod, not just on it. Impervious to rain, snow, ice, broiling sun, and humidity, they are a lifetime investment in deep satisfaction, and require no more care than any synthetic fiber rod. Prices for Battenkill rods start at $164 (rod only).

Orvis Madison Fly Rods—These impregnated bamboo fly rods have exactly the same flawless action of the corresponding Battenkill models. All Orvis rods are built by hand, inspected and tested for perfection of structure and action, and only then, after passing these tests, are graded Battenkill or Madison, solely on the basis of subtle variance of grain, coloration, and uniform perfection of appearance. Special-purpose rods, such as the Flea and Midge, have counterparts equivalent to Madison grade rods referred to as MCL Flea and MCL Midge. So, the Madisons are magnificent rods and great bargains at considerably lower prices than the two-tip, specially selected Battenkills. Prices for Madison Rods start at $143 (rod only).

Orvis Graphite Fly Rods—For fly-rod construction, High Modulus Graphite is too stiff for full-length flex "action" and is more brittle—susceptible to breakage. Some manufacturers use an admixture of glass fiber (at 87¢ a pound) with graphite fiber (as much as $100 a pound) to produce more flex and protection from breakage. Orvis, however, uses Low Modulus Graphite, which, unadulterated, produces a fly rod with beautiful flex action, protection for finest tippets, maximum tensile strength, terrific thrust, lightest weight, smallest diameter, and almost ageless resistance to fatigue.

Although Orvis Graphite Rods are designed for specific line weights, they will comfortably handle two and sometimes three line sizes, a characteristic unique to graphite. Graphite rods are supplied with cloth

C.F.O. Fly Reel

sacks and aluminum rod cases. Price range for Orvis Graphite Fly Rods is from $135 (rod only) to $250. As with all Orvis rods, the graphite rods can be purchased as complete outfits, including reel, fly line, and backing. Corresponding prices for complete graphite outfits are from $187 to $400.

Orvis Classic Fly Rod—This is a special three-piece rod in limited edition of just 200 rods. Each comes with special limited edition CFO Reel, engraved with matching serial number, milled from solid aluminum bar stock. This rod is built to be fished, but is splendid to look at in its handsome green-felt-trimmed polished mahogany presentation chest. Rod, reel, and matching six-weight line are fitted into the chest that carries an engraved brass plate, with the outfit's limited edition number. Price: $675. Also available in handsome saddle-stitched leather carrying case, 34 inches long, in place of presentation chest at $600.

Orvis 5-Foot, 1⅛-Ounce Graphite Spinning Rod—A one-piece rod for 1/16-ounce to ¼-ounce lures with Orvis 50A Spin Reel (51A for left-handers), prewound with 160 yards of 2# line. Prices: $161 (complete outfit), $130 (rod only).

Orvis 7-Foot, 4⅞-Ounce Graphite Spinning Rod—A two-piece rod with fixed reel seat, for ¼-ounce to ¾-ounce lures, with Orvis 100SS Spin Reel (101SS for left-handers) prewound with 240 yards of 8# line. Prices: $185 (complete outfit), $155 (rod only).

C.F.O. Fly Reels—Christened in memory of Charles F. Orvis and designed with frame on one side only—incredibly light, wonderfully convenient, and beautiful. Spool removes with no awkward pinching of line. Exposed spool rim for easy thumbing. Smooth lever-adjusted drag, instantly reversible for right- or left-handed wind. Not designed for use in salt water. Four models available for lines form DT3F to WF10F. Prices: from $61.75 to $71.50.

C.F.O. Multiplier Reels—New, fast-retrieve reels for rapid recovery of slack or loose line—an important safeguard when handling big fish. A real pleasure and ease in a long day's fishing. Reversible for right or left wind. All CFO Multiplier Reels are supplied in fleece-lined suede leather case. Three models available for line weights from WF6F to WF10F. Prices: from $72.50 to $79.50.

Orvis Spinning Reels—Few moving parts, easy to maintain. Orvis spinning reels are simple, rugged, and dependable. Look alike and built alike from the baby ultralight 50A on up to the big 150S, they work very long and well. Six models available. Prices: from $35.50 to $42.95.

Working Index Fly Box

Working Index Fly Box of Wets, Nymphs, Streamers—Trout do 90 percent of their feeding under water, and 90 percent of this feeding is successfully matched with this indexed selection of seven wet patterns (three of each pattern), seven nymphs (three of each pattern), and three streamers (two of each pattern). The seven wets cover the essential color range—light, medium, dark, bright. The seven nymphs cover the mayfly, stonefly, and caddis suggestions. The streamers match the minnow varieties found in trout streams. Price: $39.80.

Rangeley Fly Books—Clipped sheepskin lining keeps flies or lures neat and in perfect order. Sturdy waterproof canvas cover with button snap. Sizes (closed): 6×3 inches, 4½×2¼ inches. Prices: $3.75, $2.10.

Orvis Leader Conditioner—A gum rubber pad with leader grip backing. Pinch your leader in a fold of gum rubber, draw the leader through, and you stretch and straighten and remove the leader's glare. Comes attached to pin-on, self-retracting reel with 14-inch cord inside. Price: $3.95.

Orvis Clipper/Knot Tyer—If needle knots, blood knots, and barrel knots have been the bane of your existence, this is absolutely the solution. One basic knot ties tippet to leader, leader to fly, and fly to leader. Complete with diagram and simple instructions. Attached to pin-on, self-retracting reel. Price: $6.95.

Orvis Angler's Clip—Here it is! The handiest, most practical tool for every fly-fisherman, always convenient and ready for use. That old favorite Angler's clip, with its sharp snippers, straight edge cutting blade, awl, and hook disgorger. Comes attached to pin-on reel. Price: $3.95.

Orvis Hook Hone—This little hook hone, on pin-on reel, is no bother. Never in the way, but always right at hand for quick touch-up of a hook point. Price: $3.95.

Orvis ArctiCreel—Utilizing the principle of the desert water bag, well known to travelers in the West, the outer bag of the ArctiCreel is soaked in water; evaporation then cools contents continually, keeping fish cool and fresh for hours, even in the hottest weather. Sizes: 10×14×4 inches (deluxe), 9×15×4 inches (standard). Prices: $10.75, $8.75.

PADRE ISLAND CO.

If Padre Island doesn't immediately sound familiar to you, perhaps the PICO lures that they manufacture will. The first hand-carved cedar PICO plugs were catching fish more than forty years ago. Today, their line of plastic lures, spoons, and plastic worms is still manufactured by skilled craftsmen with the highest quality material.

PICO Perch—This is a descendant of the original vibrating underwater lure made by Padre Island in 1933. Allow to sink to desired depth and retrieve at fast or variable speed. For black bass, pike, walleye, stripers, and other freshwater and saltwater sport fish. Available in thirty-nine colors. Lengths: 2 and 2¼ inches. Weights: ⅓ and ½ ounce.

PICO Side-Shad—The large single propeller, unusual body shape, and hook arrangement create an exceptional action that entices fish. Floats on its side like a crippled shad. Available in ten colors. Length, 2½ inches. Weight: ½ ounce.

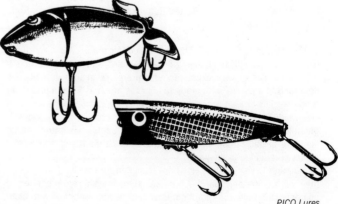

PICO Lures

PICO Pop—Deep, concave nose duplicates the sound of big fish feeding and drives others to investigate. This is a chugging, popping, and plunking lure with heavy #1 hooks large enough to land the lunkers. Casts like a bullet. Length: 3¼ inches. Weight: ½ ounce.

PLANO MOLDING CO.

The good folks at Plano do one thing, and they do it extremely well—they manufacture some of the finest tackle boxes available today. Their boxes are designed by fishermen for fishermen, and there's a Plano box to fit any fishing need.

Their line consists of tough, durable, long-lasting plastic boxes that are convenient and sensible in design. These boxes are made for lasting service and are built to take the abuse that a serious fisherman will give them. Plano boxes range in size from the super new "777" to little totes that tuck into a pocket.

#9106 Tackle Box

Plano #777 Tackle Box—Here is a spectacular new big box that will hold more lures than you can imagine. It occupies only 14¾ inches when fully opened because of the unique drawer arrangement. Front panel opens and slides under bottom drawer. Drawers pull out to make baits easy to reach. Standard box has six drawers with fifty-seven compartments. ABS construction resists most plastic baits, withstands most rugged use. Optional drawer arrangements make it possible for the fisherman to "custom design" his own box. Dimensions: 19×9½×13⅝ inches. Weight: 12 pounds.

Plano #747 Tackle Box—Exclusive with Plano, this box opens two ways. Drop front panel and three interchangeable trays pull out singly like drawers (handy for use in boats), or open top like a conventional box and cantilevered trays swing back, exposing all equipment. Standard three-tray arrangement features twenty-nine compartments, but can increase to fifty-four to accommodate any bait selection. Extra trays can be purchased separately to meet individual needs. Rugged ABS construction. Dimensions: 20⅜×11½×12¾ inches. Weight: 12 pounds.

Plano #9106 Tackle Box—This big hip-roof box has forty-two compartments in six wormproof trays that are 1½ inches deep. Two ABS drawbolt-type latches, lure-protecting Stay-Dri ribs, rugged recessed handle, and solid brass risers. Two-toned harvest gold ABS top, raw umber polypropylene bottom. Dimensions: 19½×11¼×10½ inches. Weight: 9 pounds.

Plano #1123 Magnum—Fifteen movable dividers offer up to twenty-three compartments for various tackle. Drawbolt-type ABS latch, rugged hinges, sturdy vinyl carrying strap. Wormproof. Amber Acrylite lid, corrugated harvest gold polypropylene bottom. Dimensions: 14¾×2½×11½ inches. Weight: 2 pounds.

Plano #1146 Magnum—Unique all-around wormproof box opens from either side. Thirty movable dividers (fifteen each side) can be varied to allow up to forty-six compartments. Full-size handle, two drawbolt-type ABS latches. See-through amber Acrylite lid, corrugated harvest gold bottom. Dimensions: 14¾×5×11½ inches.

QUICK CORP. OF AMERICA

Quick reels have been known for their superb functioning and quality of materials for more than fifty years. Manufactured in West Germany, these rugged reels exhibit Old World craftsmanship, but offer the latest features made possible by modern tooling and technology. The company is producing a new series of Champion skirted-spool spinning reels and free-spool casting reels. Quick rods are also available, as is Damyl monofilament line. Quick tackle is sold competitively by dealers everywhere.

Quick 3000 Champion Skirted-Spool Reel—This new reel is ideal for all heavy-duty freshwater angling and light saltwater fishing. The reel features left- and right-handed conversion as well as high-speed retrieve. The pushbutton spool is machined from the highest grade aluminum. Additional features include ball-bearing drive on the main shaft, precision-machined phosphor bronze and stainless steel gears, and internal bail release, as well as a new positive antireverse. Capacity: 250 yards of 12# line. Gear ratio: 4.25:1. Weight: 14.5 ounces.

Quick 4000 Champion Skirted-Spool Reel—This is a light saltwater reel that has the high-speed capability of really making a lure move fast through the water and of keeping a tight line on a charging game fish. Capacity: 290 yards of 15# line. Gear ratio: 4.25:1. Weight: 15.5 ounces.

Quick 5000 Champion Skirted-Spool Reel—Here is a reel designed for all types of heavy-duty saltwater fishing, including surf, boat, and pier. Capacity: 400 yards of 20# line. Gear ratio: 4:1. Weight: 20 ounces.

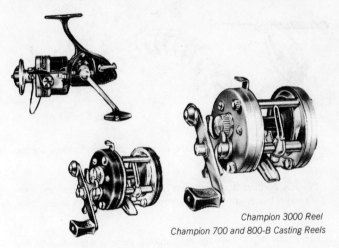

Champion 3000 Reel
Champion 700 and 800-B Casting Reels

Quick Champion #700 Casting Reel—Here is the fabulous 700, featuring silent level wind, pushbutton free-spool, and extra-long handle—counter balanced—with perfect grip; turn forward and you are instantly in gear with a smooth star drag. It's specially built for fast, no-tool take-apart and designed to handle all freshwater and light saltwater angling. Capacity: 250 yards of 12# line. Gear ratio: 3.65:1. Weight: 8.4 ounces.

Quick Champion #800-B Casting Reel—This high-speed, fast-retrieve model features stainless steel bearing drive plus a wider spool and greater line capacity. This is the all-around beauty where more or heavier line is needed. Like all Champion reels, it is salt water corrosion resistant, making it perfect for light saltwater use. Capacity: 275 yards of 15# line. Gear ratio: 4.65:1. Weight: 11 ounces.

Quick Champion Graphite Casting Rods—Introduced in 1977 to match the new Champion revolving-spool reels, these exquisite rods are available in four lengths and actions—all one-piece construction with deluxe handles that are positive-locking and self-aligning.

RAY-O-VAC FISHING TACKLE DIVISION

From Ray-O-Vac come the famous Lindy and Little Joe brands of fishing tackle. In business for forty years, the Fishing Tackle Division provides quality products and prompt service. For a buck they'll send you their chunky 80-page catalog and handbook that is loaded with good buys and good tips on tackle.

Lindy Catfish Rig—Soft, flexible, tasty, plastic body. Can be fished in heavy brush without snagging. The ridges and cross ridges form pockets to hold your favorite Lindy Cheese Baits. Colors: mustard yellow, blood red, and black. Packed three per card. Price: $1.80/card.

Lindy Cheese Bait—Available in 10-ounce tubs. Three types: bleeding bait, blood/cheese bait, and soft natural cheese bait. Price: $1.15.

Lindy Cra-Z-Spin Single—A great new spinner bait, made even better, that uses the new Cra-Z-Spin or bubble blade for high vibration. Sizes: ¼ and ⅜ ounce. Available in six colors. Price: $1.50.

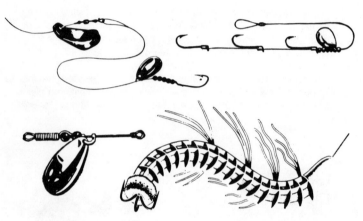

Lindy & Little Joe Products

Lindy Cra-Z-Spin Tandem—Same as above, but with tandem blades. Price: $1.65.

Little Joe 11-Inch Worm Harness—Available in Colorado- and propeller-style blades with choice of three finishes and hook sizes. Price: 50¢.

Lindy Flikker Rig—These rigs are extremely versatile and will please any spin fisherman. Can be cast, trolled, or drift fished. Available in three finishes and two hook sizes. Specifically designed for minnows, nightcrawlers, or leeches. Price: $1.60.

Little Joe Tru-Spin Single-Blade Indiana Spinners—These versatile spinners are available in six sizes and three finishes. Prices are the same for all sizes, but vary by finish. Prices: 20¢ (nickel or fluorescent red); 25¢ (gold).

Little Joe Wire Fish Baskets—Five different models available, ranging in size from 13×18 inches to 14×27 inches. Two are floating models. Prices: from $3.35 to $5.75.

HANK ROBERTS

In 1946, Hank Roberts started a tackle business by hand-tying and selling level and tapered leaders. The following year, he added hand-tied flies to this list of wares, and soon after began hiring and training people to help him sustain his growing business. Today, his company is a major producer of fine flies, fly-tying materials, and tools and kits. While his headquarters are in Boulder, Colorado, where his business began, most of the flies are tied by the skilled hands of Mayan Indians at his factory in the mountains of Guatemala.

The Hank Roberts line of flies has become famous for durability, and one reason is that no bobbins are allowed to be used during the tying process. Instead, when material is to be added to a fly, half-hitches are used—sometimes as many as twelve or fourteen such knots in the tying of a single fly. This makes for a fly that is going to last and catch many fish before it begins to deteriorate.

In addition to fly tackle, fishing vests and shirts are available from Hank Roberts. Descriptions of these will be found in Chapter 8.

No. 500 Jig-Making Kit—It's easy and fun to make your own jigs. Lots of lead jig heads with hooks already molded in, in sizes of ¼ ounce down to the tiny fly rod model of 1/124 ounce, are included in this kit. Other materials are various colors of feathers, hair, and marabou, along with bottles of paint in red, black, yellow, and white. Comes complete with instructions. Price: $17.50.

No. 150 Fly-Tying Kit—A medium-priced kit that includes an excellent vise, bobbin, hackle pliers, and a good selection of furs, feathers, hackles, hooks, and all the things necessary to tie flies. Comes with instructions. Price: $24.95.

Bass Bush Bugs—Tied with deer hair—full and brushy—left untrimmed. A high-floating, tried and tested bass-getter. Comes in the four most popular patterns. Price: $23.40/dozen.

Bass Mini Bugs—Mini-sized and ultralight for real fly-rodding fun. While terrific for bass, don't forget big trout love them, too. Five excellent patterns. Price: $19.80/dozen.

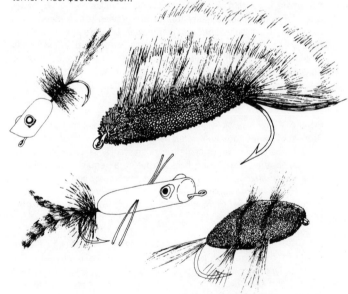

Bass Bugs and Poppers

Pop-It Popping Bugs—Made of high-floating and durable Dylite. The hump is molded in for security. Comes in six of the most sought after colors. Perfect for all panfish. Price: $9/dozen.

Slim Jim Popping Bugs—A slimmed-down popper with tantalizing wiggling rubber legs in the right sizes for most panfish. Made of Dylite in five excellent colors. Price: $10.80/dozen.

Bass Streamer Fly—Ring-eye hook so a spinner may be attached if wanted. Widely forked tail and heavy shoulder hackle for that fish-tantalizing action. Six color combinations available. Price: $12/dozen.

Double A Vise—An improved and redesigned, lever-operated style. The jaws have been tapered to hold firmly the smallest of hooks, and the vise shank is grooved so that it may be rotated to inspect both sides of the fly while tying. Price: $17.

Half-Hitch Tool—Nicely machined and polished from solid aluminum. Makes tying half-hitches easy. Comes in two sizes: extra fine and fine, medium and large. Price: 70¢.

Whip Finisher—A fast and convenient way to finish the head of a fly. This handy tool conceals the end of the thread under successive wraps, thereby preventing unraveling. Made of stainless steel and aluminum. Sizes: large and small. Prices: $4.35, $3.45.

RYOBI AMERICA CORPORATION

A major Japanese manufacturer and worldwide exporter of rods and reels, Ryobi is a name that is showing up more and more in American tackle shops and mail-order catalogs. Their skirted-spool spinning reels are finding favor among anglers everywhere.

Powerful DX Series Spinning Reels—New reels feature reduced weight and compact size. Built for convenience and long-lasting use. Precision engineering and handsome styling. Features include ambidextrous folding handle, Beric alloy master gear for increased durability, aluminum die-cast spools, light-touch retrieve with ceramic line roller, triple ball bearings. Dual end support main gear and antireverse lever that can be easily controlled, ever under a heavy load. Five models available, from the tiny DX-1 ultralight with its 4.75:1 retrieve to the big DX-5 with a capacity of 251 yards of 22# line.

Adventure Series Casting Reels—All major components of these reels are made from stainless steel to prevent rust. Side plates are made from rugged polycarbonate. All possible measures have been taken to eliminate the chance of rust. The rugged one-piece frame design adds even more durability. Ryobi has also succeeded in eliminating line backlash with its patented antibacklash device. Three models available, ranging from the Adventure-40 with a capacity of 196 yards of 9# line, to the big SD-101 with a capacity of 655 yards of 33# line.

Ryobi Fly Reels—Handsome and lightweight reels for the discriminating fly-fisherman. Modern, practical, and made to last a long time, they come with smart, protective, felt-lined, waterproof plastic cases. Smooth, adjustable drag system with ratchet, removable spool, rapidly convertible for ambidextrous use. All parts are protected against corrosion. Color: smoky gray satin. Available in two sizes. The 444 will hold 30 yards of 5# to 7# line. The 455 is designed to hold 30 yards of 8# or 9# line.

DX Series Spinning Reel

SHAKESPEARE

Another name well known and long respected in the fishing-tackle trade, Shakespeare manufactures a broad line of top-quality rods and reels for every type of fishing in fresh and salt water, as well as monofilament lines. Their new Ugly Stik rods carry one of the best warranties we have seen, and their skirted-spool spinning reels are finding favor among anglers everywhere.

Shakespeare trolling motors and depth-finders can be found in Chapter 3.

Model 2400 Spinning Reel—Ultralight spinning reel with skirted spool to prevent line tangles. Features two ball bearings for smooth action. Converts quickly for left or right handles. Manually operated, stainless steel bail. Gear ratio: 5:1. Capacity: 180 yards of 6# mono.

Model 2410 Spinning Reel—Skirted-spool freshwater reel with stainless steel bail, convertible handle, efficient disc-drag system, dual ball bearings, and high-speed retrieve. Gear ratio: 4.5:1. Capacity: 270 yards of 8# mono.

Model 2450 Spinning Reel—Large-capacity, skirted-spool reel for surf casting and other saltwater duties. Same features as other reels in 2400 series. Gear ratio: 4.1:1. Capacity: 400 yards of 12# mono.

Model 1980 President II Bait-Casting Reel—Free-spool casting reel with cast control and centrifugal brake for accurate, trouble-free casting. Two shielded ball bearings on spool pivots. Large gear set reduces friction. Features star drag with large washers. Gear ratio: 5:1.

Model 1700II Spin-Cast Reel—This reel features ceramic pickup pin, stainless steel eyelet to protect line, star drag that won't twist line, rubber disk for better casting control, all metal construction. Filled with Super 7000 mono. Gear ratio: 4:1.

Shakespeare Single-Action Fly Reels—These reels have lightweight aluminum frames, chromed line guides, adjustable drags, and changeable spools. Five models are available to handle AFTMA line sizes from #6 to #12.

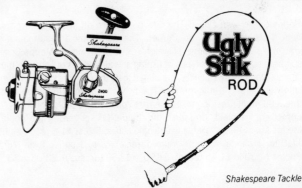

Shakespeare Tackle

Shakespeare Ugly Stik—This is a new series of rods manufactured by the exclusive Howald process. Rods have an inner spiral of graphite and an outer fiberglass filament from butt to tip. The rods are virtually unbreakable under normal fishing conditions. The series includes two spinning rods, one pushbutton rod, two bait-casting, two saltwater spinning, a trolling model, and a saltwater fly rod. All rods carry two warranties. First, any rod can be returned within thirty days for full refund. Second, if you should break an Ugly Stik while fishing during the first five years, Shakespeare will repair or replace the rod at no charge.

Super 7000 Monofilament Line—A smooth and supple line with Guide Glide coating that resists abrasion. Has excellent knot strength and flows easily for long casts.

SHELDON'S, INC.

This company is the American home of Mepps Original French Spinners—those fantastic lures that seem to be on display at tackle shops and marinas wherever you go.

We have used Mepps lures throughout North America and have taken just about everything from bluegills to big king salmon with them. They're well built and they do exactly what they were designed to do—catch fish.

As you might expect, their catalog is another quality item that lists their entire line of lures and offers many helpful fishing tips to readers. Photos of Mepps catches throughout the catalog attest to the versatility and success of these lures. The catalog also includes Mepps award information and a *Field & Stream* Fishing Contest entry blank.

Normally, this catalog would cost you half-a-buck, but our good friend T. Layton "Shep" Shepherd (The Mepps Man) will send you a free copy if you tell him you read about Mepps in *The Great Outdoors Catalog*.

Mepps Lure

Mepps Spoon—This spoon, new for 1977, is really fantastic. Field-tested by Mepps' extensive field-test team for two full years, the staff reported, "This new spoon is the best-designed, greatest fish catcher to be introduced in a long time." See the natural flutter for yourself. These spoons produce terrific action at all speeds. Simple to use at any depth, crawling over the bottom or jigging in deep water. Colors: gold or silver plating, rainbo and redbo scale. Sizes: ⅕, ⅓, and ½ ounce. Prices: $1.85, $1.95, $2.05.

Mepps Comet with Dots—The new dot pattern on Mepps Comet spinners adds sparkle to the Comet. The dots almost reach out and grab 'em. The wide range of weights and sizes makes Mepps Comet spinners suitable for all types of fishing and all species of fish. The blunt convex blade revolves easily, causing it to go through the water with very little wobble and a minimum of line twist. A spiral "bumblebee body" threaded on the inside makes it easy to detach and replace hooks. The Comet comes plain, dressed with squirrel tail, or trailing the popular Mepps Mino. Also available with single hooks. Sizes: #1 to #5. Weights: 1/10 to ½ ounce (plain or dressed treble), ⅐ to 1 ounce (with Mino). Prices: $1.30 to $1.75 (plain), $1.90 to $2.50 (dressed), $2.05 to $3.50 (Mino).

Mepps Tandem Killers—When talking big fish, real lunker hunters refer to Mepps Musky Killers and Giant Killers. They're designed specifically for the big ones. Now, both models are available with weighted tandem hooks. Two exceptionally sharp, double-strength round-bend treble hooks are designed to eliminate short hits and hold onto a trophy once hooked. Tied with a generous amount of throbbing and pulsating long dressing, every movement is accentuated. With extra weight for casting, the tandem Musky Killer weighs 1 ounce and the tandem Giant Killer 1½ ounces. Prices: $4.10 (Tandem Musky Killer), $5.10 (Tandem Giant Killer).

Mepps Killer Kits—These lure kits offer assortments of proven spinners for a given species of fish. Fishermen can buy an attractive kit of six lures with no waste, uncertainty as to size, or chance for dissatisfaction.

Kits available are the Trouter, Basser, Piker, Lunker, and Coho. All but the Coho Killer Kit are available with plain or dressed hooks. Prices: $8.55 (plain Trouter), $12.10 (dressed Trouter), $9.50 (plain Basser), $13.10 (dressed Basser), $11.25 (plain Piker), $15.55 (dressed Piker), $13.65 (plain Lunker), $20.25 (dressed Lunker), $11.65 (plain Coho).

SHURKATCH FISHING TACKLE CO., INC.

Shurkatch offers an assortment of fishing tackle, some terminal gear and netting products. They also produce a line of gaffs and gigs, as well as some ice-fishing equipment.

Fish Bag—Made with aluminum clamp with vertical swivel for attaching to the side of a boat. All hardware plated to resist corrosion. Mesh: ¾ inch. Diameter: 9 inches. Length: 32 inches. Price: $2.40.

Minnow Bucket Nets—Wire hoop is D shaped. Made of polyethylene mesh, 3½ inches wide by 4 inches long. Overall length is 11 inches. Price: 30¢.

Minnow Seine Poles—A pair of strong aluminum tubes, with clips to fasten on each end of a minnow seine, make it much easier to operate a seine, as they give the seine full support from top to bottom on each end. Poles can be left attached to the seine and the seine rolled up around the poles for storage. (Patent applied for.) Price: $6/pair.

Heavy Landing Nets—Polyethylene net with ¾-inch mesh. Hoop is ¼-inch galvanized, 15 inches in diameter. Hardwood handle is 48 inches long. Price: $4.

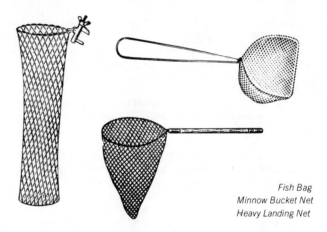

Fish Bag
Minnow Bucket Net
Heavy Landing Net

SOUTH BEND TACKLE

This division of Gladding Corporation manufactures a large line of rods, reels, line, and accessories for both freshwater and saltwater fishing. South Bend is an old name in quality tackle. Their gear is designed and tested by some of the world's most experienced anglers and is built to rigid specifications.

South Bend 725 Spinning Reel—This sturdy and dependable, all-metal, ultralight reel has bronze bearings, multiple-disk drag system, selective antireverse, sturdy precision-coined metal gears, and is corrosion resistant throughout. Gear ratio: 4.2:1. Capacity: 200 yards of 4# line.

South Bend 730 Spinning Reel—This newly designed, all-metal, freshwater reel features multiple-disk drag and plenty of line capacity for any freshwater or light saltwater chores. Corrosion resistant throughout. Gear ratio: 3.5:1. Capacity: 225 yards of 8# line.

South Bend Reels

South Bend 750 Spinning Reel—Saltwater deep jigging or trolling, bridge or pier fishing, coho or chinook, this husky reel is one of America's values. Rust-resistant finish, heavy-duty bail, rugged drag. Also has folding crank and die-cast spool. Gear ratio: 3.5:1. Capacity: 250 yards of 15# line.

Finalist 1122 Single-Action Fly Reel—Famed Finalist performance at an economy price. Great for value-wise veterans or for young beginners. Rugged aluminum construction. Quick-change, 2½-inch-diameter spool holds up to 35 yards of #5 fly line.

Oreno-Matic 1140 Fly Reel—This popular automatic fly reel features smooth, silent winding, effortless free stripping, foldaway chromed brass retrieve trigger, automatic brake, safety lock, coin-slotted takedown screw. Weight: 9.5 ounces. Capacity: 35 yards of #6 fly line.

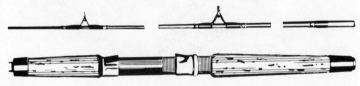

Outdoorsman Spinning Rod

Outdoorsman Spinning Rod—Two-piece, tubular fiberglass rod. Cork rear and fore grips, anodized aluminum fixed reel seat. Four hard chrome-plated guides and tip-top. Available in 6½ or 7 feet, fast taper or Power-Flex.

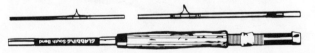

Outdoorsman Fly Rod

Outdoorsman Fly Rod—Sensitive yet tough action. Quality workmanship and parts. Specie cork grip, anodized aluminum locking reel seat, full-wrapped ferrule, five snake guides, hard chrome-plated stripper, and tip-top. Lengths: 8 and 8½ feet. For #7 and #8 fly line.

STORM MANUFACTURING CO.

From Storm comes a line of extremely realistic lures, designed to imitate various types of bait fishes found in rivers, lakes, and reservoirs throughout North America. Additionally, they offer vibrating lures, rattle lures, and spinner baits.

Their small catalog is quite descriptive and informative, covering design concepts and fishing techniques, as well as specifications for all their lures.

ThinFin Silver Shad—This lure was designed to provide the most realistic simulation of a natural shad. It has the characteristic swayed belly and extremely thin body that is shared by all members of the shad family. Three sizes are offered to better match the sizes of the preferred bait fish for any particular area, and all are available in ten colors. The floating/diving series and sinking series lures have a gloss-painted finish. The Super series is Brite-Metal finished for additional brightness and flash of metallic finishes on an etched scale pattern. Weights of the floater-diver and Super series are ⅕, ⅜, and ½ ounce. Weights of the sinking model are ¼, ½, and ⅝ ounce. Lengths: 2½, 3, and 3½ inches. Prices: $2.70, $2.80, $2.90.

Shiner Minnow—This lure represents a studied combination of the physical contours of live minnows with the characteristic "change-of-pace" swimming motion common to these small bait fish. Two sizes are available to permit you to closely match the size of locally abundant minnows preyed upon by the game fish you are after. The gloss-painted series offers an extremely durable and realistic finish, while the "Super Shiner" series features the highly reflective Brite-Metal finish with etched scale patterns. Weights: ⅛ and ¼ ounce. Lengths: 2½ and 3½ inches. Prices: $2.70, $2.80.

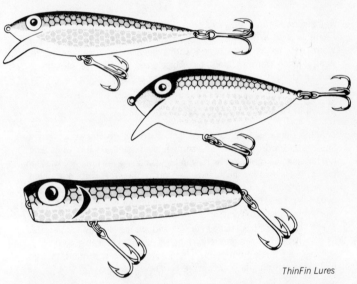

ThinFin Lures

Chug Bug—Since most topwater strikes occur within 3 to 5 feet of the point at which the lure first strikes the water, a good topwater lure must have its best action at the beginning of the retrieve. This lure has been designed to lie horizontally on the water's surface with its mouth cupped to catch the water with the slightest tug on the line, causing it to throw out a spray ahead of the lure with a noisy chugging sound and to cause sufficient drag against the lure to keep it from moving very far. Another effective characteristic is the continuous gurgling action achieved with a steady, continuous retrieve, making it a productive topwater lure from the time it hits the water, throughout the retrieve, until it reaches the rod tip. Available in fifteen colors and color combinations. Length: 3½ inches. Weight: ⅜ ounces. Price: $2.80.

STRADER TACKLE, INC.

From Capt. Jim Strader comes an assortment of lures for use in fresh and salt water, including plugs, spinner baits, and the new Rattleworm Heads—slip sinkers with built-in rattle chambers.

Diamond Rattlesub—A subsurface floating/diving lure for all saltwater fish. Imitates finger mullet. Also effective for freshwater striped bass. All colors glitter with molded-in finish. Sound chamber with rattle. Cycolac body. Colors: blue, silver, gold, and bronze. Weights: ½ and ¾ ounce. Price: $3.

Diamond Rattlesub

Rattletrap

Rattletrap (Pat. Pend.)—The only absolutely weedless spinner bait with built-in rattle. Catches bass, pike, and pickerel in heaviest cover. Colors: blue, black, red, and purple, with contrasting or coordinated skirts. Weights: ¼ and ½ ounce. Price: $3.

Rattleworm Heads (Pat. Pend.)—A proven fish-attracting, rattling sound chamber with slip sinker casting weight enclosed. Rear cup protects worm and makes Texas rigged worms weedless. Translucent colored heads match worms. Colors: blue, black, red, and purple. Weights: ¼ and ½ ounce. Packaged four per card. Price: $2/card.

ANTON UDWARY, JR.

Anton operates a personalized tackle service, dealing exclusively in fine cane fly rods, fly reels, and some related items. He has no catalog, but provides a list of what he has on hand at any given time. He wrote to tell us, "As agents for new rods by Carlson, Jenkins, Leonard, and Uslan, we accept good cane fly rods as part payment on any new or used cane fly rod. We also buy fly rods and related items for resale—be it a single piece or extensive collection."

His listings are updated as needed and are mailed free to interested fly-fishermen. Repairs and refinishing services are available, too.

Here's a sample from one of his recent lists. Keep in mind, though, that these lists change as items are bought and sold.

Hardy "Palkona"—7-foot 2-inch, 3½-ounce two-piece, one tip, case, medium action, #5 lines, nearly new. Price: $110.

C. W. Jenkins—7½-foot, 3¾-ounce, two-piece, two tips, bag and case, #5 or #6 lines, built on tapers by late Everett Garrison. Brand new. Price: $300.

H. L. Leonard #40—8-foot, 4⅛-ounce, two-piece, two tips, bag, case, #6 lines. Good all-around rod, current style winds, cane color. Brand new. Price: $320.

Model 175A Tackle Box—This aluminum box is an economy tackle toter, featuring three trays with twenty-nine compartments. Size: 17½×7×6¾ inches. Weight: 2½ pounds.

Model P-8 Mini-Box—This aluminum pocket box has two trays with seventeen compartments in all. It opens from either side. Size: 8×5×2⅛ inches. Weight: ½ pound.

UNCLE JOSH BAIT CO.

This is the company where all those great pork rind baits come from. Uncle Josh pork rinds come in a wide variety of sizes and shapes and can be used in an infinite number of ways. Perhaps the most popular

use is in conjunction with a weedless spoon. But they're also great for adding action and fish appeal to jigs, spinners, and even bare hooks.

Also available from Uncle Josh are several lures, salmon eggs, and catfish baits.

Uncle Josh King-Size Striper Hook—An extra-strong bait made especially for striped bass and other saltwater fish. Nickel hooks won't corrode, pee , or discolor the rind. Length: 4¾ inches. Width: ⅝ inch. Colors: white, red, and yellow. Hook sizes: 3/0 and 5/0. Packed three to a jar. Price: $1.65/jar.

Uncle Josh Bass Strip—Increases the effectiveness of any good lure. Guaranteed against spoilage and defects. Length: 4 inches. Width: ⅜ inch. Colors: white, green, red, yellow, black, blue, purple, and chartreuse. Packed ten in a jar. Price: $1.40/jar.

Uncle Josh Spin Tail—Long split tail with more wiggle and action. Very thin, but tough. Length: 2¼ inches. Width: 5/16 inch. Colors: white, green, red, yellow, black, purple, and chartreuse. Packed twelve in a jar. Price: $1.40/jar.

Uncle Josh Pork Skirt—Adds extra-fast wiggle to any spoon, spinner, or jig. Extremely thin, 2-inch tail cut into ⅛-inch ribbons. Length: 3 inches. Width: ⅝ inch. Colors: white, green, red, yellow, black, purple, and chartreuse. Packed eight in a jar. Price: $1.40/jar.

Uncle Josh Pork Rind Kicker—Designed especially for use with pork rind. Erratic action creates lifelike movements of the pork rind. Available in assorted colors, and equipped with 2/0 Mustad hook. Weight: ⅓ ounce. Length: 2½ inches. Price: $1.15.

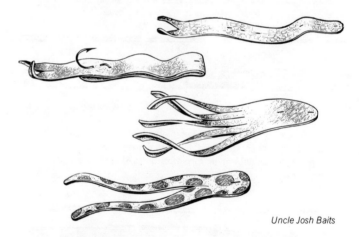

Uncle Josh Baits

VAL-CRAFT, INC.

The precision-made Valentine Fly Reels are available from this company. These are high-quality reels that come with a money-back guarantee. All parts are warranteed against defects in materials and construction for the life of the reel. And all reels come with a leather zippered reel case with belt loop.

What is unique about these reels is their planetary gear system. The line is cranked in as with any other single-action reel, but when the line runs, the crank plate remains stationary. Only the knob rotates and can be controlled by tightening or relaxing fingertip pressure on the knob. No more banged-up knuckles when a big fish heads the other way.

Valentine Fly Reel—Made of tempered gold-anodized aluminum alloy—much stronger, lighter, and less brittle than a casting. Bearings are bronze, and line guards are stainless steel. Since all parts are corrosion resistant, this is an excellent saltwater reel, too. The planetary gear system incorporates a retrieve ratio of 1½ to 1. An improved new friction

Valentine Fly Reels

brake utilizes a Teflon disk for cooler, smoother, and stronger variable drag. No-tool takedown. Extra spools can be dropped in for fast line change. Three models available. Sizes: 3½-, 3¾-, and 4-inch diameters. Weights: 7½, 9, and 9½ ounces. Line capacities: WF7F + 150 yards of 20# backing, WF9F + 200 yards of 20# backing, WF11F + 300 yards of 20# backing. Prices: $60, $68, $75. Extra spool prices: $12.60, $13.50, $14.50.

VARMAC MANUFACTURING CO. INC.

If you build your own rods, you are probably already familiar with Varmac's fine guides, tip-tops, reel seats, and rod handles. If you haven't done any rod building but want to get into this rewarding and money-saving hobby, you'll certainly want to check out the Varmac catalog.

The company has recently introduced the new line of Alumac guides and tip-tops, all featuring a diamond-hard ring of aluminum oxide. These highly polished ceramic rings are so hard they eliminate grooving forever. Each Alumac Ring is enveloped in a resilient shock absorber of high-density polyethylene. These guides are available individually or in matched sets.

Freshwater Alumac Guides—U-shaped stainless steel wire frame. Aluminum oxide ceramic ring in polyethylene shock absorber with stainless steel retaining ring. Sizes: 6, 8½, 10, 13, 16, 20, and 28 millimeters. Prices: from $1.04 to $2.96.

Freshwater Alumac Guide

Saltwater Alumac Braced Guides—Same as above, but with stainless steel brace. Sizes: same as above. Prices: from $1.27 to $3.04.

VLCHEK PLASTICS CO.

From Vlchek comes the well-known line of AdVenturer tackle boxes and bait buckets. These are lightweight, rugged, and durable plastic products, precision made to last and serve. We have been using Vlchek products for a number of years and can recommend them highly.

AdVenturer #2277 Tackle Box—Seven quick-draw, white ABS interchangeable drawers have ninety-six roomy, worm-resistant compartments. Drawers also have exclusive fingertip releases for fast, easy removal. Hinged front panel tucks under bottom drawer out of the way. Opened, the 2277 requires only 1.73 square feet of deck space. Totally rustproof. Luggage handle padlock tab. Dual positive latches and sound-dampening rubber feet. Overall size: 19½×10⅜×15 inches. Drawer size: 15-9/16×8-13/16×1⅜ inches. Color: two-tone bamboo and smoke olive. Price: $61.95.

AdVenturer #2233 Tackle Box—Saves space two ways. Drop front panel to use three easy-sliding, interchangeable drawers with thirty-two compartments. Push fingertip.release to raise cover and drawers that provides access to large storage area. Exclusive linkage design saves 25 percent of deck space required by other boxes of similar size. Rustproof linkage. Dual positive latches. Fully recessed luggage handle. Padlock tab. Pat. Pending. Size: 19½×11½×11¾ inches. Price: $50.95.

AdVenturer #1986 Select-O-Matic Tackle Box—Push a key, and a covered tray swings open. Push another button and another tray opens. Exclusive design makes tackle selection a pleasure. This hip-roof box is molded of jet green, chemically resistant materials. Rustproof. Tongue and groove construction with rain gutters. Twin padlock tabs. Top trays have clear "see-through" lids. Easily accessible bottom section holds larger gear. Covers interlock so box can be lifted without spilling, even if latches are not fastened. Six trays and forty compartments. Size: 18½×10¼×10⅜ inches. Price: $48.88.

AdVenturer #1703 Tackle Box

AdVenturer #2000 "Cartridge Loader"—Furnished with nine color-coded "cartridges," which fishermen can label and pack with any desired combination of tackle. Lift-out tray can be placed in cover when box is open. Size: 19×10¾×10⅛ inches. Price: $48.80.

AdVenturer #1703 Tackle Box—Designed to carry up to ninety-three spinner baits, this vertical Lure Arranger also has space below for pork rind jars, small utility boxes, etc. The smoke transparent lift-out rack is not affected by vinyl skirts and soft plastic lures. Positive latch. Fully recessed luggage handle. Lures won't spill even if closed box is accidentally upset. Size: 16½×8¾×7½ inches. Price: $18.95.

Velure Fly Box #V-401F—This foam-lined box holds flies, poppers, bass bugs, etc. Size: 8×4×1-7/16 inches. Price: $2.90.

AdVenturer Bait Bucket #10F2—Floats upright and won't sink even when full of water. Keeps bait cool and lively. Insulated Thermo Pail is strong enough to sit on. Molded of yellow super-strength, corrosionproof poly foam with high-density polyethylene liner. Air pump slot. Aluminum handle with poly grip. Capacity: 10 quarts. Price: $9.

WEBER TACKLE CO.

We go back a long way with Weber and their extensive line of fine fishing tackle. The company goes back farther than we do, having been established in 1933, and is known far and wide for their superb tackle. Weber still offers many of the successful items that appeared in their 1933 catalog, and they have added considerably to the line.

We have several boxes full of Weber poppers and flies. Their "Mr. Champ" wobbler is a favorite, too, for both freshwater and saltwater fishing. Our big saltwater tackle box carries about a dozen Weber Hoochy Trolls that have proved their worth in the Atlantic and the Pacific. And the Weber Fun-Kits (for flies, jigs, spoons, poppers, etc.) are just that—fun.

The list could go on and on, but why don't we show you a few items. instead?

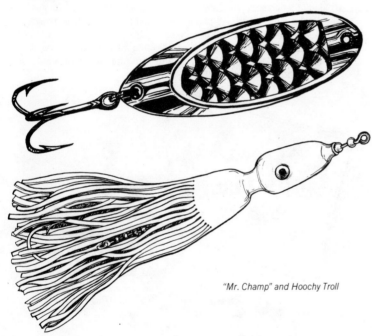

"Mr. Champ" and Hoochy Troll

"Mr. Champ"—The versatile lure in sizes for ultralight to trolling. For salt and fresh water. Deadly metal blade that goes right down to prime fishing depths fast. Unique elliptical blade design casts easily and smoothly, travels farther. "Mr. Champ" won't twist the line—it wobbles. Solid brass blades are superbly machined, and brilliantly plated. Available with tags or plain. Most weights are highly recommended for jigging. Let lure sink to the bottom, raise rod tip with a quick jerk, and then let it sink again. Blade finishes: nickel and gold. Fluorescent colors: green, blue, red-orange, chartreuse, and pink. Flashback colors: gold, green, red, silver, and blue. Tags: white and yellow. Weights: 1/12, ⅛, ¼, ⅓, ½, ⅞, 1, 1¾ ounces.

Hoochy Trolls—Lifelike squid-type lure in fish-attracting colors. For general saltwater trolling and casting. Also good for large freshwater fish. Lead-weighted head, shaped like streamlined squid. High-strength stainless steel beaded chain securely molded into head, mounting rings at both ends. Hoochy Firetail with wiggling tentacles molded of polymeric vinyl plastic for extra flexibility and livelier action. One-piece head and tail skirt drawn snug over squid head, forming sleek skintight sheath. All metals specifically chosen for saltwater fishing. Sizes: 5, 6, 7,

and 12 inches. Weights: ½, 1, 2, 3, 4, and 6 ounces. Colors: blue horizon, white, purple, neon pink, neon red, orange, chartreuse, red-orange, squid beige, and pink shrimp.

Muskrat Lures—"The Three Rats" do not constitute a new fable; they are proven deadly lures. Dressed with genuine natural northern deer hair by hair-tying specialists with know-how and muscle to produce a lure that's lifelike, durable, and effective. The heads are skillfully "sculptured" hair with a set of stiff whiskers and two securely attached beady eyes. And each has a long, flexible, black vinyl tail. The Papa and Mama Muskrats have a free-wheeling, heavily tied bucktail "rump." Three models available: Papa, Mama, and Baby Muskrat. Lengths: 12, 8, and 6 inches.

Weber Fun-Kits—These kits are economical to buy and save you money in the long run, since with them you can make your own lures at great savings. And they are fun kits. Each kit contains everything you need to make dozens of lures. Types of kits available are fly, ice fishing, jig, popper, spoon, and spinner. Price: $9.95.

WILLE PRODUCTS CO.

We always enjoy learning about new ideas that work, especially when they apply to our enjoyment of outdoor sports, and it seems that some of the simplest ideas—the ones that make us say, "Why didn't I think of that?"—are the ones that appeal to us most.

Well, the folks at Wille Products have some dandy ideas that they have put their time and money into to develop products for making angling more convenient. The one that appeals to us most is their new-fangled tackle box called "The Bait File." While it is certainly something that any fisherman could put to good use, the traveling fisherman should find it particularly handy. It's a tackle tote that makes good sense, and the price is right. What more could you want?

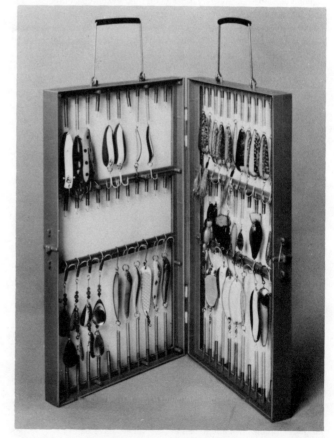

The Bait File

We recently received the two we ordered, and they are going to become a permanent part of our luggage. They're just the right size and shape for air travel carry-on luggage. They're also flat enough to slide under the seat of a car or to be packed inside a suitcase.

The Bait File—Built of rugged polystyrene with all stainless steel accessories, this new idea in tackle boxes makes all lures immediately accessible, prevents them from wear-deterioration, and eliminates tangling. The Bait File will handle flies, plugs, and spoons with perfect ease. The basic unit will store sixty-six lures. Additional panels are inserted through a master hinge system, which eliminates the need to purchase a second storage container for additional equipment. Panels are 20 inches high and 12 inches wide. Depth is 1½ inches. Prices: $24.95 (basic unit), $12.65 (basic insert), $17.50 (dodger insert).

Jr. Bait File—Just like its big brother, but this one measures only 6×10 inches. In it there's room for twenty-eight lures. And, like the larger model, this one has the same unique master hinge system that allows the addition of inserts to increase the capacity without buying another tackle tote. Prices: $13.95 (basic unit), $5.95 (insert).

WRIGHT & MCGILL CO.

Popular Eagle Claw fishing tackle is manufactured by Wright & McGill. The line includes rods, reels, and terminal tackle for all types of fishing in fresh and salt water.

We have used quite a bit of Eagle Claw tackle for years. Among our favorite rods are the Eagle Claw Northwest Steelhead models that are light and sensitive enough to handle delicate egg clusters, yet tough enough to land big chinook salmon. And we use dozens of different styles and sizes of Eagle Claw hooks, because they are top-quality and durable hooks we can depend on.

Some of the new products from Wright & McGill include their Blue Pacific skirted-spool spinning reels (see Gander Mountain) and Granger Graphite Blue Diamond fishing rods.

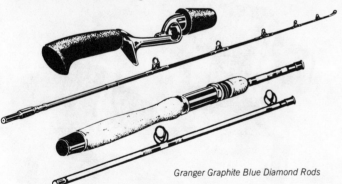

Granger Graphite Blue Diamond Rods

Granger Graphite Blue Diamond Rods—These rods are constructed of 3M Brand 100 percent unilateral carbon fibers with absolutely no glass filler introduced into their composition. It is this important manufacturing process that gives every Blue Diamond rod the greatest strength with a smooth, forceful power and the lightest possible weight. With the first few casts of the Blue Diamond rod, you'll experience an increase in casting power with a minimum of effort. Your casting motions are noticeably smoother, more controlled, and easier. The recoil motion of the Blue Diamond fly rod is quickly dampened, which produces only the slightest sine wave with almost no transmission of rod vibration to cause unwanted oscillations to the still moving fly line. The extra-sensitive characteristics of these rods not only makes casting a thing of ease and enjoyment, but provides a notable increase in touch and feel in all phases of your fishing. The Blue Diamond line includes two casting rods, five spinning rods, one fly-spin combination rod, and nine fly models. All come packed in a screw-top aluminum case with cloth inner liner.

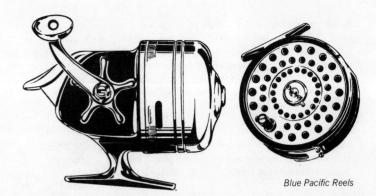

Blue Pacific Reels

Eagle Claw Pro Worm—These rods were originally designed for the professional fisherman with proven worth in tournaments around the country. Now, the new Pro rods are offered to all fishermen who fish for big fish. These rods are built strong, stiff, and powerful for fishing down deep among the weeds, brush, and snags, but they have a sensitive tip that lets you feel the strike. The rods feature high-density bonded tubular glass construction, hard high-luster finish, black/red nylon wraps over yellow nylon, nickel silver hookkeeper, and ceramic guides. One piece. Length: 5 feet 8 inches.

Eagle Claw Blue Pacific Spinning Reels—Adjustable wide-range multidisk drag reduces line friction. Heavy-duty pickup bail with chromed stainless finish to make it rustproof. Ball-bearing construction gives your reel smooth, long-wearing operation. Folding aluminum handle. Six models available, ranging from ultralight to heavy saltwater.

Eagle Claw Blue Pacific Spin-Casting Reels—All-metal precision-gear construction gives this reel smooth-running and long-wearing operation. Features include chromed wide-range star drag, built-in antireverse system, instant pickup, stainless steel rotors, and epoxy finish for durability. All parts are chemically treated for corrosion resistance. Available in three models, ranging from light to medium-heavy duty. All reels come loaded with line.

Eagle Claw Blue Pacific Fly Reels—If you're a fly-rod fisherman, you'll appreciate these beautiful new single-action fly reels. They are precision-built for long, smooth, dependable operation. The drag is adjustable for both braking and striking directly from the reel without snapping the leader. The spool is easily detached by a simple latch mechanism. These fine reels are handsomely finished in Eagle Claw brown and gold, and the hard chromed line guards complete the refinements. Four models available, from small to extra large.

Eagle Claw Blue Pacific Trolling Reels—These new reels are the result of years of research and development by the people at Wright & McGill. Outstanding design features on all models include dependable full-range drag system, spool and bearing tension adjustments, ball-sealed lubrication ports, chrome-plated brass spools, and durable stainless steel reinforced side plates. The series includes three level wind models, two freshwater and two saltwater reels.

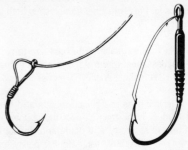

Eagle Claw Steelhead Rig
Eagle Claw Weighted Weedless Worm-Hook

Eagle Claw Steelhead Rigs—Take your pick—steelhead on eggs, bobbers, yarn, or chenille. These rigs do the job. Here's a 21-inch unlooped nylon leader tied to an Eagle Claw short-shank, up-eye hook. This snell gives the versatility you steelheaders need. The special midshank tie can be used with bobbers, eggs, or yarn. The unlooped snell lets you set up any type of rig you want. Packed twelve snells to the handy plastic pocket pack. Sizes: #4 through #3/0.

Eagle Claw Weighted Weedless Worm Hooks—Long, plain shank, weighted, weedless hooks with threaded weight makes the attachment of plastic worms easy, and they stay on your hook. Lets you fish down deep among the snags. Bronze finish. Sizes: #2 through #5/0.

Eagle Claw Worm Master Hooks—Southern sproat worm holder hook with kinked shank, ideal for Texas Rig. Finishes: blued or bronze. Sizes: #2 through #5/0.

ZAK TACKLE MANUFACTURING CO.

This company offers a line of lures, including spinners, spoons, plugs, and soft plastic baits. Additionally, their catalog includes a number of trolls and several items that are the inventions of owner, Felix Zak.

"Flipgun" Fish Hook Remover—Specifically designed for the small, hard-to-remove, deeply embedded hooks. With this hook remover there is no need to touch the fish or see the hook. Carries an unconditional guarantee. A tremendously popular gift item for fishermen and relatives.

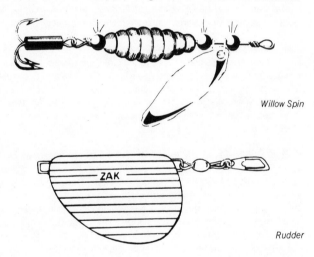

Willow Spin

Rudder

Willow Spin—A bright, rippled, fluorescent red body with pearlescent beads on top and bottom. Blade is flashy willow leaf type that spins close to the body of the lure. Red attractor tubing on #8 Mustad treble hook. This lure is used extensively for steelhead, as well as for trout and other game fish.

Twirl & Troll—An all-purpose light rod spinning and trolling rig, with three bright flashing propeller-type blades shaped to create minimum water drag. Tremendous for trout and other game fish in both lakes and streams. Length: 7 inches.

Rudder—Tough, red fluorescent plastic. The right size to satisfy most fishermen's needs. Stainless steel wire molded in with top-quality snap swivel attached. Length: 2¼ inches. Width: 1⅜ inches.

Indiana Baby Troll—Designed for the smooth action and flash of the well-known Indiana blades. Fishermen all over the country know the quality and productiveness of this type of blade and troll for lake and larger stream fishing. Has maximum fish-catching ability, combined with very little drag. Four medium-size nickel-silver blades. Length: 21 inches.

ZEBCO

Now a division of Brunswick Corporation, this firm was originally known as Zero Hour Bomb Company, and it produced the world's first closed-face spin-casting reel, which was the invention of a Texas watchmaker, R. D. Hull. Experimenting with fishing line wrapped around a beer can, Hull eventually developed the reel that was to revolutionize fishing in America. That was way back in 1948 and 1949. Since then Zebco has become the largest manufacturer of spin-cast reels in the world, producing over 30,000 units a day in thirty-three different models.

Zebco Omega Series Reels—This series of three reels, representing Zebco's top-of-the-line spin-cast offering, is easily identified by the distinctive styling that is characteristic of Zebco's entire product line. The colorful three-color band on stainless steel covers and power handles make these reels look as good as they work.

The Omega One is the heavy-duty model, featuring stainless steel ball bearings for long life and smooth retrieves, unique brake and feather-cast system, precision alloy drive and stainless worm gears, dual ceramic pickup, polished stainless covers for maximum protection, and wide-range double-cam star-actuated drag. Comes loaded with 14# DuPont Stren mono.

The Omega 33XBL is a conventional-size ball-bearing reel for all-around freshwater fishing. It features interchangeable handle, smooth stainless ball-bearing action, special alloy drive and stainless worm gears with 3:1 ratio, dual ceramic pickups, ultrasensitive wide-range drag, and polished stainless covers. Comes loaded with 10# DuPont Stren mono.

The little Omega 113 is the ultralight in the series. Weighing only 4 ounces, this professional model features precision, self-lubricating hardened metal gears. It has a tough Lexan body with polished stainless steel covers, highly sensitive multidisk drag and silent, selective antireverse. Comes loaded with 6# DuPont Stren.

Zebco Omega Reels

New Hi-Speed Cardinal Reels—Two new heavy-duty, fast-retrieve versions of the Zebco Cardinal 6 and 7 have been added to the line of popular Cardinal open-faced spinning reels. The 6X is a heavy freshwater/light saltwater reel with a super-fast 5:1 retrieve. It holds up to 230 yards of 12# line. The 7X is a heavy freshwater/medium saltwater reel that also sports a fast 5:1 ratio and holds up to 220 yards of 17# line.

All Cardinal reels feature stainless steel ball bearings, smooth Swedish steel worm, and bronze drive gears. They have multidisk drag systems with exclusive stern-mounted click-stop control. They are corrosion resistant and have dual bail springs with hard chrome-plated bail roller. Easy to change, one-piece snap-off spools.

CHAPTER THREE

WATERCRAFT, OUTBOARDS, AND BOATING ACCESSORIES

There are so many manufacturers of watercraft and boating accessories, and so many types of watercraft—from fishing tubes to yachts—that it would take an entire book, or perhaps several, to catalog them completely. Since most of our readers are fishermen, hunters, and campers, we have chosen companies and products that are of particular interest to these outdoors people. Consequently, this chapter is heavy on canoes, utility boats, bass boats, and multipurpose runabouts, and light on yachts.

We think we have listed a good mix of boats and boating accessories, and we're sure you will find items of interest to you. There should be plenty of products listed that will make your boating even more enjoyable than it already is.

The Fishing Fleet

AMF CRESTLINER

Here's a company that has plenty to offer the outdoorsman. They manufacture aluminum and fiberglass boats, ranging in size from 12 feet 1 inch to 23 feet 6 inches with standard and optional features sure to please the most discriminating boater.

The Fishing Fleet—Five boats—Voyager, Admiral, Commodore, Super Seaman, and Sportsman—make up this group of rugged aluminum boats that are ideal for fishing and hunting duties. Standard features include aluminum-enclosed motor mounts, nonskid floor surfaces, vinyl-covered solid seats, completely welded hulls, interior nonglare comfort surface, dry-drainage systems, and solid aluminum corner castings. Options include dead grass paint, console with mechanical steering, stern pan, and mooring cover. The smallest in the fleet is the 12-foot 1-inch Sportsman that is rated for a maximum 10-horsepower engine and load capacity of 555 pounds. The 18-foot Voyager is the largest, and this one will take engines in the 50- to 55-horsepower range and can haul more than half a ton.

ALLIED SPORTS CO.

From the Bass Mann who manufactures that great line of Tom Mann lures (see Chapter 2), comes the Fish Tracker and Humminbird depth-sounders and fish locators, as well as accessories for same.

Fish Tracker Sixty—The perfect sonar/locator for the occasional angler or the family runabout, the Fish Tracker offers high quality at budget prices. You'll find many of the same fine performance features as in the Humminbird line—super-bright flasher light and large sunshield for easy reading, the patented "Night Lighted" front panel for night reading, a positive noise rejection system to suppress false outside signals, and a high-speed 2-inch titanate transducer. Attractive, rugged ABS case. Complete with power cable, transducer and cable, mounting bracket, and complete instructions. Price: $99.95.

Humminbird Super Sixty—After its introduction in 1974, this unit quickly became a favorite with the bassin' man. Ideal for bass fishing because of its super-sensitive definition in shallow water. Reads in depths of as little as 1 to 60 feet. Reads to 120 feet on second revolution and up to 200 feet by adding 120 feet to the third revolution. Offers the pinpoint accuracy and resolution that pros demand in a sounder tough enough to give you years of flawless service. Guaranteed one year. Operates from your boat's 12V system.

Tom Mann Bird Trap—This portable conversion unit makes any Humminbird or Fish Tracker sounder completely portable. Attractive, rugged case, completely waterproof. Two 6V lantern batteries not included. Prices: from $49.95 to $59.95.

Humminbird

ALUMACRAFT BOAT CO.

From this company comes a line of rugged aluminum canoes, johnboats, semi-V fishing, and bass boats. We have spent a lot of hours fishing for walleyes and white bass in Wisconsin from an Alumacraft semi-V, and have used that same boat for duck hunting in Ohio. These are watercraft built to take it.

Alumacraft Quetico Canoes—Hulls and all parts of these canoes are made from heat-treated 6061 T-6 marine alloy aluminum. Bow and stern stems are made of .090-inch aluminum. Aluminum extruded keels

Quetico Canoe

and gunwales. Tunnel-designed contoured carrying yoke. Coast Guard approved flotation sealed in bulkheads. Ten models available for cruising or whitewater canoeing. Lengths: from 15 feet to 18 feet 5 inches. Weights: from 63 to 85 pounds. Prices: from $319 to $369, FOB plant.

Alumacraft Johnboats—These boats feature heavy-duty preformed extruded ribs extended up hull sides for greater strength. More and heavier ribs give added strength. Heavy-duty cast aluminum knee casting supports transom. Sturdy 1⅜-inch-thick transom with specially treated plywood inboard extending full width and depth of transom. Aluminum inboard motor pad. Seats with 1-inch front and back flange for easy securing of portable seats. Gas-resistant foam flotation. Made from 5052 alloy aluminum. Fourteen models available from 12 to 18 feet for outboard motors from 5 to 40 horsepower. Prices: from $209 to $599, FOB plant.

Bass Pro

Alumacraft 15-Foot Bass Boats—These new bass boats are constructed of high-quality 5052 aluminum. The three models have 15-foot flat bottoms and all-aluminum hulls. Each has three fold-down seats, fold-down bow lights, stowaway stern lights with brackets, console steering, gas-resistant flotation in floor and sides, bow storage compartments, rod holders, twin-shank bow eyes, floor and deck carpeting. The Bass Deluxe also includes all-aluminum floor under heavy-duty marine carpeting, 6-inch bow cleats, locking storage, trolling motor pad, bow casting platform, and live well under driver's seat. The Bass Pro, in addition to all of the above, features adjustable seat pedestals and casting platforms fore and aft. All models have 20-inch transoms. The Bass Standard

model is rated for maximum 50 horsepower, the Deluxe and Pro for 65 horsepower. Weights: 400, 420, 490 pounds. Capacities: 950, 1,040, 1,025 pounds. Prices: $1,149, $1,339, $1,549, FOB plant.

APOLLO DISTRIBUTING CORP.

From Apollo comes the Triton outboard motor. Three models are available, all featuring a telescopic leg for shallow water clearance and adjustment to any transom height, full engine rotation, single-adjustment transom bracket, and pressure die-cast, precision propellers. All three engines come with a 3½-gallon deluxe auxiliary tank with OMC type interchangeable connectors. Triton engines are guaranteed for one year against manufacturing defects.

Triton 4 Horsepower Outboard—Single cylinder, loop scavenger, two stroke, air cooled. Drive: forward, with full 360° reverse. Weight: 32½ pounds. Price: $289.95.

Triton 5.5 Horsepower Outboard—Portability and fuel-miser economy make this one a great fishing model. Single cylinder, loop scavenger, two stroke, air cooled. Drive: forward, with full 360° reverse. Weight: 34 pounds. Price: $339.95.

Triton 7.5 Horsepower Outboard—This engine has solid state ignition, sealed in epoxy—no dust, no humidity—so it starts when you expect it to. Single cylinder, loop scavenger, two stroke, air cooled. Drive: forward, with full 360° reverse and neutral. Weight: 36 pounds. Price: $399.95.

AQUABUG INTERNATIONAL, INC.

AquaBug and SuperBug ultralight outboard motors are economical little kickers, quality made of the best materials to give you years of faithful service. And don't let their low prices scare you off. These motors are sold directly to the consumer, thus eliminating middleman markups. They are excellent fishing motors and are ideal for powering small johnboats and canoes, or for use as trolling motors on larger craft.

AquaBug—At 11 pounds, it weights less than 2 gallons of fuel. With 35 pounds of thrust, it approaches the top performance of any 2-horsepower motor, yet it trolls at an extremely low speed all day without missing a beat or fouling a plug. Features include heavy-duty muffling, four-way angle adjustment, underwater exhaust, aluminum gear case, stainless gears and bearings, weedless aluminum 6-inch prop, aluminum drive shaft, self-draining carburetor, and easy-pull recoil starter. Price: $189.95, plus $7 for postage, handling, and insurance.

AquaBug

SuperBug—At 18 pounds, it weighs only as much as 3 gallons of fuel, yet it carries 70 pounds of thrust. Features include integral long-range tank, twin transom clamps, extra-long folding tiller, stainless steel drive shaft and anodized aluminum cover, three-bladed high-thrust prop, tiller-mounted throttle, and balance-point carrying handle with spare shear pins and cotter pins. Price: $289.95, plus $10 for postage, handling, and insurance.

BAYLINER MARINE CORPORATION

Bayliner's line includes twenty-eight models of trailerable power boats, including some of the biggest tow-along models around. Five of their boats are outboard models; the rest are available with a variety of single and twin sterndrive options, featuring Mercury and Volvo engines.

Bayliner 1900 Quartermaster—Don't let the luxury fool you; underneath it all there's a hard-charging performer. The deep-V hull gives you a smooth ride and precise handling, which makes it a natural for fishing. Creature comforts are well taken care of, with plush poly carpeted deck, vinyl upholstered sleeper seats, and a unique aft bench seat that folds out of the way when not in use. There's a safety glass walk-through windshield, bow rail, running lights, full canvas—all standard. Centerline: 17 feet 17 inches. Weight: 1,150 pounds. Maximum horsepower: 150. Price: $2,850.

Bayliner 1950 Jamaica—This is Bayliner's most deluxe tri-hull runabout. Spacious, comfortable, and smooth riding, the Jamaica offers spirited performance no matter which power option you choose. The vinyl upholstered sleeper seats fold down full length, and there's plenty of room for the entire family in the bow seating area and on the stern quarter seats. Standard features include full canvas, full deck hardware, transom bait well/coolers, bilge pump, blower, and more. Centerline: 18 feet, 7 inches. Beam: 89 inches. Weight: 2,000 pounds with 130 Volvo.

Fuel capacity: 36 gallons. Price: $7,350 with 130 Volvo. Five other power options available.

Bayliner 2150 Liberty Fisherman—This boat is as good looking as it is efficient. It's pure function in the cockpit: a self-bailing fiberglass inner liner, aerated bait well, rod holders, and boack on the transom, an insulated fish well with teak hatch. Up forward is a lockable cabin. The ice box is accessible from the cockpit. Centerline: 19 feet 7 inches. Beam: 93 inches. Weight: 2,500 pounds with 130 Volvo. Fuel capacity: 40 gallons. Water capacity: 20 gallons. Price: $9,095 with 130 Volvo. Two other power options available.

Bayliner 2550 Saratoga Fisherman—An all new model, this boat provides offshore fishing capabilities and weekend accommodations for even the most serious tournament fisherman. The nonskid fiberglass inner liner is uncluttered for fighting the big ones. There's a large fish well molded into the transom and covered with teak, a fish well in the cockpit floor, and teak rod racks. The forward cabin features V-berths, galley, and a portable head. The boat is designed for easy maintenance, which means you spend more time fishing. Centerline: 24½ feet. Beam: 96 inches. Weight: 4,200 pounds with 200 Volvo. Fuel capacity: 96 gallons. Water capacity: 20 gallons. Price: $12,795 with 200 Volvo. Four other power options available.

BECKSON MANUFACTURING, INC.

One of the handiest things to come along since the bucket, and infinitely more efficient as a boat bailer, is Beckson's Thirsty-Mate vinyl bilge pump. These pumps are lightweight and portable—ideal for any size boat—and are available in four sizes. Different attachments are available to make the Thirsty-Mate an all-purpose pump that can handle all the routine pumping jobs on board.

The Thirsty-Mate can pump water out of bilges, sump tanks, and

1900 Quartermaster

other places at the rate of 5 gallons per minute, transfer gasoline or diesel from one tank to another, or pump oil from inboard or sterndrive engine crankcases when it needs changing.

Diaphragm Pump DP2—Pumps 16 gallons per minute. Two-position handle and adjustable frame permits up to sixteen variations in stroke direction. Mounts vertically on bulkhead or horizontally on deck without the need for special brackets. Made of corrosionproof marine plastic, pump uses Model FH-1½ flexible wire reinforced vinyl hose. Pump comes complete with handle and storing clips. Length: 9 inches. Width: 6¼ inches. Weight: 2 pounds. Price: $39.50.

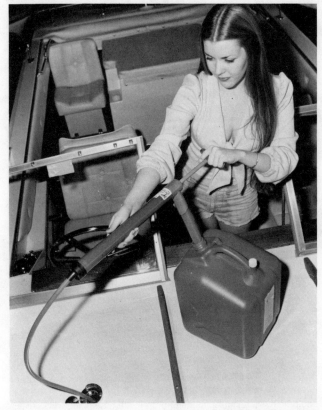

Transferring Water with Thirsty-Mate

BIG JON, INC.

From this company, near the salmon and lake trout waters of Lake Michigan, come the Big Jon downriggers and accessories. There are seven models of downriggers and sideriggers, manually and electrically operated.

If you want to get your baits and lures down deep to where the lunkers lurk, Big Jon has a downrigger to fit your needs and your budget, whether you enjoy your trolling in the Great Lakes, the big reservoirs, or in the salt chuck.

D100 Downrigger—This is the economy model, but it is manufactured with the same care and precision as all downrigger products from Big Jon. It comes equipped with a shot-pin positive lock for the reel, 150 feet of 150# braided stainless steel line, a Big Jon Multi-Bead Release, a 4-pound plastic-coated cannonball, and 4-inch-square base plate. The solid fiberglass rod is 18 inches long, with a sturdy Lexan tip that was specifically designed for downrigger fishing. The unit is built of polished aluminum and all working parts are of durable stainless steel. This model will fit all Big Jon base plates. Recommended for off-transom use only. Price: $78.95.

D400J Downrigger

D400J Downrigger—This is a deluxe unit that is ready to go fishing. It comes equipped with a true drag/clutch to help prevent cannonball loss. Features include 200 feet of braided 150# stainless steel line, a Big Jon line release with three precise settings, a footage counter, a plastic-coated 7½-pound cannonball, and a 4-inch-square mounting plate. It also has a shot-pin positive lock for the reel. The rod is polished stainless steel and is 20 inches long, with a Lexan swinging tip that permits the angler to use this unit over the stern or side of the boat from the same sturdy base plate. The unit is built of polished aluminum and all working parts are of durable stainless steel. Price: $153.

ES1000 Electric Siderigger—This is a unique new trolling downrigger that comes in two parts. The first unit is a deluxe manual downrigger with all the Big Jon quality features built right in. It comes complete with 300 feet of stainless steel wire, footage counter, mounting plate, release, ball-bearing tension clutch, shot-pin stop, 8-pound cannonball, and a demountable handle. When you want the ultimate weapon at a later date, you can purchase the motor kit, which includes a powerful 12V motor, a strong gear box, and a weatherproof switch box. This unit simply bolts on and the manual handle is removed. Prices: $220 (deluxe downrigger), $235 (drive unit), $455 (electric complete).

BLUE HOLE CANOE CO.

On Tennessee's Cumberland Plateau, Blue Hole builds their canoes with aircraft aluminum upper structures and rugged ABS Royalex hulls and tests them in nearby whitewater. Their original model, the 16-foot Blue Hole, has been joined recently by two new 17-foot 3-inch Wild River models. These canoes are handled by more than 100 dealers in the eastern half of the United States and several on the West Coast.

Blue Hole 16-Foot Canoe—The keelless hull shape of this craft provides a fast-reacting, responsive canoe. Specially designed gunwale deflects high waves, yet offers free passage to dumped water. Each lightweight seat is mounted on straight, twin thwarts, giving the canoe strength and kneeling clearance. An oversize center thwart on the canoe center of gravity is positioned for solo portaging. Grab-handles at each end are integral features of the deck plates. Structurally critical thwarts, deck plates, and grab-handles are 6061 T-6 aluminum alloy. Beam: 34 inches. Center height: 14 inches. Bow height: 25 inches. Weight: 70 pounds. Price: $465.

New 17-Foot 3-Inch Wild River Canoes—Two models available—one for whitewater, one for wilderness cruising. Model 17A features the same whitewater outfitting as the 16 foot and has an additional midship thwart. The Model 17B features full-width molded and foam-injected cruising seats, dropped slightly for seated comfort. The balanced center thwart is standard, while the new rolled-edge deck plates maintain the

Blue Hole Canoe on a wilderness cruising trip

designed-in drainage vents like those found in the whitewater models. Width: 36 inches. Depth: 15 inches. End height: 25 inches. Weight: 78 pounds. Prices: $495 (17A), $480 (17B).

BOATMEN'S INDUSTRIES, INC.

If, as the late Arnold Gingrich said, fishing is the most fun you can have standing up, the folks at Boatmen's Industries are doing their best to make it just as enjoyable sitting down. What they offer the fisherman is just about any kind of seat you might want for your fishing machine, from their little fiberglass Bass Boat Seat, right up to their big Bermuda Fishing Chair.

All arms, back supports, and pedestal assemblies on their products are manufactured of anodized aluminum. The mildew-resistant vinyls are sewn with Dacron thread to prevent breakage at the seams. Only high-density, extra-firm polyfoam is used and tacked with stainless steel staples. Only nylon zippers are used to prevent any type of corrosion and to ensure their durability. So if you're looking to outfit a fishing boat, you should be interested in what this firm has to offer.

No. 1120 Folding Chair—Overall width: 27 inches. Seat width: 20 inches. Weight: 22 pounds. Gimbal available. P ice: $95; gimbal $18 extra.

No. 2216-GA Chair—Overall width with arms: 23 inches. Seat width: 16 inches. Weight: 32 pounds. Price: $170.

Reversible Ice Box Seat and Back—This ideal seat for open fishermen combines the comfort of a padded seat and back with the convenience of a pivoting back rest, enabling the user to face fore or aft. The heavy-duty insulated ice box underneath has chrome-plated brass and stainless steel hardware. The aluminum hinges are guaranteed for two years.

Box dimensions: 21 inches wide by 42 inches long by 20 inches high. Weight: 66 pounds. Price: $432.

The Bermuda—This model, the largest of Boatmen's family of fishing chairs, is designed with the sport fisherman in mind. It features a fiberglass molded seat, back, and footrest; three-position gimbal; two rod holders; removable cushions; and heavy-duty pedestal as standard equipment. All anodized aluminum parts are assembled with stainless steel fasteners. Price: $850. Head rest $73 extra.

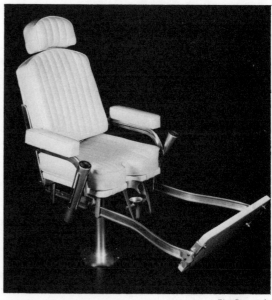

The Bermuda

60

BREMER MANUFACTURING CO., INC.

Bremer manufactures fine accessories for boating enthusiasts. They have a small catalog available that includes several dozen items to make your boating and fishing more convenient. Here's a sampling.

Two-Way Outboard Bracket—Ideal for mounting that auxiliary trolling motor, this bracket is spring-loaded with lock in either up or down position. All aluminum and stainless steel. Will handle up to 20-horsepower motor. Raises a total of 11 inches. Painted white over zinc chromate. Weight: 14 pounds. Price: $59.

Extension Handle

Extension Handle Model TG-2—Just the ticket for shifting your weight forward in a small boat or for operating an outboard from a standing position. Rubber hand grip, stainless steel clamp, 2-foot aluminum handle. Painted blue. Price: $10.

Stowable Motor Lift—Easy to stow, this 22-inch motor lift is made of lightweight aluminum. Fits all large outboards. Simple thumb-screw adjustment. Weight: 1.75 pounds. Price: $18.

Stowable Motor Lift

BROCKS ELECTRONICS CORPORATION

Marine electronics is the specialty of this company, which produces the Seafarer 3 Depth-Sounder/Fishfinder and the Seaspot 2 hand-held radio direction finder, among others.

Seafarer 3 Depth-Sounder/Fishfinder—If you're serious enough about fishing to consider sonar, you're doing more than sightseeing on the water. You might as well pick up professional gear to match your own feeling for the sport. The Fishfinder is a professional tool, built for strength and designed for accuracy and versatility—on the North Atlantic or on a tricky lake backwater. Instead of stabbing in the dark with a pencil beam of 18°, you'll be scanning the bottom with a 45° swath, and at a powerful 150 kHz. Depth ranges: 0-60 feet, 0-60 fathoms. Input voltage: internal—9V (Ever-Ready #276, NEDA #1603); ship's power—12V-40V DC (self-regulating). Solid state circuitry—fifteen transducers, nine diodes. Polystyrene case, oyster white or light gray. Weight: 3½ pounds. Price: $169.

Seaspot 2 Hand-Held RDF—Compact and lightweight, the Seaspot 2 is a hand-held radio direction finder specifically designed for the demanding accuracy of marine navigation. It is infinitely tuneable to AM broadcast stations and marine and aero beacon bands worldwide, without the need of additional modules. This unit is completely portable and can function without reference to ship's heading. A liquid prismatic compass mounted on the unit is capable of being read to 1° of its inherent calibrated accuracy and doubles as a high-quality hand-bearing compass.

Seafarer 3

The unit is powered by an internal battery that also supplies illumination for the compass and is rechargeable from the ship's 12V system. The case is constructed of rigid, extruded PVC with end panels and removable handle of molded phenolic. Compressed rubber gaskets ensure environmental protection of circuitry. Comes complete with detachable bearing compass, stethoscopic headset, recharging assembly, and simple bulkhead stowage bracket. Price: $199.

CHRYSLER CORPORATION

For the outdoorsman who enjoys his sports on the water, Chrysler has a lot to offer, from boats to outboard motors, to a complete line of marine powerhouses, including sterndrives, gasoline and diesel inboards, and jetdrives. They also offer a fleet of bass boats, described below. But for our money, one of the niftiest machines to come along in a good while is the Chrysler Funster. There are two models—the C-142, and the larger C-164. They're dandy boats for the outdoor-oriented family—great for fishing, camping, or just fun on the water.

Chrysler 6—A compact, manual-start outboard with specially calibrated carburetor to help keep fuel costs down. Exhaust tuning, precision porting, and extra-efficient prop deliver uniform, all-speed power and performance. BIA-certified 6 horsepower @ 5,000 rpm. Two-cycle. Weight: 49 pounds (add 1⅓ pounds for 20-inch motor leg). Gear ratio: 15:23. Price: $575 (15 inches), $590 (20 inches).

Chrysler 55—One of the most innovative new outboards on the water today, this engine has bigger piston displacement than any other motor in the 50- to 55-horsepower range. Performance, power, acceleration, and dependability—all in a single, simple, lightweight, fuel-saving outboard motor. Great for fishing and family boating. Features Super-Power-Charging for a full-speed super-charging effect, smooth idling and top performance at all speeds. It has breakerless, modular Magnapower ignition with just two moving parts under its forged-steel flywheel, along with a high-output alternator to make starting and idling easy and smooth. Separate coils for each cylinder. All high-tension circuitry, coils, wires, and plugs enclosed. Precision tuning of carburetors and exhaust. BIA-certified 55 horsepower @ 5,000 rpm. Two-cycle. Weight: 183 pounds. Price: $1,700.

Pro Bass Runner 15—Chrysler's new bass fisherman features both fore and aft casting platforms, a molded-in livewell, and more built-ins than offered previously on comparable models. Beam: 56 inches. Overall: 15 feet 1½ inches. Maximum horsepower: 60. Capacity: 1,000 pounds. Weight: 753 pounds. Price: $2,195.

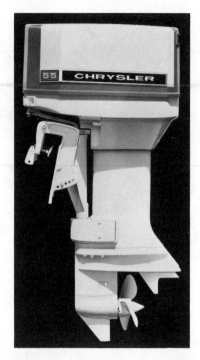

Chrysler 55

C-142 Funster—This is a 16-foot all-around funabout with cathedral hull and wide-open space from stem to stern. Instantly converts from utility boat to fisherman, to family picnic craft. Ideal as a day cruiser or camping boat. Standard features include twin jump seats aft, poly-pile carpeting on floor and sides, deluxe side console with sport wheel, pilot/fisherman swivel seat (also mounts forward on optional swivel base), forward side rails, splashwell curtain, and running lights. A variety of options are available to turn this into any kind of boat you want it to be. Centerline: 16 feet 2 inches. Beam: 76 inches. Weight: 830 pounds. Maximum horsepower: 105. Price: $2,355.

CLINTON ENGINES CORP.

Seven models of compact outboard motors are available from Clinton: four lightweight motors with integral gas tanks and three deluxe motors with remote fuel tanks. Motors with integral tanks come in 1.5, 2, 3.5, and 7.5 horsepower. Deluxe models are available in 5.5, 7.5, and 9 horsepower. These are economically priced outboards that are ideal for a wide range of duties, from pushing canoes and small inflatables, to trolling, to powering johnboats and semi-V fishing and utility boats.

Clinton engines are manufactured in the United States and carry a one-year warranty. There are 10,000 Clinton service centers throughout the country.

Clinton K-150—Here's a new standard lightweight outboard that offers more features for less money: automatic recoil starter, air-cooled engine with integral 1-quart fuel tank, four-position transom adjustment, underwater exhaust, forged alloy steel connecting rod, and aluminum semiweedless prop. Engine: 1.5 horsepower, single cylinder, two-cycle. Weight: 14.5 pounds. Price: $209.

Clinton K-350—This is the intermediate compact with dependable power to get you there. And it throttles down to perfect control when you arrive. Features die-cast aluminum connecting rod and two-blade propeller. Engine: 3.5 horsepower, single cylinder, two-cycle, air cooled. Weight: 34 pounds. Price: $219.

Bass Runner 105—The Chrysler Bass Runner fleet is topped off this year with the Bass Runner 105, a 16-foot super-performance hull with modified cathedral design and wide pad keel. Standard features include plush poly-pile carpeting, low-slung fold-away pilot/mate bucket seats, fore and aft platforms with adjustable swivel fold-down chairs, two live wells with freshwater/aerator pump systems. Safety engine "kill" switch, lockable rod/tackle storage and console with sport wheel are also standard, as are molded tackle trays, no-snag cleats, and plug-in electrical outlet and battery storage for trolling motor. Centerline: 16 feet 3 inches. Beam: 72 inches. Weight: 925 pounds. Maximum horsepower: 105. Price: $2,820.

C-142 Funster

Clinton K-550—40 pounds of fishing fun, with 2½-gallon remote fuel tank, this engine has one-hand steering and throttle, and five-position transom adjustment. Other features include magneto-spark advance ignition, automatic recoil starter, forged aluminum connecting rod, and three-blade semiweedless prop. Engine: 5.5 horsepower, single cylinder, two-cycle, air and water cooled. Price: $309.

Clinton K-900—A true fisherman's outboard, with 6-gallon remote fuel tank, this engine features forged aluminum connecting rod, solid state ignition with spark advance, and automatic recoil starter. Twist-grip throttle, three-position pull choke, and full shift mean convenience and performance. Engine: 9 horsepower, single cylinder, two cycle, air and water cooled. Weight: 49 pounds. Price: $515.

K-550

COMPASS ELECTRONICS CORP.

This company offers two lines of depth-finders. Their Sensi-Depth 3 and Sensi-Depth 4 are LED (flasher type) depth-finder/fish-finders, preferred by most sport fishermen. Their Digi-Depth line is comprised of five digital readout depth-finders, including their newest model, the Digi-Depth 99.

Sensi-Depth 3—A depth-finder/fish-finder featuring brilliant LED (light-emitting diodes) readout and a large scale that reads at a glance. Two depth ranges are 0 to 60 feet or 0 to 60 fathoms. Built-in noise suppressor is fully adjustable to eliminate false echoes. Separate brightness control on LED readout for night running. A loud depth alarm you can

Digi-Depth 99 and Remote Display

set from 4 feet to 50 fathoms is an excellent aid for fishing and navigating. Anything coming within range will set off the alarm. Comes complete with power cable and combination transducer/transom mount bracket with 20-foot transducer cable. Built to last with high-impact Cycolac case. Colors: nonglare black and white. Price: $189.50.

Digi-Depth 99—Bright, easy-to-see readout, reads to 99 feet or 60 fathoms plus (usable to 100 fathoms under good conditions). Optional remote display unit installs anywhere. Manual override to automatic gain control. Adjustable alarm operates at any depth from 2 feet to 60 fathoms. Small and compact. Dimensions: 5¾×3×3½ inches. Price: $299.50. Remote display unit $159.50 extra.

COSOM

Cosom offers deluxe mushroom anchors made of cast-iron core and encased in a thick plastic shell that will not chip or peel. For stowing the anchor when not in use, Cosom also makes a Boat Anchor Rest.

Cosom Mushroom Anchors—Two important features enhance the holding power of these anchors: concentration of weight in the upper portion of the shaft and a bowl-shaped base. These features cause the anchor to readily tip over upon touching bottom and the base flange to dig in quickly for excellent holding power on most bottoms. A favorite anchor for lake fishermen, the Cosom Deluxe Mushroom Anchor has flexible edges to prevent scratching or marring boat finishes. Colors: red, white, or yellow. Weights: 6, 10, and 16 pounds. Prices: $10.65, $13.65, $18.15.

Cosom Boat Anchor Rest—Attaches easily to the bow of most fishing boats with mounting plate provided. The rugged chrome-plated steel rest accommodates all mushroom-style anchors. Price: $12.

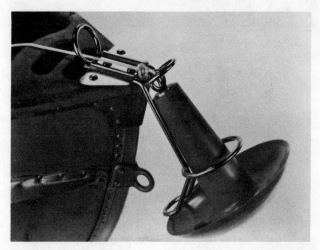

Mushroom Anchor and Anchor Rest

JACK DICKERSON'S, INC.

Jack specializes in fishing tackle (see Chapter 2). For the boater, he offers several brands of fish-finders, electric trolling motors, and boating accessories.

Pfleuger Deluxe Trolling Motor #M15—Fishermen need not be engineers to own and operate this fine trolling motor. Get six to eight hours out of a 12V, 60-amp battery. Three-speed switch with alternate forward or reverse switch all at your fingertips. High-torque permanent magnet motor. Smooth-pitch prop and 180° swivel motor. Adjustable transom bracket. Dickerson's price: $62.

Lowrance Fish-N-Float—For pinpoint accuracy use this float kit that contains six marker buoys, complete with cords and weights. Dickerson's prices: $9.95, two kits for $18.50.

EDMUND SCIENTIFIC CO.

An Edmund product of interest to boaters is described below. For other Edmund products see Chapters 2, 4, 5, 7, 11, and 12.

Navigation Kit—All the instruments most often used by navigators, including a standard marine sextant, artificial horizon, 18-inch three-arm protractor, parallel rules, time-speed-distance computer, metal dividers, and instructions. Price: $66.50 postpaid.

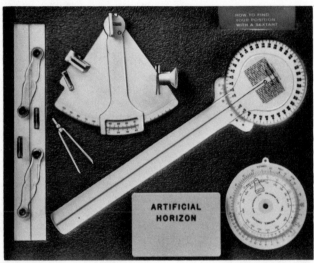

Navigation Kit

EVINRUDE

Certainly, Evinrude is one of the mighty giants of the boating world, manufacturing an extensive line of outboard motors that have gained the respect and confidence of countless thousands of boaters and fishermen over the years.

The best way to shop for an Evinrude is to look up "Boat Dealers" in the Yellow Pages of your phone directory and find one who handles Evinrude. Then stop by and pick up descriptive literature that will give you all the specifications on the various model outboard motors. Meanwhile, here are a few Evinrudes to browse over.

Evinrude 6 HP—Anglers who find the Evinrude 6 within their reach will find that Evinrude engineering comes through again. The new Evinrude 6 averages 20 percent fuel savings at the midrange speeds used by most fishermen to get to their fishing spots. This popular engine is the smallest in the line with full gearshift, twist-grip throttle, and the new water pumping indicator. Like the larger members of the Evinrude outboard family, it now features Firepower Breakerless C.D. Ignition, which makes this smooth alternate firing twin run smoother and more economically than ever before. Shaft lengths: 15 or 20 inches. Weights: 54 or 55 pounds. Prices: $575, $590.

Evinrude 15 HP—Evinrude's portable fleet also harbors the 15 horsepower—a pacesetter in compact take-along fishing motors. Consistent timing of the Firepower Breakerless C.D. Ignition provides extreme smoothness at slow-trolling or idle speeds and provides much more voltage for easy starting. It also makes for a substantial increase in spark plug life in tough, all-day trolling situations. Available in standard or long shaft and in manual or electric start models. Weights: from 72 to 82 pounds. Prices: from $840 to $995.

Evinrude 25 HP—Long a favorite among anglers who take their sport on larger rivers and bay waters, and with commercial fishermen who demand and expect a workhorse outboard, the 25 tops the line of Evinrude portable fishing power. This new compact motor tips the scale at a hair over 100 pounds, yet boasts being a "kissin' cousin" to the Evinrude 35

Evinrude 115 V-4 is Bill Dance's Choice

Evinrude 140 V-4 Drives 21-Foot Deck Craft

HP with the same displacement and same powerhead construction—but it runs a little slower and with a little less power. Boasting an edge in fuel economy of 28 percent in the cruising range over the all-time favorite 25 HP it replaces, and a performance edge of over 10 percent, this new engine now features Firepower Breakerless C.D. Ignition for smooth, consistent timing and a water pumping indicator. It is available in standard and long shaft models, with either manual or electric start. Weights: 101 to 106 pounds. Prices: $965 to $1120.

Evinrude V-4s—The Evinrude V-4 family has long provided versatile power and dependability for boaters. Now, the 140 HP (as well as the other 25-inch V-4s) has a new noise- and vibration-reducing midsection and a new gearcase. Additional power over the previous 135 HP is derived from a tuned megaphone and a larger expansion chamber in the inner exhaust housing.

Other high-styled V-4s are available in seven additional models, including 140, 115, and 85 horsepower in 20- or 25-inch transom models with either Power Trim and Tilt or manual trim.

All Evinrude V-4 motors have a new connecting rod made with a wider web that spreads the load over a larger number of bearing needles, thus increasing crankpin bearing/journal life. Features for Evinrude V-4s are low profile, patented pressure back piston rings and water shield exhaust, Firepower Breakerless C.D. Ignition, adjustable bolt-on stern brackets, through-tilt pin steering, power-assisted shift, and Power Pilot remote control with a combined start and choke switch. Prices start at about $2,150 for the 85 HP, $2,300 for the 115 HP, and $2,475 for the 140 HP.

FIN & FEATHER MANUFACTURING CO.

Here's a company that had a great idea for small-water boating and did something about it. They built the Electric Feather, which is a perfect little boat for the duck marsh or bass pond. It's small, light, portable, quiet, and powered by a custom-built Shakespeare trolling motor. What's more, the price is right.

The Electric Feather—With this craft, anglers can silently stalk fish in stump-filled weed beds or rocky shallows. Duck hunters can reach their blinds, set out the blocks, and hunt right from this modern-day pirogue. Powered by a heavy-duty electric trolling motor built into the stern and operated by remote controls, the boat provides eight to twelve hours of fishing on a fully charged, standard 12V battery. All controls are conveniently located in the cockpit so that even when the lone fisherman is busy casting or landing a fish, controls can be reached quickly and operated with one hand. A flip of the switch provides instant power, forward or reverse. A second switch permits low, medium, or high speeds up to 10 miles per hour. Slight pressure on the control stick turns the Electric Feather's bow right or left, exactly in the direction the angler wants to go. Ruggedly built of hand-laid fiberglass with a wide, flat bottom and wraparound gunwale, the sleek hull offers stability and safety. Weight: 67 pounds. Length: 12 feet. Beam: 38 inches. Bow height: 8 inches. Depth amidships: 12 inches. Colors: hunter green, cobalt blue, yellow, red, camouflage olive drab overspray. Price: $389 (without battery).

The Electric Feather

FISH HAWK ELECTRONICS

Fish Hawk represents a large line of electronic aids to fishing, including depth-finders, temperature meters, and oxygen analyzers. Portable and permanent models are available. These are quality devices, designed and manufactured for accuracy, durability, and long life.

Fish Hawk 404—Here is the sonar flasher with all the features, all the rugged quality that could be built into a long-life fishing/navigational instrument for ocean and big-lake use. A quality two-speed motor gives 60-feet or 60-fathom readings at the flick of a switch—easily readable on a clearly marked dial face. There's an audio alarm, and it even has two different tones for feet and fathoms. And the Fish Hawk 404 has Waller's superb Magnum Titanate Transducer System for the exclusive combination of wide-cone sound under water and fine-line readout on the dial. Other features include lighted dial for night use, solid-state electronics, and sturdy gimbal mount. Head is removable in seconds. Electronics are sealed from rain and spray. Nonglare dial face has deep sunshade. Wires direct to 12V system. Price: $313.95.

Digital Depth/Light Density & Temperature Meter—With an instrument to provide scientifically accurate measurement of underwater light density, fishermen now have a virtually foolproof guide to selection of lure color. This new Waller product provides light density reading, plus water temperature readings, plus positive digital readout of depths for both. This is the digital depth meter for the great majority of fishermen. Solid-state electronics. Sturdy, extra-heavy probe. Complete with long-life 9V battery. Price: $69.95.

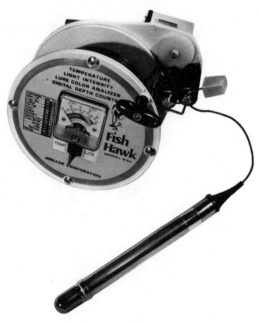

Digital Depth/Light Density & Temperature Meter

GANDER MOUNTAIN, INC.

In addition to the following items of interest to boating enthusiasts, Gander offers products that are found in Chapters 2, 4, 5, 7, 8, and 9.

In the boating area, the company carries Minn Kota electric trolling motors, Eska and Mighty Mite outboard motors, Pyrawa inflatable boats, Stearns Sans-Souci flotation vests, Lowrance depth-sounders, Riviera downriggers, and an assortment of accessories.

Old Pal Marine Battery Box—Protect your battery from damaging spray and bilge; prevent acid from damaging boat and gear. Molded of durable

Minn Kota 65 Trolling Motor

high-density polyethylene, this battery box measures 11¼×7½×10¼ inches. Strap doubles as carrying handle. G.M. price: $5.97.

Battery 4-Amp Charger—Charge 6V or 12V batteries in five to fourteen hours. With automatic circuit breaker, voltage selector switch, and rate of charge dial ammeter. Rugged steel case, power cord, and two alligator clips. G.M. price: $17.97.

Minn Kota 65—This is a big electric motor with up to 18 pounds of thrust to easily handle the big boats. Features twist-grip handle, has four-speed control, convenient forward-reverse switch, one-piece 30-inch steel shaft, rugged die-cast ten-position bracket with dual clamps. G.M. price: $124.97.

GARCIA CORP.

Garcia makes a line of fish-finders that we have sampled below. Garcia fishing tackle can be found in Chapter 2. Be sure to check out Chapter 4 for their firearms.

Garcia Electro-Sonic 9260A Fish-Finder—This is the perfect portable for the bass fisherman, with 60-foot scale for close-up detail of bottom structure. Long-life flasher gives clear readings even in direct sunlight. Range: to 120 feet. All solid state. Modular components for easy service. Uses either 6V lantern batteries or 12V boat current. Fully adjustable transducer bracket. And 20 feet of transducer cable is included.

Garcia Flasher/Recorder

Garcia Electro-Sonic 9350A High-Speed Fish-Finder—Accurate readings to 45 knots. Dual range—reads to 300 feet at normal trolling speeds and 100 feet on high-speed mode. Ultrabright, long-life flasher for clear readings. Permanent or portable mounting. Transducer can be through-hull, no-hole, or transom mounted. Includes noise filter. Comes with 20 foot of transducer cable.

Garcia 9500A Flasher/Chart Recorder—Flashes to 480 feet. Chart-records in eight close-up increments—60-foot increments from 0 to 240 feet, 120-foot increments from 0 to 480 feet. Outstanding performance at a modest price. Flip-up window for direct notation on paper. Swivel-tilt mount, easily removable. No-hole, through-hull, or transom transducer mounting. Includes 20 feet of transducer cable.

GLEN-L

If you're a do-it-yourselfer, you might want to consider building your own boat. In that case, you won't want to overlook Glen-L's catalog of boat plans. From this company you can order plans, full-size patterns, and frame kits for a variety of boats, ranging in size from small punts and rowboats to cruisers and houseboats.

See Chapter 10 for information about Glen-L recreational vehicle kits.

Mr. John—This boat can be built as either an 11-foot 9-inch or 13-foot 7-inch hull. Details for building both are shown on the plans, which are particularly simple with concise instructions. Included are methods of cutting your material from the listed plywood, fastening schedule, material listings, types of glues, etc., along with step-by-step building procedures. Beam: 4 feet 4 inches. Hull depth: 1 foot 5 inches. Weights: 145 pounds (12-foot model), 165 pounds (14-foot model). Maximum horsepower: 20. Complete plans plus patterns for bow piece, transom, and each of the frames, instructions, and material list. Price: $8.

Duck Boat and Duck Boat Too—Duck Boat is a double-ender for paddles and Duck Boat Too is for lightweight outboard motors. Either can be inexpensively and simply constructed from plywood. Duck Boat specifications: 14-foot length, 3-foot 11-inch beam, 1-foot 1-inch depth, 96 pounds. Duck Boat Too specifications: 12-foot 4-inch length, 3-foot 11-inch beam, 1-foot 1-inch depth, 88 pounds. Complete plans and full-size patterns for each of the frames, stem, and transom (on Duck Boat Too), details and instructions for building either model. Price: $8.

Hi-Rider—Here is a no-compromise, no-nonsense, no-cabin boat that's got everything you've searched for in a great sport craft. Complete plans and full-size patterns for this 20-foot deep-V boat are $30. Using a frame kit to build your Hi-Rider makes the construction easier and faster. Kit includes all bulkhead/frame units preassembled, transom fully framed, sheer harpin perimeter members, stem, complete plans with instructions, bill of materials, and fastening schedule. Price: $240.

GRUMMAN BOATS

In addition to manufacturing some of the finest aluminum canoes and utility boats afloat, Grumman promotes canoeing and water safety at every opportunity. Toward that end, Grumman offers three booklets that are free for the asking— #002 "Learn To Canoe Directory," #090 "Rent-A-Canoe Directory," and #897 "Group-Camping-By-Canoe."

We have used Grumman canoes for years and have had experience with more than a half-dozen of their seventeen models, our favorite being the rugged and roomy Sportcanoe that is a great craft for river or lake, hunting, fishing, and camping. We are excited about the prospects of Grumman's new generation of high-performance utility boats—so much so, in fact, that we recently ordered one. We think they are going to find favor among outdoorsmen everywhere.

Grumman Double-End Canoes—The Double-End is the most versatile canoe, just as easy to paddle in the current of a stream as the flat water of a lake. Grumman has compromised the sheer at the ends to reduce wind effect. The tumblehome-beam combination achieves optimum dryness in rougher water. Grumman offers ten distinct models to satisfy your particular uses. Determine your most frequent trips and focus on the model—from 13 to 20 feet—that will best carry the equipment and people you plan for and on the waters you intend to canoe. Lightweight models: 13, 15, 17, and 18 feet. Standard weight: same as lightweight, plus 20' and 20' Peace Canoe. Weights: from 44 to 67 pounds (lightweight), 58 to 117 pounds (standard). Prices: from $342 to $391 (lightweight), $321 to $534 (standard).

Shallow-Draft Grummans—Satisfying the particular requirements of whitewater canoeists, Grumman's three shallow-draft models are constructed of .050-inch marine aluminum, and have additional ribs which, by technical measurement, impart greater strength. The expressly designed and extruded aluminum keel, actually installed back to back, affords little surface for river currents to grab. Thus, if you're working left, while a current is trying to push you right, you'll be glad you have a Grumman shallow-draft keel that minimizes the effect. Lengths: 15, 17, and 18 feet. Weights: 74, 81, and 91 pounds. Prices: $363, $384, $404.

Grumman Square Sterns—Three models available for those who plan to use a motor more frequently than a paddle. Fishermen and hunters should look into their greater capacity and extra strength. The square stern itself boasts a special transom cap of .090-inch aluminum to integrate the inherent strengths of the gunwales, hull skins, and transom. Grumman's spray rails will deflect waves and chop while underway. The back seat, under which the closed-cell flotation material is located, is positioned forward from the stern for easy operation of nonreversible motors. Lengths: 15, 17, and 19 feet. Weights: 77, 85, and 112 pounds. Prices: $370, $391, $507.

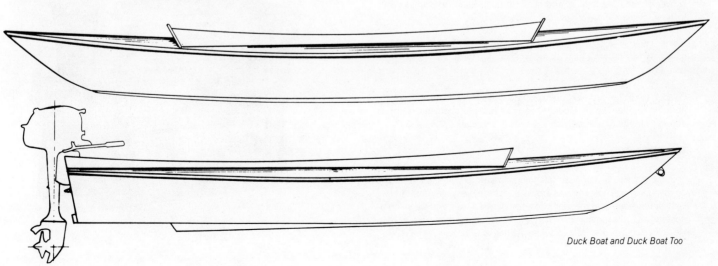

Duck Boat and Duck Boat Too

Grumman 3.8 High-Performance Utility Boat

The Sportcanoe—An everything-for-everybody boat, the Grumman Sportcanoe is virtually the most versatile watercraft available for family fun, fishing, duck hunting, river running, and float trips. The design means high performance in a utility cartopper. The craft rows easily and can be paddled, poled, or powered by an outboard motor. Standard features include three seats, spray rails, bow deck, closed-cell flotation, resilient motor pads astern, aluminum oar locks (two pairs), and special bulb т keel for strength and stability underway. Length: 15 feet 3 inches. Beam: 43 inches. Weight: 112 pounds. Price: $479.

Grumman 3.8 High-Performance Utility Boat—First of the new generation of Grumman boats, this model is 12 feet 4 inches in length and was designed by naval architect William Shaw, whose Pearson Yachts are respected and popular throughout the world. The new Grumman 3.8 already meets the U.S. Coast Guard level flotation requirements not due to become effective until August 1978. Two longitudinal steps running fore and aft parallel to the V-bottom provide additional lift underway. Hard chines of extruded aluminum assure good stability and buoyancy in turns, while at the same time reducing skidding. Though qualified to carry a 10-horsepower outboard, the 3.8 performs very well with a 6-horsepower. Hull material is marine aluminum. Beam: 54 inches. Transom height: 15½ inches. Capacity: 614 pounds. Weight: 147 pounds. Price: $497.

Rowing Rig—This accessory will add speed and power to long trips, convenience to solo fishing, and health through exercise. Clamps easily to the gunwale. Oars not included. Price: $58.

Motor Bracket—Fits all double-end Grummans and easily clamps to gunwales without structural changes. Clamps on with outboard pad to port. Price: $22.

Pontoons—5 feet long extruded, closed cell, dense foam with tough, abrasion-resistant finish. Mounted on aluminum crossbars that clamp to gunwales in minutes to provide extra safety and stability. Price: $57.

HEATH CO.

For years Heath has been offering radio and electronics kits for the do-it-yourselfer. Their line has grown to include everything from timing lights for the weekend mechanic to color television sets and stereo components. For the boater who wants to save money, there are several Heathkit depth-sounders with prices starting at $59.95.

Heathkit Dual-Range Depth-Sounder—Shows depth, type of bottom, schools and individual fish, and submerged objects. A high-pitched "beep" alerts you to shoals or objects projecting above any preselected depth from 5 to 240 feet. Has switch-selected 0- to 60-foot and 0- to 240-foot ranges. Electronically controlled motor, fixed noise rejection circuit, polarity protection, and super-bright neon indicator. Water-resistant Cycolac case with glare-free bezel and sunshield. Available with through-hull or transom transducer and 15 feet of cable. Price: $89.95.

The Seeker—A straight line/white line, charting depth-recorder. A supremely sensitive and dependable fishfinding aid that shows you exactly where they are. An important navigation aid for following coastline depths when operating in any weather. Easy to install and easy to use. Extra-wide beam transducer covers a larger area of water, so you get a better and wider picture of what's below. Three ranges—5 to 200 feet, 200 to 400 feet, and 400 to 600 feet. White line control lets you adjust the bottom indication to a fine line so objects or fish close to the bottom can be distinguished easily. Available with through-hull or transom-mount transducer. Price: $289.95.

The Seeker

HOLSCLAW BROTHERS, INC.

This company has been in business for fifty-four years and offers a wide selection of trailers for towing your boat to your favorite fishing, hunting, and camping spots. All trailers feature baked enamel finish. Parts are precision-made. Rollers are easy to adjust exactly to fit your boat bottom. Tilt-tongues have positive-lock action. Every roller has bushings for noncorrosive long life. Tie-down hooks on winch stand make it simple and quick to secure bow to trailer with winch rope.

Large, extra-heavy gauge tubular steel axle keeps wheels in perfect alignment. Wheels have centerless ground axle, high-speed tapered roller bearings, improved double-lip grease seals on inside of wheel and rubber O-rings around dust cap to seal out water. Trailers are equipped with hydraulic shock absorbers with variable-pitch coil springs or slipper-type leaf springs so both heavy and light boats get a soft ride.

Model A-600 Trailer—For flat or semi-V boats up to 14 feet. Equipped with 2×3-inch galvanized tongue that adjusts forward or aft for tongue load. Other features include three-leaf springs, plug for car with quick connectors, 8-inch demountable wheels, 4.80-8 Load Range "A" high-speed tires. Track: 46 inches. Overall: 13 feet 3 inches to 14 feet 3 inches. Capacity: 600 pounds.

Model E-2000 Trailer—This trailer will handle exceptionally wide boats, keeping them low to the ground for easier loading and unloading. Features include 6-foot longitudinal roller supports, tilting tongue with adjustable keel rollers, 6:1 winch with rope and forged hook, leaf springs with drop axle, plug for car with quick connectors, heavy-duty adjustable winch stand that adjusts up or down, back-up plates on axle for 10-inch mounting brakes only, 13-inch demountable wheels, 6.50-13 ST Load

Model A-600 Trailer

Range "C" high-speed tires, chrome hub caps. Track: 81 inches. Overall: 19½ feet. Capacity: 2,000 pounds. For boats up to 18 feet.

RAY JEFFERSON

This company probably needs no introduction to most boaters and boating fishermen, since it has been in the marine electronics business for thirty-five years and has become one of the leaders in the field. The Ray Jefferson catalog is certainly worth owning, because it not only covers their extensive line of equipment and accessories, but it is loaded with solid information. From it you will learn how a depth-finder works, how to distinguish objects with a depth-finder, how to navigate with a depth-finder, and much more. So send them a buck and the catalog will

A sampling of the extensive Ray Jefferson line of Marine Electronics

be yours. Then, if you find that you want more information on any of their equipment, you can write for the detailed specifications you require.

Model 575 Structure Beeper/Flasher—This is a highly sensitive, precision transistorized flashing neon light indicator designed specifically for the structure fisherman. The unit features an extra-large expanded dial that shows the exact depth of underwater structure and drop-offs. It searches out, finds, and shows the places where fish are likely to be found. It reads to 70 feet and will read as deep as 140 feet under favorable conditions. An audible "beeper" is built into the unit, which sounds off to indicate fish or objects under the boat at preset depths from 5 to 60 feet. It operates off any 12V source and comes complete with indicator unit, gimbal mounting bracket with swivel base and three-wing thumb screw, transducer, and 20 feet of cable with mounting bracket, 20 feet of power cord, and clear vinyl "foul-weather" cover. Price: $179.95.

Model 90 Fishing Thermometer—A precision electronic unit encased in a rugged weather-resistant plastic case made of virtually indestructible Cycolac. The unit gives instantaneous water temperature and depth readings. It is compact, portable, battery operated, and extremely lightweight. Comes complete with electronic thermometer probe and 100 feet of probe wire. Price: $39.95.

Model 400 Depthmeter—This rugged, practical, easy-to-read depthfinder is a completely transistorized, two-range, direct reading-type unit, powered by a self-contained mercury battery. Giving pinpoint accuracy from 0 to 12 feet and from 0 to 120 feet, this unit comes complete with transducer, less batteries. Price: $119.95.

Model 115 "Battery Guard" Battery Charger—Completely automatic, this unit is an AC-DC converter that monitors up to three 12V batteries with its built-in, self-contained battery equalizer. When connected to a 110V AC source, it maintains voltage constantly. It cuts on automatically when battery energy level drops and shuts off completely when full power is restored. No "trickle charge." So it never overcharges. Price: $159.95.

JOHNSON OUTBOARDS

Another of the giants among outboard motor manufacturers, Johnson is known everywhere for their rugged and dependable motors. The Johnson line includes thirty-nine models, from 2 to 200 horsepower, and two new electric trolling motors for 12V and 24V systems. If you're interested in learning more about Johnson outboards, especially the smaller ones, we suggest you drop by your nearest dealer and pick up the Johnson catalog. Here, we're going to give you a sampling of their larger engines.

Johnson V-4 Motors—Name your boating pleasure and chances are there's a Johnson V-4 that will measure up to your needs—from high-speed running to just trolling along, and everything in between.

There's a new premium V-4, the Sea-Horse 140. It gets extra power from double-drilled exhaust ports and an all-new midsection, à la the V-6s. And it has a new air silencer to keep everything Johnson quiet. It is available in standard length with manual trim or power Trim'N'Tilt and in the new extra-long transom size with T'N'T. Both T'N'T models are equipped with stainless steel "SST" props, and heavy-duty 12-amp alternators.

Johnson's popular Sea-Horse 115 comes in three models: standard and extra-long versions with factory-installed T'N'T, and a standard shaft model with manual trim. And Johnson has three 85-horsepower V-4s: the Sea-Horse 85 with standard shaft and distinctively styled Javelins with the added feature of T'N'T, in standard and extra-long versions.

Features include low-profile design, MagFlash CD ignition, tuned exhaust, pressure-back piston rings, water-shield silencing, fuel-saver throttle linkage, command center single-lever control, through-tilt-pin

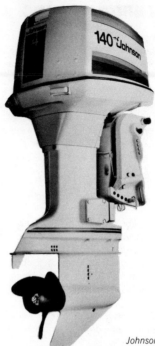

Johnson Sea-Horse 140 V-4

steering, through-hub exhaust, temperature-controlled cooling, and Lyfanite saltwater protection. Prices: from $2,220 to $2,570 (85 horsepower), $2,370 to $2,720 (115 horsepower), $2,545 to $2,995 (140 horsepower).

Johnson V-6 Motors—If big power is the name of your boating game, these exciting V-6 packages can put you in the major league of outboard performance. And that means total performance—speed, load pushing "quick-out-of-the-hole" thrust—plus fuel efficiency. Racing versions of the Johnson V-6 have won races throughout the world.

There is a choice of two Johnson V-6s: the Sea-Horse 200, and the new Sea-Horse 175, offering more boaters the chance to move up to Johnson's brand of V-6 quality. Both are available with standard 20-inch shafts, or in extra-long 25-inch versions. Power Trim'N'Tilt is standard.

The Johnson V-6 has opened up the convenience of outboard power to a fast-growing number of larger hulls. With 149.4 cubic inches, the 200 develops full power at only 5,250 rpm, the 175 at a leisurely 5,000 rpm. Their efficient power/weight ratios add more to their performance story. And all this power sits neatly on the transom, adding more usable space and new degrees of tilting, steering, and maintenance convenience to high-power boating.

Features include full 90° V-6 design, dual MagFlash CD ignition, dual tuned exhaust, three carburetors with double-drilled ports, pressure-back piston rings, water-shield silencing, fuel-saver throttle linkage, command center single-lever control, through-tilt-pin steering, through-hub exhaust, power remote T'N'T, pressure-temperature controlled cooling, and Lyfanite saltwater protection. Prices: $3,190 (175 horsepower, 20-inch shaft), $3,240 (175 horsepower, 25-inch shaft), $3,340 (200 horsepower, 20-inch shaft), $3,390 (200 horsepower, 25-inch shaft).

HANS KLEPPER CORP.

Klepper, of Rosenheim, West Germany, is the oldest maker of folding boats in the world. The company was founded in 1907 by Mr. Johann Klepper, and with the exception of Eskimos, these folks are the oldest manufacturers of kayaks, too.

In the United States, Hans Klepper Corporation is the importer, distributor, and supplier to Klepper dealers throughout the country. This company is also the New York area retailer and the mail-order supplier.

Assembling an "Aerius-20"

The folks at Klepper are experts on kayaks and kayaking and can lead you to a nearby dealer or provide you with mail-order information. Be sure to write for their brochure.

If you've never considered kayaking, keep in mind something that Klepper's manager told us: "The majority, by far, go camping, fishing, river touring, vacation paddling, bird watching, sailing or exploring. The minority, 15 percent or less, would be whitewater kayakers. Television programs have really brainwashed the innocent through programs of extreme events."

If you haven't noticed, the number of kayakers is growing tremendously, and courses in kayak handling and safety are being offered in a number of areas.

Klepper "Aerius-20"—This is the flagship of the Klepper Foldaway fleet. Seaworthy? Well, Dr. Hans Lindemann crossed the Atlantic in a Klepper Aerius II in 1956. These kayaks are amazingly compact, folding into three packbags. Assembly is quick and easy—from fifteen to thirty minutes. Patented snap-lock fittings throughout—no small parts. Hypalon rubber and cord hull with sponsons, framework, two padded contour seats, two wooden backrests, rudder bracket, and mast bracket are all included. Colors: blue and gray. Weight: 89 pounds. Price: $699.

Klepper Kamerad TS—This handcrafted, handmade fiberglass kayak is a stable, strong two-seater with solid center plate and a new cockpit design with space for three persons. Comes with two wood seats, two wood backrests, four short flotation tubes. Length: 16 feet. Width: 31 inches. Weight: 67 pounds. Colors: red deck, white bottom, or yellow/white. Price: $499.

Klepper Tramp S—This single model kayak is tailor-made for the sportsman who enjoys many different trips. Very stable, fast, and turns well. Comfortable in cockpit. Strong, durable fiberglass design. Stores

gear nicely. Ready for white water, and often preferred for high-volume rivers because of good buoyancy. Length: 14 feet. Width: 25 inches. Weight: approximately 40 pounds. Colors: red/white, yellow/white. Price: $380.

Spray Cover for Aerius-20—For rough water and cold weather. Closes cockpit. Fits to coaming with clips. Price: $69.

Klepper #E24 Whitewater Paddle—A top-quality paddle that can be disassembled for easy storage. Price: $55.

Two Klepper Singles on mountain river

LOWRANCE ELECTRONICS MANUFAC-TURING CORP.

Another company offering a line of top-quality electronic fishing aids, Lowrance has been one of the leaders in research and manufacturing in this field. If you write for their catalog, be sure to request a copy of their "New Guide to the Fun of Electronic Fishing." And for a buck they'll send you the Lowrance Fishing Calculator and Key to Sonar Signal Interpretation. Their Expert Anglers Collection includes booklets on black bass by Homer Circle, panfish by George Laycock, saltwater fish by Milt Rosko, salmon and trout by Erwin Bauer, and walleye and sauger by Parker Bauer. These can be purchased separately for $1 each or $4.95 for the set.

LFG-175 Bluewater Pro Depth-Sounder—This new, low-priced sonar features a narrow signal bulb for superb resolution on the dial. Range is 0 to 100 feet. Rugged ABS plastic case. Built-in suppressor system eliminates false signals due to electrical interference. Sonar unit supplied less transducer. Dimensions: 8 inches high by 5 inches deep by 10½ inches wide. Weight: 2½ pounds. Price: $114.95.

LFG-225 Bluewater Pro Depth-Sounder—This new, low-priced sonar is designed for rugged performance in fresh or salt water. Dual depth-range accuracy and fish-finding effectiveness. Ranges are 0 to 60 feet and 0 to 180 feet. Patented variable pulse length suppression system eliminates electrical or cavitational source with no loss of sensitivity. Will operate at speeds in excess of 65 miles per hour. Narrow signal bulb adds greater resolution to signals for easy reading and interpretation. Supplied without transducer. Dimensions and weight same as LFG-175. Price: $164.95.

LFG-175 Depth-Sounder

LUND AMERICAN, INC.

These boatbuilders offer fiberglass boats ranging in size from 13 feet 9 inches to 21 feet 2½ inches, aluminum boats from 12 feet 1 inch to 20 feet and canoes from 15 to 17 feet. Lund manufactures some of the toughest fishing boats around and offers some innovative designs in such boats as their Pike Boat Deluxe and their new rendition of an old design—The Snipe.

Lund 315 Guide Special—Here's an easy-to-own fiberglass fishing boat with swivel pedestal seats and rod racks. Will handle outboards up to 25 horsepower and can carry 765 pounds. Centerline: 14 feet 10 inches. Beam: 64 inches. Bow depth: 26½ inches. Stern depth: 22½ inches. Transom height: 15 and 20 inches. Weight: 415 pounds. Colors: turquoise or marsh brown/white seats. Price: $935. Add $10 for 20-inch transom.

V-19 and V-21 Offshores—For people who see beauty in function, Lund's new Offshore Fisherman models have to be among the most beautiful boats on the water. It's easy to see that the new V-19 and V-21 Offshores were carefully designed by people who understand fishing. Cockpits are self-bailing, and they have a one-piece fiberglass liner with nonskid floor. Surrounding the center control console is plenty of walk-around roominess. There's a 55-gallon fuel tank, a deep-V hull for big-

The Snipe

water comfort, a transom designed to handle two high-horsepower outboards, lots of storage, and many smaller details like the reversible driver's backrest, a below-floor channel for control cables, and inboard mounting of all cleats and chocks. Options include a full canvas top. The V-19 will handle outboards up to 175 horsepower and the V-21 is rated for 220 horsepower. Sterndrive models also available. Prices: $4,585 (V-19), $5,069 (V-21).

Pike Boat Deluxe—This is a fisherman's boat with a flat floor, easy walk-around layout, convenient motor-control console, built-in rod lockers along both sides and a third locker in the bow. There's an aerated live well for your bait or your catch, a convenient light for night fishing, and comfortable padded swivel chairs. It's an 18-foot fishing platform with the comfort and dry-boat seaworthiness of a rugged Lund aluminum hull. Beam: 70 inches. Bow depth: 34 inches. Stern depth: 20 inches. Transom height: 20 inches. Maximum horsepower: 75. Capacity: 1,695 pounds. Weight: 643 pounds. Color: buff (exterior), buff/saddle tan (interior). Price: $2,199.

The Snipe—Fifty years ago, people who needed a multiuse boat came up with this design. It had plenty of stability for fishing and hunting comfort. It was nimble and easy to handle, with a sleek hull shape that rowed and motored easily. Its extra bow depth added capability in rough water. Yet, this great little boat had one disadvantage—wood construction. That meant too much weight and too much maintenance. Today, Lund is adding the advantages of famous Rhino-Tuff aluminum construction to this proven design. The result is the Snipe—a boat you can pole through the cattails or power with a 10-horsepower outboard. It's a rugged boat you can knock around with almost no regard for maintenance—a Lund boat that will last you a lifetime. Length: 14 feet. Beam: 46 inches. Bow depth: 28 inches. Stern depth: 15 inches. Capacity: 525 pounds. Weight: 147 pounds. Price: $549.

MARINER OUTBOARDS

This division of the Brunswick Corporation is offering a new line of outboards that is built for rugged dependability and destined to find a long line of followers among outdoors people everywhere.

There are twenty-one different Mariner models available, from 2 to 85 horsepower.

Mariner 2—Only 20 pounds, yet built with the same care and attention as the big Mariners. Lean, light, tough, reliable. Tuck it in the trunk of your car. Clamp it on an inflatable raft, canoe, or small runabout. Use it as an auxiliary trolling motor. Water-cooled, compact loop-charged powerhead; single carburetor with fixed high-speed jet for balanced fuel/air mix; dependable magneto ignition, super-protected against saltwater corrosion. Full 360° steering. Low profile. Features include water-resistant flywheel low-tension ignition, heat-treated aluminum alloy piston, stainless steel drive and propeller shafts, manual choke, adjustable co-pilot, and integral 1-liter gas tank. Price: $250.

Mariner 8—Like all Mariner outboards, the 8 horsepower is much more than just transportation for work or fun. It's what you can't see that makes the big difference—like saltwater corrosion protection from stainless steel in driveshaft, prop shaft, clamp screws, fasteners, and all corrosion-critical areas. Low-profile design. Features include two-cylinder, high-torque, loop-charged powerhead; water-resistant flywheel low-tension magneto ignition; single carburetor with fixed high-speed jet; manual choke; four tilt positions; separate 24-liter (6.34-gallon) tank; twist-grip throttle; shift lever with forward, neutral, and reverse. Weight: 58 pounds. Price: $570. Long shaft model: $580.

Mariner 15—Engineered for pleasure cruising and fishing, the 15 horsepower is compact but powerful and operates smoothly at any speed, from idle to full bore. Drainless crankcase recirculation system reuses unvaporized fuel. Reed valve intake improves engine efficiency for better fuel economy. The rugged four-port, loop-charged powerhead is designed for day-after-day use—even abuse. Thermostatically controlled water cooling system keeps engine temperatures even. Low-tension ignition for fast, sure starts over and over again. Positive, responsive steering with tiller handle co-pilot. Superb maneuverability—even in tightest spots with forward, neutral, and reverse gearshift. Two-cylinder engine with manual choke and manual start. Completely adaptable to optional remote controls. Weight: 82 pounds. Price: $780. Long shaft model: $790.

Mariner 15

Mariner 28—Mariner engineers call it the most practical outboard they've ever produced. Versatile midrange performance, surprisingly powerful for its size, perfect for rugged everyday use. This engine is quick and easy to maintain because of its basic uncluttered design. Popular Mariner features for low-maintenance cost and long life include built-in saltwater corrosion fighters like stainless steel for the drive and prop shafts, clamp screws, and fasteners in corrosion-critical areas. Available in manual or electric start models. Completely adaptable to remote controls. Long shaft models available. Weight: 99 pounds. Prices: from $965 to $1,070.

MICHI-CRAFT CORP.

"Canoes are our specialty," say the people at Michi-Craft. They offer a line of quality aluminum canoes—twenty-six models in all—at economical prices. And to the original owner of any Michi-Craft canoe they offer a lifetime warranty against hull puncture in normal use on the water. Additionally, they offer a five-year warranty against any defects found in materials or workmanship in their heat-treated models, and a one-year warranty on their standard models.

Michi-Craft L-12 Square Stern—Take it fishing, hunting, or into small corners of your water world. This sturdy sportster takes an outboard up to 3 horsepower, plus lots of cargo, thanks to its 44-inch beam. This heat-treated canoe features an exterior keel, three ribs, and a hull thick-

Safety Pontoons

ness of .032 inch. Length: 11 feet 9 inches. Depth amidship: 12 inches. Weight: 54 pounds. Capacity: 700 pounds. Price: $334.

Michi-Craft L-17 Lightweight Double—Here's a double-ender in the length that many wilderness canoeists prefer that is just right for those trips where portages are necessary. This heat-treated aluminum canoe features six ribs, exterior keel, and .032-inch hull thickness. Length: 17 feet. Beam: 36 inches. Depth amidship: 13 inches. Weight: 62 pounds. Capacity: 790 pounds. Maximum horsepower: 5. Price: $346.

Safety Pontoons—These pontoons can be left attached while the canoe is portaged or cartopped. Paddling is easier, because the pontoons ride above the water. They're made to fit most all canoes and they provide greater floatability and more peace of mind. It's almost impossible to tip a canoe equipped with them—even when weight is unevenly distributed. Prices: $66 (for maximum 38-inch beam), $75 (for maximum 48-inch beam).

MIRRO MARINE DIVISION

From Mirro comes the popular Mirro-Craft line of aluminum boats that includes something for everybody—from their 12-foot Economy Topper to their 21-foot 2-inch Express Cruiser. For those who prefer fiberglass, they manufacture Rally fiberglass runabouts in lengths from 15 to 19 feet and Cruisers fiberglass boats for fishing, camping, and, of course, cruising.

Mirro-Craft also has a brochure of fishing tips by Homer Circle called "How To Catch More Fish from Your Mirro-Craft," and it is available free on request. It includes tips on catching the twelve most popular game fish.

Mirro-Craft 14-Foot Resort Boat—This model is popular with both rental operators and fishermen who like an aluminum boat that is rugged yet easy enough to handle for cartopping. Standard features include four vinyl-coated aluminum unitized seats, level foam flotation, skidproof flecked-paint interior, oar sockets, transom handles, bow eye, drain plug, and reinforced transom with two knee supports. Beam: 57 inches. Bow depth: 25 inches. Maximum horsepower: 25. Capacity: 845 pounds. Weight: 182 pounds. Color: yellow hull/black and red stripes. Price: $529.

"Mister Musky" Fishing Boats—The newest models from Mirro-Craft, these boats are available in 14- and 16-foot lengths and should appeal

Cruisers Bonanza Utility Day Cruiser

to both musky hunters and bass anglers. Standard fishing equipment on both models includes two swivel fishing seats, an upholstered helm seat, a 35-quart removable wet well, a 7-foot 4-inch hinged rod stowage locker, anchor and line locker, hinged gear locker, three storage pockets, and full-length tackle shelves. Other boat features are a midships console with mechanical steering, deck cleats, bow eye, ski tow rings, transom motor well, and vinyl-coated nonskid flooring. Both models are equipped with Mirro-Craft's exclusive level foam flotation. The 14-foot model has a 63-inch beam, 30-inch bow depth, weighs about 400 pounds, can carry 1,000 pounds, and takes long shaft outboards up to 45 horsepower. The 16-foot model has a 72-inch beam, 34-inch bow depth, weighs about 530 pounds, can carry 1,350 pounds, and will take long shaft outboards up to 80 horsepower. Optional on both models is a navigational light set that includes a cockpit courtesy light. Prices: $1,049 (14-footer), $1,349 (16-footer).

Cruisers Model 192 Sportsman—Here's a practical yet well-equipped, trailerable fishing machine. A V-hull center-console design, the Sportsman is rated for up to 180 horsepower in either single or twin outboard installation. Console features lockable radio and tackle stowage compartments, a tinted Plexiglas wind screen, and two swivel/sliding helm fishing seats. Other features include a 25-gallon foamed-in aluminum fuel tank with electric gauge, removable aft bait well, four rod holders, built-in storage for six rods, aft stowage compartments, complete hardware, stainless steel bow rail, bow anchor and rope locker, rack and pinion steering, treated teak trim, and electric single-trumpet horn, as well as factory-wired, switched, and fused navigational lights. The Sportsman has level foam flotation and is self-bailing. Centerline: 18 feet 11 inches. Beam: 90 inches. Weight: 1,600 pounds.

The Rushton is a great duck boat

OLD TOWN CANOE CO.

If there is a canoe in your future, this is certainly a company you will want to become familiar with. Old Town manufactures a vast line of canoes in Oltonar multilaminate, fiberglass, and wood. They also build kayaks and several specialty boats.

Their catalog also lists books on canoeing, gives addresses of magazines of interest to canoeists, and contains information on eight free publications that they will send on request.

Old Town Chipewyan Canoes—Old Town forms the hulls of these multipurpose craft from single sheets of their exclusive Oltonar multilaminate. This amazing material comprises three basic layers: an outer skin of tough, colorfast, weatherproof, cross-linked vinyl; specially layered inner laminates of ABS to impart strength and stiffness to the hull (extra layers are added in key points that will undergo the most stress and suffer the most abuse); and a core of expanded, closed-cellular foam to provide integral flotation and insulation against noise, cold, and heat.

The Chipewyan is a superb performer both in flat and in moving water, and it should be considered by those who anticipate rough going. It is particularly able to withstand collisions with rocks and ledges and will slide over underwater obstructions without grabbing. Any dents suffered in the hull either will "self-heal" if the canoe is left out in the sun, or they may be removed easily by gentle heating.

There's a wide choice of models, from the Chipewyan-12 lightweight pack canoe to the deep-hull Chipewyan-18. The Chipewyan-17 handles best with heavy loads and has the highest capacity of all Oltonar canoes. It's a great expedition craft.

These canoes need no special maintenance, can be stored outside in all climates, and can give years of dependable service. There are six models in all, ranging in length from 12 to 18 feet and weighing from 40 to 79 pounds. Prices: from $425 to $545.

The Rushton—Here is a fine, featherlight craft for those who enjoy fishing or exploring remote mountain ponds or other bodies of water normally inaccessible to the sportsman. Large enough to hold one paddler and his gear, Rushton also is a great canoe for youngsters. Both hull and deck unit are of reinforced fiberglass construction. Flotation comprises polyurethane foam expanded under the inwales and thwart of the deck unit, and ethafoam installed under decks and used as seat. Sportsmen prefer a 52-inch whitewater paddle with this craft. Length: 10½ feet. Width: 27 inches. Bow height: 15½ inches. Depth: 10 inches. Weight: 19 pounds. Price: $330.

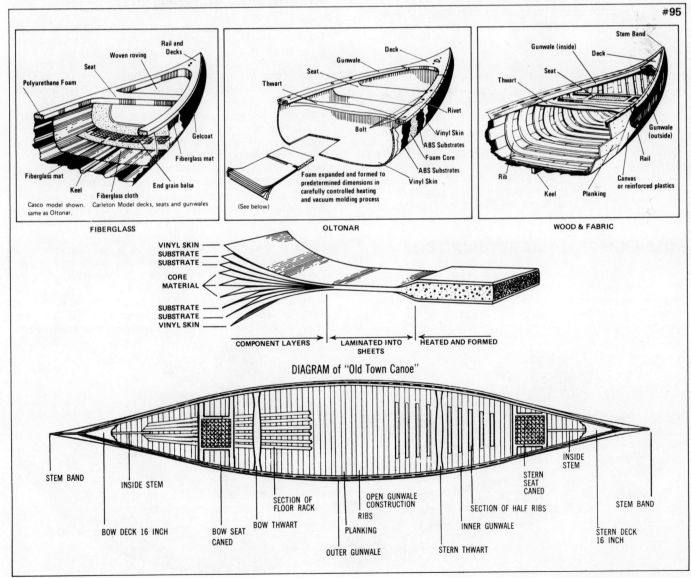

Construction of Old Town Canoes

PENGUIN INDUSTRIES, INC.

Penguin offers a variety of marine products as well as the popular Hoppe's line of gun care products and accessories for hunters and shooters.

Check Chapter 4 for other Penguin products.

Rod Rigger—Keeps your fishing rods handy, yet out of the way. Holds four rods. Mounts anywhere. Price: $3.95.

Boat Hook Holders—Keep your boat hook at the ready but safely out of the way. Spring steel clips with plastic coating. Convenient storage for fishing rods when not in use, too. Price: $3.95.

Paddle Holders—Mount easily to side of boat to give maximum uncluttered deck space. Spring steel clips with plastic coating. Price: $4.95.

Rubber Mooring Snubber—Extra-strong rubber absorbs shock and prevents jarring. Keeps boats properly positioned, regardless of weather conditions. Price: $3.95.

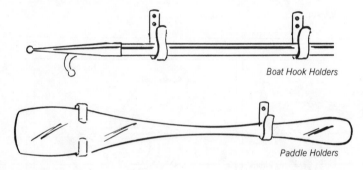

Boat Hook Holders

Paddle Holders

Military Signal Flare Kit—Projects a 15,000 peak candlepower red star to altitudes of approximately 500 feet. Will withstand all environments. Package measures 3½×6×⅝ inches, in resea able flexible polyethylene bag. Kit folds flat to the size of a cigarette pack. Contains lanyard for attaching launcher and bandolier of cartridges to clothing or life raft. Price: $15.45.

POLAR KRAFT MANUFACTURING CO.

This company has been building aluminum heavy-duty work boats and commercial fishing boats for years. T ey incorporate this know-how into the design and manufacture of some rugged aluminum fishing and hunting boats. Their line includes semi-V hulls, johnboats, and bass boats.

Bass Fisherman 40—This is a fine boat for the price-conscious bass angler. The boat features running lights, carpet, livewell, two fiberglass swivel seats, one swivel seat box, gas tank box, a pair of rod holders, Teleflex stick steering, and universal kit. Length: 14 feet. Beam: 56 feet. Weight: 250 pounds. Capacity: 710 pounds. Rec. horsepower: 10 to 40. Price: $990.

Bass Fisherman 44—A bit more boat than the Model 40, this boat offers the fisherman such features as running lights, carpet, three fiberglass swivel seats, one swivel seat box, gas tank box, one adjustable pedestal, Teleflex stick steering, and universal kit. Length: 15 feet. Beam: 61 inches. Weight: 310 pounds. Capacity: 945 pounds. Rec. horsepower: 20 to 50. Price: $1,042.

Bass Fisherman 51—This is the top of the Bass Fleet from Polar Kraft, and it features running lights, carpet, livewell, one pair of ice runners, steering console, two upholstered swivel seats with arms, one fold-down upholstered swivel seat, one swivel seat box, gas tank box, one adjustable pedestal, a pair of rod holders, Teleflex mechanical steering, and universal kit. Length: 16 feet. Beam: 68 inches. Weight: 440 pounds. Capacity: 1,215 pounds. Rec. horsepower: 20 to 85. Price: $1,668.

RIVERS AND GILMAN

This is Maine's oldest manufacturer of fiberglass and Royalex canoes. Their's is the Indian Brand, and they offer seven different models, ranging from 11 to 18 feet, both square stern and double-enders.

16-Foot Penobscot Square Stern—This fiberglass canoe is truly a versatile craft—handles like a canoe yet motors very well. This is Rivers and Gilman's answer to the modern version of the famous Grand Laker, an old-time fishing craft used on Maine's larger lakes by guides and camp owners for years due to its large load capacity and stability. A full-length chine serves as a splash rail at the bow and stabilizes the canoe at the stern while motoring, and is especially helpful on turns. The transom width of 15 inches, plus an oversized stern seat, makes this canoe very comfortable to operate under all circumstances. Its exceptional stability and maneuverability make it an excellent river or lake canoe. Beam: 38¼ inches. Capacity: 850 pounds. Maximum horsepower: 5. Weight: 108 pounds. Price: $349.

17-Foot Princess—This fiberglass canoe is of classic design—round bottom, and narrow, high ends. The Princess will be especially appreciated by the more experienced canoeist, yet it is not necessarily limited to him or her. Extremely fast, it's a beauty for cruising or pleasure paddling. Basically, not designed for extended camping where large amounts of gear are to be carried, this canoe has been used for afternoon outings and weekend trips where ease of paddling is very helpful.

Bass Fisherman 51

Beam: 35¾ inches. Depth: 12½ inches. Capacity: 650 pounds. Weight: 84 pounds. Price: $309.

18-Foot Chief—Here's a fiberglass canoe that has exceptional stability and maneuverability since it is standard without keel and has a large load capacity with a minimum of draft. You will find it an excellent river or lake canoe. You will also find its ease of getting around sharp corners and ability to side-slip unsurpassed for stream canoeing. The Chief is an excellent choice for running rough white water because of its long length, flat bottom, and wide beam. This is the work horse that will handle the extended trips and still provide comfort. Beam: 38¼ inches. Depth: 12 inches. Capacity: 850 pounds. Maximum horsepower: 5. Weight: 90 pounds. Price: $319.

SHAKESPEARE

A company celebrating its eightieth birthday in 1977, Shakespeare has long been recognized for its quality fishing tackle. They also offer a line of fish-finders and electric trolling motors. Be sure to check out Chapter 2 for their fishing tackle.

DF-3 Scanmaster Depth/Fish-Finder—Efficient, easy-to-own unit with many features. Lightweight and attractive. Locates depths and structure to 100 feet. Single on/off gain control. Tilt head for easy viewing. Operates on single 12V battery or two 6V batteries (not included). Has 15-foot transducer cable and suction cup mount. Exclusive curved bracket ensures direct aim to structure. Rubber feet prevent sliding or marring finishes. Two holes in base of battery holder for permanent mounting.

DF-2 Scanmaster Depth/Fish-Finder—Popular on big water where the DF-2's 200-foot range is necessary. Sturdy ABS plastic housing protects solid-state electronic components. Pedestal base for turning DF-2 for easy viewing also permits easy removal for overnight storage. Metal bracket can be permanently mounted to console. Transducer with 24-foot cable can be mounted permanently on stern or through the hull. Separate on/off gain and filter controls for fine tuning. Operates from boat's 12V electrical system.

Wondertroll 52 Motor—This is the lightest of the Shakespeare trolling motors, made to operate dependably and efficiently for years. Forward and reverse control for getting into and out of small, fishy-looking coves and other small places. It has two preselected fishing speeds, and adjustable aluminum bracket has co-pilot feature to keep you on course—you can use both hands to fish. Chrome-plated 33-inch motor shaft resists corrosion. Permanent magnet motor produces up to 8 pounds of thrust. High and low speeds. Recommended for use with 12V battery.

Wondertroll 888 Bow Mount Motor—Remote-controlled bow mount motor with lots of features for a small investment. Has same quality, dependability, and ease of operation as other Wondertroll fishing motors.

Chrome-plated tube adjusts from 28 to 36 inches. Stationary head has night light and lighted motor direction indicator. Efficient, cool running 12V motor with permanent magnets. Smooth, easy steering with ball bearing and sleeve bearing located in steering assembly. Full-folding bow mount has hold-down latch to secure motor in stowed or running position. Single pull of lanyard releases latch so motor can be used or placed in stowed position. Foot pedal provides remote-control steering. Three-position speed control and on/off switches placed on foot pedal for convenience. O-rings protect seals from moisture damage. Battery cable runs from front or rear of pedal. Has 54-inch control cable. Low, medium, and high speeds produce 3.5, 5.5, and 12 pounds of thrust. Comes completely assembled, ready to be installed.

612 "Hot 12" Motor—Improved model of the Wondertroll 612 features convenient pushbutton on/off switch in the handle. Three speeds have been carefully tested and have been determined the best for all-around fishing conditions. Circuit breaker prevents motor damage from a fouled prop. Easy-to-reach reset button on motor head restores power. O-ring seals protect switches and motor from water and moisture damage. Built-in night light for changing baits without struggling with another light. Replaceable zinc sacrificial anode in the skeg protects motor from corrosion. Heavy, chrome-plated 36-inch motor tube. Sturdy die-cast aluminum bracket features six running positions. Replaceable props are reinforced with fiberglass. Low, medium, and high speeds produce 6, 11, and 17 pounds of thrust.

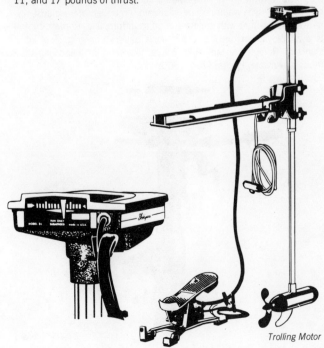

Trolling Motor

SUZUKI INTERNATIONAL (U.S.A.), INC.

The respected Suzuki name is now on a line of outboard motors that includes nineteen models ranging in horsepower from 2 to 50. All are built to take rugged saltwater use with corrosion-resistant stainless steel and die-cast alloys and special protective finishes. Currently, these motors are marketed only in the twelve Western states.

Suzuki DT 4.5 Outboard—This is the little motor with big motor features. All the performance of Suzuki's larger outboards is engineered into the DT 4.5's water-cooled, 69.8cc, single-cylinder, two-stroke motor: reed valve induction, Mikuni carburetion, sealed flywheel magneto ignition, and underwater exhaust. A trouble-free centrifugal pump provides efficient cooling. Standard equipment includes full forward-neutral-reverse gearshift, easy-pull recoil starting, and easy access choke control. The integral 2.5 liter (0.7 U.S. gallon) fuel tank has a convenient external fuel shutoff valve and fuel filter. Twist-grip throttle has a tension adjustment to let you set speed, plus a kill button mounted in the grip end. The DT 4.5 is also equipped with Suzuki's "Auto Slant" feature, which allows the motor to tilt up automatically on contact with an underwater obstruction. A handy tool kit is included. Short-shaft and long-shaft models available. Prices: $380, $395.

Suzuki DT 9.9 Outboard—This powerful twin-cylinder, two-stroke outboard is perfect for fishing boats up to 16 feet. The 256cc engine features Mikuni carburetion, reed valve induction, fuel filter, and water cooling for freedom from overheating, even during continuous low-speed operation. The DT 9.9 is designed for easy operation with all controls within reach: throttle and kill button, easy-pull recoil starter, choke, and rubber-covered gearshift. For night running, a 12V, 80W lighting coil is standard. Battery charging is available as an optional extra. Smooth, quiet operation is assured with soundproofing on the engine shroud and special shear mount to absorb vibration. While reversing, the transom locks automatically in place. Remote fuel tank capacity is 6.1 U.S. gallons. Motor comes complete with tool kit. Available in short-shaft and long-shaft models. Prices: $695, $710.

Suzuki DT 16 Outboard—This 16-horsepower motor is lightweight and built for power with a 284cc, water-cooled, twin-cylinder, two-stroke motor. Extra performance is attained with Suzuki's special reed valve induction, high-performance Mikuni carburetor, and auto advance magneto ignition. For low-speed cooling efficiency, a special displacement-type water pump is standard. An underwater exhaust system works together with engine shroud soundproofing. Remote control is available as an optional extra, as is battery charging. Tool kit is standard. Remote fuel tank holds 6.1 gallons. Short-shaft and long-shaft models available. Prices: $785, $800.

DT 4.5 Outboard

Suzuki DT 25 Outboard—Just right for fishing, this motor is built for performance with a 447cc, twin-cylinder, two-stroke motor. Pointless electronic ignition, reed valve induction, and efficient Mikuni carburetion are standard. The DT 25 is available in two versions. The standard model features a fully enclosed easy-pull recoil starter and 12V, 80W lighting coil. The DT 25E has dependable electric starting with emergency recoil starter, neutral start interlock, larger Mikuni carburetor, and 12V, 80W battery-charging alternator. Available in short-shaft and long-shaft models. Prices: from $895 to $1,010.

TER MAR, INC.

Ter Mar is the company that produces that popular little kicker, the Mighty Mite II, which is the offspring of the famous Mighty Mite that was a favorite among small boat fishermen for over thirty-five years.

Mighty Mite II—This outboard motor features improvements over its predecessor such as a new recoil starter, enclosed gas tank, and high-impact molded shroud. It is a water-cooled lightweight that excels as an auxiliary motor for larger boats and the main power workhorse for inflatables, canoes, kayaks, and small fishing boats. Easy to tote and economical to operate. Features include float-type carburetor, adjustable three-position transom mount, large-capacity water pump for efficient cooling at trolling speeds, super-iron oilite precision gears for longer life, completely water-cooled system with underwater exhaust, and linear polyethylene molded gas tank that prevents rusting. With one-quart integral gas tank, this 1.7-horsepower motor weighs in at a mere 17½ pounds. Price: $189.95.

Mighty Mite II

TRAILEX

Since 1963, Trailex has been manufacturing aluminum boat trailers. They have a trailer to fit just about any need you might have, whether you want to tow a small johnboat, canoe, bass boat, or a big open fisherman.

K.D. Dolly—This lightweight anodized aluminum hand dolly enables you to easily maneuver your loaded trailer. It is shipped via United Parcel Service directly to your front door with freight charges prepaid. The dolly can be taken apart for storage by simply removing a pin. Or it can be left assembled to hang on the garage wall. Price: $49.80.

TX-200 Trailer—This model will handle light canoes up to 18 feet. It has a capacity of 200 pounds. Standard equipment includes 7-foot web strap, adjustable bow stop, 480 × 8-inch 2-ply demountable tires and wheels, aluminum suspension system, and all required safety and lighting equipment. Assembly is accomplished through the use of T-bolts

TX-4000A Ro-Lo-Der Trailer

that slide into slots to permit infinite adjustability. All aluminum component parts are guaranteed for three years. This model can be broken down and shipped via UPS. Price: $259.

TX-4000A Ro-Lo-Der Trailer—This trailer permits ramp loading with minimum submersion. Equipped with over fifty rollers for hull and keel support, the Ro-Lo-Der will conform to all hull contours through its unique straddle roll mount design. It is capable of carrying power boats up to 24 feet and has a capacity of 4,000 pounds. Trailer weight: 840 pounds. Price: $2,020.

WOOD MANUFACTURING CO.

In the heart of America's bass country, within 200 miles of such famous lakes as Bull Shoals, Reelfoot, Eufaula, Lake of the Ozarks, Table Rock, and others, this company turns out the popular Ranger line of bass boats.

The firm has been in business for only eight years, but for the past five years their boats have been selected as the official boats for the B.A.S.S. Masters Classic Tournament. So to call these professional bass boats would be no exaggeration.

There are fifteen models of Ranger boats available, all equipped with level flotation.

Ranger 205A—This boat is specifically designed for the big engine enthusiast to use with the outboard in the 175- and 200-horsepower range. The hull is of the high-performance type that has become so popular among fishermen. The design provides an exceptionally smooth ride, and the rough-water handling characteristics make it an extremely seaworthy boat. Two livewells, power pedestals for front and rear fishing seats, rod storage compartment, two large dry storage compartments, and key locks for compartments are the standard features you want for a comfortable and carefree day of fishing. Length: 20 feet 1¼ inches. Beam: 77 inches. Transom height: 22¼ or 24¼ inches. Weight: 1,200 pounds.

Ranger 1776 Super A—This boat features a high-performance hull to provide more speed without an increase in horsepower and a higher transom for higher placement of the outboard motor to take advantage of this hull design. First introduced during 1976 and named to com-

memorate the nation's 200th anniversary, it has become most popular among those fishermen wanting just an extra touch of performance. Some of the many standard features are two livewells, key lock compartments, rod storage, dry storage, Poly-turf main deck, deluxe running lights, rack and pinion steering, power pedestals, and competition steering wheel. Length: 17 feet. Beam: 74¾ inchesm Transom height: 22½ inches. Weight: 900 pounds. Maximum horsepower: 115.

Ranger 1750—This boat is fun for the entire family. For the fisherman it has two padded fold-down fishing seats, one forward and one aft, both mounted on power pedestals. Each fishing position has its own livewell with optional aerator system. Forward of each console is a bench-type upholstered seat for lounging. Under each of these seats is a compartment for storage. Built on the 175A high-performance hull, the Ranger 1750 "Fish-'n-Play" is a dream boat for the water sports family. Length: 17 feet. Beam: 74¾ inches. Transom height: 21 inches. Weight: 900 pounds. Maximum horsepower: 115.

Ranger 205A

CHAPTER FOUR

GUNS, SHOOTING ACCESSORIES, AND HUNTING GEAR

Some of the items described in this chapter and in Chapter 5 can be purchased by mail, but many of them cannot be, since their shipments are regulated under the Gun Control Act of 1968. Firearms, ammunition, and components so regulated must be ordered through holders of Federal Firearms Licenses.

Of course, many of the firearms in this chapter and ammunition and components in Chapter 5 will be available from local dealers, but if you find something in *The Great Outdoors Catalog* that isn't carried by your local dealer, you can still get it legally by having it delivered to your dealer. Dealers usually charge a fee of about $5 for this service. Always check with your dealer first. Then you can either have him order the product for you, or you can order the product yourself, giving explicit instructions to the company along with a copy of your dealer's Federal Firearms License.

If you are ever in doubt about the legalities of a firearms transaction, by all means contact your nearest agent of the Alcohol, Tobacco, and Firearms Division of the Internal Revenue Service. We do not recommend, however, that you send for a copy of the 1968 Federal Gun Control Act, simply because it is about as clear and concise as you might expect any document of the IRS to be. Instead, we're going to provide you with a good, readable summary of the act that was prepared by the staff of *The American Rifleman* magazine, which we are reproducing here with their permission.

Highlights of the Gun Control Act

The Federal Gun Control Act of 1968 restricts interstate, but not intrastate, sales and trades of firearms, ammunition and components as defined under the act, to transactions between Federal licensees.

The act defines as firearms, and accordingly restricts, all types of rifles, shotguns and handguns manufactured since 1898, except for air and CO_2 guns and replicas of pre-1898 firearms which are not designed or redesigned to fire rimfire or centerfire fixed ammunition, or for which ammunition is not currently manufactured or readily available in the U.S.

The interstate restriction also applies to all frames or receivers for firearms (except those for legal replicas) made since 1898, and all ammunition, including .22 cal. rimfire and component "cartridge cases, primers, bullets or propellent powder designed for use in any firearm" as "firearms" is defined by the act.

The restriction does *not* apply to barrels (without actions), stocks, sights, triggers and trigger assemblies, magazines, springs and screws and other parts, excepting frames or receivers. Ammunition restrictions do not apply to percussion caps, flints, matchlock fuse or black powder for use in pre-1898 arms or replicas thereof.

The restriction also does *not* apply to antique firearms classified as curios or relics "including any firearm with a matchlock, flintlock, percussion cap or similar type of ignition system" if manufactured in or before 1898, or replicas of such firearms, provided the replicas are not designed or redesigned to fire rimfire or centerfire fixed ammunition, or provided they use rimfire fixed ammunition no longer made in the U.S. or "readily available in ordinary channels of commercial trade."

Under the Federal Gun Control Act, individuals may mail rifles or shotguns that they own legally under Federal, State, and local laws to a licensed manufacturer, dealer, or importer for "repair or customizing." Handguns, while covered by the same provision, cannot be mailed because of U.S. Postal regulations but may be sent by common carrier. Licensees may return such firearms or a "replacement firearm of the same kind and type" to the sender.

—*The American Rifleman*
Reprinted with permission

ALBRIGHT PRODUCTS CO.

Cal Albright manufactures the "Fast-Fit" trap butt plate that will be of particular interest to those of you who enjoy doing your own custom stock work or gunsmithing, or those who plan to have a gunsmith build a custom gun. Target and varmint shooters might also want to know that Albright provides precision barrel fitting service as well. The company carries a large stock of Douglas Premium and Shilen barrels for rebarreling and Mark-X actions, too. And Cal tells us that most jobs can be handled without the usual delays.

"Fast-Fit" Trap Butt Plate—This plate is easy to install with the exclusive fitting flange. It is shaped and contoured to minimize the effect of recoil. Large door opening provides ample space to carry cleaning rod and patches, screwdriver, hunting license and game tags, compass, matches, emergency first aid or survival supplies, spare cartridges, etc. Door is actuated by two springs for smoother action and added protection against breakage in the field. Length: 5⅛ inches. Width: 1¹¹/₁₆ inches. Weight: under 3 ounces. Price: $24.95.

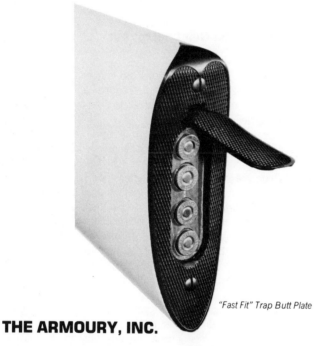

"Fast Fit" Trap Butt Plate

THE ARMOURY, INC.

If you are among the many outdoors people who are taking up muzzle-loading firearms for target shooting or hunting, you'll want to dig into the Armoury's catalog of black-powder guns and accessories. Their line includes cap-and-ball revolvers, percussion and flintlock pistols and rifles, a double-barrel percussion shotgun, and accessories. A number of their guns are available in kit form, too.

Their new powder flasks are the first American made since before the Civil War and are made of the highest-quality materials.

Model S101 12-Gauge Double-Barrel Percussion Shotgun—A beautifully designed shotgun with modified and full chokes. Its tastefully engraved side locks and English browned barrels make it a superb-quality shotgun. Wooden ramrod is brass tipped and capable of taking a brush or worm. Weight: about 6 pounds. Price: $191.25.

Model R135 Enfield Musketoon—The Enfield, one of the most outstanding military percussion rifles, due to its exceptional accuracy and known reliability was often sited as the finest infantry rifle of the nineteenth century. Seasoned walnut stock with sling swivels. Round, high-luster blue barrel. Heavy-duty percussion lock. Graduated military leaf sight. Brass furniture. Caliber: .58 Minie ball. Barrel: 24 inches. Overall: 40¼ inches. Price: $207.25.

Model S101 Shotgun

Model R135 Enfield Musketoon

Model R120 Kentucky Percussion Rifle

Model R120 Kentucky Percussion Rifle—A deluxe Pennsylvania-style rifle. Comes in .45 caliber and has large brass patch box, case-hardened percussion lock with flash shield on bolster. Walnut stock is full length, one piece. Octagonal barrel is 36 inches long. Mountings are polished brass, and there is light engraving on the lock plate. Weight: 6½ to 7 pounds. Price: $179.50.

Model KR140 Hawken Rifle Kit—Its well-figured walnut stock is perfectly inletted. Sights are installed. Patchbox and fore-end are fitted. Wood requires finish sanding. Metal parts require polishing. Barrel: rifled, 29 inches. Overall: 45¾ inches. Calibers: .45, .50, and .54. Weight: about 9 pounds. Price: $128.50.

Model KP20 Percussion Pistol Kit—The inletting on this kit is superb, with parts going into place with very little effort. All metal screws and holes are fully drilled and tapped and fit correctly into place. With this kit you can build an authentic and beautifully finished Kentucky pistol very similar to the original. Barrel is .44 caliber, deep rifled, and 10 inches long. Overall: 15 inches. Weight: 44 ounces. Price: $49.95.

Model SS36 Cap and Ball Revolver—Police model, .36 caliber, fluted cylinder, steel frame. Barrel: 5 inches. Overall: 10½ inches. Weight: 38 ounces. Price: $99.50.

Model SL36 Cap and Ball Revolver—Police model, .36 caliber fluted cylinder, steel frame. Barrel: 7½ inches. Overall: 13 inches. Weight: 41 ounces. Price: $99.50.

Model ST36 Cap and Ball Revolver—Sheriff revolver with a steel frame and engraved cylinder. Barrel: 5 inches. Overall: 10½ inches. Weight: 39 ounces. Price: $97.50.

Silhouette Decoy

ASHLEY PRODUCTS

This company offers a line of folding field goose decoys and decoy kits, if you want to save a few bucks by assembling and painting your own.

Standard Canadian or Blue Goose Field Decoys—Compact, foldable, and lightweight goose decoys. All are completely self-contained for portability. Field set up or take down only requires wing nut operation after hardware alignment. All parts remain attached to the decoy at all times. Waterproof laminated wood veneer decoys are painted with flat non-sheen paint. All metal parts are specially finished to resist rust and eliminate glare. Length: 23½ inches. Height: 9 inches. Stacking height: about 3½ inches per dozen. Weight: 7 pounds/dozen. Prices: $2.75 each, $29/dozen (one or two dozen), $27/dozen (3 dozen or more).

No 1B Decoy Kit—Complete except for paint. Same hardware as Standard Canadian. Order paint separately. Prices: $2.25 each, $19.50/dozen (one or two dozen), $17.50/dozen (three dozen or more).

No. 3B Paint Kit—Canada goose only. Four colors, ½ pint each. Sufficient for painting three-dozen silhouettes. Instructions included. Price: $8.50.

BEEMAN'S, INC.

Robert and Toshiko Beeman handle a huge line of precision airguns and accessories, yet they endeavor to provide personal service. They generally are able to ship orders on in-stock items within forty-eight hours and they use United Parcel Service whenever possible to reduce transportation time to two to five workdays for the forty-eight contiguous states.

Their 84-page catalog is also a sourcebook filled with technical reference material, specifications, and complete product descriptions on some sixty different models of airguns and thirty different types of airgun pellets.

Beeman/Webley "Hurricane"—An exciting successor to the Webley Premier, the Hurricane incorporates some of the time-tested Webley features with a longer barrel and such refinements as micro-click rear sight and a hooded front sight. The barrel is 8 inches long, but thanks to the Webley design with the barrel mounted over the compression chamber, the overall length is kept to a manageable 16³/₁₆ inches. Good grip angle and checkered thumbrest grips make the Hurricane feel and point like a fine target firearm. Available in .177 or .22. Weight: 2.4 pounds. Velocities: 539 feet per second (.177), 410 feet per second (.22). Price: $69.95.

BPA Model 6 Air Pistol—An amazingly effective antirecoil mechanism causes this gun to just sit there motionless as it discharges. A special match foresight has interchangeable inserts that combine with the four rotating rear sight notches to give twelve sighting combinations. Caliber: .177. Length: 16 inches. Weight: 3.2 pounds. Velocity: 420 feet per second. Price: $99.95.

BPA Model 6 Air Pistol

Beeman's Original Model 10 by Diana—While this is an interesting pistol to use for pest control, plinking, or firearms training, its designed purpose is ISU target competition. Every detail is concerned with accuracy and shooter comfort and control. The finish is a carefully sand-blasted nonreflective one. The grip provides maximum hand support and is adjustable three ways: bottom "shelf" raises, lowers, tilts, and has a novel extension that can be adjusted rearward to support the heel of the hand. The trigger is adjustable six ways. The pistol has a refined two-way recoilless piston similar to that used in the Beeman Model 6. Caliber: .177. Length: 16½ inches. Weight: 3.3 pounds. Velocities: 435 to 500 feet per second. Accuracy: .040 inch. Price: $299.50.

Beeman/Webley Hawk Mark III—One of England's most popular air rifles has been improved. A direct successor to the Hawk Mark II, the Mark III features a fixed barrel available in either .177 or .22 caliber, with sleeker, more modern lines. It retains the unique Webley nonmetallic piston rings that are self-lubricating for long life and consistent wear. Sights are the same positive micro-click rear that are in the more expensive Osprey. Windage and elevation knobs have clear, easy-to-read graduations. The safety is automatic—it is engaged every time the rifle is cocked, making this an ideal rifle for training beginners. Length: 41 inches. Weight: 6½ pounds. Velocities: 725 feet per second (.177), 550 feet per second (.22). Price: $66.95.

Beeman/Feinwerkbau Rifle

Beeman/Feinwerkbau 124-127 Rifles—Construction details of these rifles are most interesting and often unique. A slightly heavy barrel plus the super-precision rifling that has put the FWB match rifles at the top are at least partly responsible for the unusual accuracy these rifles exhibit. The receiver is a single, beautifully machined tube containing the mass of all the key working parts. The model 124 is .177 caliber and model 127 is .22. Length: 43½ inches. Weights: 6.7 pounds (124), 6.6 pounds (127). Velocities: 780 to 810 feet per second (124), 620 to 680 feet per second (127). Available with beech stock or deluxe walnut. Prices: from $139.98 to $173.50.

Beeman's Silver Jet Pellets—High-velocity sporting pellets available in .177, .20, and .22 caliber. Pellets per box: 500, 300, and 250. Price: $3.59/box.

Silver Jet Pellet

BLUE AND GRAY PRODUCTS, INC.

This company provides products for all shooters and special products for muzzle-loader enthusiasts. No matter whether you enjoy shooting modern arms or the smoke belchers, Blue and Gray has something you can use.

Stock Finish—Provides a hard, durable, high-gloss finish that can be rubbed down if desired to a soft appearance. Easy to apply. For the finest of finishes on all wood surfaces. Price: $1.95/2-ounce jar.

Wax Guard—This specially blended formula, containing silicone, carnauba, and beeswax, is designed to give a hard protective finish that will not readily scuff off. It produces a glossy, water-resistant coating of long-lasting beauty. Price: $1.50/2-ounce jar.

Metal Cleaner—Designed to remove oily films, light grease, dirt, etc., to prepare your metal for application of bluing or browning. Price: $1.50/2-ounce jar.

Gun Bluing—A true chemical blue. It reacts immediately on contact to create a fine professional blue-black finish. Price: $2.98/2-ounce jar.

Target Stand—Clips and cross bars are instantly adjustable to accommodate up to a 19×24-inch target. All parts solid steel. Assembles in fifteen seconds. Can be packed conveniently. Price: $3.95.

Target Stand

Patch Lubricant—Especially designed for use with all guns shooting a patched ball. It does not burn, creates no residues, reduces buildup and fouling, produces no odor, eliminates caking and hardening, rust and corrosion. Price: $2.98/8-ounce tube.

Pistol Patch—Formulated for revolvers. Will not melt or jar out at high temperatures, nor will it stiffen. It leaves no residue, reduces buildup and fouling while providing protection against rust, corrosion, and binding. Price: $2.98/8-ounce tube.

Mini-Maxi Ball Grease—Will promote extended shooting periods. The reduction of caking and hardening facilitates cleaning. It protects indefinitely against rust and corrosion. Price: $2.98/8-ounce tube.

BG-73—This lubricant provides long-lasting protection for all metal. It will not evaporate or harden over an extended period. Excellent protection against moisture, wear, rust, corrosion, and binding. Price: $2.98/8-ounce tube.

Black Powder Gun Cleaner—With pure silicone this product cleans, polishes, protects, and preserves. Polishes up to ten times longer than wax. Protects all metal, wood, and fiberglass. Lubricates up to twenty times longer than oil. Price: $3.98/14-ounce can.

Muzzle-Loader Bore Cleaner—Makes cleaning simple using only patches and cleaning rod. It dissolves black-powder residue and fouling. Price: $1.98/2-ounce jar.

Powder Horn Valve—Available in either brass or black finish. Ideal for making your own powder horn. You need only bore horn to proper size opening and cement in place. Price: $3.50.

Powder Horn Valve

Speed Shell Kit—A special molded high-impact styrene tube with a watertight snap cap designed to help the muzzle-loader gain speed and accuracy in reloading. Available in .36, .44, .45, .54, and .58 calibers. Kit contains four speed shells, patching material, and cap box. Price: $2.95.

BROWNING

To say that we're Browning fans would be something of an understatement. Just some of the Browning products we own that come readily to mind are two rifles, a shotgun, a bow, two sleeping bags, and several pairs of boots.

This is a company that makes durable, reliable, and eye-catching products for outdoors people. Be sure to see Chapters 6, 7, 8, and 9 for more of what they have to offer.

Superposed Presentation Series—Although there may be a few Grade I Browning Superposed Shotguns on dealers' racks, when this inventory is exhausted the Superposed will be offered in Presentation Grades only.

For years Browning has offered the American sportsman specially engraved Custom Superposed Shotguns on special order. Unfortunately, these guns usually took a year or more to deliver. And the purchaser did not know the final cost of the gun until it was delivered. In an effort to eliminate these uncertainties, Browning is now offering the Presentation Series. This is a choice of four basic receiver engraving styles to which you add your choice of engraved animal or bird scenes. You also can specify other options, including stock dimensions, stock finish, forearm configurations, extra barrels, initial or name engraving, and the like. The Presentation Series Superposed Shotguns offer you the opportunity to order custom specifications with much quicker delivery time, and at clearly defined prices. You should have your Presentation Grade Superposed in six months or less after the order is placed. These shotguns are available in 12, 20, 28, and 410 gauges. Prices range from $2,690 to $6,290 in the four grades. Other options and extra barrels will increase these prices.

Automatic-5 Shotguns—If years of dependable service under every known condition will prove the excellence of a product, few of any type (not just guns) have so remarkably passed the test as the Browning Automatic-5. These guns are in the hands of more than two million sportsmen the world over.

The Automatic-5 uses the force from a fired shell to eject an empty case, cock, and reload the gun automatically. Loading is equally conve-

nient for right or left hand, even with gloves. The straight sighting plane is sharp and distinct from receiver to muzzle. A cross-bolt safety is conveniently located just behind the trigger. All parts are carefully machined and hand fitted, and all exposed metal is hand polished before being blued to a durable and penetrating blue-black luster. The five models include a 3-inch Magnum 12 Gauge, Light 12 Gauge, 3-inch Magnum 20 Gauge, Light 20 Gauge, and Buck Special 12 Gauge. There is a wide selection of barrel lengths and chokes. Prices: from $374.95 to $394.95.

B-SS Side-By-Side Shotguns—There is something about uncasing a side-by-side on a crisp fall morning that thrills both man and boy. The heft and balance is a promise of the excitement to come, whether it's a fast-swinging shot at exploding quail or a measured bead on a gaudy squawking rooster. And all the qualities that make the side-by-side a favorite of many gunners have been captured in the sleek Browning B-SS.

Choose the favored 12 gauge or the trim little 20. With 26- or 28-inch barrels, either is a sweet upland game field gun. The 12 Gauge Model with 30-inch barrels is right at home in a waterfowl blind. All current models have 3-inch chambers; chromed, single mechanical trigger; automatic safety; and automatic ejectors. Stocks and full beavertail forearms are select walnut with deep, clean-cut hand checkering of twenty lines to the inch. Weights are from 6 pounds 14 ounces (20 gauge with 26-inch barrels) to 7 pounds 7 ounces (12 gauge with 30-inch barrels). Price: $359.95. A new 20-gauge Sporter Model with single selective trigger and straight grip stock is now available for $369.95.

Browning 78

Browning 78—One, clean, well-placed shot. That's the creed of the Browning 78. It's a single-shot rifle, chiseled right out of the year 1878 in Utah Territory. A clear descendant of a famous and highly accurate single shot invented by John M. Browning in 1878—the famous Model 1885 High Wall. Features include classic falling block action, exposed hammer, crisp grooved trigger, ejector system, and low profile sling swivel studs. Barrels are round or octagonal. The .45/70 Government comes only with a 24-inch octagon bull barrel. All other calibers feature 26-inch barrels. Stocks are high-grade walnut with excellent grain. No shortcuts in polishing are taken on the 78. Calibers: .22-250, 6mm Remington, .243 Winchester, .25-06 Remington, .30-06 Springfield, 7mm Remington Magnum, .45-70 Government. Price: $362.95.

Jonathan Browning Mountain Rifle—If you've got your eyes on a blackpowder rifle, consider this one. You'll find Browning quality along with some exclusive features, such as a remarkable trigger system that is two triggers in one. The secret to this trigger system is a roller bearing sear that makes the trigger let-off remarkably smooth and dependable. The single set trigger design gives you the choice of a standard trigger or a

sensitive set trigger. For the standard trigger simply cock the hammer and squeeze the trigger, and the trigger pull will let off crisply at about 4 to 5 pounds. If the shooting situation calls for a carefully planned, down-range shot, cock the hammer, push the trigger forward, and the trigger is sensitized to provide a beautiful, light let-off. You can preadjust the set trigger pull from 2 ounces to 2 pounds. Other features include a super-strong breech plus, convenient hooked breech for easy barrel removal, traditional styled adjustable sights, and traditional half stock with semicheek piece. Stock has hand-rubbed oil finish. Calibers: .45, .50, and .54. Price: $274.95.

B-SQUARE CO.

This company has a catalog that is full of interesting products for the hobby gunsmith, firearms enthusiast, and reloader. Be sure to check Chapter 5 for more B-Square products.

Dovetail Mount for 1-inch Scopes—Fits all grooved receivers and adaptors. Does not chew up dovetail or bases. Uses large socket screws for tightest clamping. Fits flat tops and high tops without filing (stays on Nylon 66s). Matching finish. No knobs. No slots. No protrusions. Weight: 1½ ounces. Packaged two rings with wrench. Price: $11.95, plus 50¢ shipping.

Side Mount for M-94 Winchester—This Side Mount will mount any 1-inch-diameter scope, including high-power variables. Early rifles made prior to 1946 will require two rear holes to be drilled and tapped (the M-94 mount can be used as drill jig). Otherwise, no drilling or tapping required. Weight: 2½ ounces. Price: $14.95, plus 50¢ shipping.

M-94 Side Mount

Cross Hair Square—This simple tool will square up your scope or front sight in seconds. Accurately sets the scope vertical reticle position. Accurately determines front sight ramp vertical. No need to remove action and barrel from gunstock. Vertical index is square with the bore. Fits into receivers of most bolt-action centerfire rifles. Price: $3.95, plus 50¢ shipping.

Bolt Jeweling Fixture—Holds Mauser, Remington 721 and 722, Springfield, M-70 Winchester, Enfield, and Japanese rifle bolts. Kit includes universal bolt-holding fixture with spotters, compound, and extension holder. Price: $21.95, plus $1 shipping.

BUSHNELL OPTICAL CORP.

Bushnell manufactures a wide range of optical instruments for active outdoorsmen. In addition to telescopic sights for rifles and pistols, they offer spotting scopes, shooting glasses, and bore sighters.

Bushnell photographic lenses can be found in Chapter 10 and Bushnell binoculars in Chapter 11.

Bushnell Riflescopes with BDC—Bushnell's new riflescopes with BDC, their patented bullet drop compensator, eliminate half the guesswork of scope aiming. When you take aim with a standard scope, you really are mentally estimating the range and then estimating the bullet drop at that range to determine how high over your target to hold your cross hairs. BDC automatically compensates for bullet drop—so it eliminates half the guesswork at any range.

Once your scope is zeroed in, simply twist the range knob to dial the estimated distance, aim dead on, and fire. Once you've practiced a few times, it takes only about a second to set the dial at the estimated distance from your aiming position. The calibrated compensation dial lets you hold dead on for better aiming and fewer mistakes at 50 yards up to 500 yards.

BDC is available on most Bushnell riflescope models, at no extra charge, and you'll be getting the same famous quality you've come to expect from Bushnell.

Bushnell Riflescope with BDC

Spacemaster Zoom Telescope—Zoom at will from wide, bright 20-power to the detailed close-up of the 45-power. Handy, lightweight, compact—perfect for rugged field use. Amazing clarity and brilliance. Achromatic color corrected, fully hard-coated optics. Maximum eye comfort for prolonged viewing. Fingertip fast focusing. Comes with protective lens cap. Standard thread tripod mount quickly attaches to camera tripod or shooter's stand. Length: 11⅝ inches. Weight: 36 ounces. Price: $135 for Spacemaster without eyepiece, $64.50 for 20X–45X Zoom eyepiece.

Spacemaster Zoom Telescope

Spacemaster Fixed Power Telescope—Same optical quality and body features as Zoom, but with fixed power eyepiece, interchangeable if you wish—in seconds. Eyepieces available: 15X, 20X, 20X wide angle, 25X, 40X, and 60X. Prices: $135 for Spacemaster without eyepieces, $29.50 for each fixed-power eyepiece.

Sentry Fixed Power Telescope—With design inspired by Spacemaster, the Sentry is ideal for all-around use. Its small size and added carrying ease make it the favorite for field use of trophy game hunters and rifle marksmen. Eyepiece available: 20X, 32X, and 48X. Length: 12⅝ inches. Weight: 25.4 ounces. Prices: $72.50 for Sentry without eyepieces, $27 for each fixed-power eyepiece.

Bushnell Custom Shooting Glasses—These glasses not only shield from powder, gases, wind, and dust, but act as a positive aid to better shooting as well. They are free of distortion and aberration. Extra-large lenses and lightweight frames designed to ride high on the bridge of the nose offer an obstruction-free view when the head is in sighting position. Nose

TruScope

pads are easily adjusted to fit the individual. Glasses have gold-plated wire frames and are enclosed in a handsome reinforced case that combines protection with good looks. Lens colors: yellow, green, and gray. Prices: $32.95 (yellow), $27.95 (green or gray).

TruScope Pocket Bore Sighter—It happens to the best. Sometimes a scope gets knocked out of alignment. A test shot would give you an idea if you were zeroed in—and spook the game for miles around. At the range, sighting-in test shots are on the paper and should require only minor adjustments for the desired point of impact. This pocket-size bore sighter gives you the flexibility to carry it in your pocket. Rugged plastic case; comes complete with weatherproof cap and adjustable arbor that fits .243 to .308. Two other arbors available. Prices: $24.95 for TruScope and adjustable arbor, $6.95 for extra arbors.

Professional Portable Bore Sighter—An invaluable aid to serious hunters and shooters for aligning and rechecking riflescopes and iron sights. This most precise unit built with quality provides unusual flexibility and fits all rifles and handguns. Made from lightweight metal and finished in a mar-resistant, glossy black. Order expandable arbors separately. Arbors available: .22 to .270, 7mm to .35, .35 to .45 caliber. Prices: $32.95 for Bore Sighter, $6.95 for each arbor.

CAPITOL PLASTICS OF OHIO

CAP-LEX gun cases are manufactured by this company. These cases are molded of rugged ABS plastic that is soil resistant and easy to clean, lightweight yet extremely durable. Each case is lined with inert, double convoluted polyurethane foam to provide proper cushioning for the contents.

Single- and multiple-gun cases are available for rifles, shotguns, and pistols. See Chapter 2 for Cap-Lex fishing rod cases.

The Bengal Two Match Rifle/Shotgun Case—Provides maximum protection and is large enough to hold two rifles with scopes, two shotguns, or any combination. Dimensions: 52 inches long by 13 inches high by 4½ inches deep. Price: $80.39.

The Bengal

Pistolero I Handgun Case—Compactness is the key word for this small, sturdy case. It will securely hold two standard-size handguns with ease. Its size also makes it handy for transporting other small, valuable items. Dimensions: 14 inches wide by 9 inches high by 3½ inches deep. Price: $30.37.

CHALLENGER MANUFACTURING CORP.

Challenger manufactures custom-fitted cases made from the highest-quality luggage-type material. These cases are dust and moisture resistant and are equipped with positive safety locks. They're reinforced throughout to provide maximum protection of contents. Challenger cases are made for rifles, pistols, shotguns, and spotting scopes.

The Competitor Four-Gun Pistol Case—A handsome luggage-type case ideal for transporting your favorite target guns to and from the range. Dimensions: 18×13×4 inches. Weight: 4½ pounds. Price: $29.55.

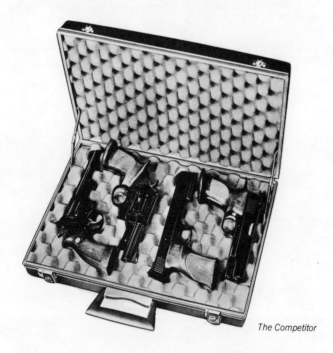

The Competitor

Spotting Scope Case—This is an ideal case for transporting your spotting scope in the field and to and from the range. It is large enough to accommodate all models. Dimensions: 22×10×5¼ inches. Weight: 4½ pounds. Price: $37.95.

The Matchmaster—This is an exciting new, super-large take-down, two-gun case, wide enough to accommodate two complete shotguns and at least one set of extra barrels for each. Dimensions: 37½ ×20×4½ inches. Weight: 10 pounds. Price: $84.75.

Carbine Case—A special, newly designed case for carrying any popular carbine being manufactured. Dimensions: 41×9×3¾ inches. Weight: 8 pounds. Price: $59.75.

Muzzle-Loader Case—Here's a case long enough to handle those Kentucky rifles. Dimensions: 60×10×4½ inches. Price: $79.95.

CLEAR VIEW MANUFACTURING CO., INC.

This company manufactures the Clear View "See Thru" mounts that allow use of rifle scope and iron sights with the scope mounted on the rifle. If you want that kind of versatility, you will want to send for their brochure that describes the various models of mounts available.

Model 101 Mount

Clear View Mount Model 101—Designed to fit 95 percent of all high-power rifle and scope combinations. Unique engineering design provides for clear "See Thru" sighting when using your iron sights. Mounting screws offer no obstruction to full-view sighting. Model 101 is strong enough to withstand recoil from magnum-size loads. Price: $13.50.

Clear View Mount Model 104—Fits all .22-caliber rimfire rifles with grooved receivers. Price: $7.95.

Clear View Mount Model 336—For Marlin Models 336, 444, 36, 62, and Glenfield 30. Price: $14.95.

COLT INDUSTRIES

Sam Colt began putting his name on fine firearms 141 years ago, and that name went on to become synonymous with precision craftsmanship. Even in today's mechanized world, every firearm manufactured by this company is hand honed, filed, and tested by a skilled assembler. Each gun is test fired and inspected by a master gunsmith before it gets the Colt name.

In addition to the legendary Colt handguns, the company also offers the superior Colt Sauer rifles. Here's a sampling of what you will find in the Colt catalog.

Single Action Army—This is the essential Colt—simple in design and ruggedly built with a minimum of moving parts. This revolver is made of the finest steel throughout, with a color case-hardened frame to protect it from wear. And like the 1873 original, it's built the Colt way, featuring three hammer positions, each one with a purpose: one for carrying, one for loading, one for firing. Other features include Colt blue finish or nickel (7½-inch barrel only), black composite rubber stocks (walnut on 7½-inch nickel only), fixed rear square-notch sight, and fixed front blade sight. Calibers: .45 Colt, .357 Magnum. Barrel lengths: 4¾, 5½, and 7½ inches. Overall: 10⅛, 10⅞, and 12⅞ inches. Prices: from $311.95 to $366.95.

Single Action Army

Python—If you're thinking seriously about a double-action magnum handgun, here's one to consider. The Python is laser-boresighted to hold center-of-impact variation to a minimum, and like all Colt revolvers, each one is proof-fired with special high-pressure ammunition. Features include ventilated rib, fast-cocking widespur hammer, full-shrouded ejector rod, Colt blue or nickel finishes, checkered walnut stocks, fully adjustable rear sight, and ramp front sight. Barrel lengths: 2½, 4, and 6 inches. Overall: 11¼ inches with 6-inch barrel. Caliber: .357 Magnum. Prices: $339.95 to $369.95.

Python

Gold Cup National Match—This is definitely the automatic for the serious targetshooter. It has everything you need to score your best: the exclusive Colt Accurizor barrel and bushing that tightens groupings by up to 100 percent over conventional automatics; Colt-Elliason adjustable rear sight; adjustable, wide, grooved trigger; undercut front sight. Features include checkered walnut stocks, Colt blue finish, and grip and thumb safeties. Barrel length: 5 inches. Overall: 8¾ inches. Weight: 38½ ounces. Caliber: .45 A.C.P. Price: $314.95.

Gold Cup National Match

Colt Sauer Standard Rifle—This bolt-action sporting rifle features a bolt with internally cammed lugs for positive lock-up, and a barrel that is locked into the receiver, not just threaded. The single stack box magazine precisely feeds each cartridge into the chamber. The trigger has an exclusive roller bearing sear that means crisp and consistent pull. The sum of these elements is fantastic accuracy. The American walnut stock has a Monte Carlo cheekpiece and rosewood fore-end tip and pistol grip cap, and it is fitted with a black recoil pad. The receiver is drilled and tapped for scope mounts. Barrel length: 24 inches. Overall: 43¾ inches. Calibers: .25-06, .270, .30-06. Price: $599.95.

Colt Sauer Drilling—This is both a versatile field gun and an heirloom. The Drilling's 12-gauge double bore, combined with a .30-06 or .243 barrel beneath, makes it an ample fowling piece and a capable big-game rifle. The stock is select European walnut, oil finished. The receiver is hand engraved with a traditional animal motif and scrollwork. Barrel length: 25 inches. Overall: 41¾ inches. Price: $1,908.95.

Colt Sauer Drilling

EARL T. CURETON

Earl makes powder horns, and from what we've been able to learn, he does a fine job. His prices are some of the lowest we've seen for quality craftsmanship. He uses an exclusive aging and coloring process, and his horns come with turned wooden plugs and stoppers. Standard-grade horns are fine quality, but without decoration. Deluxe-grade horns come with decorated spouts.

No. 2 Caphorn—This is a small, standard-grade horn with a plain, rounded wood end for carrying percussion caps. Length: 3½ to 4 inches. Price: $5.25.

No. 3 Priming Horn—Standard-grade horn for carrying powder to prime the pan. Turned wood end. Length: approximately 5 to 6 inches. Price: $7.15.

No. 5 Medium to Large Horn—Standard-grade horn, usually 10 to 14 inches. Price: $14.25.

No. 9 Small Powder Horn—Deluxe-grade horn. Length: approximately 8½ inches. Price: $16.90.

No. 11 Combination Matched Set—Deluxe-grade powder horn and priming horn. Price: $36.10.

Powder Horns

DAYTON TRAISTER CO.

Those who want to sporterize military rifles will find the Mark II Trigger Mechanisms manufactured by this company of interest. In addition to these triggers, several other items are offered that the hobby gunsmith should find useful.

Mark II Trigger Mechanism—Exclusive patented rolling sear-block design gives your converted military rifle faster lock time and increased accuracy with a uniform, crisp trigger pull that's adjustable from 2 to 6 pounds. These triggers feature all-steel construction and a permanently welded frame. All operating parts are hardened and honed. Mechanisms are fully polished and blued. The Single Stage model replaces issue trigger and requires no alteration. The Speedlock model requires bolt alteration only. Enfield mechanism fits .303 P-14 and .30-06 P-17, Remington Models 30 and 30S, and adapts to others. Springfield mechanism fits Models 03 and 03A3, Japanese Arisaka 6.5 and 7.7, Winchester Model 54, and adapts to others. Mauser fits M-98 and all identical actions as well as most Models 93 through 98. Prices for Speedlock: $15 (Enfield), $13.50 (Springfield and Mauser). Prices for Single Stage: $12.50.

Curl Cut Tool—This is a barrel inletting tool, simple in design for precision fitting of rifle barrels to stocks. Three sizes of cutters to fit into con-

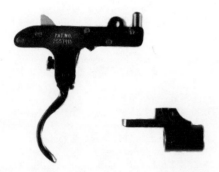

Enfield Speedlock Kit

tour of all barrel channels by holding tool at different angles. Cutters are easy to sharpen on flat stone or piece of fine emery cloth. Price: $3.75.

Tru-Feed Kit—Prevents jamming of softnose cartridges in Enfield rifles and provides smoother feeding. All stainless steel with no welding of receiver ledge or magazine ramp required. Price: $1.75.

DECKER SHOOTING PRODUCTS

As we put this book together we kept a list of products we wanted to order as soon as time (and bank account) permitted. The Decker Rifle Vise is a priority item on that list, and if you are at all serious about shooting, we think you'll want to send for the brochure that shows some of the many uses of this unique and useful tool.

Decker Rifle Vise—Fittings are machined 1½-inch selected soft wood, free of objectionable knots and defects. The base is machined of 1³⁄₁₆-inch high-density particle board. This sturdy, rugged, almost indestructible vise weighs 17 pounds. It is 32 inches long by 8 inches wide by 10 inches high. The clamp assembly is brass-plated. And it is shipped completely assembled. The vise is available in right- or left-hand models. It is neatly upholstered with Naugahyde covering sponge padding wherever it comes in contact with the gun. Use it while cleaning rifles and shotguns to prevent scratching, marring, or dropping the gun. Secure the gun while removing screws or installing sling swivels. Use the vise while inletting stocks or fitting barrels and actions. Mount sights and bore sight your rifles with the aid of this tool. You can also remove the two cap nuts that secure the rear section of the vise and use a rifle rest bag or sand bag to prop the butt stock while the forestock rests in the vise, and you have a dandy zeroing rest to use on the range. Shipping weight: 19 pounds. Price: $24.95 plus shipping.

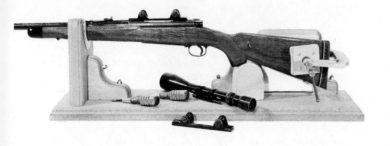

Decker Rifle Vise

EDMUND SCIENTIFIC CO.

Several items in the Edmund catalog should prove useful to shooters and hunters. For other Edmund products, check Chapters 2, 3, 5, 7, 10, and 11.

Precision-Built Ear Valves—These devices protect against the harmful high frequencies of loud noise, yet you can hear a whisper. Unlike with ear plugs, the ear canal remains open to normal air circulation, reducing possible problems of dizziness and temperature change. Special formula silicone-rubber ear insert assures maximum comfort. Last indefinitely. Universal size fits most ears. Price: $5.95 postpaid.

Polyethylene Gloves—Soft, lightweight, they protect hands from harmful or dirty substances. They resist solvents, chemicals, and detergents. Many uses for the hobby gunsmith and particularly useful for hunters when field dressing game. Sizes: medium and large. Price: $3.25/package of 100 postpaid.

Telephoto Zoom Spotting Scope—This precision optical system has thirteen fully coated elements in eight groups that resolve images to brilliant clarity. Just twirl focusing knob (focuses 300 feet to infinity) and zoom in, bringing objects up to fifty times closer. Weight: 2 pounds 1 ounce. Price: $189 postpaid.

Tripod for Above Scope—Newly designed, low-level tripod with folding legs and adjustments. Price: $56.95 postpaid.

Telephoto Zoom Spotting Scope and Tripod

EDWARDS RECOIL REDUCER

In addition to the Edwards Firearms Recoil Reducer manufactured by this company, a new Snap Cap is now available.

Edwards Recoil Reducer—The Recoil Reducer is an ingenious device that works on the principle of Newton's Laws of Motion. An object in motion can only be stopped by an object in motion from the opposite direction of equal or greater force. The reducer meets the force to shorten the length of recoil and to control barrel bounce by adjustment. The adjustment feature allows the individual shooter to adjust the device according to his physical structure or the characteristics of the gun. The reducer is a precision instrument that does not alter the stock or change the external appearance in any way, and adds only about 5½ ounces each after

Recoil Reducer

drilling. Many of the top competitive shooters use one or more of these Recoil Reducers in all of their guns. The Recoil Reducer can be installed in any gun and is 100 percent guaranteed if installed exactly according to instructions without alteration of the reducer. It has been on the market for more than eleven years and is covered by two U.S. patents. Price: $30 (single installation), $60 (double installation), plus $4 shipping and insurance.

Edwards Snap Cap—Designed to protect the firing pin and to keep moisture out of the chamber of firearms. It is made of solid material, having a cavity filled with a moisture-absorbent compound. Made to last a lifetime. Price: $3.

REINHART FAJEN, INC.

This is a gunstock company, manufacturing stocks for most all guns except muzzle-loaders. Fajen stocks are available semifinished or completely finished. According to Reinhart Fajen, they have what they believe to be the largest custom stock department in the United States.

If you're sporterizing a military arm, planning to restock your favorite rifle or shotgun, or if you're a hobby gunsmith, you ought to have the Fajen catalog on file. They will send you information on their line of stocks free of charge, but their big color catalog will cost you three bucks. We recommend the catalog, as it not only gives you a good look at the Fajen line, but is also quite a sourcebook on gunstocks.

Semifinished "Aristocrat" Stock—This stock is completely shaped and 85 percent machine inletted. Thin swept sides ahead of grip allow for more trigger-finger freedom. Special streamlined grip for positive, natural positioning of trigger hand. Cheekpiece for right- or left-handed shooter. Grades: from Utility to AAA Fancy. Prices: from $21.95 to $102.

Finished "Regent" Varmint-Style Stock—The completely finished and checkered stock features straight line pull and straight line recoil for complete control and comfort. Distinct lightweight style for scope-equipped rifles only, includes positive streamlined grip. Lightweight, wide-angle cheekpiece for full face support. Scope height comb just clears the cocking piece, with heel ½ inch higher sloping down and away from cheek. Cheekpiece for right- or left-hand shooters. Grades: from Supreme to AAA Fancy. Prices: from $177.50 to $286.50.

Semifinished "Aristocrat"

Finished "Regent"

Thumbhole Trap Stocks—This stock is available for certain pump and over/under shotguns. It has the straight line pull and straight line recoil for complete control and comfort. It has a wide-angle cheekpiece, with full cheek support for comfortable, positive alignment and minimum recoil effect. Grades: from Supreme to Extra Fancy. Prices for semifinished stocks: $46.50 to $93 (pump), $52.50 to $100 (O/U). Prices for completely finished stocks: $165 to $237 (pump), $260.50 to $336.50 (O/U).

Butt Cartridge Trap—This trap is wide enough to take up to the .532-inch base diameter belted magnum cartridges. It is ¹¹/₁₆ inch wide with a ⁹/₁₆ inch radius across cover. This width calls for a larger radius and more width at the bottom of the butt than Fajen stocks and others normally have. For this reason, a Fajen stock that will have the magazine trap installed should be special run to incorporate this extra width. Cartridge trap may also be installed in reverse, so that sling swivel stud is to the rear near the butt plate if cartridges are not too long. This is generally no problem with the Monte Carlo stocks. Prices: $35; $60 if furnished and installed in a Fajen semifinished butt, including special run charges.

FALLING BLOCK WORKS, INC.

This company currently offers three models of single-shot rifle actions. Each action is of original design by Falling Block Works, but the classical contours of the actions are apparent. The actions are well engineered, produced from the best modern materials, and manufactured by the best production methods. The resulting actions are simple, rugged, and reliable.

Each action is a true falling block action, operated by a finger under-lever. The receiver is a one-piece investment casting made of chrome moly steel. The barrel shank is threaded and the rear of the action recessed for easy and secure stock attachment. A stock bolt is provided with each action.

Stocks for Models H and J are available from Reinhart Fajen, Inc.

Model H Falling Block Action—"The Plains Pattern," suitable for all rimmed cartridges from .22 Hornet through .45-70. Overall thickness: 1⅜ inches. Sidewall thickness: ³/₁₆ inch. Approximate weight: 41 ounces. Price: $99.

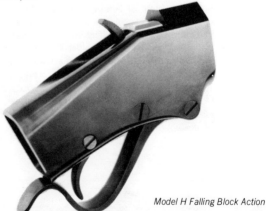

Model H Falling Block Action

Model J Falling Block Action—"The Frontier Pattern," suitable for all rimmed cartridges from .22 Hornet to .45-70. Features bushed, gas-proof firing pin. Overall thickness: 1⁵/₁₆ inches. Sidewall thickness: .160 inch. Approximate weight: 34 ounces. Price: $120.

Model K Falling Block Action—New for 1977, this action is similar to the Model J, except smaller. Features bushed, gasproof firing pin. Overall thickness: 1.040 inches. Sidewall thickness: .145 inch. Approximate weight: 27 ounces. Price: $105.

G. & H. DECOYS, INC.

G. & H. offers a broad line of fine decoys as well as other products of interest to waterfowlers. Their nesting shell goose decoys can be turned into floaters by the addition of G. & H. Detachable Goose Floats. And in the hard-to-find department, the company has blue-winged and green-winged teal decoys available.

G & H Products

Field Stake Goose Decoys—Hollow super-impact plastic bodies with removable, folding reinforcement stakes. These decoys are lightweight, stackable, and easy to carry. Patented snap-on heads provide quick easy setup in the field. Bodies are 20 inches and heads are custom painted for an authentic, natural look that will bring them in every time. Four each long, short, and feeder heads to the dozen.

Floating Goose Decoys—Full-bodied, 22-inch floating geese of high-impact polyethylene are lightweight and durable and feature a unique weighted keel that guarantees self righting. Raised feather detail is authentically hand painted with nonglare material. Patented snap-on heads (nine short neck and three long per dozen) make transporting easier and are adjustable for a more realistic spread on the water.

Field Stake Mallard Decoys—Hollow super-impact plastic bodies with removable, folding reinforcement stakes are lightweight, stackable, and easy to carry. Patented snap-on heads. Bodies 20 inches long have raised feathers and are hand detailed with nonglare paint in natural colors. Four feeder and eight regular heads to a dozen.

Standard Mallard Decoys—Custom manufactured in the United States of high-impact polyethylene for lightweight durability. The 16-inch decoys have raised feathers and are hand detailed. Unique keel design is weighted to assure self righting. Packaged six drakes and six hens.

Teal Decoys—Ideal for special early teal seasons or as additions to regular decoy spread. Rugged and lifelike, these 11-inch teal are available in green wing or blue wing, each with raised feather body and hand detailing. Packaged six drakes and six hens.

Bluebill Decoys—Lifelike and ruggedly constructed, these 15-inch scaup decoys will attract all diving ducks and others, too. Raised feath-

ers and quality hand painted. Self righting, line adjustment hook keel. Packaged six drakes and six hens.

Decoy Anchors—This new concept in decoy anchors allows the hunter to vary the weight by filling or emptying (with sand, gravel, etc.) so that they accommodate and hold in place all size decoys. Weather-resistant band secures anchor for storage.

GANDER MOUNTAIN, INC.

Among Gander's claims to fame is that this company is the world's largest supplier of rifle scopes, handling such brands as Tasco, Weaver, Leupold, and Redfield. Additionally, Gander's fall-winter catalogs carry numerous other well-known brands of gear for the hunter and shooter.

For other Gander Mountain products, see Chapters 2, 3, 5, 6, 7, 8, and 9.

Trapmaster with Trius Trap—Now you can throw clay targets from the comfort of the chair mounted on the fully portable, takedown, easy-to-set-up base. Trapmaster comes apart at the center pivot, seat folds down for easy portability in car trunk. Weight, complete with Trius Trap: 36 pounds. G.M. price: $69.97.

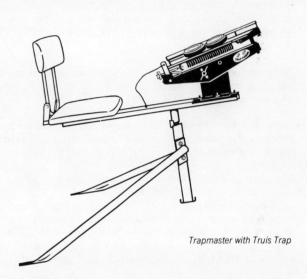

Trapmaster with Truis Trap

Outers 1001 Target Trap—A lightweight, completely portable trap that throws perfect singles and doubles. Fully adjustable for angle of flight and variety of spring tension. Calibrated to fifteen different degrees of loft, allowing variations of flight from a high, looping throw to a flat, bullet-like throw. Comes with unique hold-down frame, leaving the lone shooter/operator free to trip the trap from a distance. G.M. price: $29.97.

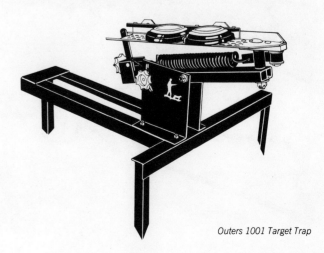

Outers 1001 Target Trap

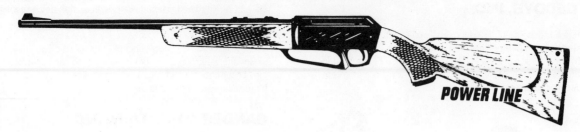

Daisy 880 Air Rifle

Gander's Decoy Painting Kit—Everything you need to paint those old battered decoys you've had for years, or great for touching up nicks and scratches. Instructions included. Decoy drawings key the colors to the parts that are to be painted. The paints are authentically matched to the duck or goose. Kit will paint twenty-four duck or twelve goose decoys. Kits available: mallard, pintail, bluebill, and Canada goose. G.M. price: $8.47.

Outers Gun-Cleaning Kits—Everything you need to keep your firearms in top, match condition—all in a compartmented case. Kits include strong aluminum alloy rods with palm rest handles, bronze bristle brush, patches, solvent, and gun oil. Rifle and pistol rods feature rotating ball-bearing swivel handles. G.M. prices: $4.27 (pistol), $4.47 (rifle and shotgun).

Outers Silicone Gun Cloth—18×18-inch cloth impregnated with 100 percent silicone removes fingerprints, prevents rust, corrosion, and salt spray damage. Washable. G.M. price: $1.07.

Outers Stock Finishing Kit—Refinish your favorite gun's stock with this kit for a durable, handsome finish. All necessary materials, plus instructions. G.M. price: $2.17.

Outers Gun Blue Kit—Touch up worn spots on metal of your gun. Includes everything you will need. G.M. price: $2.17.

Gunline "Camp Perry" Checkering Tool Set—Contains a two-edge spacer, three-edge spacer, border-vex, 90-degree V-edger, 90-degree pointer, long venier, rule with gauge, and complete instructions. Sets available for 16, 18, 20, or 22 lines per inch. G.M. price: $19.97.

Gunline Barrel Bedding Tool—An indispensable part of the gunstocker's tool chest, this tool makes barrel bedding easy. An absolutely fine, chat-

terless finish can be cut with this tool. It is primarily a finishing tool. It also is first rate as a groove cutter under heavy pressure. It is safer to use than a gouge since its hardened, cushioned multicutters shave rather than dig under the wood. Sizes available: 5/8, 11/16, and 3/4 inch. G.M. price: $4.17.

Shaper File Set—Includes three shaper files, shapes D, E, and F. This set is handy in shaping bolt handle recesses, cheekpieces, etc., on the gunstock. G.M. price: $9.97.

Daisy 880 Pump-Up Air Rifle—A new, more powerful BB rifle—longer lever makes it easier than ever to achieve maximum power with ten strokes, less for indoor target shooting. Super-strong molded Monte Carlo stock. Sights are ramp front and open rear with adjustments for elevation and windage. Crossbolt trigger safety. 100-shot BB magazine with magnetic pickup. Overall: 37¾ inches. G.M. price: $36.97.

GARCIA CORP.

The Garcia Sporting Arms line includes Sako, Rossi, Astra, and Star firearms. For other Garcia products, be sure to check Chapters 2 and 3.

Sako Deluxe Sporter—A truly beautiful sporting arm, with all the features of a standard Sako Sporter, plus a finish that's like a blue-black mirror, a European walnut stock with contrasting rosewood forearm and grip cap, rich inlays in the trigger guard and floorplate, and a fitted recoil pad. Available in eleven popular calibers, from .222 to .375 H&H Magnum. Weights: from 6½ to 8 pounds. Barrel lengths: 23, 23½, and 24 inches.

Rossi Gallery Model—The famous shooting gallery .22—its dependability made it the favorite of galleries for more than fifty years. And these Rossis are made the way the old dependables were—machined steel,

Sako Deluxe Sporter

Bronco

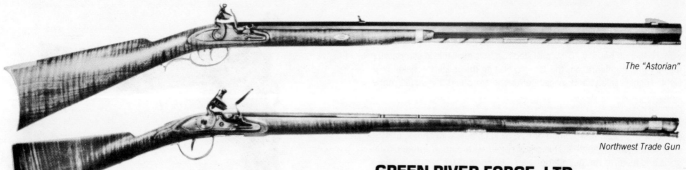

The "Astorian"

Northwest Trade Gun

precision fitted on the inside for a slick, smooth action, and beautifully finished on the outside. The Gallery Model is made in two great versions: the classic standard model with 23-inch barrel and the new Gallery Carbine with 16¼-inch barrel. The tubular magazine of either version holds twenty Short, sixteen Long, or thirteen Long Rifle .22 rimfire cartridges interchangeable, and that short, snappy pump action shucks 'em through without a hitch. Quick takedown for handy packing on a vacation or camping trip. Weights: 5½ pounds (carbine), 5¾ pounds (standard).

Rossi Overland—A re-creation of the old favorite "hammer gun," brought up to date with modern steels to make it perfectly safe for use with today's high-pressure loads. Available in both 12 and 20 gauge, each with 3-inch Magnum chambers. All have solid matted rib, double locking lugs, and full beavertail forearm. Barrel length: 20 inches. Chokes: IC/M (12 gauge), M/F (20 gauge). Weights: 7 and 6½ pounds.

Bronco—No frills, no trimming—just plenty of rugged backbone. It's the ideal barn gun for the farmer. And for the trapper, it's just as perfect. Weighing only 3 pounds in .22 and 3¾ pounds in the new over/under, a Bronco can be carried all day long without fatigue. It's a great boat gun, too. The crackle-finish, one-piece stock and receiver can't rust, and the .410 bore barrel, loaded with 3-inch slugs is a powerful piece of shark repellant. The Bronko takes down for ease in packing or storage, and it has a crossbolt safety just above the trigger.

Astra 357—Potent, powerful, and smooth as silk. Chambered for the hot .357 Magnum, this superbly balanced, large-frame revolver also handles the popular .38 Special, making it equally suitable for the serious target shooter and for the sportsman looking for the ultimate in a hunting handgun. Available with 3-, 4-, 6-, or 8½-inch barrel. The 4-inch and longer models have square butts and are supplied with comfortable, hand-filling oversized grips. The 3-inch version has the more compact round butt with magna-style grips. Length overall with 6-inch barrel is 11¼ inches. Weights: from 37 to 41 ounces.

Star FRS—This is a totally delightful handgun for plinking or informal target shooting. The FRS is light enough to be comfortably carried, yet it has enough weight for steady holding. The 6-inch barrel, in addition to its longer sighting plane, also gives the FRS a slightly muzzle-heavy balance that further aids accuracy. The sights are fully adjustable for both windage and elevation, and three separate safeties—half-cock, thumb, and magazine—are incorporated. It's a safe, reliable, accurate, and pleasant-to-shoot handgun. Available in blue or chrome.

Star Model PD—One of the most potent, practical handguns ever made, the Star PD is chambered for the sledgehammer .45 ACP and has the same capacity (eight rounds) as the U.S. Government model, yet it weighs nearly a pound less, as well as being smaller in every dimension. It's just a fraction over 7 inches long and weighs only 25 ounces. It has fully adjustable rear sight, ramp front sight, positive thumb safety, grooved nonslip front strap, and checkered walnut grips. Available in blue or chrome.

GREEN RIVER FORGE, LTD.

The owners of Oregon Gun Works recently purchased this company from Frank Straight and moved it from Bellevue, Washington, to Springfield, Oregon. Their rifle makers are Gary Ruxton and Asher Hamilton. Gary is one of the finest young craftsmen in the United States and has been building the "Astorian" rifle and the Northwest Trade Gun for Green River Forge for some time. Asher is a gun maker who has been turning out some very fine work for Oregon Gun Works. Their guns are muzzle-loaders, both flint and percussion.

The Hudson's Bay Factor's Pistol—This is a first-quality pistol in all respects with a degree of inletting and fit very few custom pistols can match. It comes in smoothbore, 20 gauge (595 ball), or .50-caliber rifled barrel—both barrels are hooked breech for easy removal. The smooth bore is deadly at 15 to 20 yards. Price: $350, plus $3 postage and insurance.

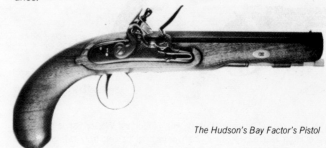

The Hudson's Bay Factor's Pistol

The "Astorian"—One of the historic guns of the really early fur trade days that saw deadly service with the lonely few who went west in the footsteps of Lewis and Clark, Manuel Lisa, and John Jacob Astor in the far Northwest. The Astorian is stocked in the finest walnut and features a truly rainproof lock. Comes in flint or percussion (if you insist) with 32-inch octagonal barrel. Calibers: .45 and .50. Furniture: brass. Weight: 8½ pounds. Prices: $450 (fine standard-grade walnut), $475 (figured fancy grade), plus $5 postage and insurance. Available also in kit form for $210, plus $5.

Northwest Trade Gun—So close to the original that Green River Forge is supplying guns to several museums and historic sites. And these superb guns are shooters. Each Sitting Fox lock is timed and tuned for fast, sure ignition. Dragon sideplate, all steel, big bow trigger guard, and the historically correct two sets of "wedding rings" are taken directly from an original Belgian Trade Gun that was specifically made for the American Fur Company trade. Two barrel lengths offered: 36 and 30 inches, either in smoothbore 20 gauge or .50-caliber rifled (36 inches only). Each gun is hand fitted and finished with over fourteen coats of hand-rubbed old-style finish. Prices: $450 (smoothbore), $465 (rifled), plus $5 for postage and insurance. Also available in kit form for $210 or $220, plus $5.

HIGH STANDARD

Since 1932, High Standard has produced quality firearms for America's sportsmen. Their line includes pistols and revolvers for the discriminating target shooter, as well as handguns for the hunter and camper.

Olympic ISU—Chambered for .22 Short, this target pistol meets all the requirements for use in the international rapid-fire events. Equipped with a 6¾-inch barrel with integral stabilizer, it is available in standard or military grip configuration, the latter providing the military bracket rear sight. Trigger, safety, and magazine release are blued. Finish is Trophy Blue. Price. $213.50.

Sport King—An ideal sidearm featuring accuracy in a plinking-style gun. Available in the standard blued or new nickel finish, with choice of 4½- or 6¾-inch barrel lengths. This pistol comes with hard, durable plastic grips and features the pushbutton barrel takedown standard throughout High Standard's family of .22 pistols. Chambered for .22 Long Rifle. Prices: $112.50 (blue), $122.50 (nickel).

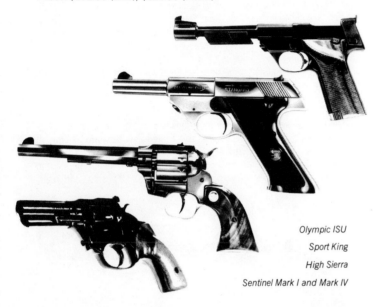

Olympic ISU
Sport King
High Sierra
Sentinel Mark I and Mark IV

High Sierra—The newest of the High Standard Western-style revolvers, the High Sierra, with its 7-inch octagonal barrel, truly brings out the flavor of the frontier. A steel frame revolver, with a custom blue finish, complemented by hand-rubbed walnut grips, this revolver features gold-plated trigger guard and backstrap, and the gun is accompanied by its own walnut presentation case. Available with single or dual cylinders, fixed or adjustable rear sight. Calibers: .22 Long Rifle or .22 Long Rifle/.22 Magnum. Prices: $133, $143.

Sentinel Mark I and Mark IV—A completely redesigned and improved version of the .22-caliber Sentinel revolver which, for years, filled the needs of sportsmen throughout the country. At home in the field or in camp, it's now a steel-framed revolver with classic styling, chambered for .22 Long Rifle (Mark I) or .22 Magnum (Mark IV). Available in 2-, 3-, or 4-inch barrel lengths with fixed or adjustable rear sights, in Trophy Blue or nickel finish with wraparound American walnut stocks. Prices: from $114.50 to $138.

DON HUME LEATHER GOODS, INC.

Don Hume manufactures holsters, belts, and accessories that have won the acclaim of law enforcers and sportsmen throughout the country. These are heavy-duty leather goods, made of thick leather that stands up under rugged use, and crafted for long life and durability.

Jordan River Holster and Belt—This set is not only accepted by police as regulation equipment, but is also popular with sportsmen. The features incorporated in the holster assure the wearer that the gun will be in the right position and readily available when needed. This combination has been tested and proven for many years as to its efficiency and comfort. The belt is 2¼ inches wide and is fully lined. The holster features

Jordan River Holster and Belt

metal in the loop contoured to the hip, muzzle plug to limit gun wear, and custom molding to fit the weapon. Finishes: plain, basketweave, and Hi-Gloss Clarino. Colors: black, brown, and tan. Holster prices: $19.65 (plain), $21.65 (basket), $23.65 (Clarino). Belt prices: $17.85, $19.45, $21.75.

Tom Threepersons with Thumb Break—This holster is made with 1¾- and 2¼-inch belt loops for handguns with 4-inch barrels. It is available in black or tan, in plain, basketweave, or Hi-Gloss Clarino finish. Prices: $14 (plain), $15 (basket), $16.50 (Clarino).

Garrison Belt—This rugged belt is constructed from 1/10-ounce saddle leather and has heavy cast buckle. Width: 1¾ inches. Available in black or tan, plain or basketweave. Prices: $9.25 (plain), $10.50 (basket).

IVER JOHNSON'S ARMS, INC.

For years, Iver Johnson handguns and long guns have seen action from traplines to target ranges. Their line now includes four single-action and eight black-powder revolvers.

Cattleman Buckhorn Magnum—Here's the single-action you big bore fans have been waiting for, manufactured from forgings in exactly the same fashion as its original predecessor of 100 years ago. No castings are used on any Cattleman revolver. The Buckhorn features a specially designed frame with adjustable target sights. It is a handy and versatile weapon, ideal for the handloader. The backstrap and trigger guard are made from highly polished solid brass, complementing the beautifully color-case-hardened frame. The precision rifled ordnance steel barrel is available in 4¾, 6, and 7½ inches in the .44 Magnum. The .357 Magnum and .45 Long Colt calibers come with 5¾- and 7½-inch barrels. Prices: $166.95 (.357 and .45 Long Colt), $191.25 (.44 Magnum).

Cattleman Trailblazer—A great idea in .22-caliber rimfire revolvers. In a matter of seconds your favorite shooting iron converts from an economical plinker to a serious varmint-hunting weapon with the interchangeable cylinder in .22 Winchester Magnum. A big, heavier-built gun with the exact same finish and quality found on the magnum revolvers. The highly polished brass backstrap and trigger guard is complemented by deep rich color-case hardening on the forged frame. With adjustable rear sights, it is available in 5½- or 6½-inch barrel lengths. Weight: approximately 2½ pounds. Price: $132.

Model 1851 Navy .36-Caliber Revolver—The famous 1851 Navy is a gun that served both sides in the Civil War, and it found its way into the hands of many frontiersmen opening up the great boundaries of our Western frontier. It is manufactured from the finest modern ordnance steels with a highly polished brass backstrap and trigger guard. The frame and loading lever are finished in beautiful color-case hardening, complementing the deep rich custom blue on the remaining metal parts. Barrel length: 7½ inches. Overall: 13 inches. Weight: 2 pounds 9 ounces. Price: $80.95.

Model 1860 Army .44-Caliber Revolver—This gun needs no introduction to any avid gun enthusiast. It played a significant role in American history as both a military and civilian weapon. It is built to handle the most severe black-powder loads. The cylinder is authentically roll engraved, and grips are finely figured oil-finished walnut. It's a fine black-powder revolver that will be a highlight in any collection as well as a pleasurable and accurate weapon to own and shoot. Price: $98.

The Police Pocket Model Revolver—Historically, the Pocket Model was the official sidearm of the New York Police Department. No effort has been spared to reproduce this historical gun right down to the last detail. Quality craftsmanship is evident throughout its construction. Caliber: .36. Barrel lengths: 4½ and 6½ inches. Price: $98.

Iver Johnson Revolvers

KOLPIN MANUFACTURING, INC.

Every hunter and shooter ought to have a Kolpin catalog, because in it you will find an extensive line of gun cases of every imaginable design; there's something to accommodate any firearm you own. Kolpin also offers several accessory items and a complete line of archery cases and accessories.

Be sure to check Chapters 6 and 8 for other Kolpin products.

#700 Sandbag Rifle Rests—For benchrest shooting or sighting-in, these rests are contoured to snugly hold your rifle. Funnel flap on bottom allows you to fill it with dry sand. Combination of front and rear rest provides maximum stability. Price: $8.50.

#600 Sandbag Rifle Rest—This rest is long enough that only one rest is required to steady your rifle. Same construction as #700. Price: $5.

#4 Web Shotshell Belt—This is a 2-inch-wide olive web with leather retaining strap, metal buckle, and single row of twenty-five elastic loops. Adjusts to fit all waists. For 12-, 16-, and 20-gauge shotgun shells. Price: $4.95.

#4 Deluxe Web Shotshell Belt—Heavy web belt is instantly adjustable from 28 to 46 inches with special Velcro fastener. Elasticized shell compartments securely hold twenty shells of any gauge, completely enclosing shells except for bases. Color: marsh tan. Price: $8.

Sandbags

#357 Hanger Holster (Pat. Pend.)—So many firsts put this extraordinary pistol case in a class by itself. It is a three-in-one pistol case. Two Velcro straps allow the case to attach to the bottom rung of a hanger for convenient storage in a closet. With the special belt loop it can also function as a versatile holster. The full-length zipper coils also allow the case to lie completely flat when open, thus enabling the shooter to use it as a pad on which to lay his gun. Case lengths: 7, 10, 13, and 15 inches. Prices: from $11.50 to $12.50.

#99 Closet Gun Glove—This case combines two exciting Kolpin features. First it allows you to store your gun out of the way, securely and safely. Second, the heavy-duty YKK nylon-coil zipper runs the full length for easy access. The patented "Envelope" design means your gun will never slide out the end or fall to the bottom of the case, even with the zipper open. Lengths: 40, 44, 48, and 52 inches. Price: $16.

#84 Deluxe Reloader's Pouch—Here's another two-in-one bargain from Kolpin. This tan canvas pouch features a top compartment that holds a full box of shells, while the bottom compartment has a zippered bottom that can hold more than 100 empties. Price: $9.

#72 Four-Box Shell Carrier—Handcrafted of beautiful brown, top-grain cowhide leather with matching leather handles. Ideal for carrying shells on the shooting range. Price: $14.

#72E Vinyl Shell Carrier—With the same features offered on the #72, this case is made of heavy black expanded vinyl. Price: $6.30.

GEORGE LAWRENCE CO.

This company is known primarily for the fine holsters they manufacture to fit all popular revolvers and pistols. But they offer a number of other quality leather products of interest to hunters and shooters, too. Located in Portland, Oregon, the George Lawrence Company was founded when Oregon was a rugged territory and Portland was no more than a small inland port. That was in 1857, so this company puts years of experience into the leather goods they make.

No. 3 Rifle Cartridge Belt Slide—For all rifle cartridges. One-piece leather folded and stitched to form belt loop. Oiled, with twelve cartridge loops. Price: $11.55.

No. 111 Leather Shotgun Carrier—The safe, handy device that takes the load off your arms, yet keeps your shotgun ready for action. Has ¾-inch adjustable strap with wide shoulder pad. The holder is metal

No. 3 Belt Slide

reinforced and has nonslip rubber tread. Available in plain unoiled leather with nickel hardware. Price: $12.95.

No. 11B Game Carrier—For carrying small game and birds over shoulder or belt. Total length: 36 inches. Shaped body 12 inches long, 3½ inches wide at ends, and 2½ inches wide at center. Double and stitched, tan leather and six pliable lace strings on each end. Hand-stamped basketweave only. Unoiled. Price: $14.95.

No. 2 Pronghorn Rifle Sling—This sling is 2¼ inches wide over the shoulder area to give better stability and comfort. Tapers to fit 1-inch swivels only. Lined over shoulder with suede for better gripping. Has solid brass post and screw on one end while other end of sling is adjustable and has laces. Oiled. Finishes: plain, basketweave, and flower design. Prices: $14.95, $19.95, $24.95.

No. 52 Holster for Automatics—Open-end holster with safety strap and snap-covered clip pocket. Oiled. Finishes: plain, basketweave, flower design. Prices: $26.95, $31.75, $37.35.

LEUPOLD & STEVENS, INC.

Some of the finest telescopic sights and mounts to be found anywhere come from Leupold & Stevens. They manufacture seventeen models of fixed-power and variable-power scopes, including a new 20X target scope introduced in 1977.

Their 20-page catalog, which describes their entire line, is free for the asking.

Leupold Vari-X III 1.5×5 (1½- to 5-power)—This scope's 1.5X power setting is particularly helpful for hunting whitetail deer, since they often are taken in fairly heavy cover. Also, because a large field of view makes it easier to get on target fast, this magnification is often used when hunting dangerous game. The settings up to 5X are excellent for longer shots. Price: $154.50. Add $14 for dot reticle.

Leupold Vari-X III 2.5×8 (2½- to 8-power)—This scope is excellent for all types of big-game and varmint hunting. It offers a versatile range of magnifications in a compact package (approximately the same size as Leupold M8-6X fixed-power scope). Price: $174.50. Add $14 for dot reticle.

Leupold Vari-X III 3.5×10 (3½- to 10-power)—The extra power and adjustable objective feature makes this scope the optimum choice for the year-round shooter who enjoys every phase of shooting from big-game and varmint hunting to target shooting. Price: $199.50. Add $14 for dot reticle.

Vari-X III 1.5x5

Vari-X III 2.5x8

Vari-X III 3.5x10

Leupold M8-2X (2-power)—This is a new, exceptionally long eye relief scope, redesigned to be more versatile. The eye piece is now adjustable. With an eye relief of 10 to 24 inches it can be easily mounted ahead of the chamber opening on Winchester Model 94s and other rifles where forward mounting is desirable. Its new shorter length, plus the noncritical eye relief, makes it an excellent choice for handguns. Price: $79.50.

Leupold M8-4X (4-power)—Light, compact, and modestly priced, this scope has what many big-game hunters consider to be the optimal combination of a generous field of view and magnification. In fact, the M8-4X is, by far, the most popular of all Leupold fixed-power scopes. Price: $101.50. Add $14 for dot reticle.

Leupold Target Scopes—Today, target matches are being won with five-shot groups measuring as small as .100 inch at 100 yards. It takes sights designed and manufactured for extreme accuracy to accomplish this. Leupold target scopes provide the resolution to clearly see bullet imprints at 100 or 200 yards. Changing conditions, such as wind or mirage movements, can be readily seen also. The compact 15-inch length and generous eye relief of these scopes permit taking advantage of all the benefits of receiver mounting. Weight has been pared down to a minimum to allow for maximum rifle weight. They are excellent target scopes and the M8-16X also can be used for long-range varmint shooting. Its more modest 16X power, which doesn't magnify minor movements as much, sometimes can be desirable. Target scopes available with cross hair or conventional dots only. Powers available: 16, 20, and 24. Price: $219.50. Add $14 for dot reticle.

.45 ACP "Gold Cup" Mount

.45 ACP "Gold Cup" Mount—Leupold is the first to admit that the mounting of a scope sight on the slide of a Colt .45 "Gold Cup" National Match is most unusual. Unlike their regular "STD" mounts, the .45 Ring Mount is actually a pair of special rings only. But like all their mounts, the Ring Mount is precision machined from tough cold-rolled steel to assure solid strength, positive alignment, and slip-free grip. The height of the rings is designed to allow trouble-free discharge of spent cases and to be compatible with the Leupold "Golden Ring" 2X scope. The company warns that preparing the slide for the rings is not a do-it-yourself project, since the cross slots must be cut on a vertical milling machine. Price: $24.

LYMAN

Lyman has been offering top-quality products to shooters and hunters since 1878. Their extensive line now extends through telescopic sights and mounts, iron sights, chokes and compensators, and a number of muzzle-loading rifles and handguns.

Lyman is a major producer of reloading tools and bullet molds. You won't want to miss their products for the reloader described in Chapter 5. The company also offers a number of publications for the hunter, shooter, and reloader. So why not drop them a note and ask for their latest catalog that will show you everything they have to offer?

Lyman Black-Powder Guns

New Lyman Brown Bess Musket—At the beginning of the Revolutionary War, America had few facilities for manufacturing guns. Luckily there were many British muskets available that had seen service in earlier colonial wars against the French and Indians. The Brown Bess Musket was the mainstay of the U.S. forces during the early stages of our Revolution. Lyman's Brown Bess is a faithful replica of the "New Land Pattern" in .75 caliber. The 42-inch barrel and lock are brightly polished, while the walnut-finished stock and rich polished brass trigger guard combine to produce a classic American flintlock. This one fires either the .715 round ball and patch or bird shot in all sizes. Overall: 59 inches. Weight: 10½ pounds. Price: $324.95.

1853 Enfield Rifle Musket—The original three-band rifle musket saw extensive service during the Civil War. Lyman's replica is finely fitted and will serve its owner equally well on the range or resting over the fireplace. Features include one-piece walnut stock, color-case-hardened percussion lock, blued round barrel with blackened brass barrel bands, brightly polished steel ramrod, and brass furniture. The tangent rear sight is adjustable for elevation to 900 yards. Fixed iron front sight. Caliber: .58. Barrel length: 39 inches. Overall: 55 inches. Weight: 9 pounds. Price: $249.95.

New Model Army .44—This rugged replica of Remington's 1858 New Model Army .44 has been the favorite of target shooters and other experienced muzzle-loaders. The sturdy top strap, besides strengthening the basic frame design, provides an excellent platform for installation of an adjustable rear sight. Features include a deep blue finish on the machined steel frame, barrel cylinder, and loading lever. The trigger and hammer are color-case hardened. The trigger guard is polished brass and the two-piece grips are well-finished European walnut. Barrel length: 8 inches. Overall: 13½ inches. Weight: 2 pounds 9 ounces. Price: $134.95.

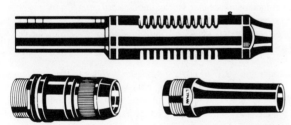

Cutts Compensator and Tubes

The Cutts Compensator—This device offers perfect pattern control and maximum recoil reduction (up to 40 percent) by venting excess expanding gases away from the shot charge as it leaves the muzzle. Due to its superior patterns the Cutts has long been a favorite of skeet shooters the world over. The wide variety of interchangeable choke tubes available will turn any single barrel pump or autoloader into a truly versatile firearm. It consists of three basic parts: the adapter, the expansion chamber, and the choke tube. Extra tubes are available at a small additional cost. There is an adjustable tube available for 12 gauge only. Prices: $33 (complete with adapter wrench and any single tube of your choice), $44 (as above but with adjustable tube for 12 gauge), $22 (12 gauge adjustable tube only), $9 (any additional tube).

Lyman 3-9 Variable Scope—This new hunting scope is designed to perform flawlessly under the most adverse conditions—from deep woods to the Rocky Mountains. Yet, its classic uncluttered lines will enhance even

the most beautiful custom rifle. This scope has a precise optical system, derived from the world-renowned Lyman Target Scopes and contained within a lightweight and fog-free scope body. Length: 12 inches. Weight: 14 ounces. Tube diameter: 1 inch. Click values: ½ inch at 100 yards. Field of view: 39 feet at 100 yards (3X), 13 feet at 100 yards (9X). Price: $139.95.

Lyman Scopes and Sights

Super-Targetspot Scope—Exceptional brilliance and sharp definition permit this scope to perform superbly in target shooting and extra-long-range varmint shooting. In the higher powers (15X and over) it works equally well for target spotting and eliminates the need for a spotting scope. The lower powers are recommended primarily for varmint shooting, while the 15X and 20X are the leading choice of small-bore and high-power target shooters. The 25X and 30X are strictly for benchrest or the highly experienced target shooter and should be purchased only by those who are sure that they require an instrument of this power. All are parallax adjusted from 50 feet to infinity with graduations that permit an ultrafine degree of adjustment. Windage and elevation adjustments (¼-minute clicks) are precise for the smallest of long-range adjustments. Super-Targetspots come complete with mounts and bases. Price: $239.95. Add $12.50 for dot reticle. Mahogany carrying case: $29.95. Sunshade: $4.95.

No. 16 Folding Leaf Sight—Designed primarily as an open rear sight with adjustable elevation, a leaf sight makes an excellent auxiliary sight for a scope-mounted rifle. It folds close to the barrel when not in use, and can be installed and left on rifle without interfering with scope or mount. Two lock screws hold the elevation blade adjustments firmly in place. Available in three heights. Price: $5.50.

Series 53CS Shotgun Sight—When you use your shotgun for slug shooting, you need a rear sight that provides quick, accurate shooting. The

Series 53 Shotgun slug sight turns your bird gun into a deadly deer gun at 100 yards. Sights can be fitted to most slug-shooting shotguns. Price: $7.

No. 25 Bases—Permit the installation of dovetail rear sights, such as the Lyman No. 16 Leaf Sight, on rifles that do not have dovetail cut in the barrel. They also supply a higher line of sight when needed. The No. 25 base is mounted by drilling and tapping the barrel for two 6-48 screws, which are supplied with base. Price: $3.50.

No. 18 Screw-on Type Ramp—The screw-on ramp is designed to be secured with a heavy 8-40 screw, but may be brazed on if desired. Screw-on ramps are ruggedly built and extremely versatile. They use A-width front sights and are available in three heights: low, medium, and high. Prices: $11 (complete with sight), $6 (less sight).

No. 3 and No. 28 Hunting Front Sights—Identical except for bead size, these sights are equipped with a standard ⅜-inch dovetail. They are available in one base width (F) and are designed to be used directly in the barrel dovetail. The ¹/₁₆-inch bead is the most popular but some shooters prefer the wider ³/₃₂-inch bead for fast shooting. Bead colors: ivory and gold. Price: $4.75.

MALLARDTONE

Mallardtone makes a variety of calls for crow, coon, squirrel, turkey, predator, quail, chukar, pheasant, deer, and waterfowl hunting. They are well made to last and to serve, and each call is tested by an expert to make sure it is "suitable for the most discriminating customer."

Duck Call
Pintail Whistle

Model M-5-DC Duck Call—Made of the finest materials available. The barrel is of American black walnut, assuring beauty and lasting durability, and is polished to a high luster. Price: $5.95.

Model M-250-PTC Pintail Whistle—Same materials and craftsmanship as all Mallardtone calls. Price: $2.95.

Duck Calling Record—Expert calling instructions on a 45 rpm record. Price: $2.50.

MARBLE ARMS CORP.

Marble Arms offers a number of products of interest to hunters and shooters, including scope mounts, sights, cleaning kits, and accessories.

Sporting Rear Sight—This sight is available in full buckhorn, semibuckhorn, or flat top for every rifle manufactured. Will fill the need of every hunter. Reversible notch piece gives choice of U or V notch. Can be ad-

Sporting Rear Sights

justed for height. Long-blade and short-blade models available. Prices: $5.50 to $6.50.

No. 14R Modern Contour Ramp—For late model Remington 725, 740, 760, 742, and others. Distance between mounting screws is ⁹/₁₆ inch. Two standard 6-48 screws furnished. Price: $6.

No. 71 Ramp and No. 71A Hood—Traditional front sight ramp base available in sweat-on or screw-on models. Five heights available. Two standard 6-48 screws furnished. Prices: $5.60 (ramp), $1.40 (hood).

Shooting Goggles—These new shooting goggles provide maximum eye protection at minimum cost. Remarkably light in weight, yet ruggedly built. Available in amber or green. Price: $2.39.

Model 400 Hearing Protector—Offers outstanding protection for the serious shooter. Designed to reduce harmful high-frequency and impact noise, this ear muff allows the wearer to hear warning signals and sound in the speech frequency range. Easily conforms to all head and ear contours. Adjustable suspension band is heat-treated aircraft aluminum alloy and ear cups are high-impact plastic with cold-resistant vinyl ear seals. Weight: 9 ounces. Price: $12.50.

Marble's Non-Freeze Oil—A product of Marble's continuing research to ensure reliable operation of hunting equipment when it is needed most. Excellent for extreme-temperature use. Keeps sports equipment functioning freely in any kind of weather. Price: 69¢.

MARKSMAN PRODUCTS

Marksman air guns and accessories ought to be familiar to anyone who has browsed around the air gun departments of any discount department stores anywhere. These products are great fun for any shooter and are excellent training aids for beginners. You should be able to find competitively priced Marksman air guns and accessories locally. You can also write Marksman for their latest catalog.

Marksman No. 1010 Repeating Air Pistol—With the heft and feel of a real .45, the 1010 is easy to operate with a cocking slide and two safeties. The side latch must be released from its notch before cocking, and the crossbolt safety blocks the trigger until ready to fire. No CO₂ cartridges and no loss of power. The 1010 is time tested for years of wear.

No. 1010 Air Pistol

Marksman 740 Air Rifle—The 740 combines constant shooting power, advanced design, positive safety features, and excellent accuracy potential in one precision-made repeating BB air rifle. It also shoots .177-caliber pellets and air gun darts (must be loaded one at a time). For BB shooting, the 740 has a large-capacity magazine holding over 100 BBs. Cocking is simple with easy "breaking" action. The 740 uses a permanent spring-activated power supply and velocity is delivered at over 450 feet per second. Features include ramp front sight and adjustable rear sight, automatic safety, handsome simulated walnut-finished checkered stock of sturdy molded material.

MARLIN FIREARMS CO.

Marlin is one of the giants of the firearms industry and certainly an important part of American firearms history. Best known for a line of top-flight lever-action rifles, Marlin also produces autoloaders and bolt-action rifles in .22 and .22 Winchester Magnum calibers, as well as shotguns and the Glenfield line of economy-priced .22s.

Marlin 336C—All Marlin 336 models are available in the famous .30/30 caliber, the first smokeless powder cartridge made for sporting use. The 336C is also available in .35 Remington, a cartridge long preferred for hunting in heavy woods. Features include a lever action with side ejection, solid top receiver, gold-plated steel trigger, deeply blued metal surfaces, and receiver top sand-blasted to prevent glare. Stock is two-piece American black walnut with full pistol grip and fluted comb, grip cap, white butt plate and pistol grip spacers, and tough Mar-Shield finish. Sights are adjustable semibuckhorn folding rear and ramp front with brass bead and Wide-Scan hood. Receiver is tapped for scope mount or receiver sight. Offset hammer spur for scope use is adaptable for right- or left-hand use. Six-shot tubular magazine. Barrel: 20 inches with Micro-Groove rifling (twelve grooves). Overall: 38½ inches. Weight: about 7 pounds. Price: $144.95.

336C

39A

99M1

Glenfield Model 10

Marlin 336T—The traditional western version of the 336, known as the "Texan" and famous for its fine balance and fast handling. Straight grip styling makes the Texan an ideal saddle gun. Other features same as the 336C, except available in .30/30 Winchester only. Weight: about 6¾ pounds. Price: $144.95.

Marlin 336A—Back by popular demand, this old favorite is made for hunters who prefer a longer barrel on their 336. Features include sling swivels and leather carrying strap and a traditional half-magazine tube. Other features same as the 336C, except this one has a five-shot capacity and is chambered for .30/30 Winchester only. Weight: about 7 pounds. Price: $151.95.

Marlin 1895—Here's Marlin's re-creation of the original 1895 .45/70 repeater. Adopted by the U.S. Army over 100 years ago, the .45/70 has always been classed as one of the finest heavy-cover cartridges ever developed for big-game hunting. The 1895 uses the basic Model 336 lever-action system especially designed to feed and eject the larger .45/70. Features include a four-shot tubular magazine, two-piece American black walnut stock, adjustable semibuckhorn folding rear sight, brass bead front sight, solid top receiver tapped for scope mount or receiver sight, and offset hammer spur. Barrel: 22 inches. Overall: 40½ inches. Weight: about 7 pounds. Price: $209.95.

Marlin 444—For big-game hunters who want smashing knockdown power combined with the fast, smooth Marlin lever action, this big-bore stopper features a 22-inch barrel that makes for quick handling even in heavy brush, Micro-Groove rifling, American black walnut stock, machined and heat-treated steel forgings, solid top and side ejecting receiver, detachable sling swivels, and leather carrying strap. Sights are same as .336. Caliber: 444 Marlin. Capacity: four-shot tubular magazine. Overall: 40½ inches. Weight: about 7½ pounds. Price: $163.95.

Marlin Golden 39—Its design is so basic and clean it has been a favorite for eighty-four years. Iron-sight shooters will find the 39 receiver clean, flat, and sand-blasted to prevent glare. Scope shooters will appreciate the screw-on scope adapter base that provides a neat, versatile way to mount either a .22 or high-power scope. Features include tubular magazine with new patented closure system that holds 26 Short, 21 Long, or 19 Long Rifle cartridges. Stock is two-piece American black walnut—pistol grip on 39A and straight on 39M. Barrel: 24 inches with Micro-Groove (sixteen grooves). Overall: 40 inches. Weight: about 6½ pounds. Price: $134.95.

Marlin 49 Deluxe—The luxury .22 autoloader with the classic customized look, features handsome scrollwork on both sides of the receiver, a damascened bolt, American walnut stock and forearm handsomely checkered, a white line spacer on the butt plate, and 18-shot tubular magazine. Sights are open rear and ramp front. Receiver is grooved for tip-off mount. Caliber: .22 Long Rifle. Barrel: 22 inches with Micro-Groove (sixteen grooves). Overall: 40½ inches. Weight: about 5½ pounds. Price: $79.95.

Marlin 99M1 and 989M2 Carbines—Styled after America's most popular carbine, the fast-handling 99M1 and its clip-loading version, the 989M2, feature the lightning-fast Marlin auto action. These slick shooters are ideal for small game or plinking. Features include Monte Carlo American black walnut stock with full pistol grip, white butt plate spacer, sling swivels, adjustable and removable open rear sight, ramp front sight, and receiver grooved for tip-off mount. Caliber: .22 Long Rifle. Barrel: 18 inches with Micro-Groove (sixteen grooves). Overall: 36¾ inches. Weight: about 5 pounds. Price: $69.95.

Glenfield Model 10—One of America's most popular single shot .22 rifles. A great gun for getting a beginning shooter off to a good start. Simple and safe to use, the 10 takes only one .22 cartridge at a time, and it must be cocked by hand before it can be fired. Its big T-shaped cocking knob is easy to grip, even when wearing gloves. Perfect first rifle for boy or girl. Barrel: 22 inches. Overall: 40 inches. Weight: about 4½ pounds. Price: $39.95.

MASTER LOCK CO.

Master has developed an excellent firearms locking system that is worthy of any gun owner's attention. Other Master locks can be found in Chapter 11.

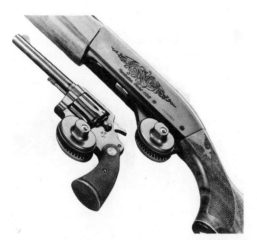

No. 90 Master Gun Lock

No. 90 Master Gun Lock—You may not have room for a locking gun cabinet, but you still can safeguard guns stored in a closet or on an open wall rack. The No. 90 Gun Lock discourages theft and prevents accidental firing of stored firearms. An exclusive, patented system clamps this lock securely to both sides of the trigger guard, effectively blocking trigger action. To assure maximum security, these locks are self-adjusting to suit each firearm and feature a key operated pin tumbler locking mechanism. Cushioned pads protect the gun's finish. These locks are also available keyed alike so a single key can control several guns. Price: $5.95.

MICHAELS OF OREGON

This is where all those Uncle Mike's brand swivels, slings, and shooting accessories come from. They have an extensive line of swivels, some of which would be difficult or impossible to find elsewhere. And they have accessories of interest to the black-powder buff as well as to the modern arms enthusiast.

QD 115 Mini-14—Direct replacement for factory-equipped nondetachable swivels on the Ruger Mini-14. Special front adapter fits band, eliminating need to dismantle gun. Price: $6.95.

QD 115 SG Sling Swivel—Split band in four diameters, mounts easily on single barrel or over/under shotguns without special tools or dismantling. Not for 10, 28, or .410 gauge. Price: $8.95.

QD 115 MCS Sling Swivel—Universal pump, auto magazine cup adapter with special tool for quick and easy installation. Fits pumps and autos except Browning 2000, Winchester 1400, Ithaca 37, Savage 30, Sears 21 and 30, or Stevens pumps. Price: $6.95.

Cease Fire! Gun Lock—A key-operated device that rotates and locks into the breech recesses provided for the locking lug of bolt-action rifles. When gun is locked, key is replaced by a red tag that cautions: "Stop! This gun is locked." Fits most popular bolt-action centerfire rifles. Price: $9.95.

New Style Possibles Bag—Made of soft suede leather with a traditional beavertail flap and buckskin fringe. Handy Velcro tab holds flap in place. Loops inside are handy for holding nipple wrenches, powder measure, capper, etc. Generous inside pocket for small items such as extra nipples, caps, etc. Shoulder strap is adjustable. Price: $15.95.

Possibles Bag

Do-It-Yourself Ramrod Kit—Make your own individual ramrod to the desired length from dowel or fiberglass rod. Or repair or beef up factory rods. Kit includes two solid brass end tips, one tapped 10 to 32 inches and the other tapped 8 to 32 inches, plus unique small jag for Hawken-type rifle breeches to fit any attachment made, plus cross pins. Installation is simple. Rod material not included. Price: $2.95.

S. D. MYRES SADDLE CO.

This firm, in business for eighty years, offers a line of holsters and belts, none of which are factory mass produced. They have made custom holsters to fit all types of guns, including special models for Gen. George S. Patton, Nikita Khrushchev, Harry S. Truman, and many others.

See Chapter 8 for more Myres products.

Model 604 Quick Draw Holster—The 600 series "Quick Draw" holster was originally designed by S. D. Myres for Tom Threepersons, famous Western peace officer. It features a high-ride, full-welted design, and canted belt loop for quick draw. Available with belt loop sizes up to 2½ inches, and in plain, basketweave, or carved designs. Prices: $17 (plain), $20 (basket), $27 (carved).

Model 604 Holster

Model 3TB Border Holster—Modified Border Holster with thumb break features galvanized steel reinforcement, heavy welt, welt plug, two-position safety strap, hand-stitched plug bottom. Prices: $30.25 (plain), $33.75 (basket), $40.25 (carved).

Model 331 Flap Holster—Custom designed and hand fitted as each order requires. They may be ordered to fit any age gun, any caliber, any barrel length. Available in any belt width and either cross-draw or regular at no extra charge. Prices: $29.50 (plain), $34.50 (basket), $43.50 (carved).

crease the already extensive line of replica arms, to offer more stainless steel options, and to provide a complete line of black-powder cartridges.

Their full-color catalog is a work of art and a genuine browser's delight—and at $1 it's a bargain.

Zouave Rifle—One of the most accurate .50-caliber military percussion rifles ever produced, it features a fine walnut-toned stock, deep-blued barrel, case-hardened lock, elegant brass fittings, and patch box. The Zouave Rifle is a harmonious symphony of wood and metal. Barrel: 32½ inches. Overall: 48½ inches. Price: $150.

Zouave Rifle, Zouave 1864 Carbine, J. P. Murray Artillery Carbine, Zouave Rifle Powder Flask, Mini-Ball Sealer

NAVY ARMS CO.

It was the idea of Val Forgett, Jr., when he founded this company in 1957, to manufacture quality replica firearms for the growing numbers of black-powder shooters in this country—firearms manufactured with the most modern materials and technology that would be safer to use and easier to own than the original collector's pieces.

His plan to put black-powder guns in the hands of the shooter of average means was certainly a success, and today Navy Arms offers a complete range of muzzle-loading replicas, as well as accessories and some popular early-American cartridge arms. Plans for the future are to in-

Zouave Model 1864 Carbine—This carbine in .58 caliber is considered by many as one of the most thoroughly perfected percussion rifles. The carbine is an ideal, fast-handling, brush-busting percussion carbine with precision-rifled ordnance steel barrel, finished in a deep luster blue that handsomely contrasts with the color-case-hardened lock. Barrel length: 22 inches. Price: $150.

J. P. Murray Artillery Carbine—Copy of the carbine used by the Southern Artillery Units during the Civil War, this carbine has been carefully reproduced with a browned barrel in .58 caliber. Barrel length: 23½ inches. Price: $135.

Zouave Rifle Powder Flask—For all .58-caliber rifles, this is a faithful reproduction of the Civil War Peace Flask, showing the clasped hands of friendship and the American Eagle surrounded by stars. The central adornment shows military arms used throughout the centuries. Price: $15.

Mini-Ball Sealer—This lubricant is designed to help seal the ball, prevent rust, and keep fouling soft for an indefinite period. It creates no residue, produces no odor, and inhibits the rust and corrosion normally associated with black powder. Price: $1.98.

Buffalo Hunter—A big-bore percussion rifle designed with the hunter in mind. An ideal choice for primitive weapons hunting, because the giant 500-grain slug will give that one-shot knockdown power. Pack a gun that packs the punch—a big .58 Buffalo Hunter. The wood is a handsome walnut color with a generous amount of tasteful hand checkering. The lock and hammer are color-case-hardened for lasting beauty, complementing the rich, deep blue of the precision-rifled barrel. Price: $160.

12 Gauge Magnum Deluxe Double Barrel Percussion Shotgun—This gun is classic in design with the styling reminiscent of the early English and French doubles. It is a rabbit ear sidelock configuration with a forward-locking pin holding the barrels. A fast-handling beauty with traditionally hand-checkered walnut stock, blued barrels, and polished locks. Barrels are choked IC and M. This magnum beauty will shoot all 12-, 10-, and light 8-gauge equivalent percussion loads. Patent breech with removable breech plugs. Barrels: 28 inches. Weight: about 7½ pounds. Price: $225.

Charleville Pistol—The famous French Model 1777 flintlock pistol, as made by Charleville and other arsenals. This arm was so well liked by the colonial troops it served as a model for the first martial pistol made by the U.S. Government after the war. The Navy Arms replica is a beauty with gleaming brass frame, polished steel barrel, and finely finished walnut stock. Caliber: .69. Barrel: 7½ inches. Weight: 2 pounds 14 ounces. Price: $125.

Harper's Ferry 1855 Dragoon Pistol—Developed at Harper's Ferry Arsenal as a holster pistol for the U.S. Mounted Rifles, this pistol was later fitted with a shoulder stock and designated the Springfield Pistol Carbine Model 1855. This beautifully crafted percussion weapon of walnut, modern ordnance steel, and polished brass in .58 caliber fires the standard 500-grain Minie ball. Originally issued in pairs and designed to be carried in saddle holsters, it is a true horse pistol. Length: 11¾ inches. Price: $95. Optional shoulder stock: $30.

Colt Walker Model 1847—This big, powerful, .44-caliber revolver is the famous magnum developed with the help of Capt. Sam Walker of the U.S. Mounted Rifles and saw extensive service in the Mexican War. The largest of all Colt revolvers and authentically reproduced, it weighs a mighty 4 pounds 8 ounces, with an overall length of 15¾ inches. Six-shot with handsomely engraved cylinder and barrel marked "U.S. 1847." Price: $130.

Buntline Model Dragoon—The popular Third Model Dragoon will now be offered as a Buntline model, complete with shoulder stock and 18-inch barrel. A beautiful set to delight the most avid collector or shooter. Complete with holster to hold both pistol and shoulder stock. Price: $195.

NIKKO FIREARMS

From this company comes the exquisite line of Golden Eagle shotguns and rifles. The shotguns currently being produced are over/unders in three grades and in field, trap, and skeet models. The Model 7000 is the only rifle available at this time. It's a bolt action, chambered for all the most popular calibers.

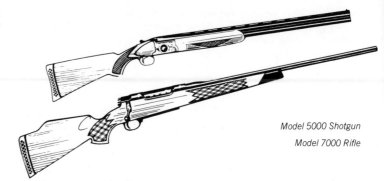

Model 5000 Shotgun

Model 7000 Rifle

Golden Eagle Model 5000 Grade I—This shotgun is an international blend of the fine gunsmithing talent, skill, materials, and design from around the world to bring you a sporting firearm that stands out as something special. The carefully calculated stock geometry, pistol grip, semibeavertail forearm, and overall balance allows the Golden Eagle to come to your shoulder smoothly. Each Grade I is beautifully hand finished with original receiver engravings. Other features include modern box-lock receiver, precision barrels with hard chrome-plated bores and chambers, rapid-heat-dispersing ventilated rib, antibalk gold-plated single selective trigger, tang safety and barrel selector, automatic ejectors, and hand-checkered stock and forearm. Available in Field and Skeet models in 12 or 20 gauge and Trap models in 12 gauge. All models have a variety of barrel length options and each comes in its own foam-lined hard case approved for air travel. Prices: $699.50 (Field), $823.50 (Trap), $751.50 (Skeet).

Golden Eagle Model 7000 Big Game Rifle—This rifle is made without resorting to shortcuts or compromise. Its super-strong action, hammer-forged barrel, rich high-luster blue, and finely checkered, hand-bedded fancy American walnut stock all contribute to making this rifle the talking piece of your gun cabinet. All are drilled and tapped for scope mounts and also feature a shotgun tang-type safety. The bolt can be opened while the safety is engaged. The hinged floor plate with removable clip is designed for easy loading and unloading. Five hefty locking lugs ensure that the bolt is fully engaged when you close the bolt handle. Available in popular calibers from .22/250 to .458 Winchester Magnum. Prices: $379.50 (all standard and magnum calibers), $399.50 (African calibers, furnished with sights).

NORTH AMERICAN ARMS

North American manufactures two handguns that couldn't be more different from each other. One is their .22-caliber Mini-Derringer; the other is the .454 Casull, which is touted as the world's most powerful handgun. Since the latter ought to be of interest to handgun hunters, we'll describe it.

See Chapter 5 for ammunition and brass for the .454 Casull.

.454 Casull Revolver

.454 Casull—This hefty five-shot single-action revolver is what handgun hunters have been waiting for. Designed along the lines of an American classic, the .454 is constructed of the finest quality stainless steel and has a polished finish. It is chambered for the powerful .454 Casull ammunition (specially developed for this and only this revolver) and features a massive cylinder with locking notches placed to give the best lockup and safety possible. The stout frame features an ample sighting groove that's quick to line up with the ramp front sight. Its barrel is rifled with six lands and grooves for superior performance under the heavy pressures and hyper-velocities generated by the .454 Casull cartridge. It also features a classic loading gate and ejector rod design, easy takedown, deluxe hardwood grips, a spring-loaded firing pin that's independent of the hammer, and a foulproof "hammer down" safety system that fully locks the cylinder when the hammer pushes the firing pin into one of five detents on the rear face of the cylinder. All this and a crisp, clean trigger pull, too. For added versatility, the .454 Casull can also chamber .45 Long Colt cartridges. Barrel length: 7½ inches. Overall: 14 inches. Weight: 3 pounds 2 ounces. Price: $445.

NUMRICH ARMS CORP.

With more than 100 million parts in stock, Numrich is the world's largest supplier of gun parts. Their inventory includes parts for long guns, handguns, military, sporting, modern, and out-of-production arms. They carry gun stocks, pistol grips, slings, swivels, cases, locks, triggers, clips, screws, pins, springs, sights, and hundreds of other items. Additionally, they carry quite a line of muzzle-loader kits.

No collector, hobby gunsmith, or serious firearms enthusiast should be without their 140-page catalog that they'll send you for two bucks.

Here's just a small sampling of what they have to offer.

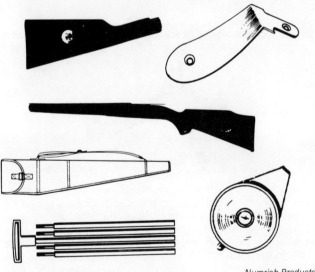

Numrich Products

Winchester 94 Stock—Genuine walnut replacement stock for the Model 94 Winchester is completely finished with gold-plated medallion of a covered wagon. Price: $19.

Winchester Butt Plates—Original-style replacement for the '92 and '94 Saddle Ring Carbine. Price: $3.75.

Military Sporter Stock—Numrich is now able to offer custom sporter stocks for the large-ring 98 Mauser. These stocks are genuine walnut, completely checkered, and have butt plate and pistol grip cap installed. Will fit any 98 Mauser with a military or sporter barrel. An ideal conversion stock for the average sportsman. No special tools required. Also available for other military rifles. Price: $45.

Rifle Case—Brand new U.S. GI heavy-duty canvas gun case with carrying strap. Will hold any U.S. military rifle, including Garand, as well as most commercial rifles and shotguns. Length: 48 inches. Price: $7.95.

Springfield Rifle Blanks—Will fit 03 and 03A1. Not inletted. Price: $4.50.

Cleaning Rod—Steel, .50-caliber rod useful for .45 caliber and over. Good for muzzle-loaders 40 inches long. Price: $1.70.

Cappers—Civil War-type cappers—the handy way to carry and store your caps. Solid brass with simplified feed system allows you to cap quickly. Round capper for rifles and pistols. Long capper with larger capacity for revolvers and rifles. Price: $4.49 each.

Hopkins & Allen Boot Pistol Kit—For the first time, Numrich is offering their famous Boot Pistol as a construction set for the home craftsman. The kit will be complete except for the final fitting and finishing. No power tools required. The underhammer action's simplicity of design provides the shooter with years of trouble-free shooting. It has gained popularity because of its balance and accuracy and is the ideal companion piece to every Hopkins & Allen rifle. Calibers: .36 or .45. Overall: 13 inches. Price: $29.95.

Minuteman Brush Rifle Kit—All metal parts are American made and fully finished. Stock is machine-inletted, drilled, and fully contoured. Needs only a bit of rasp work and sanding. Barrel is fully finished but left unblued so it can be either blued or browned. No power tools required. Available in flint or percussion. Calibers: .45 and .50. Price: $129.95.

Kentucky Long Rifle Kit—A new addition to the Numrich line of kits, this muzzle-loader features a ³⁄₁₆-inch octagonal, unblued barrel and a one-piece solid maple, 58-inch, fully machined stock. All metal parts are fully finished and, as in all other Hopkins & Allen kits, are manufactured and guaranteed by Numrich Arms Corporation. Available in flint or percussion. Barrel: 42 inches. Calibers: .31, .36, and .45. Price: $129.95.

P. S. OLT CO.

This company produces a complete line of game and bird calls, which is one of the most extensive we know of, including calls for waterfowl, pheasant, quail, chukar, dove, turkey, squirrel, coon, deer, elk, and predators. And for some birds and animals they have a selection of several different models of calls. They also produce instruction records, game call lanyards, and silhouette crow and dove decoys.

Double Reed DR-115 Duck Call—A beautifully crafted call of select American walnut with red cedar reed base. Double-reed design eliminates "blow down" and prevents distortion; all-wood construction means minimum moisture condensation. Easy to blow. Easy to adjust tone. Price: $9.95.

Big Water Duck Call K-11—This adjustable call is specially designed for calling diver ducks—blue bills, redheads, and canvasbacks. Price: $7.50.

Big Water Duck Call   *Dove Call*

Big Bay "800" Goose Call—Will bring in even the highest-flying honkers. Small difference in cost makes a big difference in calling effectiveness. Handcrafted from beautiful American black walnut. Price: $10.95.

Crow Call E-1—Favorite among crow hunters. Lightweight. Easy to blow. Tone is raucous and far-carrying. Black hard rubber. Price: $5.25.

Dove Call DV-35—Proven effective call. Has true tone and is easy to blow. Mauve color plastic. Price: $4.50.

Quail Call Q-30—Delivers persuasive whistle of quail. No reed—always in proper tone. Hard rubber. Black barrel, tan tone bell. Price: $5.50.

Squirrel Call B-10—Bellows-type call gives perfect imitation of a squirrel's bark. Easy to use. Price: $4.75.

Coon Call N-27—Produces deep guttural sound that arouses the curiosity of a hidden coon. Hard rubber. Black barrel, gray tone bell. Price: $5.50.

Clarion "600" Deer Call—Handmade from select black walnut with a fine walnut tone bell. Helps bring in deer for closer shot. A valuable assistance to any deer hunter in any weather. Price: $6.95.

Elk Call EL-45—Lures elk close for clean kill. Delivers perfect operation in all weather conditions. Black and red color plastic. Price: $6.95.

Long Range "33" Predator Call—Screaming, rabbit-in-distress call brings foxes, coyotes, bobcats, and other predators within shooting range in any season. One-piece construction from select American black walnut. Price: $6.95.

Close Range Predator Call CP-21—Use for close-range predator calling. Black plastic. Price: $8.95.

Call Lanyards—Made of durable green nylon. Single- and double-call models to keep your calls within easy reach for instant use. Prices: $1.25 (single), $1.50 (double).

ORVIS CO.

Orvis offers a number of hunting and shooting accessories. Hunting clothing can be found in Chapter 8, and the Orvis fishing tackle is in Chapter 2.

Orvis also offers annual shooting schools. All instruction, shells, use of Orvis guns (if you wish), and comfortable room, good food, and good company for three days will cost you only $325. If you want to know more, write to Miss Pam Newhouse.

Orvis Custom Shotgun—The ultimate in a personal, custom-stocked shotgun delivered to you in less than six months. This gun, made for you, will bring you that ideal gun-gunner relationship in which you will find it almost impossible to mount the gun incorrectly. It comes up already aligned, pointing where you are looking for quick, accurate shots the moment the butt of the gun reaches the proper position on your shoulder. There is no fitting yourself to the gun, so that precious seconds

are saved. The custom fitting allows you to mount the gun the same every time, and thus your percentage of hits will be greatly improved.

The Orvis Custom Shotgun is handcrafted by old-world-quality gunsmiths in Spain. The 12 gauge with 2¾-inch chambers weighs but 6½ pounds, making it one of the lightest 12 gauges available. Choice of 26- or 28-inch barrels, choked full, improved modified, modified, improved cylinder. The 20 gauge weighs only 6 pounds. It comes with 25- or 27-inch barrels and the same choice of chokes as in the 12 gauge. You can select either double triggers or single nonselective trigger. The shotgun has selective ejectors and an automatic safety. It is beautifully engraved and the stock is deluxe-grade European walnut with fine hand checkering. Price: $1,250.

PENGUIN INDUSTRIES, INC.

While the name Penguin might not be immediately familiar to some of you, certainly the company's popular Hoppe's brand of shooters' products will be. Penguin offers a complete line of gun-cleaning and maintenance products, including the famous Hoppe's No. 9 Solvent, cleaning kits, lubricants, patches, brushes, and more.

For Penguin marine products, see Chapter 3.

Game Bird Carrier—Handy way to carry game birds. Heavy plated rods shaped to fit over belt. Birds slip on easily and hang securely. Each carrier holds several birds. Price: $2.98.

Hoppe's Hunter's Seat & Deer Drag—Provides a comfortable seat that can be secured to any tree or post. Rolls to a compact bundle in seconds. Web strap, nylon rope, and reinforced vinyl seat safely support 300 pounds. Can be used as a deer drag by attaching rope to the deer with seat across hunter's chest or shoulders. Price: $9.95.

Expert's Bench Rest

Expert's Bench Rest—This well-constructed rifle rest is ideal for use on the range or in the field. The special alloy of the cast metal—painted in a handsome orange—provides stability to stay put but is light enough to carry in the field for those long-range shots. Sturdy rifle bed measures 5 inches across, 3¼ inches deep—takes widest forearms. Height extends to 8¼ inches, retracts to 5¾ inches. Screw-type pointed anchor pins (may be fully retracted) in each tripod foot assure nonslip grip on bench top. Price: $34.95.

Bench Rest Bag—A small front bag, available in leather or vinyl, made to fit on your bench rest. With wraparound taps and laces. Dimensions: 5¼ × 1⅞ × 2⅜ inches. Prices: $6.95 (leather), $5.95 (vinyl).

Orvis Custom Shotgun

"Sta-Put" Clay Target Thrower

Rifle Rest Bags—Both bags are available in leather or vinyl and are shaped and stitched to form total support for stock and barrel. Front rest is 5½×5½×5 inches. Rear rest is 4⅜×4¾×5¼ inches. This set is a must for every shooter. Easy to fill with your sand. Prices: $7.95 (front, leather), $10.95 (rear, leather), $5.95 (front, vinyl), $9.95 (rear, vinyl).

Hoppe's Shooting Stick—This field rifle rest ensures accuracy for scope shooters and all still hunting—varmints, deer, turkey, etc. A must where precise bullet placement is essential. Handy to carry, fully adjustable to 26-inch height, strong construction, lightweight. Price: $19.95.

"Sta-Put" Clay Target Thrower—Simply step on the base to force spikes into ground. Trap is then ready to launch targets. Base becomes more firmly implanted with each launch. Targets may be launched from 16 yards away. Stable, portable, lightweight. Adjustable flight—no tools necessary. Throws singles or doubles. Price: $49.95.

POLY-CHOKE CO., INC.

The Poly-Choke brand appears not only on this company's popular adjustable shotgun chokes, but also on a line of fine rifle sights, shotgun sights, and raised ribs for shotguns and handguns.

Poly-Choke Adjustable Shotgun Chokes—Nine settings at your fingertips to give you the right pattern for any range. You'll get a precision, custom installation at the Poly-Choke factory or by authorized installers throughout North America (write for list). Poly-Choke is custom fitted to your shotgun. Your barrel can be shortened or lengthened. The standard style is slim and sleek and recommended for trap. Ventilated style reduces recoil. Available for 12, 16, 20, and 28 gauge. Prices: $32.95 (standard), $34.95 (ventilated) installed, plus $2.50 shipping. Barrel only needed.

Adjustable Choke

Poly-Choke Raised Ribs for Shotguns—A truly fine raised ventilated rib for your shotgun. Ultralight (less than 2 ounces) and custom mounted. Provides a great sighting plane. Keeps barrel cool. Special top milling reduces glare and heat shimmer. Custom installation at the Poly-Choke factory or a franchised installer near you. Price includes front and mid-sight and complete installation. Installation takes four to five days plus mail time. For all over/under, pump, auto, or single-shot shotguns, in 12, 16, 20, 28, or .410 gauge. Price: $34.95, plus $3.50 shipping. Complete gun needed.

REDFIELD

Redfield manufactures a complete line of telescopic sights, rings, and bases as well as spotting scopes and accessories. In 1968 they introduced their Widefield scopes with eyepieces that allow up to 30 percent more field of view. These scopes have gained tremendous popularity among hunters, and the entire line now incorporates the sleek, low-slung functional feature called "Low Profile," which permits better cheek-to-stock fit.

Accu-Range, an optional quick range-estimator, is a feature that is available on most Redfield variable power scopes at an added charge. Redfield binoculars and monoculars are described in Chapter 11.

Scopes, Reticles, Rings, Bases, Accessories

Low Profile Widefield 2¾X Scope—An economical scope that will stand a lifetime of tough use. Ideal for close-range hunting with the popular 30/30, other brush rifles, and slug guns. Provides 55.5-foot field of view at 100 yards. Allows you to get on targets fast, even in the poor light of early dawn or dusk. Prices: $118.70 (3-inch dot), $103.80 (all other reticles).

Low Profile Widefield 4X Scope—Popular, compact, and economical. Offers the versatility needed for both close-in and moderate long ranges. The nearest thing to an all-purpose, all-around fixed power scope. Price: $132.70 (3-inch dot), $115.90 (all other reticles).

Low Profile Widefield 6X Scope—Effective in mountains or open country where reach for long-range shots is needed. Good medium- to long-range scope for flat-shooting varmint rifles, too. Prices: $145.70 (2-inch dot), $129.90 (all other reticles).

Low Profile Widefield 1¾X–5X Variable Power Scope—Perfect for fast, accurate shooting with brush or slug gun. Has a 70-foot field of view at

100 yards on low setting, yet can be cranked up to as high as 5X when targets call for longer ranges. Compact, lightweight. The most economical choice in a variable Widefield. Prices: $128, $143 (with Accu-Range).

Low Profile Widefield 2X–7X Variable Power Scope—Sleek, compact, and lightweight. As versatile a scope as you can buy if you want instant power selectivity for a variety of hunting situations. Use it at 2X for close-in brush shots, 7X for longer-range open-country targets, or in between for medium ranges. Prices: $163.60 (3- to 1-inch dot, or Accu-Range), $148.60 (all other reticles).

Low Profile Widefield 3X–9X Variable Power Scope—For the shooter who wants the most popular, versatile scope available. Unquestionably the most popular scope—either fixed or variable—with both big-game and varmint hunters. Use for long-range spotting and zeroing in on that trophy that's way out there. Turn to lower power and you're ready for woods hunting and poor light conditions. Prices: $180.40 (3- to 1-inch dot, or Accu-Range), $165.40 (all other reticles).

JR Rings—All Redfield rings have ring screws with hexagonal sockets for maximum tightening capability. Note the new streamlined design that improves the overall appearance of a Redfield scope-and-mount installation. Rings are quickly detached from the mounting base. Available in low, medium, and high heights, depending on your scope's objective diameter. Price: $17.80. Engraved and extension rings available at higher costs.

JR Bases—These one-piece Redfield dovetail design bases permit scope removal with positive return to zero. Streamlined rounding of edges for added beauty. Many different base configurations to fit almost any rifle. Price: $12.

SR Bases—These two-piece bases are designed for rifles requiring greater cartridge-loading access. Same tight-fitting dovetail design and streamlined edges. Prices: $12 for most, but some up to $21.

Regal Variable Power Spotting Scopes—These American-made, fog-proof spotting scopes assure constant focus as power is changed. And the clicker or detent positions give you "clicks" you can feel as you change power. The separated power and focus rings offer one-hand adjustment and eliminate confusion when changing power or focus while looking through the scope. Available in either 15X–45X or 15X–60X. Come with unique sighting device. Prices: $232.20, $267.90.

Sighting Device—Unique new sighting device attaches quickly to your spotting scope, enabling you to easily sight game using an open sight so that target is not lost in confusion of trees and brush. Once sight is aimed at game, scope is pointed directly at your target. Price: $4.90.

Bench Shooting Tripod—This stand is the choice for target range spotting. Provides stable base for even the highest-power spotting scopes. Comes complete with adjustable saddlehead. Price: $39.20.

Tree Mount—Screws into tree trunk, or clamps to tree branch, stump, or fence post to provide stable base for glassing distant objects in comfort. Price: $19.60.

Window Mount—Clamps quickly to window glass of car or truck to provide a steady hold for spotting scopes. Adapts to standard saddlehead or universal mount. Price: $8.

REMINGTON ARMS CO., INC.

As one of the largest manufacturers of firearms and ammunition in the world, Remington needs no introduction to the American outdoors person. Their vast line includes shotguns in semiautomatic, pump, and over/under models for field, trap, skeet, and slugs; centerfire rifles in bolt action, semiautomatic, and pump, chambered for all popular calibers; rimfire rifles in bolt-action, auto-loading, and pump models; and such specialized arms as their bench rest rifles and target rifles chambered for centerfire or rimfire cartridges.

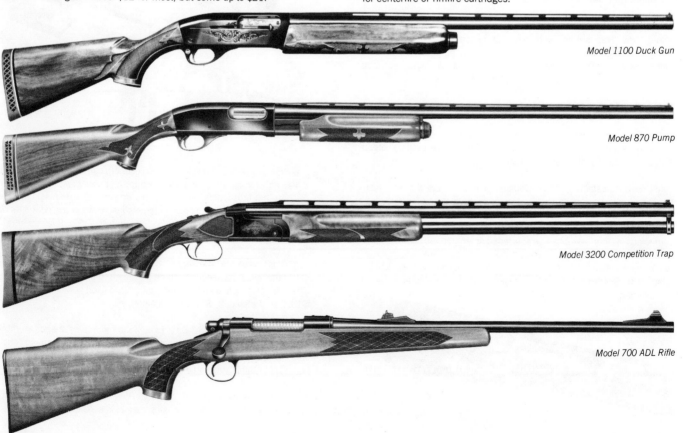

Model 1100 Duck Gun

Model 870 Pump

Model 3200 Competition Trap

Model 700 ADL Rifle

Model 760 Pump

Model 581 Bolt-Action .22

Model 541-S "Custom" Sporter .22

"Nylon 66" MB

Their annual catalog is available free at gun shops and department stores throughout the country or can be ordered by mail.

Information about Remington's ammunition and components can be found in Chapter 5.

Model 1100 Automatic Magnum Duck Gun—This shotgun is specially designed for 3-inch magnum and 2¾-inch magnum shells in 12 and 20 gauge only. It is available with ventilated rib or plain barrel and comes with recoil pad. Left-hand version is available in 12 gauge only with ventilated rib. Barrel is special Remington proof steel. Receiver is solid steel, top matted with scrollwork on chrome-plated bolt and both sides of the receiver. Barrel lengths: 28 inches (20 gauge), 30 inches (12 gauge). Chokes: modified or full. Prices: $227.95 (plain barrel), $307.95 (vent rib).

Model 870 "Wingmaster" Field Grade Pump Shotgun—Rich appearance, perfect balance, and super-dependable, lightning-fast pump action have helped the "Wingmaster" to become a popular shotgun the world over. More than 2½ million have been sold since 1950. Stocks and fore-ends are enriched and protected by the scratch-resistant DuPont RK-W wood finish. Metal parts are vibrahoned to achieve a more lustrous finish and smoother action. Functional checkering, full beavertail fore-end, chrome-plated bolt, and white line spacers enhance overall styling. Right-hand versions are available in 12, 16, 20, 28, and .410 gauge. Left-hand models come in 12 or 20 gauge. A complete choice of barrel lengths and chokes, plain barrels or ventilated ribs are available. Prices: from $197.95.

Model 870 "Brushmaster" Deer Gun—Available in 12 or 20 gauge, this gun comes in standard or deluxe models with 20-inch barrels and rifle sights. Standard model in 12 gauge only has plain stock, grooved fore-end. Choke: improved cylinder. Prices: $193.95 (standard), $208.95 (deluxe).

Model 3200 Competition Trap and Skeet—Classics in their own time, the Remington Competition guns have all the superlative features that make them stand out. The wood is selected for figure and grain and is

offered in a choice of a subdued satin finish or DuPont RK-W high-gloss wood finish. Stock, side panels, grip, and fore-end are checkered in a distinctive design. Contoured pistol grip and presentation-style recoil pad. Gilded "Competition" scroll on frame. The trigger guard and fore-end latch plate are engraved. Monte Carlo trap and standard trap stocks are offered with 30- and 32-inch barrels. Skeet guns are offered with 26- or 28-inch barrels. Available in 12 gauge. Price: $950.

Model 700 ADL Deluxe Bolt-Action Rifle—Performance and value that last. Superlative features include a jeweled antibind bolt, shrouded bolt head, low-profile positive thumb-style safety, skip-line checkering, Monte Carlo stock with cheekpiece, checkered bolt knob, easily detachable sights, and a receiver drilled and tapped for scope mounts. Available in nine popular calibers. Prices: $224.95 (7mm Remington Magnum), $229.95 (all other calibers).

Model 700 BDL "Varmint Special"—Chambered in seven popular varmint calibers. Combines all of the performance of the BDL with a heavy barrel for extreme accuracy at all ranges. Equipped with scope bases (no sights). The 700 BDL Varmint rifle chambered for .308 Winchester makes an excellent metallic silhouette rifle and meets the required specifications. Barrel length: 24 inches. Weights: 8¾ pounds (.308), 9 pounds (all other calibers). Price: $274.95.

Model 788 Centerfire Bolt-Action Rifle—A no-nonsense big-game rifle at a no-nonsense price. An incredibly fast lock time is one reason for this rifle's accuracy. A good value to start with, and lasting value in the long run, make the 788 one of the great hand-me-downs. Features include Monte Carlo stock, serrated thumb-style safety, easily removable clip magazine, blade front sight and fully adjustable U-notch rear sight. Receiver drilled and tapped for scope mounts. Left-hand versions available in 6mm Remington and .308 Winchester. Right-hand versions available in six popular calibers. Prices: $159.95 (right), $164.95 (left).

Model 742 "Woodsmaster"—The standard version autoloading centerfire rifle is available in five popular hunting calibers. Stock and tapered fore-end are distinctively checkered. White line spacers enhance ap-

Model 40-XBBR Bench-Rest Centerfire Rifle

pearance. Sights are removable. Receiver drilled and tapped for scope mounts. Barrel length: 22 inches. Overall: 42 inches. Price: $257.95.

Model 760 "Gamemaster" Pump-Action Rifle—When the situation calls for a fast second shot, the smooth pump action of the 760 allows you to operate the action while keeping the rifle in a natural shooting position. Styled for fast handling, the 760 is the only pump-action rifle available in .30-06. Also available in 6mm Remington, .243 Winchester, .270 Winchester, and .308 Winchester calibers. Barrel length: 22 inches. Overall: 42 inches. Price: $244.95.

Model 40-XBBR Bench-Rest Centerfire Rifles—Bolt-action, single shot with wide, squared fore-end for stability. Available with 20- or 26-inch stainless steel barrel to meet I.B.S. and N.B.R.S.A. 10½-pound and 13½-pound class specifications. Features a trigger adjustable from 1½ to 3½ pounds. Special 2-ounce trigger available for $55 extra. Selected walnut stock. Price: $480.

Model 40-XR Rimfire Position Rifle—For the serious competitor who wants a fine rimfire position rifle. Two-way vertically adjustable butt plate. Exclusive loading platform provides straight-line feeding with no shaved bullets. Meets International Shooting Union requirements for standard rifle. Caliber: .22 Rimfire. Price: $325.

Model 581 Bolt-Action Rimfire Rifle—Practical and economical .22-caliber rifle with strong, safe, dependable action. Extra-fast lock time increases accuracy. Full-size Monte Carlo stock. Five-shot removable clip magazine handles Short, Long, or Long Rifle Cartridges. Extra five- and ten-shot clips available. Also available in left-hand version. Barrel length: 24 inches. Prices: $79.95 (right), $84.95 (left).

Model 541-S "Custom" Sporter Bolt-Action Rimfire Rifle—This rifle is a classic 22, sure to become a great hand-me-down. It is designed along the line of its big-game cousins, with similar features and outstanding value. Features include American walnut stock; thin pistol grip; fine-line checkering; matching rosewood colored fore-end tip, grip cap, and checkered butt plate; DuPont RK-W wood finish. Decorative scrollwork engraving enhances appearance of specially blued receiver and bowed trigger guard. Adjustable match-type trigger; low profile safety; artillery style bolt, with six locking lugs; double extractors. Receiver grooved for tip-off scope mounts. Price: $199.95.

"Nylon 66" MB Rifle—Stock and fore-end of durable, supertough DuPont Zytel structural nylon in Mohawk Brown. Blued barrel and receiver cover. Tubular magazine feeds through buttstock and has a capacity of fourteen Long Rifle cartridges. Barrel length: 19⅜ inches. Overall: 38½ inches. Weight: 4 pounds. Price: $84.95.

Model 572 BDL Deluxe Pump-Action Rimfire Rifle—A favorite pump-action 22. The pump action works easily with speed and smoothness. By removing the inner magazine tube, the pump action converts to a single-shot rifle. Replacing the tube makes it a repeater again. Features include custom checkering, DuPont RK-W finish, and big-game-type

sights. Trim design and fine balance. Barrel length: 23 inches. Overall: 42 inches. Weight: 5½ pounds. Price: $114.95.

Model XP-100 Long-Range Pistol—A unique single-shot, centerfire, bolt-action pistol chambered for the 221 Remington "Fire Ball" cartridge. Designed to reduce whip, jump, and recoil. Extremely accurate. One-piece stock of DuPont "Zytel" nylon. Universal grip fits left- or right-handed shooters. Internal fore-end cavities for addition of weights. Match-type grooved trigger. Ventilated rib. Rifle-type rear sight. Two-position thumb safety. Receiver drilled and tapped for scope mounts. Barrel length: 10½ inches. Overall: 16¾ inches. Weight: 3¾ pounds. Price: $184.95.

SAFARILAND LTD., INC.

This is another company offering a large line of leather products for shooters. They manufacture some outstanding leather holsters, belts, slings, cases, and accessories that will be of interest to many of you. Some are for black-powder arms, while others are for modern weapons.

Civil War Holsters—Designed by the early craftsman for all cap and ball black-powder revolvers. All detailing is authentic and, just as it was then, the front flap is held securely over a solid brass retainer. This holster is to be worn in the classic "reverse draw" position. Features a 2-inch stitched-on belt loop, and the leather is Safariland's finest grade. Available in black or brown, CS or US insignia. Price: $23.95.

US or CS Cap Pouch—Authentically reproduced and detailed, this pouch was designed to carry the cap portion of a soldier's ammunition. Available in black or brown, CS or US insignia. Price: $10.95.

Civil War Shoulder Bag—Has three separate compartments and was designed to be worn loose over the shoulder. Construction is of Safariland's finest top-grain cowhide and high-quality standards. Its uses are as varied as your imagination. Available in black or brown, US or CS insignia. Price: $39.95.

Model 82 Gun Rugs—Safariland offers rich, fully lined gun rugs in 7-, 11-, 14-, and 17-inch sizes to accommodate most handguns. The outside is cut from the finest suede and each rug is lined with supple flannel padding. Prices: $7.95, $8.95, $9.50, $10.95.

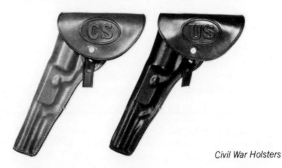

Civil War Holsters

SAVAGE ARMS DIVISION

Another major firearms manufacturer, Savage also produces such familiar rifles and shotguns as Anschutz, Fox, and Stevens. Their line includes rimfire and centerfire rifles for hunting and target shooting and pump, side-by-side, over/under, and single-barrel shotguns.

Anschutz Model 1413 Super Match 54—The superb Super Match 54 action is satin smooth, with a large loading platform and a single-stage adjustable trigger. There's a new combination hand stop/sling swivel, hook butt plate for right- and left-handed use and an adjustable cheekpiece. Other outstanding features are an adjustable butt plate with lateral and cant adjustments, plus horizontal and vertical. There's the new No. 4840 adjustable palm rest, adjustable pistol grip base, and hand-filling beavertail fore-end. Caliber: .22 Long Rifle. Barrel length: 27½ inches. Overall: 50 inches. Weight: 15½ pounds. Price: $626.45.

Anschutz Model 1413

Anschutz Models 1433

Savage Model 99-CD

Savage Model 2400

Savage Model 24-C

Savage Model 333-T

Savage Model 30 Field Grade

Stevens Model 72 "Crackshot"

Anschutz Models 1433 and 1533 Center Fire Rifles—These bolt-action rifles are of true European styling that will appeal to the most serious American shooters. These excellent rifles feature stocks of one-piece select walnut—Mannlicher type with cheekpiece. Hand-cut checkering. European oil finish. Double-set or single-stage trigger is optional. Receivers grooved for scope mounts and drilled and tapped for bases. These little sporters boast all the custom features as well as Anschutz traditional quality. Available on special order only. Calibers: .22 Hornet (M. 1433) and .222 Remington (M. 1533). Barrel length: 19¾ inches. Overall: 39 inches. Weight: 6½ pounds. Price: $517.

Savage Model 99-CD Lever Action Rifle—Time-tested design plus added features that will appeal to the most serious shooter are combined in the 99-CD detachable box magazine rifle. As a final touch, the Savage Signature medallion pistol grip cap highlights the top of the Savage lever-action line. Features include a select walnut stock with a high Monte Carlo cheekpiece and deeply fluted comb. Stock and grooved fore-end are hand checkered and have swivels. Detachable hooded ramp front sight, adjustable rear sight. Truly a long-awaited addition to the Savage tradition of quality. Barrel length: 22 inches. Overall: 41¾ inches. Weight: 8¼ pounds. Calibers: .250 Savage, .243, and .308. Price: $249.50.

Savage Model 99-358 Lever Action Rifle—Much recent demand for a rifle in a caliber with brush-bucking performance has necessitated the introduction of this new rifle. A fast-handling rotary magazine rifle with straight stock, recoil pad, grooved fore-end for firmer control, fitted with swivel studs. Barrel length: 22 inches. Overall: 41¾ inches. Weight: 7 pounds. Caliber: .358 Winchester. Price: $225.

Savage Model 111 "Chieftain" Rifle—Time-tested design plus added features will make this bolt-action rifle appeal to the serious hunter. Features include a detachable box magazine, select walnut stock with high Monte Carlo cheekpiece and hand-checkered pistol grip and fore-end, a deep gloss finish, quick adjustable sling strap with swivels, detachable hooded ramp front sight, and adjustable rear sight. Available in five popular hunting calibers. Barrel lengths: 22 inches (standard calibers), 24 inches (Magnum). Overall: 43 and 45 inches. Weights: 7½ to 8¼ pounds. Prices: $240 (standard), $250 (7mm Magnum).

Savage Model 2400 Shotgun/Rifle Combination—This high-quality combination gun is truly a quality, custom-grade firearm with turkey or big-game capabilities. Features include select walnut stock, recoil pad, highly polished and blued metal, selective single trigger, solid matted rib with blade front and folding leaf rear sights. Suitable for scope mounting. Barrel length: 23½ inches. Overall: 40½ inches. Weight: 7½ pounds. Gauges/Calibers: 12/.222, and 12/.308. Price: $550.

Savage Model 24-C Camper's Companion—At 5¾ pounds, it's 1 pound lighter and 4 inches shorter than other 24s. When stored in special case, it measures just 5×22 inches. The case has handles for carrying and thongs for tying to pack or saddle. Trap door butt plate flips out for quick access to a shotgun shell and ten .22 cartridges. Case included. Gauge/Caliber: 20/.222. Price: $107.50.

Savage Model 242 Shotgun—This new .410 gauge over/under sports a deluxe stock and fore-end of select walnut. Has two-way top opening lever, swings either way for right- or left-handed use. Ideal for pest control or small-game hunting. Chambers: 3 inches. Barrel length: 24 inches. Chokes: full/full. Overall: 40 inches. Weight: 7 pounds. Price: $124.50.

Savage Model 333-T Trap Gun—When a shotgun is fired as much as most trap guns, dimensions, balance, and dependability are paramount. The 333-T excels in these areas. It has a rugged top breech lock-up, similar to that of guns selling for much more. The finely polished surfaces, both inside and out, assure smooth operation. Other features include an extra-wide ventilated rib, selective trigger, extractors, manual top tang safety, recoil pad with Monte Carlo stock. Wood is select walnut. Barrels: 30 inches. Overall: 47 inches. Chokes: I.M. and F. Weight: 7¾ pounds. Price: $525.

Savage Model 30 Field Grade Pump Shotgun—The Field Grade offers the same basic quality as the more deluxe 30X. Trim solid-steel receiver houses a fast, dependable action. From the handfilling walnut slide handle to the checkered walnut stock with fluted comb, the 30 Field Grade is a pleasure to handle and shoot. Interchangeable barrels available. Comes in 12, 20, and .410 gauge. Varied choice of barrel lengths and chokes. Price: $147.

Fox Model B Double Barrel Shotgun—For sheer beauty of design, fine balance and fast handling, nothing equals a double—the traditional sporting gun. And there isn't anything like the Fox B. Standard equipment includes ventilated rib, checkered select walnut stock with fluted comb, beavertail fore-end, and two triggers for split-second choice of chokes. Gauges: 12, 20, .410, with 3-inch chambers in 12- and 20-gauge models. Varied choice of barrel lengths and chokes. Price: $199.50.

Stevens Model 94-Y Youth Model Shotgun—Top lever opening. Has shorter stock with rubber recoil pad. Barrel: 26 inches. Overall: 40½ inches. Weight: 5½ pounds. Gauges: 20 and .410. Chokes: modified (20) and full (.410). Price: $60.50.

Stevens Model 72 "Crackshot" Rifle—This unique falling-block action is a pleasure to handle, shoot, or simply admire. It has balance, smooth functioning, and safety. This popular .22 rifle is truly in the great Stevens tradition. It features an octagonal barrel, case-hardened frame, walnut stock, and fore-end with oil finish. Barrel: 22 inches. Overall: 37 inches. Weight: 4½ pounds. Price: $75.

Stevens Model 89 Rifle—This little single shot has the balance and feel of a traditional Western carbine. Featuring Western-style lever action with a rugged Martini-type breech block, automatic ejection. Hammer must be cocked by hand, independent of the lever, prior to firing. Ideal for that young beginner. Barrel: 18½ inches. Overall: 35 inches. Weight: 5 pounds. Caliber: .22 Rimfire. Price: $51.50.

SHERIDAN PRODUCTS, INC.

For the shooting pleasure of young and old alike, Sheridan offers several models of pneumatic and gas-powered rifles, as well as a selection of air gun accessories and ammunition.

Blue Streak Model CB Pneumatic Rifle—A superbly crafted rifle that meets the demands of discriminating target or small-game shooters. Full-length Mannlicher stock is made of genuine hand-rubbed walnut with a proper heft and balance. All working parts are precision engineered to assure accuracy and dependability—and backed by Sheridan's reputation as the leader in the pneumatic rifle industry. Pump action permits the shooter to determine the exact amount of velocity required for each shot. Single shot, 5mm (.20 caliber). Equipped with standard open sights. Price: $63.75.

Silver Streak Model F Gas-Powered Rifle—In answer to an increasing demand Sheridan now has available a companion line to their famous

pneumatics for those who enjoy or need faster shooting or who can't or just don't like to pump up an air rifle. Lightweight and compact. Standard open sight. CO₂ powered, bolt-action, single shot. Price: $66.75.

"333" Targetrap—Newly designed, this Targetrap is ideal for indoor and outdoor use with NRA air rifle targets AR-1 and AR-2, and pistol target B-32. The 6×7-inch opening will also accommodate many other targets. Also usable for standard velocity .22 Long Rifle practice. Features include wall hanger and flat base for placement anywhere, handle for portability, sturdy construction with durable enamel finish. Dimensions: 13½ inches high, 7¼ inches wide, 5 inches deep. Price: $26.

SMITH'S GAME CALLS

This company produces a number of game calls and game-calling instruction records, as well as hunting accessories and a line of inexpensive inflatable crow decoys.

Call of the Wild Caller

Call of the Wild Game and Bird Caller—Bring game to your camera or gun with this all-transistor, high-powered record player, game and bird caller. Four-speed, weighted turntable with dual-range governor-controlled motor. Operates on flashlight batteries. Has provision for microphone for calling. Speaker equipped with special mounting bracket and 25-foot cord. Built-in record holder will not scratch records. Available with either inside or outside volume-control switch. Strong steel cabinet with baked enamel finish. Price: $142.50.

ST-17 Box Turkey Call—This call will imitate the gobbler on one side and the hen calls on the other side. By shaking this box call the imitation gobble of the tom turkey can be made. This call comes complete with a sliding silencer to keep the call quiet while you walk through the woods. It also has a built-in chalk holder. Price: $9.95.

Inflatable Crow Decoys—Enjoy your next crow shoot with these inflatable decoys. It's no longer necessary to carry a bulky sack of decoys; a complete set can now be carried in your hunting coat. Equipped with heavy wire legs. Slightly oversize for better visibility. Prices: $1.50 each, $8.10/half-dozen, $15/dozen.

Blue Streak Model CB
Silver Streak Model F

SMITH & WESSON

Horace Smith and Daniel Baird Wesson first joined in partnership in 1852 and pioneered many developments in sporting arms and accessories. In 1854, this team invented the rimfire cartridge, and for years to follow all rimfire ammunition manufactured in the United States was produced under license from Smith & Wesson. Since then, many Smith & Wesson rounds—from .22 rimfire to .357 Magnum—have become standards among American sportsmen.

The company is best known, though, for its fine handguns. Smith & Wesson handguns have been manufactured since the 1850s, and today the company offers twenty-nine different models of revolvers and pistols. Additionally, the Smith & Wesson line includes shotguns, air guns, and hunting and shooting accessories.

Model 14 K-38 Masterpiece—This is a favorite handgun of many sportsmen. It features a microhoned barrel and mirror blue finish and has checkered walnut service stocks with S&W monograms. Front sight is a ⅛-inch plain Patridge type. Rear sight is the S&W Micrometer Click Sight that's adjustable for windage and elevation. Barrel lengths: 6 and 8⅜ inches. Overall: 11⅛ inches with 6-inch barrel. Weights loaded: 38½ and 42½ ounces. Caliber: .38 S&W Special. Capacity: six rounds. Price: $153.

Model 29 .44 Magnum—This powerful revolver is favored by many handgun hunters. It features the smooth and reliable S&W double action as well as the crisp single action demanded for long-range accuracy. It has a checkered target-type hammer and grooved target-type trigger. Stocks are special oversize target type of checkered Goncalo Alves, with S&W monograms. Sights are the same as the Model 14, with a white outline notch on the rear sight. Barrel lengths: 4, 6½, and 8⅜ inches. Overall: 11⅞ inches with 6-inch barrel. Weights: 43, 47, and 51½ ounces. Capacity: six rounds. Finishes: blue or nickel. Prices: $268 (4 or 6½ inches), $276 (8⅜ inches).

Model 34 .22/32 Kit Gun—Here's a great little handgun for small-game hunting, target shooting, or plinking. It has all the famous S&W features. Front sight is a ¹/₁₀-inch serrated ramp; rear is a S&W Micrometer Click Sight, adjustable for windage and elevation. Checkered walnut service stocks are available with round or square butt. Barrel lengths: 2 and 4 inches. Overall: 8 inches with 4-inch barrel. Weight: 24½ ounces with 4-inch barrel. Caliber: .22 LR. Capacity: six rounds. Price: $137.50.

Model 78G Pellet Pistol—Here is a quality air pistol that can be enjoyed by the entire family. The superior craftsmanship of this popular CO₂-powered pellet pistol provides the high performance and safety features expected from Smith & Wesson. A copy of the famous S&W Model 41 .22 caliber Autoloading Target Pistol, it has the same balance and design, the same heft and feel. And within pellet gun range, accuracy isn't much different either. Two power settings make this pistol adaptable to a wide variety of uses from basement target shooting to long-range plinking and small-game hunting. It has a positive cross-bolt safety, Patridge, front sight, and fully adjustable rear sight. Barrel length: 8½ inches. Weight: 42 ounces. Caliber: .22 Pellet. Velocities: 420 feet per second (high), 320 feet per second (low). Price: $41.

Model 1000 Autoloading Shotgun—Behind the good looks, the superb balance, swing, and pointing characteristics of this great shotgun is a superior design with unmatched features that have been proven in season after season of trouble-free shooting performance. Whether your choice is 12 gauge or 20 gauge, the lightweight, 2¾-inch chambered Model 1000 is really four guns in one. Easily interchangeable barrels, in five chokes and four lengths provide the Model 1000 owner with a full range of shooting pleasure, from skeet to white wings to deer. Barrels are proof-tested chrome molybdenum steel. Receiver is lightweight, high tensile strength aluminum alloy, with scroll engraving on both sides. Stock and fore-end are select American walnut. Barrel lengths: 26 to 30 inches. Weights: from 6½ to 8 pounds. Prices: from $287.95.

Model 14 K-38 Masterpiece
Model 34 .22/32 Kit Gun
Model 78G .22 Pellet Pistol

STURM, RUGER & CO., INC.

This company is one of the major American firearms manufacturers, producing traditionally styled single-action revolvers, cap and ball revolvers, double-action revolvers, automatic pistols, popular bolt-action rifles, autoloading rifles, and single-shot rifles.

Ruger firearms are stocked and sold by thousands of dealers throughout the United States and Canada, and in many foreign countries.

.44 Caliber Old Army—This is a top-quality, black-powder, cap and ball revolver designed by Ruger engineers and manufactured of superior materials. Experienced black-powder shooters and hunters who have tested and used the Old Army have been lavish in their praise for this percussion revolver that has all the features everyone has been asking for. It features stainless steel nipples for standard caps, American walnut grips, cylinder frame and cylinder of chrome-moly steel, coil springs throughout, adjustable target rear sight, and ramp front sight. It is available in high-polished blue finish or stainless steel. Barrel length: 7½ inches. Weight: 46 ounces. Prices: $125 (blue), $175 (stainless steel).

New Model Super Blackhawk—One of the world's truly great handguns, the Super Blackhawk is widely regarded as one of the finest, most advanced single-action revolvers ever produced. Exactingly designed and built to take advantage of the power of the .44 Magnum cartridge, the Super Blackhawk provides the hunter with a capability for special situations. Features include walnut grips, high-polished blue finish, adjustable rear sight, and ramp front sight. Barrel length: 7½ inches. Overall: 13⅜ inches. Weight: 48 ounces. Price: $180.

New Model Blackhawk—The mechanism of the New Model Blackhawk and Super Blackhawk is based on the same unique (patents pending) mechanical principles as the New Model Super Single Six. The massive Blackhawks, however, are designed and engineered expressly for use with modern centerfire revolver cartridges. In the New Model single actions, the hammer has only two positions—all the way forward, and fully cocked. The firing mechanism includes a transfer bar—a component usually found only in the double-action revolver. The loading gate, when opened, depresses the upper arm of the gate detent spring which in turn lowers the cylinder latch, allowing the cylinder to be turned manually for loading or unloading. When the gate is closed, the arm of the gate detent spring returns to its upper position and allows the cylinder latch to be engaged and disengaged by the hammer in the normal way. The New Model Blackhawk features walnut grips, adjustable rear sight, and ramp

Ruger Old Army Revolver
Ruger New Model Blackhawk
Ruger Standard .22 Automatic Pistol
Ruger No. 1 Light Sporter

front sight. Barrel lengths: 4⁴/₈, 6½, and 7½ inches. Calibers: .30 Carbine, .357 Magnum, .357/9mm Parabellum Convertible, .41 Magnum, .45 Colt, .45 Colt/.45 A.C.P. Convertible. Prices: $154 (Convertible models), $164.50 (.357 stainless steel), $134.50 (all others).

Standard .22 Automatic Pistol—Designed and constructed to be the choice of knowledgeable shooters, this autoloading pistol is unsurpassed for reliable performance, balance, and all-around handling qualities. In an independent laboratory test, a Ruger Standard Model was fired 41,000 times with no malfunctions, no parts failures, and with no measurable wear. Grips are Butaprene-type hard rubber with exceptional impact resistance, black gloss finish, and sharp diamond checkering. Features include a detachable, nine-shot clip magazine; grooved trigger; square-notch rear sight; Patridge-type front sight, and polished and blued finish. Barrel lengths: 4¾ and 6 inches. Overall: 8¾ and 10 inches. Price: $87.50.

No. 1 Single Shot Rifle—This rifle combines modern, engineered design with the luxury of a finely finished and closely fitted mechanism. Beyond the physical characteristics of the firearm itself is the challenge of a single shot—it is the type of firearm that puts to a test the skill and marksmanship of the hunter, and which requires practice and presence of mind to master. The action of this rifle belongs in the under-lever, falling-block category and follows in many respects the Farquharson design. In all mechanical details, however, the Ruger No. 1 action is completely new and is in no sense a replica of any older action. Particular care is taken in the fitting and finishing of the No. 1. The contours and dimensions of the stock have been carefully worked out to combine correct sporting appearance with the high comb required for use with telescopic sights. All metal parts are polished and blued with special care, and receiver and stock are individually fitted. The receiver and all action parts are made of hardened alloy steels and the functioning of the action is practically frictionless. Five different models available are the Light Sporter, Medium Sporter, Standard Rifle, Special Varminter, and Tropical Rifle. The No. 1 is chambered for a complete range of popular calibers from .22/250 to .458 Winchester Magnum. Prices: $295 (all models), $170 (barreled action, blued), $145 (action only).

M-77 Bolt Action Rifle—In creating this rifle, the key objectives have been quality and performance, regardless of cost. However, design and engineering experience, plus the application of advanced manufacturing techniques have made it possible to achieve these objectives and, at the same time, to offer the Model 77 at a price that makes it an outstanding value. With many unique and significant advances in design and construction, the M-77 offers an excellent standard of performance and reliability while preserving the classic tradition of form and balance. Superior strength has been conclusively proven in extensive field and laboratory tests where the stresses imposed by actual shooting have been duplicated, multiplied, and accurately measured. The M-77 is available in two action lengths—Short Stroke and Magnum. The scope mount bases are built into the solid steel of the receiver. They are actually part of the rifle and do not depend on small screws and separate mounts to hold the scope securely in alignment. A ramp-type, gold bead front sight and folding leaf adjustable rear sight are standard on the basic model. The barrel/action assembly of the Model 77 is precisely fitted to the stock and is secured by the exclusive (patented) Ruger diagonal-front-mounting-screw bedding system. Stock is American walnut, selected for grain, and handsomely and durably finished, with sharp-diamond hand checkering. The M-77 is available in most popular calibers from .22/250 to .458 Winchester Magnum. Prices: from $230 to $370 (M-77 rifles), $172.50 to $237.50 (M-77 barreled actions, blued).

TASCO SALES, INC.

Now a major producer of sportsmen's optics, Tasco has added greatly to its line of rifle scopes, spotting scopes, and other optical instruments over the years. Their optical line for the shooter is among the most complete to be found. They produce scopes for .22 rifles, centerfire rifles, and even for muzzle-loaders. They have a complete range of fixed- and variable-power scopes and a variety of spotting scopes from which to choose.

#632V Scope
#705 Scope
#1860 Scope

Tasco #632V Utility 4X Scope—Fully coated eight-lens optical system. Opti-Centered with 30/30 reticle and attached ring mounts. HUALF/MINUTE CLICK STOPS. Fits all .22 rifles with grooved receivers. Fogproofed. Haze filter caps included. Price: $46.95.

Tasco #630V Zoom Utility 3X–7X Scope—Target marksman or small-game hunter, you'll always be on target with the Zoom Utility. Fully coated eleven-lens optical system. Opti-Centered 30/30 range-finding reticle, parallax corrected, half-minute click stops. Fogproofed. Attached ring mounts fit all .22-caliber rifles with grooved receivers. Haze filter caps included. Price $42.95.

Tasco #627W Super Marksman 3X–9X Scope—Now you can hunt with a zoom-powered rifle scope that's waterproofed against all weather conditions. No matter where the game is, no matter what the weather is, the Super Marksman will do the job. A large 40mm objective lens centers your target with edge-to-edge crispness in an Opti-Centered 30/30 range-finding reticle. Fully coated ten-lens system is shockproof. Fogproofed by nitrogen. Quarter-minute click stops. Haze filter caps. Price: $74.95.

Tasco #619W 4X–12X Zoom Scope—Here's Tasco's top-performance zoom-action rifle scope. Preset the fast focusing ring on the large 40mm objective bell from 25 yards to infinity. When you've spotted your game, the zoom action smoothly moves the image from 4-power through 12-power without losing its crisp focus. Tasco's exclusive single plane 30/30 range-finding reticle gives you distance information to help you make your best shot. Durable one-piece construction, guaranteed fog-proof, waterproof, shockproof, and anodized. This ten-lens system has quarter-minute click stops, Opti-Centered reticle, and haze filter caps. Price: $109.95.

Tasco #702W 6X–18X Zoom Scope—A lightweight, powerful zoom scope with cross hair reticle, features quarter-minute click stops and is waterproof, fogproof, shockproof, and anodized. Price: $129.95.

Tasco #705 6X–18X Target Scope—Fully coated ten-lens optical system. Opti-Centered cross hair reticle. This variable target scope has powers of 6, 8, 12, 14, 16, and 18 with clear images at all powers. When used with base spacing of 7 inches, it has quarter-minute click stops. Target style mounts fit standard available bases. Recoil spring, clamp ring, and screw-in dust caps are standard equipment. Price: $199.95.

Tasco #1860 Early American Styled Rifle Scope—This is a long, solid brass, 4X, ¾-inch tube. In 1860, a telescope for rifles was already a familiar shooting aid. Today, Tasco presents the return of this original in its 1860 solid brass model. Faithfully reproduced in detail, this scope has the advantages of today's improved optics—full coating, fog-proofing, and more efficient mounting system. Length: 32½ inches. Fits Hawken, Plains, Pennsylvania Half-Stock, F.I.E. Zoauve, and Kentucky rifles. Price: $159.95.

Tasco #1903 Early American Styled Rifle Scope—Similar to above in a lighter and more compact design. Length: 18½ inches. Fits Savage Model 72 and Gallagher. Price: $119.95.

Tasco #8T Spotting Scope—If you demand a razor-sharp target image, you'll like this spotting scope with its large 60mm objective lens, revolving turret, and four par-focal variable power eye lenses in 15X, 30X, 40X, and 60X that keep the image in focus. Camera tripod adaptor. Resolving power: 2.5 seconds. Styrofoam fitted and gift packed. Price: $279.95.

Tasco #22T Zoom Spotting Scope—Big 40mm objective lens for extra-bright and extra-sharp images. Color corrected, fully coated lenses, and wide field of view in this 15X–45X zoom scope. Sturdy tripod has rubber-tipped 8-inch folding legs and pan head tension adjusting screw. Price: $69.95.

Tasco Scope Guide—The lightweight Tasco rifle scope collimator kit uses the internal optics of the rifle scope in conjunction with a light-gathering lens built into each of the included scope aperture caps. There are separate kits for centerfire or rimfire and air rifles. While sighting through the scope, slight thumb changes for the windage and elevation adjustments bring the sighting grid pattern and reticle into quick alignment. The pocket-size kits are compact and easy to use for those unexpected, on-the-spot readjustments. Price: $9.95.

THOMPSON/CENTER ARMS

In addition to manufacturing several superb muzzle-loading firearms, T/C also produces the ultramodern Contender pistol, as well as shooting accessories and parts for their black-powder firearms.

Contender Hunting Handgun—A perfect companion for those secluded places—for the woods, the open fields, the saddle, the deer camps—the Contender packs snugly on the hip and does the job of pistol, rifle, and shotgun all rolled into one. Made to the highest standards of American manufacture, the Contender is a true sports pistol. It was designed expressly for those sportsmen who take their shooting seriously and for the professionals—the trappers, hunters, and guides who require a small, high-performance firearm that is dependable under all conditions. Contender offers the simplicity and strength of a single-shot, break-open design, coupled with the unique features of interchangeable barrels in a wide selection of calibers—both rimfire and centerfire, from the .22 right up to the heavy magnums. Barrels available currently number twenty-three. Grips and fore-ends are of select American walnut. Standard models have Patridge rear sight with ramp front sight. Bull barrel models are available with or without sights. Barrel: 10 inches. Overall: 13½ inches. Weight: 43 ounces with standard barrel. Prices: from $155. Extra barrels: from $57 to $67.

Lobo 1½X Handgun Scope—A mighty 7¾-inch midget, the Lobo was designed for those Contender owners who take their handgun shooting seriously. Manufactured to T/C specifications, this handgun scope will stand up to the jarring recoil of the .44 Magnum and the other heavy calibers offered in the Contender. Price: $44.50.

Patriot Pistol—Made in America to American standards of manufacture, the Patriot is a composite design. Its carefully selected features were inspired by traditional gallery- and dueling-type pistols. With discretion, modern metals and manufacturing methods have been used to improve the shooting qualities of the piece, yet it still retains its full flavor of antiquity. Featuring a hooked breech, double-set triggers, first-grade American walnut, adjustable (Patridge-type) target sights, solid brass trim, beautifully decorated and color-case-hardened lock with a small dolphin-shaped hammer, the Patriot is geared to win the heart of the most selective shooter. Caliber: .45. Weight: 36 ounces. Price: $125.

Contender Pistol with Lobo Scope

Hawken Rifle

Hawken Rifle—Similar to the famous Rocky Mountain rifles made during the early 1800s, the Hawken is intended for serious shooting. Precision rifled for ultimate accuracy, the Hawken is available in cap-lock or flint-lock models. Featuring a hooked breech, double-set triggers, first-grade American walnut, adjustable hunting sights, solid brass trim, beautifully decorated and color-case-hardened lock, it captures the romance of the original. Best of all, it's made to American standards of manufacture. Calibers: .45 and .50. Prices: $205 (cap lock), $215 (flint lock).

TREAD CORP.

The wise outdoorsman will properly insure all outdoor gear against theft, and in the event of a burglary should get something close to the market value for any gear stolen and determined irretrievable, if the insurance has been kept up to date and the coverage has been increased according to the rate of inflation. But all the insurance in the world won't protect equipment from theft. A Treadlock Security Chest will.

As your insurance agent will tell you, firearms are "target" items in any burglary—they are number one on the thief's shopping list. So if you value those guns, you had better have them securely locked away.

Treadlock Model 600 Security Chest—The new upright version of the original Treadlock Security Chest provides vertical storage for all your valuables. Built like a miniature Fort Knox, it provides positive security for your home or office. It comes equipped with vertical felt-faced mountings for twelve rifles or shotguns, plus an easily accessible storage shelf at the top of the cabinet. Three narrow shelves are also built into the reinforced steel door. Features include 12-gauge welded steel construction, two-point sliding bar lock secured by one high-security pad-

Model 600 Gun Chest

lock (included), three heavy-duty concealed hinges, and two-coat textured finish. For added security, the chest may be easily bolted to the floor or wall. Dimensions: 24 inches wide by 17 inches deep by 63 inches high. Weight: 225 pounds empty. Price: $412.

Treadlock Model 101 Horizontal Security Chest—Rifles and shotguns are placed on horizontal, removable racks in the top and bottom of the chest. When the chest is closed and the cushion (optional) is in place, the chest becomes a comfortable seat or bench for the family room or recreation room. Features include 12-gauge welded steel construction, sliding Steel-Pin locks with Medeco security inner cylinders that prevent tampering, welded piano-type hinge inside the chest, and two-coat texture finish. For added security the chest may be easily bolted to the floor. Dimensions: 52 inches long by 24 inches wide by 17 inches high. Weight: 180 pounds. Prices: $305 (chest), $32 (top rack), $29 (bottom rack), $61 (vinyl cushion).

TRIPLE-S DEVELOPMENT CO., INC.

This firm is manufacturing the new Wickliffe '76 Falling Block Single Shot Rifle. They offer standard and deluxe grade, and for the hobby gunsmith or the shooter who wants only a barreled action he can stock himself, these are available, too.

Wickliffe '76 Falling Block Rifle

Wickliffe '76 Falling Block Single Shot Rifle—A combination of beauty, balance, and rugged simplicity that made the early falling block single shots famous, the Wickliffe '76 is a product of the best of modern materials and firearms engineering. Assembled and finished to the highest standards of American gunsmithing, the Wickliffe '76 is a single-shot falling block that is more than just a copy. Barrel is diamond lapped, 4140 chrome moly. Select-grade American walnut Monte Carlo stock and semibeavertail forearm. Trigger is adjustable for over-travel and sear engagement. Butt plate and grip cap are of black tenite with white spacers. Choice of two barrel lengths and weights. Standard calibers: .22 Hornet, .22-250, .223, .243, and .308. Deluxe calibers: same as standard, plus option for .30-06. Rifle prices: $298 (standard), $372 (deluxe). Barreled action prices: $205, $216.

WEATHERBY, INC.

More than twenty years ago, Roy Weatherby designed the Weatherby Magnum rifle that has since become a favorite among hunters throughout the world. During the past two decades, the Weatherby line has come to include the extremely accurate Mark XXII .22 semi-automatic rifle, the Patrician pump shotgun, the Centurion automatic shotgun, the exquisite Regency O/U shotgun, and a number of hunting and shooting accessories.

In 1970, Weatherby introduced the Vanguard—a medium-priced rifle with all the quality craftsmanship and materials expected to be found in a Weatherby firearm.

Following is a sample of what can be found in the Weatherby catalog.

Mark V Weatherby Varmintmaster—This rifle is available in the popular .22/250 and the hot .224 Weatherby Magnum. The .224 is a new magnum cartridge designed specifically for varmint shooting. The only belted varmint cartridge in existence, it is not a modification of any other existing cartridge. The Varmintmaster action is a scaled-down version of the popular Mark V action, with six precision locking lugs. Stock is

Mark V Weatherby Varmintmaster

.300 Mark V Weatherby Magnum

Weatherby Vanguard

Weatherby Patrician Pump Shotgun

Weatherby Regency Field O/U

American walnut, hand-bedded to assure precision accuracy, with durable finish, quick detachable sling swivels, basketweave checkering, and Monte Carlo cheekpiece. Barrel lengths: standard 24 and 26 inches (#2 contour). Overall: 43¼ and 45¼ inches. Weight: 6½ pounds. Prices: $449.50 (standard barrel contour), $459.50 (#2 contour).

.300 Mark V Weatherby Magnum—The .300 Weatherby Magnum has a combination of more foot-pounds of energy, muzzle velocity, and flatter trajectory than any other .30 caliber rifle manufactured today. With four factory-loaded bullet weights ranging from 110 to 220 grains, it is also the most versatile Weatherby rifle on the market. This rifle features the Mark V action with nine locking lugs that have almost doubled the shear area of the lugs found on conventional bolt-action rifles. The cartridge case head is completely enclosed in the bolt and barrel. Barrel lengths: standard 24 and 26 inches (#2 contour). Overall: 44½ and 46½ inches. Weight: 7¼ pounds. Prices: $469.50 (standard contour), $479.50 (#2 contour).

.460 Mark V Weatherby Magnum—This is the rifle for the person who wants the absolute maximum in knockdown and stopping power for the world's largest and most dangerous game. In addition to other Mark V features, the .460 action includes hand honing, fully checkered bolt knob, damascened bolt and follower, and custom engraving·on floor plate. The .460 stock is of French walnut. Barrel length: 26 inches. Overall: 46½ inches. Weight: 10½ pounds. Price: $679.50.

Vanguard—Here is a medium-priced rifle with the Weatherby touch. The Vanguard action is based on one of the most highly acclaimed designs in the gun industry. The bolt face is recessed and it in turn is recessed into the barrel, forming three concentric bands of steel around the cartridge case head. In the event of cartridge case failure, the Vanguard also features a completely enclosed bolt sleeve to prevent escaping gases from blowing back through the bolt into the shooter's face. Other features include gas ejection ports, two massive bolt lugs, and a side-operated safety lever. The action has a knurled bolt knob and hinged floor plate. Receiver is drilled and tapped for scope installation. Trigger is fully adjustable, and hammer-forged barrel has a glass-smooth bore with optimum dimensional uniformity from breech to muzzle. Stock is select American walnut and is hand-bedded. It sports a Weatherby butt pad, rosewood fore-end tip and pistol grip cap, white line spacers, and the traditional Weatherby diamond inlay. The Vanguard is guaranteed to shoot a 1½-inch three-shot group at 100 yards, or it never leaves the factory. Calibers: .243, .25-06, .270, 7mm Magnum, .30-06, .300 Winchester Magnum. Barrel length: 24 inches. Overall: 44 inches (.243), 44½ inches (all others). Weight: 7 pounds 14 ounces. Price: $299.50.

Weatherby Mark XXII Deluxe—Here is the perfect companion to the Weatherby big-game rifles. Although lighter and handier, as befits a .22, it has the same basic feel and balance, the same pointing characteristics as the world-famous Weatherby Magnums. It is manufactured with flawless precision. The design and finish of wood and metal are of the highest order. Features include a single-shot selector, shotgun-type tang safety, nonskid rubber butt pad, single-pin takedown, Monte Carlo stock, and rosewood fore-end tip. Stock is of select walnut and is hand checkered. Receiver is precision grooved for dovetail scope mounts. The rifle is available in five-shot and ten-shot clip or fifteen-shot tubular magazine models. Action is semiautomatic. Caliber: .22 LR. Barrel length: 24 inches. Overall: 42¼ inches. Weight: 6 pounds. Prices: $179.50 (clip), $189.50 (tubular).

Weatherby Patrician Pump Shotgun—The Patrician establishes new criteria for speed, dependability, and beauty in a pump shotgun. The super-fast slide action operates on double rails for precision and reliability—no twists, no hang-ups. In every detail, this is a consummate example of the gunmaker's art. It is available in 12 gauge only, with 2¾-inch chamber, and comes in either field or trap models. Stock is fine-line checkered American walnut. Barrel lengths: 26, 28, and 30 inches. Chokes: skeet, improved cylinder, modified, full. Prices: $249.50 (field), $299.50 (trap).

Weatherby Centurion Automatic Shotgun—With unique "Floating Piston" action, the Centurion is a new concept in gas-operated automatics. The piston floats freely on the magazine tube, completely independent of every other part of the action. There is nothing to get out of alignment. The Centurion is a magnificent combination of modern concept and classic design. It is available in field or trap models, in 12 gauge only, with 2¾-inch chamber. Barrel lengths and chokes are same as the Patrician (above). Figured American walnut stock is hand checkered. Prices: $289.50 (field), $339.50 (trap).

Weatherby Regency Shotgun—This is perfection in a shotgun. The graceful Regency receiver houses a strong, reliable box lock action, yet it features side lock-type plates to enhance the beauty and carry through the fine floral engraving. The hinge pivots, the center of any O/U, are made of a special high-strength steel alloy. The locking system employs the time-tested Greener cross-bolt design. All internal parts are hand fitted and hand polished. Every Regency is equipped with a matted, ventilated rib and bead front sight. The trap model incorporates a wider rib with a center bead as well. Additionally, the trap barrels are mated with double ventilated side ribs. The beautifully hand-checkered American walnut stock features a contrasting rosewood grip cap and diamond inlay. The trap model is available either with or without the Monte Carlo stock. Other features include single selective trigger, selective automatic ejectors, and slide safety. Field and skeet models are available in 12 or 20 gauge; trap models are 12 gauge only. Chambers: 2¾ inches (12 gauge), 3 inches (20 gauge). Barrel lengths: 26, 28, 30, and 32 inches. Prices: $799.50 (field), $849.50 (trap).

W. R. WEAVER CO.

This company is one of the major manufacturers of telescopic sights for firearms—the very popular Weaver Scopes. They offer a complete line of scopes for .22s and high-power rifles, as well as their innovative Qwik-Point sight for shotguns, .22s, and centerfire rifles.

Weaver K4 Scope—An excellent scope for all-around hunting. Ample magnification for long shots in open country, but not too much for easy off-hand use close in. This 4X-power scope features quarter-minute graduated adjustments and a 26-foot field of view at 100 yards. It is available with a choice of five different reticles. Price: $72.50. Add $10 for dot reticle.

Weaver K6-W Scope—Wider-View narrows down the Big Country. With as much as 40 percent more viewing area than ordinary scopes, Weaver Wider-Views have been catching a wider part of the public eye each year. This 6X-power scope is for big-game hunting that requires long shots over wide open country, yet it's also an effective scope at moderate ranges with a field of view of 25 feet at 100 yards. It features quarter-

K 4 Scope
T10 Scope
Qwik-Point R-1

minute graduated adjustments, and is available with a choice of five reticles. Price: $97.50. Add $10 for dot reticle.

Weaver V7 Scope—This 2.5X–7X-power scope offers a well-balanced power range for the shooter who hunts both in brushy country and open country and needs a variety of magnifications. The V7, however, is no larger than most 4X-power scopes. Features include quarter-minute graduated adjustments, a big 40-foot field of view at 100 yards on lowest setting, and 15-foot at 7X. Available with a choice of five reticles. Price: $94.95. Add $10 for dot.

Weaver V9-W Scope—This is Weaver's most versatile Wider-View scope. With its 3X–9X range it adapts easily from an extremely effective varmint scope at higher powers to an all-range hunting scope. All you do is match power to terrain and set Range Focus at the 200-yard setting. Features include quarter-minute graduated adjustments, 36-foot field of view at 100 yards on 3X and 14-foot on 9X. Five reticles available. Price: $119.95. Add $10 for dot reticle.

Weaver T10 Scope—This 10X scope is for the silhouette shooter who wants more magnification without losing too much field of view. And it is popular with varmint and target shooters as well. Features include quarter-minute graduated adjustments and 11-foot field of view at 100 yards. Reticles: cross hair, Dual X, Range-Finder, and Dot. Price: $150. Add $10 for dot reticle.

Weaver Qwik-Point R-1—No magnification, but rather an optical sight that throws a blaze orange sight right out there on the target. For super-fast short-range shooting with centerfire rifles. Accurate in dim light or heavy cover. Focus is universal and eye relief is infinite. Adjustments are ¼-inch clicks at 40 yards. Price: $44.95.

Weaver Qwik-Point S-1—Keep both eyes open. Swing gun up naturally. Don't look at the gun or the Qwik-Point; look at the target. See the dot out there, not on the end of the barrel? No lining up of eye, bead, and target. A precise, fast sight for all kinds of shotgun shooting—birds, trap, and skeet, or deer hunting with slugs or buckshot. Price: $44.95.

Weaver Accu-Point—A new way to improve accuracy with most steel-ribbed shotguns. An optical sight—which means no magnification or restricted field of view—the Accu-Point has a blaze-orange dot that pinpoints the center of the target. A perfect trainer for beginners; an added advantage for experts. Price: $14.95

WESTERN GUNSTOCK MANUFACTURING CO.

Here's a company that specializes in stocks the way you want them, and they manufacture stocks for a variety of popular rifles and Remington XP-100 pistols. The selection of woods is large and five grades are available. The brochure is available for $1 (refundable) and color photos of any three stocks or blanks will be sent for another dollar.

Western "Thumbhole" Stocks—No cast-off, close grip with finger grooves. Wide fluted forearm, 2¾ to 3 inches wide. Nonfluted styles also available. Grades: 2X, 3X, 4X, and 5X. Prices: $48, $58, $76, $96. Walnut/maple lamination: $85. Exotic tip and cap: $90.

"Bullpup" Stocks—These stocks are made for the Remington 600 and XP100 actions using the XP100 trigger assembly. Most stocks will not have fore-end tops installed. Prices: same as Western "Thumbhole" stocks.

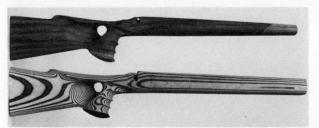

Western "Thumbhole" Stock

"XP100" Stock

"XP100" Stocks—Three styles available for standard-weight barrels, heavy barrels, and heavier for larger cartridges. The heavier stocks are priced higher due to special selection to accept heavy recoil. Grades: 3X, 4X, and 5X. Prices: $56, $76, $96. Walnut/maple laminated: $85.

WILLIAMS GUN SIGHT CO.

Williams is another company that every serious shooter and hobby gunsmith ought to be familiar with. They offer a large line of firearms accessories and sights of all kinds.

Their catalog is well worth the $1 price. We have found their service to be quick and efficient.

Williams Shotgun Ramp—For 12-, 16-, and 20-gauge shotguns, the new Williams shotgun ramp elevates the front sight so you can easily sight in your shotgun for slugs. And if the gun shoots high, as so many of them do, the ramp will correct it. Easily installed. Price: $4.75.

Williams QD Shotgun Swivels—Offered in a variety of sizes to fit most 12-, 16-, and 20-gauge shotguns. Set includes QD stock swivel, barrel adapter, and QD front swivel. Price: $8.95.

Williams 5D Receiver Sights—For big-game rifles, .22s, and shotguns. Positive windage and elevation locks. Lightweight, strong, and accurate. Williams quality throughout. Rustproof. Available for a large variety of rifles and shotguns. Price: $10.50.

Williams "Guide" Straps—Made from selected, evenly sized leather, ⅞ inch wide, with snug-fitting stitched keepers. Enables you to carry your rifle safely, yet ready for instant use. Easily adjustable by means of rust-resistant buttons. Finishes: plain, basketweave, and carved. Prices: $5, $5.45, $8.15.

Williams Foolproof Receiver Sights—Internal micrometer adjustments have positive internal locks. The Foolproof is strong, rugged, and dependable. The alloy used to manufacture this sight has a tensile strength of 85,000 pounds. Yet the Foolproof is light and compact, weighing only 1½ ounces. Most rifles are now being drilled and tapped at the factory for installation of the Foolproof. Price: $18.50.

Williams Hammer Extensions—Positive, faster, and safer—a must when a telescopic sight mounts over the hammer, and necessary when eye relief is critical. Not a gadget, but an improvement that gives absolute hammer control and more speed. Easy to install—just one set screw. Excellent for either right- or left-handed shooters. Price: $4.25.

WINCHESTER-WESTERN

As their catalog states, Winchester is more than a gun—it's an American legend. Certainly one of the most influential firearms manufacturers in America's history, Winchester produced that first seventeen-shot repeating rifle more than a century ago. And today, the offspring of that Model 1866 are sought after by sportsmen throughout the world.

There are legends aplenty in the Winchester line—the ubiquitous Model 94 Lever Action, the famous Model 70 in all its variations for hunting everything from varmints to elephants, the favored Model 12 shotgun, the elegant and reliable Model 101 over/under, and the classic Model 21 double-barrel shotgun, to name just a few.

Their line also includes .22 rimfire rifles, match rifles, and a vast selection of ammunition and components. Be sure to see the Winchester-Western listings in Chapter 5.

Model 94 Rifle—This lever action is the original Western carbine. Selected by well over four million hunters in the last eighty-three years,

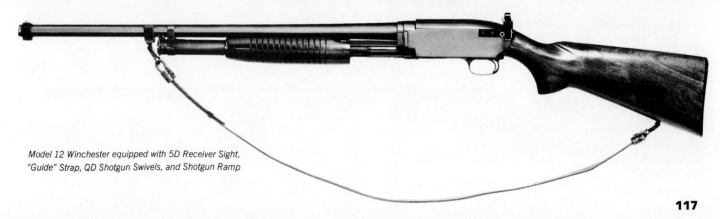

Model 12 Winchester equipped with 5D Receiver Sight, "Guide" Strap, QD Shotgun Swivels, and Shotgun Ramp

this famous lever-action carbine offers the same crisp, lean look as in 1894—and the same features that have made it truly an American legend. The Proof-Steel barrel is cold forged to give durability and accuracy unheard of back in 1894. And the rugged steel carrier can really take it. Stock and fore-end are of solid American walnut. An all-weather, wear-resistant finish over rich wood tones assures a handsome appearance in the field and at home. Barrel: 20 inches. Overall: 37¾ inches. Weight: 6½ pounds. Caliber: .30-30 Winchester. Capacity: 7 rounds (6 in magazine, 1 in chamber). Price: $140.95.

Model 70 Rifle—The Winchester Model 70 is a versatile bolt-action rifle famous for its trophy-winning performance, both in the field and in championship target competition. It combines the many features and innovations expected by today's hunter—such as a three-position safety—and is available in a wide selection of calibers to handle every type of game. Features include a steel receiver with integral recoil lug machined from precision forgings, Proof-Steel barrel that's cold forged from a chrome molybdenum blank under 200 tons of pressure, and an antibind, engine-turned bolt also machined from solid chrome moly with integral double-locking lugs and recessed face. Solid American walnut

stock has cut checkering, pistol grip cap, and black fore-end tip with white spacers. Monte Carlo cheekpiece. Detachable sling swivels. Drilled and tapped for scope mounts and receiver sights. Price: $265.

Model 70 Varmint—Same features as above, but equipped with a special, heavy barrel for extra accuracy. Calibers: .22-250, .222 Remington, and .243 Winchester. Barrel: 24 inches. Overall: 44½ inches. Weight: 9¾ pounds. Price: $280.

Model 70 African—This rifle, chambered for .458 Winchester Magnum, is built to deliver a knockdown punch to the biggest of all game. It comes with special African open rear sight and rubber recoil pad. Barrel: 22 inches. Overall: 42½ inches. Weight: 8½ pounds. Price: $455.

Model 670 Rifle—Offered with a 4-power Weaver Scope at an attractive combination price, substantially lower than if scope and rifle were purchased separately. Calibers: .243 Winchester and .30-06. Barrel: 22 inches. Price: $229.95.

Model 190 Rifle—This is a semiautomatic rimfire offering performance, features, and styling usually found only in higher priced .22-caliber

Model 94 Rifle

Model 70 Rifle

Model 70 Varmint

Model 70 African

Model 9422 Rifle

Model 52D Rifle

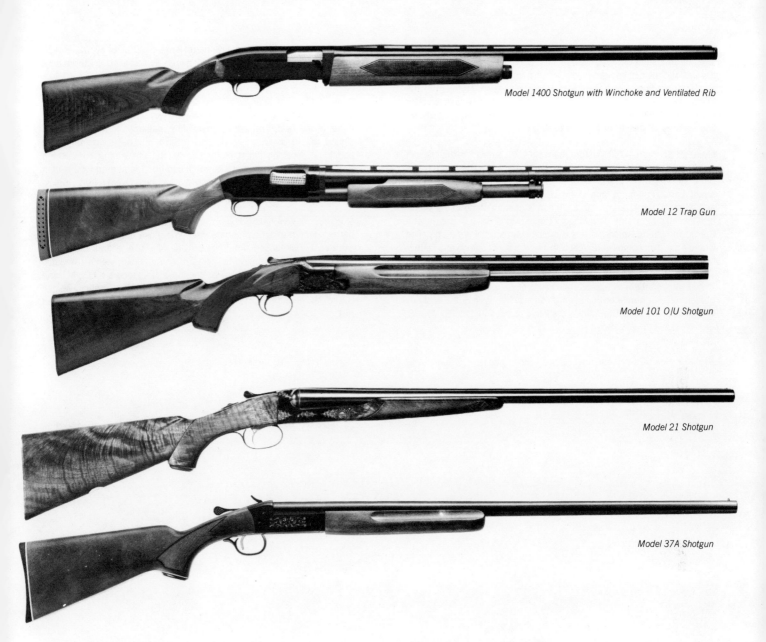

Model 1400 Shotgun with Winchoke and Ventilated Rib

Model 12 Trap Gun

Model 101 O/U Shotgun

Model 21 Shotgun

Model 37A Shotgun

rifles. Pistol grip stock. Crisply styled forearm. Adjustable, open elevator rear sight and ramp front sight. Capacity: 17 Long or 15 Long Rifle cartridges. Barrel: 20½ inches. Overall: 39 inches. Weight: 5 pounds. Price: $69.95.

Model 9422 Rifle—This is a real "son of a gun"—an authentic descendent of the legendary Winchester Model 94. It offers the same classic Western styling, plus high strength, balance, and quality materials. Calibers: .22 Rimfire and .22 Winchester Magnum. Barrel: 20½ inches. Overall: 37⅛ inches. Weight: 6¼ pounds. Prices: $169.95 (9422), $174.95 (9422M).

Model 52D Rifle—The Model 52 has been a consistent winner in small bore match shooting for over fifty years. The Model 52D has a free-floating, heavyweight, counterbored barrel and a trigger adjustment to 1 pound. Also available in International Match and International Prone models by special order. Caliber: .22 Long Rifle. Barrel: 28 inches. Overall: 46 inches. Weight: 11 pounds. Price: $325.

Model 1400 Winchoke Shotgun—This is a semiautomatic field gun with the barrel adapted to accommodate three Winchoke tubes, supplied at no extra charge. Its light weight makes it easy to carry and point. A

pushbutton carrier means faster loading. And its self-compensating gas-operated system reduces recoil. Features include a high-strength, corrosion-resistant aluminum alloy receiver; a Winchester Proof-Steel barrel; crossbolt safety; handsome, sure-grip checkered American walnut stock and fore-end. Available with plain barrel or ventilated rib. Winchokes included are I.C., M., and F. Barrel: 28 inches. Overall: 48⅝ inches. Gauges: 12 and 20. Weights: 6½ to 7¼ pounds. Prices: $224.95 (plain barrel), $244.95 (vent rib).

Model 12 Trap Gun—The present Model 12 is precisely like the "old" Model 12—superior in pointability, balance, and performance. Chrome molybdenum steel receiver. Winchester Proof-Steel barrel. Cut checkering on selected American walnut. Crisp, clean trigger pull. Engine-turned bolt and carrier. Available with standard or Monte Carlo stock. Equipped with ventilated rib. Gauge: 12. Barrel: 30 inches. Overall: 49¾ inches. Weight: 8¼ pounds. Price: $575.

Model 101 Shotgun—This over/under shotgun is superbly crafted from quality materials for top performance. Partially hand-engraved receiver and trigger guard. Barrels are made of Winchester Proof-Steel and the stock and fore-end are of finest French walnut, hand checkered, with a weather-resistant and wear-resistant high-gloss finish. The receiver is machined from a single block of steel. The safety doubles as a barrel selector for instant choice of barrels from the single trigger. Available in the widest choice of gauges, barrel lengths, and chokes in Field, Skeet, and Trap models. Also comes in a Magnum version. Included in the Winchester over/under family are the Expert, a nonengraved shotgun for the economy-minded shooter, and the Pigeon Grade, with top-of-the-line features. Prices: from $475 to $700.

Model 21 Shotgun—This custom-made double barrel offers the finest in distinctive features for distinguished sportsmen who expect to pay the price for elegance, grace, and superb performance. Engine-turned bright parts. Full-fancy and hand-fashioned walnut. Chrome molybdenum steel. Hand engraving. Each gun is custom made to the shooter's special dimensions. The Model 21 comes in Custom Grade, Pigeon Grade, and Grand American and is available on special order only. The Grand American comes complete with an extra set of barrels and leather luggage-style case.

Model 37A Shotgun—This is a single-shot shotgun designed for the budget-minded hunter or beginner. It offers all the basic qualities of any Winchester shotgun. The standard shotgun comes in 12, 16, 20, 28, and .410 gauge. Full choke. Five barrel lengths—26, 28, 30, 32, and 36 inches. Waterfowler—available in 12 gauge. Prices: $69.95 (36-inch 12 gauge), $64.95 (all other lengths).

Super-X Model 1 Shotgun—This is a rugged semiautomatic shotgun made to stand up under the pressure of heavy competition as well as the rigors of the field. The self-compensating, gas-operated system is designed to cut down on recoil and reduce muzzle jump for getting additional shots on target more quickly. Cut checkering on selected American walnut. Equipped with ventilated rib. Chambered for 2¾-inch shells. Gauge: 12. Barrel: 26, 28, and 30 inches. Overall: from 46¼ to 50⅝ inches. Price: $299.95.

Model 1200 Winchoke Shotgun—This is a slide-action field gun with barrel adapted to accommodate three Winchoke tubes, supplied at no extra cost. Twin-action slide bars provide fast, sure action. Checkered stock and extended beavertail forearm of American walnut. Available with plain barrel or ventilated rib. Winchokes included are I.C., M., and F. Gauges: 12 and 20. Barrel: 28 inches. Overall: 48⅝ inches. Weight: 6½ to 7¼ pounds. Prices: $179.95 (plain barrel), $199.95 (ventilated rib).

CHAPTER FIVE

AMMUNITION, COMPONENTS, RELOADING TOOLS, AND ACCESSORIES

Many of the products in this chapter can be ordered by mail and shipped directly to you, but some will have to be purchased or ordered through a local firearms dealer. The Federal Gun Control Act of 1968 restricts the sale of most ammunition and components. Reloading tools, case tumblers, bullet molds, and other reloading accessories, as well as some components such as shotshell wads, can be purchased by mail.

For a summary of the Gun Control Act of 1968, please turn to the introduction to Chapter 4.

BARNES BULLETS

Barnes carries 126 different weights and calibers of bullets and bullet jackets in three different thicknesses. They also produce custom weights and calibers to the customer's specifications.

They will send their complete price list on request. Meanwhile, here is a small sampling from that list, just to give you an idea.

.17 Caliber—.172, 25-grain Semi-Spitzer S.P. Jacket thickness: .030 inch. Price: $10/100.

.22 Caliber—.224, 60-grain Semi-Spitzer S.P. with .030-inch jackets. Price: $9.60/100.

6.5mm—.264, 130-grain and 150-grain Semi-Spitzer S.P. with .032-inch jackets. Price: $10.20/100.

7mm—.284, 125-grain and 140-grain Semi-Spitzer S.P. with .032-inch jackets. Price: $10.20/100.

.30 Caliber—.308, 180-grain Semi-Spitzer S.P. with .032-inch jackets. Price: $11.40/100.

.375 Caliber—.375, 350-grain Round Nose S.P. with .049-inch jackets. Price: $11.20/100.

.444 Marlin Caliber—.430, 300-grain Flat Nose S.P. with .032-inch jackets. Price: $7.50/100.

.458 Magnum Caliber—.458, 600-grain Round Nose S.P. with .049-inch jackets. Price: $17.40/100.

.600 Nitro Caliber—.620, 900-grain Round Nose F.M.J. with .049-inch jackets. Price: $32/100.

BONANZA SPORTS MANUFACTURING

Bonanza offers a substantial line of reloading tools including two presses for metallic cartridges, scales, powder measures, dies, and a number of other tools and accessories.

Model 68 Press—Bonanza engineers have developed a new and sensational reloading press. Without imitation, the new product incorporates both ease of operation and accuracy to the highest degee. Competitively priced, yet designed to give a lifetime of satisfactory service. Features include 100% visibility, upright mounting, and simple construction with ample power and strength to perform all the operations demanded in reloading metallic cartridges. Linkage pins are hardened and ground to insure precise alignment and long service. Ram is machined and fitted. Accepts any standard ⅞ inch by 14 dies. Price: $40.50.

Bonanza Co-Ax Indicator—It's a fact that bullets will not leave a rifle barrel at a uniform angle unless they are started uniformly. This tool will give a reading of how closely the axis of the bullet corresponds with the axis of the cartridge case. Sensitive indicator measures in half thousandths. Prices: $13.45 (indicator), $19.50 (indicator dial)

Bonanza Case Lube Pad—The secret of lubricating cases properly is to apply a thin film of case lubricant to the outside of the case. If too much lubricant adheres to the case, oil dents will result. With a proper amount of lube on the pad, cases can be lubricated by rolling them on the pad. Price: $2.95

Bonanaza Case-Sizing Lubricant—A high-pressure lubricant that will adhere to the case when forced into the die. With this lubricant you will scarcely feel the case enter and leave the die. Makes resizing easy and saves equipment. Price: 85¢/2-oz. bottle

Co-Ax Indicator

Bonanza Powder Funnel—This clear plastic funnel is designed so that it may be used for all calibers from .222 to .45–70 Price. $1.25. Funnel for .17 cal.: $1.25

Bonanza Large Powder and Shot Funnel—A powder and shot funnel that is made of resilient, transparent plastic. Price: $2.25.

Bonanza Funnel and Long Drop Tube—For use with 4831 and other slow-burning powders where full capacity loads are desired. By using this funnel and drop tube the reloader can add from three to eight more grains of powder, depending on the case used. Price: $2.50.

B-SQUARE

This company offers a number of useful tools for the reloader. Check Chapter 4 for other B-Square products.

Model AR-12 Case Tumbler—This is a popular model that polishes up to 200 cases at a time in its molded rubber drum with four bags of medium. Rubber barrel is guaranteed five years against wearing out. Price: $37.95, plus $2 shipping.

Model B-1 Case Tumbler—This is the professional model with heavy-duty motor and metal drum with rubber lining. It has wing nut cover and uses all types of media. It will polish over 200 cases with four bags of medium. Drum is guaranteed for five years. Price: $49.95, plus $3 shipping.

Model B-1 Case Tumbler

Deburr Lathe—A clever little hand-crank lathe with a chuck·for holding standard deburr, chamfer, or pocket primer tools. Speeds up the deburring and chamfering of both old and new cases. It eliminates the chatter and unevenness that you get with hand-held tools. Price: $9.95 (without cutters), plus 50¢ shipping.

Friction Thimble Micrometers—Accuracy to .0001 inch. Parallelism from .00005 inch. Flatness to .00003 inch. Positive locking clamp. Friction thimble for exact and repetitive readings. Carbide faces, .256 inch in diameter. Every micrometer meets federal specifications for accuracy. Cast iron frame with silver-gray enamel finish. Spanner wrench with each micrometer. Packed in specially fitted case. Two models: 0–1-inch range and 1–2-inch range. Prices: $20, $21.50.

Dial Calipers with Thumb Roll—Easily used and accurate—reading directly to .001 inch on large clear dial. Outside, inside, and depth measurements. Stainless steel, with measuring faces hardened, precision ground, and microlapped for absolute accuracy. Scale surface has satin chrome finish with clear, crisp engraved graduations in inches. Clamp for repetitive readings. Accurate to .001 inch per 6 inches. Supplied in deluxe, cushion-fitted metal case. Price: $42, plus 75¢ shipping.

Calipers

Model 75 Chronograph—It is crystal controlled and has the very latest integrated circuit and components. There are no buttons to push, no switches to turn, and no complicated procedures. It is foolproof and easy to use. Just hook up your screens and shoot. A red stop light will tell you when not to shoot. Add the total lights "on" and obtain the exact velocity from table. Nothing can go wrong. Will use any type of screen from a conductive pencil mark to the electronic types. B-Square screens are metallic printed paper screens. Screen holders are spring plastic and stretch the screens for most accuracy. Screen holders come with brackets to attach to standard conduit and camera tripods. Chronograph dimensions: 8×3×5 inches. Weight: 2¾ pounds. Price: $149.95, plus $1 shipping. Brackets: $7.95 per set, plus 50¢ shipping. Screens: $10.95/100, plus 25¢ shipping.

C-H TOOL & DIE CORP.

The C-H line includes several presses for metallic cartridges—both "C" press and "H" press designs—as well as dies and other tools of interest to rifle and pistol cartridge reloaders.

No. 204 Semi-Steel Cast Iron "C" Press—This heavy press is strong, tough, and durable. Extra-wide bowed mouth permits easy access to reloader's hand—no scraped knuckles. Reinforced throughout with ribbing and gussets for perfect rigidity. Extra-heavy toggle will not fail. Accepts all standard ⅞ inch by 14 dies. Comes with toggle, handle, universal shell holder ram, one shell holder, and universal priming arm. Weight: 11½ pounds. Price: $37.50.

No. 333-X Pistol Champ Reloading Press—An economical, semiprogressive ammunition reloading tool. Comes complete and ready to load one caliber. Capable of reloading 150 rounds per hour. Integral powder measure that is super simple to use. Easy-to-change bushings. Size and decap at the first station. Seat primer, expand and bell the case, and drop the powder charge at the second station. Seat and crimp the bullet at the third station. Calibers: .30 M1, 9mm, .38 Special, .357 Magnum, .44 Magnum, .45 ACP, .45 Colt. Comes complete with all accessories and one steel sizing die. Your choice of above calibers. Price: $114.

No. 204 "C" Press

Powder and Bullet Scale—A great value in a moderately priced scale. Chrome-plated brass beam, graduated in 10-grain and ¹⁄₁₀-grain increments. Convenient pouring spout on pan. Leveling screw on base. All metal construction. Capacity: 360 grains. Price: $15.95.

CHRONOGRAPH SPECIALISTS

If you're a serious shooter or reloader, interested in doing your own ballistics research, here's a company you should know about, because they produce a line of relatively inexpensive chronographs. Perhaps you'll find a model that fits your budget.

Model CS-100 Chronograph—Now you can really know what your reloads do besides go boom. The CS-100, while being very low in price, is no less accurate than machines costing ten to twenty times as much. It is easy to use and features a quartz crystal controlled time base; 500,000 pulse per second timing frequency; 100 percent solid-state circuitry, utilizing medium-scale integrated circuits; binary coded decimal (BCD) readout for simplicity in use; short screen spacing for less chance of missing one of the screens and wasting a shot; battery operation for complete portability; and easy-to-use velocity conversion charts. Comes complete with everything needed for checking the velocity of your handloads—chronograph, screen holders, screen cable, velocity conversion charts, ten screens, and instructions. Dimensions: 6 inches long, 4 inches wide, 2 inches high. Weight: 1½ pounds. Price: $49.95, plus $3 shipping and insurance. Extra screens: $7.50/100 postpaid.

Model CS-200 Chronograph—This is a three-decade digital counter chronograph, capable of accurate velocity measurements for pistols, rifles, and shotguns. Features include a quartz crystal controlled time base; 500,000 pulse per second timing frequency; BCD readout for simplicity in use; a screen check, powered by four inexpensive flashlight batteries; 100 percent solid-state circuitry; and complete portability. Comes complete with screen holders, screen cable, velocity conversion charts, ten screens, and instructions. Dimensions: 6½ inches long, 5¼ inches wide, 2¼ inches high. Weight: 2½ pounds. Price: $65, plus $3 shipping and insurance. Extra screens: $7.50/100 postpaid.

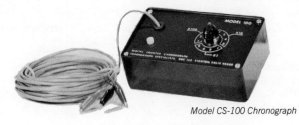

Model CS-100 Chronograph

Model CS-600 Chronograph—Here's a low-cost direct velocity counter chronograph that features a quartz crystal controlled time base; 500,000 pulse per second timing frequency; 100 percent solid-state circuitry; large, easy-to-read numerical display; automatic screen check circuit to prevent wasted shots; light weight and portability. Displays velocity in feet per second, eliminating the need for velocity conversion tables. Operates on 6V DC. Comes complete with screen holders, screen cable, fifty screens, and instructions. Dimensions: 4.25 inches deep, 6.4 inches wide, 3.25 inches high. Weight: 4 pounds. Price: $150, plus $3 shipping and insurance. Extra screens: $7.50/100 postpaid.

CORBIN MANUFACTURING AND SUPPLY, INC.

This company manufactures tools, dies, and accessories for bullet swaging—making your own bullets, including jacketed bullets, with a press and dies.

While we have been reloading rifle and handgun cartridges and shotgun shells for a number of years, and have done some bullet casting as well, we confess that we have had no experience in swaging. Certainly, it is the next logical area to explore in the fascinating hobby of precision handloading, but it has always been one of those things that "we're going to do one of these days, when we have time."

Actually, that's been a flimsy excuse for ignorance. The mysterious art of swaging has seemed to us something for the experts. But after reading Dave Corbin's Handbook and Catalog, we've learned that swaging is no more complex or mysterious than any other reloading process. Furthermore, you can make your own jacketed bullets for handgun calibers as well as .224 and 6mm rifle calibers with dies that fit your loading press. You can even draw your own jackets for .224 and 6mm out of spent .22 Long Rifle cases. For larger rifle calibers, you'll want a swaging press, such as Corbin's Mity Mite. Corbin charges $2 (refundable) for their Handbook and Catalog.

Mity Mite Swaging Press

Mity Mite System—Together with the Floating Alignment punch holder and Corbin's Mity Mite Punch and die sets, the Mity Mite comprises a powerful and accurate bullet swaging system, far superior to the use of even the most ruggedly built loading press. Features include built-in automatic ejection, horizontal operation, true zero-tolerance die and punch alignment, and a system of leverage that produces virtually unlimited power (to the maximum yield strength of the steels). Each delivery is custom built to customer orders, and a modest price attracts commercial and private users alike. The Mity Mite System can be ordered complete for any rifle caliber or any handgun caliber. Price: $150.

Matched Set of Rifle Dies—Includes three dies for Open Point Match bullets. Comes with all punches. Price: $80.50.

Matched Set of Handgun Dies—Two dies with all styles of base and nose punches. Makes many dozens of bullet styles by using two punch combinations on the same bullet. Price: $80.50.

Cannelure Tool—This is a machine to roll a crimp groove into a bullet or cartridge. The groove can be used as a crimp groove, but it also has other purposes. It is very effective in a narrow range of velocities in controlling expansion in pistol and rifle bullets. It allows more accurate

Matched Rifle Die Set

handloads in a .45 pistol and other autoloaders that headspace on the end of the case by providing a positive stop for the bullet to rest against when rolled into the cartridge case. Cannelures also identify bullets before loading as to selected weight or core hardness. The Corbin Cannelure Tool has a tool-steel roller that is hardened, adjustment for depth and for position of cannelure, and you can even put an additional roller on the shaft if you want two at once for lube grooves. Price: $19.50. Extra rollers: $6.50 each.

Powerful Vibrator Motor—Now you can make your own cartridge case or bullet jacket polisher/tumbler. Mount this motor to the bottom of a large can or bucket. Subsonic vibrations churn the contents in your tumbling medium. Complete with cord, switch, and mounts. Price: $17.50.

FEDERAL CARTRIDGE CORP.

Federal offers a complete line of shotgun shells, centerfire rifle and pistol cartridges, and .22-caliber ammunition for the shooter. For the reloader, there are shot cups, wads, empty primed shotshells, and unprimed centerfire cases for rifle and handgun calibers. And they've recently introduced some new products that should interest you.

Their catalog includes load data on their shotshells as well as complete ballistics tables for their metallic cartridges.

Premium Magnum Shotshells—For long-range shooting with large shot, it is extremely important that patterns be concentrated. These new Premium Magnums excel in this respect by using three special ingredients: copper-plated, extra-hard shot; granulated plastic shot buffer material; and a long-range plastic shot cup. The result is pellets that are much less deformed as they emerge from the gun barrel. These pellets retain velocity better and deliver denser patterns with shorter shot strings—all necessary characteristics for pass shooting or hunting wild turkey and

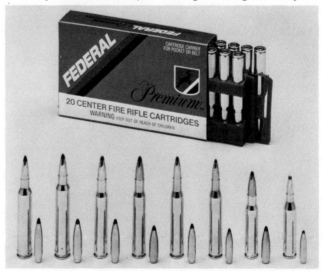

New Premium Centerfire Cartridges

fox. Retail prices on these new shells will run from about 50¢ to $1 higher than standard loads.

Premium Hi-Power Shotshells—These are truly superior high-velocity loads. Copper-plated, extra-hard shot, and a plastic shot cup deliver more pellets into the pattern area and ensure greater downrange velocity and penetration. A careful selection of powders and the gas sealing of the plastic Triple-Plus wad column add to the effectiveness of these shells. Premium Hi-Powers are an expert's load for all-around hunting of waterfowl, pheasants, and other large upland game. Expect them to cost from about 50¢ to $1 more than standard loads.

Premium Field Loads—Added performance features make these superior "light loads" for taking small game. The shot is copper-plated and extra-hard to ensure easier flight through vegetation and better penetration on game, with less feather draw. In addition, the shot pellets are less deformed on firing, thus delivering a more useful shot pattern from any degree of gun choke. A Triple-Plus wad column complements the special shot in providing effective patterns. Prices will be slightly higher than standard shotshell ammunition.

Premium Centerfire Ammunition—To increase the performance of centerfire rifles, Federal has introduced a selection of eight Premium cartridges loaded with boat-tail, soft-point bullets. Designed along principles proven repeatedly by elite marksmen, the streamlined, tapered base of the boat-tail bullet greatly reduces drag. This results in higher retained velocity, more striking energy, flatter trajectory, and less wind drift than with conventional flat base bullets. The bullets in Premium cartridges are manufactured by the world famous Sierra Bullet Company, in special production runs, exclusively for Federal to assure highest quality. Calibers/grain weights: .243/100, .25-06/117, .270/150, 7mm Magnum/175, .30-06/165, .30-06/200, .308/165, .300 Winchester Magnum/200. Retail prices for a twenty-round box of Premium centerfire ammunition is between 55¢ and 65¢ higher per box than standard ammunition.

HENSLEY & GIBBS

Jim Gibbs tells us that he's semiretired now, but that his son is continuing to run their bullet mold business. They manufacture top-quality molds that are sold in countries throughout the world. Their molds are primarily for handgun and muzzle-loader calibers, and they are no longer making one- or two-cavity molds.

Jim also said that while you can count on receiving some of the best bullet molds on the market, you will probably have to wait about six months for your order to be completed—they're that busy. You can be assured of getting the best price by dealing directly with the company, because they charge you the same prices they would charge any dealer.

The Hensley & Gibbs molds are available in four-, six-, or ten-cavity models. They also offer complete repair services. If cavity edges are not chipped beyond practical resurfacing, they can recondition most molds of their manufacture. You need only send the complete mold to them for a cost estimate.

If you want more information on their line and a list of bullet designs, weights, and mold prices, send them a note, and include a self-addressed and stamped envelope for their reply.

HODGDON POWDER CO., INC.

Hodgdon is a major manufacturer of modern smokeless powders and accessories for the reloader, but they are also the exclusive U.S. distributor of the great new "Black Powder Replica" known as Pyrodex.

Pyrodex is a powder with a harder finish than black powder; thus it's more difficult to ignite. It burns cleaner—so the shooter needn't scrub out the barrel after each shot. And an 80-grain load of Pyrodex will produce about the same velocities and pressures that 100 grains of black powder will. Like black powder, however, Pyrodex is hygroscopic—that

is, it will attract and retain moisture, which means you must thoroughly clean your barrels at the end of a day's shooting to prevent corrosion.

As for the aesthetics, Pyrodex does smoke—plenty.

As some of you may not know, there was a disastrous accident at the Pyrodex plant near Seattle, Washington, on January 27, 1977, that killed four employees, including Dan Pawlak, the young president of the company and coinventor of Pyrodex.

A new Pyrodex plant is to be built near Kansas City where Hodgdon will manufacture the powder. Meanwhile, existing equipment may be used to complete processing of a large quantity of semifinished Pyrodex now in the magazines, which would help to alleviate the heavy demand for the product.

As we go to press, the stocks of Pyrodex RS and P are depleted and others are in short supply. Dave Parker at Hodgdon told us, though, that they hope to see the first can of Pyrodex produced in the new facilities around the first of 1978.

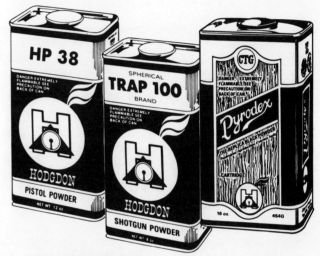

Hodgdon Powders, Pyrodex, Manuals

H4227 and H4198 Rifle Powders—H4227 is the fastest burning of the IMR series. Well adapted to Hornet, light bullets in .222, and all bullets in .357 and .44 Magnum. Cuts leading with lead bullets. H4198 was developed especially for small- and medium-capacity cartridges. Prices: $6.95/1-pound can, $50.95/8-pound keg, $119.50/20-pound keg.

H4831 Rifle Powder—Here's a new batch of the original 4831—the most popular of all powders. Use same loading data as the original surplus powder. Outstanding performance with medium and heavy bullets in 6mm, .25-06, .270, and magnum calibers. Prices: $5.95/1-pound can, $43.95/8-pound keg, $102.50/20-pound keg.

HP38 Pistol Powder—A fast pistol powder for most pistol loading. Especially recommended for midrange 38 Special. Prices: $4.95/12-ounce can, $46.25/8-pound keg, $63.50/12-pound keg.

Trap 100 Shotgun Powder—This is a spherical trap and light field load powder, also excellent for target loads in centerfire pistols. Mild recoil. Prices: $2.70/8-ounce can, $35.75/8-pound keg, $48.50/12-pound keg.

HS-5, HS-6, and HS-7 Shotgun Powders—HS-5 for heavy field and HS-6 and HS-7 for magnum field loads are unsurpassed as they do not pack in the measure. They deliver uniform charges and are dense, so allow sufficient wad column for best patterns. Prices: $5.95/1-pound can, $43.95/8-pound keg, $59.50/12-pound keg.

Pyrodex RS Replica Black Powder—For use in all calibers of muzzle-loading percussion rifles and shotguns. Price: $4.50/1-pound can.

Pyrodex P Replica Black Powder—Designed for use in percussion single-shot pistols and cap and ball revolvers. Price: $4.50/1-pound can.

Pyrodex CTG Replica Black Powder—For black-powder cartridges, CTG will duplicate black-powder loads in rifle, pistol, and shotshell. Price: $4/1-pound can.

Pyrodex/Black Powder Data Manual—New! Manual covers rifle, pistol, shotgun, and cannon. New loads, data, and information. Price: $1.

Hodgdon Data Manual No. 23—New data on Pyrodex and black powder, new section on "How To Reload for Beginners." New format and new calibers. Information on rifle, pistol, shotgun, and lead bullet loads. Price: $3.95.

Hodgdon Bullet Lube (Alox)—The answer to the gun buff's desire for increased accuracy and higher lead bullet velocity. A mixture of pure beeswax and Alox 2138F assures these results. Hollow sticks only for popular lubricators. Price: $1.65.

Case Cleaner—A proven formula. Cleans cases without etching, is non-corrosive and inexpensive. Four ounces, when diluted, cleans 1,000 cases. Price: $1.75/4-ounce bottle.

HORNADY MANUFACTURING CO.

Hornady is one of the major bullet manufacturers in the United States, offering rifle bullets, jacketed pistol bullets, lead pistol bullets, round balls, and crimp-on gas checks. They also offer a new expanded line of Frontier Cartridges for centerfire rifles and handguns.

.22 Caliber 55-Grain FMJ Bullets   .30 Caliber 165-Grain BTSP Bullets

.22 Caliber 55-Grain FMJ Bullets—The full-metal jackets on these bullets make them especially useful for the hunter who wants as little damage as possible done to pelts. Price: $5/box of 100.

.30 Caliber 165-Grain BTSP Bullets—This new bullet is sure to prove a favorite among big-game hunters who want the reduced drag and high sustained velocity of the boat-tail bullet. Price: $7.85/box of 100.

Jacketed Pistol (9mm HP) Bullets
Lead Pistol Bullets
Round Lead Balls

Jacketed Pistol Bullets—Hornady offers fourteen different calibers and weights of jacketed pistol bullets. Prices: from $4.90 to $7.10/box of 100.

Lead Pistol Bullets—Designs include bevel base wadcutter, hollow base wadcutter, round nose, and semiwadcutter, in .38, .44, and .45 calibers. Prices: from $3.65 to $4.95/box of 100.

Round Lead Balls—Here is a new item for black-powder shooters—round lead balls in twelve sizes from .350 through .570. Prices: from $2.85 to $4.35/box of 100.

Hornady Handbook Vol. II—Now in its second printing. A valuable addition to your library. Loaded with information on reloading 104 rifle and pistol cartridges. Number of pages: 512. Price: $5.95.

LYMAN

Lyman's extensive line touches on practically every phase of the reloading process. Additionally, the company offers a number of publications of interest to handloaders.

All-American Turret Press—Combines maximum speed with maximum precision. The four-station turret mounts three dies and a powder measure in reloading operation sequence. As the turret is revolved, dies remain in place and are positioned directly over the shell holder with a positive-locking audible click action at each of the stations. No single-station press can compare with the turret speed. Used with the optional Lyman No. 55 Powder Measure and the optional pushbutton primer feed, the press handles extra-high-volume reloading. The press provides maximum leverage in either up- or down-stroke operation. Standard dies for any rifle or pistol cartridge may be used. Price: $99.50.

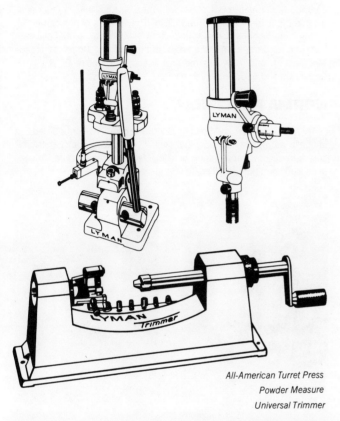

All-American Turret Press
Powder Measure
Universal Trimmer

Universal Trimmer—Simplicity and precision clearly describe Lyman's new trimmer. Its patented chuck head accepts all metallic rifle or pistol cases, regardless of rim thickness. To change calibers, simply change the inexpensive case head pilot. Prices: $34 (trimmer and one pilot). Extra pilots: $1.50.

No. 55 Powder Measure—This powder measure dispenses charge after charge of smokeless powder with consistent accuracy to a fraction of a grain. The key to this unfailing precision is the 55's unique three-sided micrometer, adjustable cavity. A 2,400-grain reservoir of clear PVC plastic resists chemical action and protects your powder from harmful light

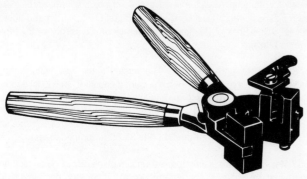

Bullet Mold

rays. An attached knocker assures a complete charge every time. Mount the 55 on your bench or any turret press. No funnel is required. Price: $31.50. Standard ⅞-inch by 14 adapter for turret mounting: $1.50.

Inertia Bullet Puller—Quickly and easily removes bullets from cartridges. Price: $12.50.

Shell Chamfering Reamer—Tapers case mouth for easier bullet seating. One size adapts to all cartridges used with jacketed or cast bullets. Price: $5.

Primer Pocket Reamer—Cleans and removes rough metal edges and carbon deposits from primer pockets. This tool is a must for all reloaders. Two sizes: large and small. Price: $5.

All-American Reloading Die Sets—These dies are designed for rapid, accurate reloading of metallic cartridges on any press with ⅞-inch by 14 thread die stations. Carefully constructed of first quality steel, AA dies are first hardened and then polished to a mirror smooth interior finish to produce a perfectly finished and sized case. AA dies come in standard two- and three-die rifle and pistol sets. Price: $16.50.

Group A Bullet Molds—Lyman's most popular group of molds, available for casting a variety of bullet sizes and designs. Available in single-cavity, double-cavity, and four-cavity models. Prices: $16, $18, $38.

Lead Pot—Cast-iron pot for melting lead alloy using any source of heat. Capacity: 8 pounds of alloy. Price: $5.

Lead Dipper—Dipper with cast-iron head is shaped for easy, accurate pouring and prevents air pockets in the finished bullet. Dipper is also used for stirring molten lead alloys. Wooden handle stays cool. Price: $5.

Ingot Mold—Used when melting down scrap lead or blending alloys. Each mold forms four, easy-to-use ingots. Price: $5.

Mold Master Bullet Casting Furnace—A heavy-duty, 11-pound-capacity electric furnace that comes complete with one ingot mold. The Mold Master is a safe and reliable furnace, designed for years of flawless service. It operates on standard household power. Calibrated thermostat regulates heat from 450° to 850° F. and controls temperature to within 20°. A lever-operated valve controls discharge spout. Prices: $79.95 (includes ingot mold), $86.95 (includes ingot mold and mold guide).

No. 450 Bullet Sizer/Lubricator—Prepares almost any cast bullet for high-accuracy reloading. One effortless stroke correctly sizes with a swaging action and pressure lubricates. It also seats gas checks. Rugged iron-steel frame casting not only provides a leakproof lubricant, but also assures a lifetime of precise bullet sizing. To change bullet diameters you simply change an inexpensive die set consisting of a top punch "G" and a sizing assembly "H & I." Price: $44 (less dies).

Lyman Gas Checks—These gilding metal caps fit the cast bullet base and protect it from hot powder gases. Easily seated during bullet sizing, the gas checks also permit higher velocities. Sizes: .22 through .45 caliber. Price: $10/1,000.

Lyman Shotshell Handbook, 2nd Edition—This is a complete update and expansion of the popular 1st Edition—the first reloading manual exclusively for the shotshell reloader. The all-new 2nd Edition is greatly expanded and in a new easy-to-read format with over 2,000 tested loads. Price: $6.95.

Lyman's 45th Reloading Handbook—Backed by Lyman's many years of experience filling the shooter's needs, this handbook is comprehensive enough for the advanced reloader, yet is clear enough to initiate the beginner. There's even a special muzzle-loading section. Price: $6.95.

Lyman Cast Bullet Handbook—This handbook contains load data on every popular rifle and pistol cartridge incorporating the most popular cast-bullet designs and weights. It also features a complete "how-to" section, pictorial listing of cast bullet designs, and a comprehensive black-powder section. Price: $6.95.

Lyman Black Powder Handbook—This new book provides the most comprehensive load information for the modern black-powder shooter. More than 20,000 shots were fired to compile the data featuring nearly every modern barrel length and most projectiles available today. Price: $6.95.

MAYVILLE ENGINEERING CO.

It's the acronym by which you will recognize this company's products. *Mec* is the brand on a line of top-quality and popular shotshell reloaders and accessories. There's a Mec machine to fit nearly any budget, from the 600 Jr. to the big, electric-powered Hustler.

Mec 600 Jr. Shotshell Reloader—Any Mec reloader can be used for reloading plastic shells, but the "600 Jr." positively masters the process. The Plastic Master is a single-stage tool, but is designed to permit rapid, progressive operation. Every step from fired shell to the fresh-crimped product is performed with a minimum of motion. An exclusive shell holder positions and holds the shell at each station. No transfer die is required. Resizing dies at reconditioning and crimping stations give your shell its proper form. Several brand-new features make this reloader a great buy: Adjusta-Guide wad feed device with vertical adjustment to permit rapid wad insertion, Spindex crimp starter with swivel action to correctly align with original shell creases, and a cam-actuated crimping station that finish forms the shell progressively and releases it from the die easily. Price: $79.20.

Hustler Shotshell Reloader—This is the completely MECanized reloader that not only gives you your own miniature reloading factory, but one that resizes to under industry standards for minimum chamber. It's one super-fast way to reload with a quality that is unsurpassed. The hydraulic system is compact, lightweight, and designed for long, trouble-free service. The motor operates on regular 110V household current and

Hustler Shotshell Reloader

the pump supplies instant, constant pressure—no slowdown, no misses. The entire downstroke and upstroke functions are utilized and synchronized to allow continuous action. Every stoke of the cylinder piston is positive and performs all operations at six reloading stations. Every downstroke produces one finished shell. The operator inserts empty shells and wads; the Hustler does the rest—automatically. Currently available in 12-gauge only, but other gauges are to follow. Prices: $618 (complete), $293.60 (reloader less pump and hose).

Mec E-Z Prime "V" and "S"—From carton to shell with security. These completely automatic primer feeds provide safe, convenient primer positioning and increase rate of production. They reduce bench clutter, allowing more free area for wads and shells. Primers transfer directly from carton to reloader, eliminating tubes and tube fillers. Model "V" fits the Mec 600 Jr. and 700 Versamec reloaders. The Model "S" is for the Super 600 and 650. Price: $20 each.

NORMA PRECISION

This division of General Sporting Goods Corporation offers a broad line of quality ammunition and components. If you write for their catalog, be sure to request a copy of their booklet, "Norma Loading Data." It contains loads and data for rifles, handguns, and shotguns.

.308 Winchester   *.357 Magnum*

Norma .220 Swift—American high-velocity cartridge developed in 1935, based on the 6mm Lee Navy round. A successful varmint cartridge, its muzzle velocity hasn't really been beaten by later developments. Soft point, semipointed, 50-grain, .224 bullet. Prices: $10.70/box of 20 (loaded ammunition), $5.10/box of 20 (unprimed brass).

6.5 Norma (6.5X55mm)—This is the Swedish and Norwegian military round of 1894. A very accurate cartridge with moderate recoil, it has become popular with target shooters in many countries and is also used widely for hunting. Available in 77-grain soft point, semipointed; 139-grain plastic-pointed "Dual Core"; and 156-grain soft point, round nose. Prices: $12.60/box of 20 (loaded ammunition), $5.45/box of 20 (unprimed brass).

.308 Winchester—This is the civilian version of the 7.62 Nato round. Ballistically close to the .30-06, it has gained popularity due to its adaptability to shorter rifle actions. Available in 130-grain soft point, semipointed boat tail; 150-grain soft point, semipointed boat tail; and 180-grain plastic-pointed "Dual Core." Prices: from $9 to $9.35/box of 20 (loaded ammunition), from $4.60 to $5.05 (unprimed brass).

.357 Magnum—This is an improved version of the 38 Special, based on test firings by Philip B. Sharpe and Douglas B. Wesson back in 1934. The round was marketed in 1935 along with the corresponding S&W re-

volver. Available in 158-grain hollow point; soft point, flat nose; and full jacket semiwadcutter. Prices: from $14.60 to $17.25/box of 50 (loaded ammunition), $8.90/box of 50 (unprimed cases).

Norma Magnum Rifle Powder—An exceptionally slow-burning, high-energy powder for highest velocity with large-capacity cases. A must for magnums. Price: $10.65/400-gram cannister.

Norma Powder 200—A fast-burning powder for small-capacity cases such as the .222, but also excellent for use with light bullets and light loads in larger calibers. Price: $10.65/400-gram cannister.

NORTH AMERICAN ARMS

If you're planning to buy the NAA Casull five-shot stainless steel revolver described in Chapter 4, you'll want to know about the ammunition for it.

.454 Ammunition—This ammunition was specifically developed for use in the .454 Casull revolver only. Loaded with a 225-grain bullet. Price: $19.50/box of 50.

.454 Brass—Primed or unprimed cases available. Prices: $9.80/box of 50 (primed), $9.30/box of 50 (unprimed).

NOSLER BULLETS

A 180-grain .308 Nosler Partition bullet once kept us supplied with caribou meat for nearly a year. Another Nosler Partition—this one a 160-grain .270—dropped a running black bear at 225 yards and subsequently helped us fill our freezer with tasty bear roasts and homemade bear sausage.

Certainly, Nosler is best known for their line of premium Partition big-game bullets that are extremely popular among hunters everywhere. But recently, Nosler developed a new Solid Base bullet that is competitively priced and is sure to find favor among all hunters, from the small-game and varmint hunter to the big-game hunter.

According to Nosler, their new Solid Base bullets are physically different from ordinary bullets. Each starts out as a solid metal bullet, cut from a solid copper alloy rod. Nosler then uses a unique impact extrusion manufacturing method that requires annealing the metal twice during the process. Shaping the bullet to its final configuration, the impact extrusion process permits precise control of length, weight, ogive design, and sectional density to achieve the optimal ballistic coefficient for a true, accurate flight path.

The solid base of these bullets, according to Nosler, serves two purposes. First, it serves as a platform for the mushroom to control expansion and thus increase penetration. Second, the solid base resists deforming during firing and creates a symmetrical gas seal between the bullet and the bore.

At the time of this writing, the Nosler Solid Base line has grown to twenty-nine bullets, all with the boat-tail design.

Solid Base .22-Caliber 60-Grain Bullet—A highly accurate .224 bullet intended for small game, the new 60-grain Spitzer will develop tight groups when used with the hotter .22 cartridges. The ballistic coefficient of .290 will help the long-range varmint shooter develop the most from his rifle. The high coefficient is the result of the boat-tail design that reduces drag and improves overall flight characteristics. Price: $5.30/box of 100.

Solid Base 6mm 100-Grain Bullet—A low-cost hunting and plinking bullet, the new 100-grain is very adaptable to deer and antelope-sized game. It has a high ballistic coefficient (.381) as a result of its boat-tail design and general efficient shape. Load data for the 6mm 100-grain Solid Base is interchangeable with the 6mm 100-grain Partition bullet

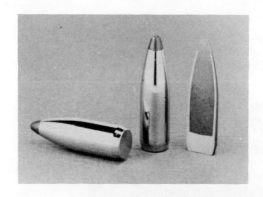

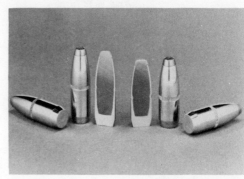

.22 60-Grain Solid Base Bullet
.30-Caliber 170-Grain and 150-Grain Flat Point Solid Base Bullets

described in the *Nosler Reloading Manual Number One*. Price: $7.50/box of 100.

Solid Base 7mm 120-Grain Bullet—The first lightweight 7mm offered by Nosler is this highly accurate boat tail. A tapered interior jacket design makes this new bullet ideal for varmints, because it will expand easily upon impact, even at long ranges. The boat-tail design, with a ballistic coefficient for this bullet of .434, conserves valuable energy for more positive stopping power at long range. Price: $7.85/box of 100.

Solid Base Bullets for .30-30s—A pair of .30-caliber flat-nose bullets for lever-action .30-30 rifles is now available in the Nosler Solid Base design and are the first bullets the company has offered for these popular rifles. The .308-inch-diameter bullets include a 150-grain flat point and a 170-grain flat point. Specifically designed for .30-30 velocities, the bullets feature a boat-tail design to retain maximum energy for more positive stopping power. This design, once found mostly in competitive match bullets, gives these new bullets less drag and a higher ballistic coefficient than regular bullets. A precision cannelure is installed in each bullet to prevent accuracy-robbing distortion caused by some canneluring operations. Prices: $8.40/box of 100 (150 grain), $8.60/box of 100 (170 grain).

OMARK INDUSTRIES

CCI and Speer are the familiar brands of ammunition and components offered by Omark, and recently the RCBS line of reloading tools has been added. So their next catalog should be loaded with goodies for the reloader.

CCI .22-Caliber Stinger

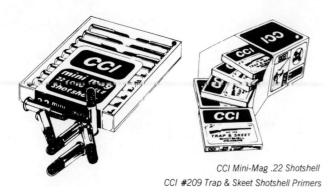

CCI Mini-Mag .22 Shotshell
CCI #209 Trap & Skeet Shotshell Primers

CCI .22-Caliber Stinger—This is CCI's newest .22-rimfire cartridge, which, according to Omark, is 25 percent faster than a regular .22. Features include a Penta-Point (HP), copper-plated bullet, and nickel-plated case. Muzzle velocity: 1,685 feet per second. Caliber .22 Long Rifle. Price: $1.95/box of 50.

CCI Mini-Mag .22 Shotshell—This shot load features 165 #12 pellets in a plastic capsule. Pistol muzzle velocity: 1,050 feet per second. Price: $1.59/box of 20.

CCI .22 Maxi-Mag—This .22 WMR features a 40-grain solid-point bullet with bonded copper jacket. Muzzle velocity: 2,025 feet per second. Price: $3.92/box of 50.

CCI #200 Large Rifle Primers—These primers give positive ignition to all calibers requiring large rifle primers—.22-250 and up. Price: $9/box of 1,000.

CCI #250 Large Rifle Magnum Primers—Best for cold-weather hunting loads or when loading slow-burning IMR and Ball powders in .22-250 through belted magnum calibers. Price: $10.20/box of 1,000.

CCI #209 Trap & Skeet Shotshell Primers—Designed for the clay bird shooter. "Engineered Uniformity" means easy feeding in automatic primer feeds. Price: $15.55/box of 1,000.

Speer Rifle Bullets—The Speer line of rifle bullets features the exclusive Hot-Cor process in which molten lead is poured into their special jackets to get a core that grips the jacket better. Speer's Mag-tip bullets have a special jacket design that ensures good expansion every time. The rifle bullet line includes sixty-six different bullets in calibers from .22 to .458. Prices: from $4.45 to $10.95/box of 100.

Speer Handgun Bullets—Speer's handgun bullets include twenty different jacketed bullets and nine different swaged lead bullets, from 9mm to .45 caliber. Prices: from $5.25 to $7/box of 100.

Speer Round Balls—For the muzzle-loading enthusiast, Speer now offers a line of round balls—ten in all, ranging in diameter from .375 to .570 inch. Prices: $3 to $4.50/box of 100 (.375 through .530 inch), $2.45/box of 50 (.570 inch).

Speer Reloading Manual—Full of facts for the reloader. Includes data and loads for all popular rifle and pistol calibers and shotgun as well. Price: $5.50.

PACIFIC TOOL CO.

This division of Hornady offers an expensive line of reloading tools and accessories for metallic cartridge as well as shotshell reloading. They manufacture two "C" presses, four shotshell reloaders, a complete range of rifle and pistol dies, powder measures, and much more.

Series II Durachrome Dies

Multi-Power "C" Press—Here's the reloading press that lets you tackle the heaviest and most difficult reloading operations with smooth, effortless power. It has the power and strength for easy case forming, full-length resizing, and bullet swaging. But the heavy-duty capabilities don't make it a specialist. Precision-ground pins of hardened tool steel and extra-close manufacturing tolerances give it the precision to handle the most delicate reloading operations with the smallest and lightest calibers. That extra precision—plus features like 7/8-inch by 14 frame threads, universal primer arm, and a ram that accepts removable head shell holders—makes this as versatile as any reloading press you can buy. Prices: $64 (complete press only), $79 (with Durachrome dies, primer catcher, and removable shell holder).

Series I and II Durachrome Dies—These dies begin as solid steel bars. Then Pacific uses the most machinery to form them to ultraprecision dimensions, in nearly indestructible "Durachrome," and finishes them with careful hand polishing. They're so well built that they come with a lifetime guarantee. Series I two-die sets are for bottleneck cartridges. Series II three-die sets are for straight-sided cartridges. Price: $16.50.

Shell Holder
Bullet Puller

Removable Head Shell Holder—Pacific shell holders snap into the ram of your reloading press and hold the cartridge in perfect alignment for all reloading operations. For changing to different cartridges, you have snap-in/snap-out convenience. There are no set screws and you do not have to change rams. Will fit Pacific and most other presses. Price: $3.

Primer Pocket Reamer—Makes GI brass reloadable by cutting away the primer pocket crimp. Available for large or small primer pockets. Made of solid steel with blued, knurled finish. Price: $4.50.

Mesur-Kit Powder Measure—It's simple, fast, and easy to use. Just screw it onto powder can and turn upside down. To drop an exact powder charge, simply move the spring-loaded charge arm. The adjustable powder tube is precisely calibrated and easy to set. Universal powder can is included, and Mesur-Kit also fits standard DuPont and Winchester cans. Complete with chart showing settings for more than 1,000 loads. Price: $10.

Aluminum Powder Funnel—All-aluminum construction eliminates static electricity and powder clinging that occurs with plastic funnels. Three sizes available: .17 caliber, .22 to .270 caliber, .28 to .45 caliber. Price: $2.

New Bullet Puller—This heavy-duty bullet puller has improved collet lock-up. Hardened steel handle pushes precision collet down over bullet to grab even the shortest bullets. Collets are hardened to last a lifetime. Collets are available in thirteen sizes. Prices: $5 (puller without collet), $3.25 (each collet).

Pacific 105 Shotshell Reloader—This machine has much more performance and quality than you would expect in a low-priced reloader. It has the operating convenience of more expensive reloaders, quality construction that will give years of service, and precision to load top-performing ammunition. Whether you're a beginner or an experienced reloader, Pacific's 105 is a truly outstanding buy. It operates in the same convenient five-station sequence as Pacific's 155 and 266 loaders. It loads all types of ammunition, resizes entire length of shell, and crimps perfectly. Quality materials include blued steel, precision-machined aluminum, and heavy-duty alloy castings. Plastic is used only in the handle grip, hoppers, crimp starter, and spring fingers. It comes completely assembled and factory-adjusted with step-by-step instructions, recommended loads, and standard charge bushings. Conversion sets are available for changing to other gauges or to 3-inch magnum capabilities. Comes in 12, 16, or 20 gauge. Price: $57.50.

Pacific 366 Auto Shotshell Reloader—This is a fantastic machine featuring full-length resizing with each stroke, automatic primer feed, swing-out wad guide, three-stage crimping with Taper-Loc for factory tapered crimp, automatic advance to the next stage, and automatic ejection. The 366-Auto comes equipped with Auto-Advance, which automatically moves the shells to the next station, but is designed also to permit the operator to resume full manual control in case of a mixup. The Shot/Powder Shut-off permits operation of the loader without dropping shot or powder. Swing-Out Wad Guide automatically swings toward the operator at the completion of each stroke. Turntable holds eight shells for eight operations with each stroke. Automatic charge bar loads shot and powder. Primer tube filler is fast and fumble-free. Right- or left-hand operation. Interchangeable charge bushings, die sets, and magnum dies. Crimp starters for six-point, eight-point, and paper crimps. Available in 12, 16, 20, or 28 gauge. Comes complete with standard bushings. Price: $339.

New Versalite Wads—With Pacific's new Versalite wad you can change the powder charge, shot charge, shell case, or all three, and Versalite automatically adjusts to correct wad length. It's designed for 10 gauge and the most popular 12 and 20 gauge cases, including Winchester AA, Federal Champion II, Remington RXP, Winchester high-brass plastic, etc. The new Versalite wads simplify reloading. The center section is engineered to avoid tipping wad during seating, eliminating a common cause of bloopers. Flared shot cup lets you slip wad over seating punch, making your reloading faster, easier, and more enjoyable. Prices: $4/bag of 200, $19/1,000 wads.

PONSNESS-WARREN, INC.

If you're shopping around for a top-quality shotshell reloader, you should send for the Ponsness-Warren catalog, because they manufacture a line of superb machines that we're sure you'll want to learn more about. They also offer some accessories, primarily for their own line of reloaders.

Du-O-Matic Model 375 Shotshell Reloader—Here's one of the most versatile machines around. It can hold tooling for one or two gauges simultaneously. With two gauges attached, it can be converted from one to the other in less than five minutes. Conversion kits for 3-inch magnums

can be installed in even less time. Factory-perfect reloads are made consistently by moving a shell encased in a full-length sizing die around the five-station loading plate. The full-length sizing dies and tooling are precision ground, then polished or richly blued. All castings are of the finest grade aluminum, precision machined and handsomely finished in baked-on black wrinkle varnish. Under normal conditions, a person can load between eight and ten boxes of shells in an hour. The Du-O-Matic will handle all types of shells—paper or plastic, high or low brass. All shells loaded on Ponsness-Warren tools are guaranteed to feed and chamber into any firearm. Available in 12, 16, 20, or 28 gauge or .410 bore. Comes complete and ready to reload one gauge. Price: $149.50.

Mult-O-Matic Reloader

Mult-O-Matic Model 600 Shotshell Reloader—This machine was designed to fill the needs of today's active trap and skeet shooters. It is a progressive tool, built to provide the high production required by serious trap shooters as well as the multiple gauge capabilities necessary for skeet. Each shell is contained in a full-length sizing die through the entire reloading operation, producing perfectly sized, top-quality reloads in every gauge from 12 to .410. One operator can readily load at a rate of 500 rounds per hour. Additional tooling sets are easily installed in five to ten minutes. A unique breakaway cam prevents damage to the indexing system, should an inadvertent jamming occur through operator error. The simple loading procedure is easily mastered, leaving more time free for your shooting sport. All full-length sizing dies and tooling are precision ground, then polished or richly blued. The castings are made of the finest grade aluminum, precision machined and beautifully finished. The Mult-O-Matic will load paper or plastic shells, high or low brass, and all shells loaded are guaranteed to feed and chamber into any firearm. Available in 12, 16, 20 or 28 gauge and .410 bore, with six- or eight-point crimp. Price: $329.50.

Size-O-Matic 800B Shotshell Reloader—This is the tool for the shooter who demands unequaled performance. It is an incredibly efficient machine. One reasonably experienced operator can load shells at a rate of 700 rounds per hour; two operators, 1,200 rounds; three operators, 1,800 rounds. The Size-O-Matic has an ingenious automatic primer feed system with no tubes to fill and primers always in full view of the operator. A full box of 100 primers loads in just seconds. Each shell is held in a full-length sizing die through the entire loading operation, affording consistently perfect reloads, guaranteed to feed and chamber into any firearm. All tooling is ground to exacting specifications, then polished or richly blued. This machine will handle plastic or paper shells, either high or low brass, with unmatched ease and speed. Available in 12, 20, or 28 gauge or .410 bore, with six- or eight-point crimp. Price: $575.

REDDING-HUNTER, INC.

Redding is another brand of reloading tools and accessories that we've been using for years. Their line has grown extensively since we first started reloading, and they now offer presses for metallic cartridges, dies, scales, powder measures, case trimmers, shotshell reloaders, and more.

Improved "C" Press Model 7—New improvements include a stronger frame for the heaviest reloading task, extremely shallow throat that eliminates deflection, stronger lower linkage, added rear mounting lug that prevents springing and bench splitting, and snap-in shell holder that can be rotated to any position. The press accepts all standard dies and all universal shell holders. Press includes primer arm for seating both large and small primers. Prices: $36.50 (press complete), $52 (press, shell holder, case lube, and one set of dies).

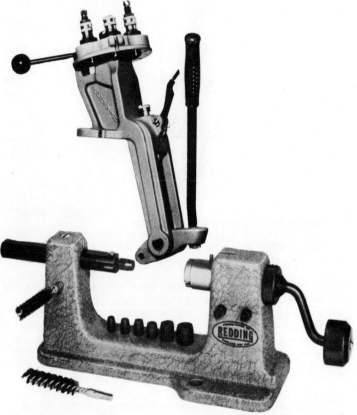

Turret Press Model 25

Master Case Trimmer Model 14K

Turret Press Model 25—Extremely rugged and ideal for production reloading. Choice of four-or six-station turrets. No need to move shell; just rotate turret head to positive alignment. Ram accepts any standard snap-in shell holder. Includes primer arm for seating both large and small primers. Prices: $84.50 (press complete), $98 (press, shell holder, case lube, and one set of dies).

Reloading Dies Model 10—Top quality, made from the best alloy steels available. Manufactured to exacting tolerances, properly heat-treated and hand-polished. No aluminum or chrome plating used. Available in usual calibers, in two-die and three-die sets. Standard ⅞-inch by 14 threads. Price: $16.50.

Master Case Trimmer Model 14K—This new unit features a universal collet that accepts all rifle and pistol cases. It is also unique in that it chamfers and deburrs the case neck at the same time it trims to length. The frame is solid cast iron with storage holes in the base for extra pilots.

Both coarse and fine adjustments are provided for case length. The case neck cleaning brush and primer pocket cleaners attached to the frame of this tool make it a handy addition to the reloading bench. Trimmer comes complete with two cutting blades, two pilots (.22 and .30 caliber), universal collet, two neck cleaning brushes (.22 through .30 caliber), and large and small primer pocket cleaners. Price: $26.50. Extra pilots: $1.25 each.

Powder Trickler Model 5—Brings underweight charges up to accurate readings, adding powder to scale pan a granule or two at a time. Speeds weighing of each charge. Solid steel, low center of gravity. Companion height to Redding scales. Price: $5.

Standard Powder Measure Model 4—Capacity from 0 to 100 grains. Powder pours directly from metering chamber into cartridge case. Metering chamber is chrome-plated, adjustable, and easily removed. Includes mounting bracket. Extra metering chambers available. Price: $16.50.

Standard Powder and Bullet Scale Model 1—Guaranteed accurate to less than $1/_{10}$ grain. Features include clearly graduated beam, 380-grain capacity, self-aligning bearings, two counterpoises, pour spout pan, and stable cast-iron base. Price: $19.25.

Super 32 Shotshell Reloader—This is a turret-type shotshell press capable of producing in excess of 300 reloads per hour. All reloading operations are performed at one station, eliminating shell handling. Resizes cases of any brass length without adjustments. Other features include a foolproof charge bar, fully adjustable wad pressure, and a tilt top that allows easy change of powder and shot. The most unique feature of this press is a quick-release die head assembly that allows a complete gauge change in seconds. Press comes complete with all necessary bushings, dies, shell holder, and crimp starter. Prices: $89.50 (12 or 20 gauge), $93.50 (16, 28, or .410), $39.50 (complete conversion kit for 12 or 20 gauge), $43.50 (conversion kit for 16, 28 or .410), $10 (die head stand).

REMINGTON ARMS CO., INC.

Besides being one of the major firearms manufacturers in the world, Remington is also one of the top producers of ammunition and components. Their annual catalog contains helpful charts and ballistics tables as well as descriptions of their products.

For descriptions of a number of Remington firearms, see Chapter 4.

"Express" Shotgun Shells—If it's a consistent performer you're after, you'll pick "Express" long-range shells for most field situations. Or make it "Express" buckshot loads or rifled slugs for bigger game. Either way, the yellow and green box brings premium quality to knockdown power. Available in 12, 16, 20, and 28 gauges and .410 bore in a variety of loads to meet all your long-range needs.

"Shur Shot" Shotgun Shells—Remington reliability and top performance are found in every "Shur Shot" shotgun shell. In the standard 2¾-inch length, these low base field loads are especially suited for game requiring shot sizes #4 or smaller. "Shur Shot" shotgun shells have Power Piston one-piece wads, Kleanbore priming, and smooth-chambering plastic hulls. Also available in 12 gauge scatter load with special wad column. The color-coded red and green box with the words Remington and Shur Shot is your assurance of quality and performance. Available in 12, 16, and 20 gauge.

RXP Trap & Skeet Loads—When the targets are clay, you need a shell that really smokes 'em. Remington RXP shotgun shells do. Everything that makes Remington hunting shotshells tough makes RXP trap and skeet loads dependable. Power Piston one-piece wads seal in the power to keep it where it counts—right behind the shot column. Specially

Cutaway view of Remington "Shur Shot" load
Cutaway view of Remington RXP load
Cutaway view of Remington Centerfire Rifle Cartridge
Cutaway view of Remington .22 Cartridge

not cause rust or corrosion. Available in seventeen calibers, from .22 Remington "Jet" Magnum to .45 Auto.

High-Velocity .22 Cartridges—High Velocity 22s are clean, because the "golden" bullets resist picking up dirt, grit, and lint when carried loose in your pocket. Shooters call them "pocket-proof." High-Velocity cartridges are designed for maximum effectiveness at specific ranges in Short, Long, and Long Rifle. High Velocity 22s have greater velocity at 50 yards than ordinary 22s have at the muzzle. Available in .22 Short, Long, and Long Rifle.

Match .22 Cartridges—Bullet shape micro-measured for consistency. Kleanbore priming and silicone base lubrication on bullets keep barrel cleaner. Special rim shape for improved ignition. Available in .22 Long Rifle Rifle Match and .22 Long Rifle Pistol Match.

Power Piston Wads—These wads are a lot more than one-piece plastic wads. They act as a container for the shot in the shell. They form an effective seal to separate shot from powder and keep moisture from the powder. They insert easily and fit exactly into reloaded shells. Special bridge construction compensates for various seating pressures, permitting a uniform crimp with different powder charges. Upon ignition, a specially designed shock absorber section cushions the shot to minimize shot-to-shot deformation. The Power Piston wad and shot leave the barrel together, utilizing the full power of the gases created by the ignited powder. The wad falls away from the shot column, its force having been transferred to the shot. The result is a better shot string and a more uniform shot pattern.

WINCHESTER-WESTERN

Winchester's legendary firearms are accompanied by their complete line of ammunition and components. Their catalog contains an abundance of helpful technical information, charts, and ballistics tables that should be of importance to any serious shooter or reloader. If you send for their catalog, request a copy of their booklet, "Ball Powder Loading Data," as well. It contains important data and loads for rifle, pistol, and shotgun. And don't forget to check Chapter 4 for their firearms.

Super-X Double X Shotgun Shells—These are magnum loads that give you full, dense patterns and can add up to 10 or 15 yards of effective distance. Specially granulated polyethylene powder added to the shot column works in combination with the Mark 5 collar to protect the shot and results in unprecedented patterns—full, dense, and right on target. This is a load that is becoming increasingly popular for turkey hunting.

Super-X Steel Shot—Nontoxic steel shot for waterfowl shooting is required by law in a small number of specified areas of the country. To meet this requirement, Winchester-Western has developed Super-X Steel Shot waterfowl loads. Available in shot sizes 1, 2, and 4 in 12 gauge, 2¾- and 3-inch magnum. Prices: approximately $9.60/box of 25 (2¾ inch), $12.30/box of 25 (3 inch).

Upland Shot Shells—Winchester-Western Upland is a shotshell designed specifically for the upland game hunter. Its characteristics of controlled power and full patterns make it especially effective for upland birds and elusive small-game animals. Available in shot sizes 4 through 9 in 12, 16, and 20 gauges.

Double A Special Skeet Loads—This is a shell for the skeet shooter who wants more open patterns. A unique wad design has the same gas sealing cup and cushioning column as in standard Double A Skeet Loads, but without the shot protecting collar. Available in 12 gauge. Price: approximately $5.10/box of 25.

Double A Handicap Trap Loads—A 12-gauge load designed for long-yardage handicap trap shooting. It has the same compression-formed

hardened shot is cushioned to stay round, fly true. Kleanbore priming, free from corrosion, means consistent ignition. And Remington powders are specially blended to burn clean and dependably. Component by component, the RXP target load is the tough, smooth-chambering shotshell that holds up to the gruelling demands of your favorite sport.

Remington Centerfire Rifle Cartridges with Core-Lokt Bullets—The advanced design of the Core-Lokt bullets locks jacket and core together. The heavy midsection and a notched jacket form the lock and give uniform expansion. Top-quality brass cases, made to precise tolerances, assure uniform powder volume and consistent performance. Progressive burning powder is specially selected for each cartridge and bullet type to assure proper velocity at safe pressure limits. The result is greater accuracy and reliable functioning, particularly in automatic rifles. Kleanbore priming provides instantaneous ignition and uniform, dependable performance. Noncorrosive Kleanbore priming will not cause rust or corrosion. Available in twenty-one bullet designs and weights in nine popular calibers.

Remington Centerfire Pistol and Revolver Cartridges—With a wide variety of calibers available, Remington offers a choice of ammunition for most handguns. REmington quality control standards call for the finest quality brass cases; bullets of exact weights and dimensions, lubricated to protect barrels; Kleanbore priming, combined with specially blended powder to match each caliber and bullet type. It all adds up to accuracy, reliability, and performance you can count on, shot after shot. Uniform crimping assures high accuracy and ideal combustion of powder. Highest quality brass is formed and machined into exacting tolerance in the manufacture of cases. Powders are selected for maximum performance in handguns. Remington quality control ensures uniform loading. Solid-head construction adds strength to the cartridge in the critical powder area. Kleanbore priming provides fast, positive ignition and will hull and components as regular AA loads, plus a special Handicap plastic wad with built-in shock-absorbing posts to help prevent pellet distortion and to maintain pattern performance from the 27-yard line. Price: approximately $5.10/box of 25.

Super-X and T22 Rimfire Ammunition—For hunting, target shooting, or plinking, Winchester-Western makes .22 ammunition for the broad requirements of today's rimfire shooters. Super-X 22 is the ideal load for a variety of small game. Now available with the recently introduced Dynapoint bullet, it gives you an unbeatable power package. Super-X Magnum 22 lets you reach out farther and shoot flatter when you are after medium-size game. T22 is a standard velocity cartridge, perfect for target shooting, shorter range hunting, and plinking.

Centerfire Rifle, Pistol, and Revolver Cartridges—Winchester-Western centerfire cartridges are available for all types of game, firearms, and every variety of hunting and shooting. There are more than 130 combinations of bullet types and weights and over 60 calibers to match your needs. Precision engineering, the finest quality components, and more than 100 years of experience assure accuracy, power, and performance.

W-W Staynless Primers—These primers are designed for fast, sure ignition, and they are noncorrosive. They are available for shotgun, large rifle, small rifle, and large and small pistol in regular and magnum.

W-W Cases—These cases offer superb quality, reliability, and maximum reload ability. The brass is custom-formulated in the Winchester-Western brass mill. All cases are designed for uniform capacity, exact chambering, and the ability to withstand neck and full-length resizing many times.

W-W Bullets—Jacketed and lead bullets come in a wide selection of types and calibers. All bullets are made to the most exacting standards of contour and structure for maximum accuracy and dependability. More than sixty different bullets are available to the reloader in calibers from .22 to .45.

Ball Powder Propellant—Winchester-Western smokeless propellants are the result of an exclusive manufacturing process that produces powder that meters evenly, burns cool and clean. And an improved, expanded line of eleven different types of propellant enables you to duplicate popular Winchester-Western factory loads and to reload many other specialty loads.

Ball Powder Loading Data Booklet—A new revised edition of this popular booklet has been published recently. Now in its third edition, the new 72-page booklet is the only complete source of reloading data available for Winchester-Western Ball Powder propellants. For your free copy, check your local dealer, or write to Edward A. Matunas, Winchester-Western, 275 Winchester Avenue, New Haven, Connecticut 06504.

ZENITH ENTERPRISES

This company manufactures one tool for the reloader, and we haven't seen anything else quite like it. If you want to eliminate problems with primers, you might want to check out Zenith's little Primer Mike.

Primer Mike—This new tool is a micrometer-type depth gauge, especially designed to assist the reloader in checking primer pocket depth and primer flushness in small arms cartridges. Easy to handle, it will help eliminate high primers, misfires, and faulty ignition. The scale is graduated in thousandths of an inch with the primer depth being indicated by a plus or minus reading. This is a precision-made, highly dependable gauge, constructed of top-quality materials. Price: $10 postpaid.

CHAPTER SIX

ARCHERY TACKLE AND ACCESSORIES

The burgeoning interest in archery has made it one of the fastest growing forms of outdoor recreation in America. Hunters are finding longer seasons and uncrowded hunting conditions available to them when they hunt with bow and arrow. Fishermen are able to find another kind of excitement hunting rough fish with archery tackle. And others have discovered that target shooting is a healthy combination of recreation, exercise, and competition.

Coinciding with the swelling ranks of archers is an industry that is booming. Many of the current big names in archery are relatively new to the business. And even the old companies are offering new lines of tackle that have undergone radical changes in design and materials.

Growing out of the recent development of the compound bow is an entire industry dedicated to producing bows that are more efficient, accurate, and powerful than their predecessors; arrows of cedar, fiberglass, graphite, aluminum, and stainless steel to fit any archer's needs; and countless hundreds of accessories, tools, and supplies to help keep bows in tune and arrows flying straight and true.

ALLEN ARCHERY

H. W. Allen holds the original patent on the compound bow, and his company produces eight different models of compounds. Also available from Allen are arrows, cases, and other accessories.

Model 7306

Allen's Compound Bow Model 7306—This is the original Allen compound bow with plenty of knockdown power. It features all-glass limbs with new laminated front face of epoxy bow glass and hard maple handles in forest colors. Draw lengths: from 23 to 31 inches. Draw weights: from 25 to 60 pounds. Let-off: 25 to 35 percent. Prices: from $115 to $125.

Allen's Speedster Model 7507—Here's knockdown power and up to 50 percent more speed and penetration in a bow priced to fit any hunter's budget. This bow weighs less than 3 pounds and features reliable, laminated, all-glass limbs, hard maple handle for all-weather comfort, and textured finish for nonslip grip. Draw lengths: 27 to 31 inches. Draw weights: 45 to 55 pounds. Let-off: 40 percent. Prices: from $79.50 to $99.50.

THE ALLEN CO., INC.

This company manufactures a variety of cases for archery tackle and limb covers for the bowhunter. They have cases available for compound bows and takedown models, as well as full-length sleeves to fit any size bow.

Model 670 Compound Bow Case—This case is of top grade expanded vinyl with ½-inch moistproof Tufflex padding and flannel lining. Features include a full-length, self-healing zipper and built-in pocket for extra string and accessories. Large enough to carry bow with quiver and arrows attached. Dimensions: 53×19 inches. Price: $31.

Model 640 Compound Bow Case—This leather-grained vinyl case with ¼-inch moistproof Tufflex padding and flannel lining has a full-length, self-healing zipper. Dimensions: 53×16 inches. Price: $18.50.

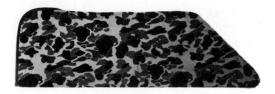

Model 130 Sleeve

Model 140 Covers

Model 130 Compound Bow Sleeve—This sleeve features camouflage material, one-third-length nylon self-healing zipper. Will fit compound bow with quiver and arrows attached. May be folded to pocket size to carry in the field. Dimensions: 54×18½ inches. Price: $7.50.

Model 140 Compound Limb Covers—These covers feature camouflage material with elastic and Velcro closures so that covers may be attached to compound bows without unstringing. Limb covers will adjust to fit most compound bows. Price: $4.95.

ANDERSON ARCHERY CORP.

Here's a company that represents more than 200 manufacturers in forty-seven countries and offers their products at discount prices. They carry a complete range of archery tackle and bowhunting accessories.

Bear Whitetail Hunter Bow—This new bow has all the compound features at a price you can afford. Double tapered, thermal bonded Epoxy-resin limbs—an exclusive Bear formula with over five years of development. Positive weight control system allows peak weights of 50, 55, or 60 pounds on the same bow. New Power-Tapered limb design. Smooth, soft, and extremely efficient fiberglass limbs. A six-wheeler design that stays tuned throughout the entire range of bow weight settings. Draw lengths: 28 to 30½ inches. Draw weights: 50 to 60 pounds. Let-off: 50 percent. A.A.C. price: $79.95.

Bear Lightarget

Jennings Super T Hunter Bow—This is a dependable hunting bow with superior performance. The successful Model T concept is supplemented by the ability to vary draw weight without changing draw length. Weight change is accomplished by simply turning the weight adjustment limb bolts with an allen wrench. This bow also maintains excellent cable clearance so that large hunting fletching may be used. Features include a textured black riser of 356/T-6 aluminum, center shot adjustment screw, laminated wood and Magna-Ply black limbs, and machined Delrin step-wheel eccentrics. Bow is drilled and tapped for sight, stabilizer, cushion plunger, and bow quiver. Maximum draw lengths: 25, 27, 29, and 31 inches. Draw weights: 25–35, 35–45, 45–60, and 55–70 pounds. Let-off: 40 percent. A.A.C. price: $129.95.

Bear-Easton Metric Magnum Aluminum Arrows—These arrows are made by James D. Easton to Fred Bear's specifications. The Sylvan brown shafts are made of a special X-7 alloy and were designed for use with compound bows. Resilient wall construction, coupled with large diameter, make them lightweight with super strength. They are coated with a hard anodic film for a long-wearing, noncorrosive life and they feature hand cresting and matched pro fletch vanes. Available in three-fletch and four-fletch models with a variety of point options, including the Bear Converta points. A.A.C. prices: $40.50 to $55/dozen.

Bear Lightarget—A fantastic new archery target that is long-lasting, lightweight, and resists the effects of moisture, insects, and small critters. Comes complete with stand, 80 centimeter printed target sleeve, sandbags for support, and interchangeable target sections for three times the target life. Target front is 32×32 inches, and entire target weighs less than 10 pounds. Stops compounds up to 70 pounds. Not for use with broadheads. A.A.C. price: $21.

BEAR ARCHERY

Fred Bear is one of the world's foremost bowhunters, and his line of archery products is extensive—covering a full range of compound and recurve bows, arrows, quivers, cases, and accessories.

The 48-page Bear Archery Catalog is chock-full of archery products, helpful information, and the addresses of major state and national archery clubs throughout the country.

Victor Tamerlane II—This is Bear's finest compound bow for the serious tournament archer, featuring new automatic tuners for easier tuning and smoother break-off, Arrowdynamic Flight System, exclusive new Glacier Vein metallic epoxy finish, and takedown design. Standard equipment includes dual-needle bearing eccentric wheels, chrome-plated idler pulley assembly, weight adjustment assembly, with case hardened or stainless steel components in critical assemblies. Bear Bristle Rest, adjustable nylon arrow plate, cover plate for bowsight, lightweight magnesium handle with standard pistol grip are other standard features. Glass color: white. Draw lengths: 27 to 31 inches. Draw weights: 30 to 55 pounds. Let-off: 33 to 36 percent, depending on eccentric wheel size. Other draw lengths and weights available on special order.

Victor Alaskan Bow—This is Bear's best compound hunting bow, with the convenience of a takedown. It features new automatic fine tuners, new Bear universal sight stage, Arrowdynamic Flight System, and new Silver Vein metallic epoxy finish. Standard equipment is similar to the Tamerlane II. Glass color: black. Draw lengths: 25 to 33½ inches. Draw weights: 35 to 70 pound peak. Let-off: 33 to 36 percent, depending on eccentric wheel size. Can be ordered in camouflage at additional cost.

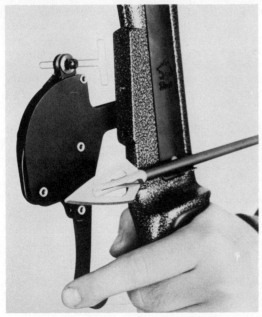
Trigger Sight

Bear Trigger Sight—A fantastic new hunting bowsight with a built-in rangefinder that automatically compensates for the distance between you and your target. No more missed shots because you misjudged the distance. Just place the sight window on your target and squeeze the sight handle with your finger until the target and sight line up. Instantly adjustable for various bow weight changes. Fits all new Bear compound and takedown bows with no drilling. Can be adapted to most other bows. Use a Trigger Sight and make your first shot count every time.

BOWHUNTERS DISCOUNT WAREHOUSE

This company caters to the bowhunter, with good prices on bows, cases, quivers, sights, and other tackle. They handle a number of top name brands, such as Jennings, Bear, Easton, Challenger, and PSE, to name a few.

Cobra Compound Bowstring Changer—Unique brass pully eliminates all wear on the nylon cord. Works well on all cable end types. Just brace one bow end and pull—the bow is in compressed position and ready for new string. Price: $4.25.

Cobra Compound Bowstring Changer

PSE 6-Arrow Hunting Quiver—This two-piece quiver fits all Precision bows. Lower piece attaches to stabilizer hole. Upper piece attaches to Killian sight holes. Stabilizer and sight can still be attached. Price: $13.95.

Protecto CB2 Case—Large enough to hold your compound bow as well as your arrows, quiver, sight, and accessories. Dimensions: 15×56×6 inches. Price: $46.

Protecto TBC027 Case—Carries takedown bow, arrows, sight, quiver, and other accessories. Individual compartments. Dimensions: 16× 38×6 inches. Price: $39.95.

Bear Polar II Economy Compound Bow—Quick weight change adjustments. Features magnesium handle with interchangeable grips, wood laminated limbs, excellent cable clearance, and built-in sight base. Drilled and tapped for stabilizer and quiver. Draw lengths: 28 to 30½ inches. Draw weights: 35 to 60 pounds. Price: $129.

BROWNING

Browning has been in the archery business for a long time, and they are currently offering a line of tackle that includes compound and recurve bows, arrows, and accessories for hunting, fishing, and target shooting.

For other Browning products, see Chapters 4, 7, 8, and 9.

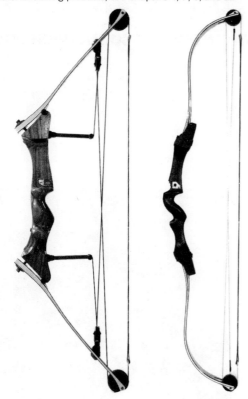

Explorer Compound Bow

Compound Cam-Lock

Explorer Compound Bow—This is the top of the fast-shooting Browning line, and is a product of the design genius of Harry Drake. Harry designed it short—only 40½ inches axle to axle—so it's easy to maneuver in thick cover, easy to carry down the trail, and fast shooting. This may surprise you, but a short compound actually shoots the same arrow faster than a long one. And this short little beauty is no exception. Adjusted to a 50-pound draw weight, Browning tested this bow with a 450-grain hunting arrow, and the chronographed velocities averaged from 195 to 200 feet per second. This hardwood handle also makes the Explorer light—only 3¾ pounds. The handle riser is equipped with three accessory insert bushings, so you can screw in a quiver and hunting stabilizers for deer hunting, and a bow fishing reel when you go after carp. Draw lengths: 28 to 29 inches. Draw weights: 45 to 60 pounds. Let-off: 40 or 30 percent. Price: $169.95.

Compound Cam-Lock—This bow combines the know-how of Harry Drake, Browning's master bowyer and holder of World Flight Records, with the sizzling power of the compound design. Its high-strength handle riser is a precision-cast alloy with a full center shot window and overdraw cutout, allowing you to shoot light, short arrows with maximum speed and accuracy. It has been predrilled for use with the Browning Super Berger Button or other popular adjustable arrow rests. It is fitted with three accessory insert bushings for quick attaching of the Browning bow quivers or other popular double-arm quivers, all popular hunting stabilizers, or even the Browning Piranha Bowfishing Reel. It has also been predrilled for the Browning Hunting Sights. It features a full pistol grip and thumb rest and a Browning Sure-Fold arrow rest. Draw length:

28 to 29 inches. Draw weights: 45 to 60 pounds (preset at 50 pounds). Let-off: 50 or 40 percent. Price: $157.95.

Deluxe Nomad Compound—This single-pulley bow has a unique draw length adjustment on the limb. By just twisting the knob a quarter turn, you can decrease or increase the draw length by ½ inch. It also has an adjustable draw weight. The select hardwood handle riser has a hand-filling pistol grip and is coated with a strong, durable, olive drab weatherproof finish. Three accessory insert bushings let you mount quiver, bowfishing reel, and stabilizers. The limbs are a high-gloss black finish fiberglass and maple lamination for flat, fast shots. Draw lengths: 28 or 29 inches. Draw weights: 45 to 60 pounds (preset at 50 pounds). Let-off: 50 or 35 percent. Price: $114.95.

CARROLL'S ARCHERY PRODUCTS

This is the birthplace of Carroll Compound Bows that are currently offered in four different models for hunting and tournament shooting. Some accessories are also available from CAP.

CAP 2000 Target Compound—The handle of this bow is made of cast magnesium and it is available in custom colors or Plastic Fantastic paint. The limbs are made of extremely durable laminated glass and hard core maple. Utility in the 2000 is paramount, but looks have not been neglected. Attractive, slotted, swept-wing side plates accentuate the beauty of the 2000. It is available in left- or right-handed models. Handle is drilled and tapped for CAP target sight. Cushion plunger and stainless steel stabilizer insert are installed. Stabilizer, soft case, and cushion plunger are furnished. The 2000 also features positive clicker ratchet and aircraft-type cables. Highly precision eccentric wheels are available in four sizes. Hardened steel axles are used in critical areas. Draw weights: up to 70 pounds. Let-off: 20 or 35 percent. Price: $310.96.

CAP 2000 Target Compound

CAP 900 Compound—This is an all-black compound, critically designed for the hunter. The improved limb design delivers speed and power with a smooth, quiet performance. There is ample cable clearance for any style of fletching. The 900 has a metal alloy handle that is drilled and tapped to accept the Carroll's and other conventional hunting sights. The bowstring is drilled for an adjustable rest or cushion plunger. Draw lengths: 25 to 32 inches. Draw weights: 30 to 65 pounds. Let-off: 35 or 50 percent. Axle to axle length: 47½ inches. Price: $175.

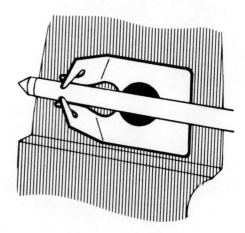

ArroGuide

J. DYE ENTERPRISES

This company offers the ArroGuide and ArroGuide 2 arrow rests for target shooters and bowhunters. If you can't find these accessories locally, you can order direct.

ArroGuide—For target archers, fun shooters, and beginners. Eliminates struggle to keep arrow on arrow rest. Improves shooting from first arrow shot. Allows archer to concentrate more on shooting form. Delicately cushions arrow at four points and helps forgive shooter's releasing faults. Fits left- or right-handed bows. Made of nylon and is self-adhesive. Price: $1.95.

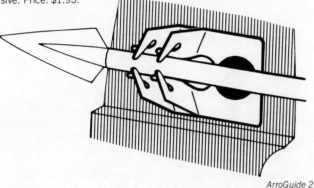

ArroGuide 2

ArroGuide 2—For bowhunting and bowfishing. Developed for quick draw and fast shots on moving targets. Snap arrow in guide and arrow stays in shooting position on bow. Shoot through it. Ideal for shooting with cold or wet hands. Price: $2.95.

GANDER MOUNTAIN, INC.

Gander Mountain's archery selection includes compound and recurve bows, fiberglass and aluminum arrows, and accessories for bowhunting and bowfishing.

For other Gander products, check Chapters 2, 3, 4, 5, 7, 8, and 9.

Jennings Twinstar Hunter Bow—This is a fine, adjustable two-wheeler. Limbs of white rock cross-laminated maple core with superior walnut wood fade out, Magna-Ply covered with reinforced tips give the Twinstar superb and quiet limbs. Aircraft aluminum handle fitted with insulated pistol grip, drilled and tapped for side mount sight and quiver; custom center shot adjustment screw included, as well as stabilizer insert and Super bow hunting rest are standard. Draw lengths: 29 to 31 inches. Draw weights: 40 to 50 pounds or 50 to 60 pounds. Let-off: 40 percent. G.M. price: $229.97.

Jennings Sidekick II—The new shorter length of Sidekick II has improved adjustable solid Magna-Ply limbs that develop a substantial performance increase for speed, recoil, and quietness. This is a durable, high-performance hunting bow. Its lightweight alloy handle, step eccentrics, and 20-pound weight adjustment are features that are usually found only on the most expensive compounds. The bow is drilled and tapped for the Delron center shot adjustment screw (included) and side mount sight and quiver (not included). Stabilizer insert and Super bow hunting rest are standard. Draw lengths: 29 to 31 inches. Draw weights: 40 to 60 pounds. Let-off: 40 percent. G.M. price: $79.97.

Ben Pearson Equalizer Bow—Designed for the tight situation that puts you in heavy cover within a few yards of your quarry. When maneuverability and speed are essential, power and accuracy a must, this bow is the one. Pearson designers took the principles of the reflexed tension and compression required to achieve acceleration in a tournament bow and compressed them into 48 inches of hunting dynamite. Handle is of select laminated hardwoods. Limbs are black Pearsonite with custom

Dacron string. Draw limit: 31 inches. Draw weights available: 40, 45, 50, and 55 pounds. G.M. price: $59.97.

Pearson Bow Fishing Outfit—Complete with tape-on reel, fiberglass arrow, harpoon head, and 50 feet of 80-pound braided nylon line. G.M. price: $8.77.

Pearson Bowhunting Sight—Four-position multicolored sight settings. Adjustable pins for windage and elevation. Double-nut locks ensure nonslip positions. Fits all bows. Comes with screws, but may be taped on. G.M. price: $7.47.

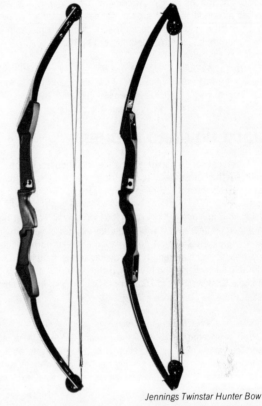

Jennings Twinstar Hunter Bow
Jennings Sidekick II

GOLDEN KEY ARCHERY PRODUCTS

This company has no catalog, but will provide descriptive literature on their arrow points and arrow rests to those who write.

Pacesetter-1 Arrow Rest

Pacesetter-1 Center Shot Arrow Rest—This all-new arrow rest brings you such standard features as precision parts, machined from the highest quality metals, polished and beautifully gold anodized; durable space-age launcher arm and reinforcement strips; positive locking vertical and horizontal adjustments of launcher arm; and calculated vertical give of launcher arm for optimal arrow flight. Complete with Redi-stick, pressure-sensitive tape with holding block drilled for permanent installation. May be used with cushion plunger if desired. Price: $11.10.

Pacesetter Hunter II Arrow Rest—This rest eliminates rest problems with such features as absolute clearance of fletching feathers or vanes, lowest possible sound level while drawing and shooting, full adjustment for height and left or right placement. It is impervious to weather, slick under all conditions, will support the heaviest shafts, can be used without a cushion plunger if desired, and lasts a lifetime, with replaceable launcher arms, if ever needed. Price: $11.10.

Futura Custom High Velocity Arrow Points—All new aerodynamic bullet design provides faster recovery of the arrow and better arrow flight by allowing more air to flow onto entire shaft and fletching, giving better steerage and higher velocity. Price: $11.10/dozen.

JACK HOWARD ARCHERY

Jack's catalog is loaded with tackle and accessories, tips, tricks, and hints for the bowhunter. Some of these products can be found nowhere else. Here's a small sampling of what Jack has to offer.

Jack Howard Hunter Bow—With the incorporation of a set-back handle, a generous deflex, and wider tips, the Hunter is very smooth drawing and completely stable. A combination of imported hardwoods used in riser section adds strength and beauty to the handle. The bow has a durable epoxy finish and is shipped complete with bow case. Length: 62 inches. Draw weights: to 70 pounds. Left- or right-handed models available. Price: $75.

Howard's Camo Release—Before you spray your bow with Howard Camo paint, simply brush on the Howard Camo Release, allow to dry, and then spray on the paint. After hunting season, you can then peel the paint off, leaving the bow looking just like new. Comes with complete instructions and enough release agent to do at least three average-size bows. Price: $1.50.

Broadhead Tip Aligner—This is a simple tool, yet it does an excellent job of placing the broadhead tops in exact alignment to centerline of the shaft. To use the aligner, you simply rotate the shaft, keeping an eye on the pointer just behind the broadhead. While the hot-melt cement is warm, you can easily align the tip, using the pointer as a guide. When tip is in alignment, you can carefully remove the arrow and dip the broadhead into cold water to set the cement. Price: $6.95.

Nylon Mesh Chest Protector—If you have problems with your bowstring catching on bulky clothing, a chest protector is the answer. It's a must

Arrow Points

when hunting in heavy down garments. Comes in large size for men and small for women. Colors: black or white. Available for right- or left-handed archers. Price: $6.95.

Pliobond—This is a very strong all-purpose adhesive that works well on nylon broadhead ferrules and plastic vanes, or any item that is normally tough to adhere. Pliobond becomes stronger with age. Prices: 60¢/1-ounce bottle, 98¢/3-ounce bottle.

Match-All Arrow Points—Four different points available in all sizes. Point styles are field, target, and blunt with tapered holes, and target with parallel holes. Prices: $1.25/dozen (field and target with tapered holes), $1.00/dozen (blunt with tapered and target with parallel holes).

Bjorn Server—Do you have a problem keeping the tension always the same on your string server? This one was made especially to lick that problem. Made from strong, light plastic. Price: $3.75.

IMPACT INDUSTRIES

Specifically for the archer, this company produces a new type of target that is lightweight, compact, portable, durable, and economical. They also manufacture a tree stand that bowhunters should find interesting. For a description of the tree stand, please turn to Chapter 11.

Promat Archery Target—This is a target ideally suited for home use as well as for shooting ranges. The heart of the Promat is a special self-sealing screen that will withstand thousands of penetrations without damage or excessive weakening due to central grouping. The material, a nylon monofilament, "remembers" its original shape, not where you hit it. Under rigorous mechanical testing, the screen was penetrated thousands of times and did not need replacement. The Promat I hunter's model weighs only 12 pounds and has a 24-inch-square target surface. The Promat II, a 36-inch model designed for beginners and groups, weighs only 15 pounds. Both models set up anywhere. They're as portable as your bow, and clean—no straw mess. The steel channel frame and support arms never need to be replaced. The strong woven backstop is the same material used in power lawn mower grass catching bags. It stops arrows without any damage to the shaft or fletching. If either the self-sealing screens or backstops should be cut, burned, or damaged, there are replacements available. Prices: $40 (Promat I), $53 (Promat II).

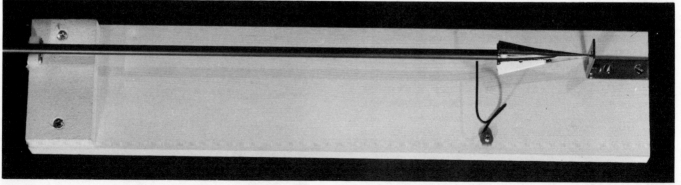

Broadhead Tip Aligner

Promat Target

JENNINGS COMPOUND BOW, INC.

A physicist by the name of Dr. Claude J. Lapp was involved in research on the efficiency of conventional bows in 1938. That research ultimately led to the creation of the first bow with pulleys. But it was Tom Jennings who convinced the archery world that the compound was a superior bow.

In 1950, Tom was designing, building, and selling handmade bows to the public under the name of S & J Archery. He built his first compound bow in 1966, and later toured the country in an effort to convince archers and state wildlife department officials of the virtues of the compound bow. Today, Jennings is the largest manufacturer of compound bows in the world. They currently offer eight different models for target shooting and bowhunting, as well as a line of compound accessories.

Arrowstar Target Bow

Arrowstar Target Bow—A rare combination of function and beauty puts the Arrowstar in a class by itself. Speed, stability, and special features exclusive to Jennings make the Arrowstar an outstanding tournament bow. Draw weight, draw length, and eccentric wheel roll-over can be adjusted for perfect arrow flight while maintaining the most cable clearance built into a compound bow. Standard features include custom riser, chromed hardware, adjustable arrow rest carriage with springy arrow rest, interchangeable black grip, laminated wood, and Magna-Ply white limbs, machined magnesium eccentrics with special bearings, machined aluminum idler wheels with bearings, and more. Draw

lengths: 23 to 33 inches (true draw 21½ to 31½ inches). Draw weights: 25 to 35, 30 to 40, 35 to 45, 40 to 50, and 45 to 55 pounds. Let-off: 40 percent.

Arrowstar Hunter Bow—The ultimate in four-wheel compound design, this bow was built for the serious bowhunter who demands perfectly tuned equipment. Fine tuning is simple with adjustments that allow you to precisely control draw weight, draw length, and eccentric wheel roll-over. Optimal cable clearance is achieved with large-diameter idler wheels. Performance and dependability make the Arrowstar Hunter the choice of discriminating bowhunters who expect the best from their equipment. Standard features include textured black custom riser, adjustable arrow rest carriage with cushion plunger and compound bow arrow rest, interchangeable wood-grained grip, laminated wood and Magna-Ply black limbs, machined magnesium eccentrics with special bearings, machined aluminum idler wheels with bearings, and more. Draw lengths: 23 to 33 inches (true draw 21½ to 31½ inches). Draw weights: 35 to 45, 40 to 50, 45 to 55, 50 to 60, 55 to 70 pounds. Let-off: 40 percent.

Six Shooter Bowquiver—This is an economical bowquiver designed for rugged use. Vinyl-coated metal brackets attach the quiver solidly and silently to the bow. The broadhead cover is molded out of special, high-impact plastic and is big enough to accommodate the largest broadheads. This quiver is especially designed to fit left- or right-handed Super T, Model T, or Sidekick II bows.

Ace-in-the-Hole Bowquiver—Here is an innovative eight-arrow bowquiver that fits all current Jennings bows. It attaches to the bow with a unique "quick release" feature. It features adjustable arrow grippers to accommodate large and small arrows, while the high-impact broadhead cover is large enough to safely protect eight big broadheads.

Buckshot Hunting Sight—This nonglare, textured black sight is a versatile sight, tough enough to withstand the roughest treatment while hunting. Positive contact between all parts stops any rattle and ensures positive alignment. It has a master adjustment, plus independent vertical and horizontal adjustments. It can be mounted to any bow on the market and features three-point hole spacing that also fits the popular Killian two-hole spacing. This sight can be instantly mounted to the front or back of recent Jennings bows by the use of furnished buttonhead screws which thread into pretapped holes.

Cushion Plunger—Totally redesigned for smooth jam-free operation, the Williamson Cushion Plunger is considered standard equipment by archers today. This top-quality product is manufactured of brass and is available in three lengths. Each cushion plunger comes as a complete package, consisting of three springs of different tensions, an adjustment wrench, and a Teflon button.

KOLPIN MANUFACTURING, INC.

Howard and Ron Kolpin have had twenty-five years of experience in bowhunting and archery, which is reflected in the ever-expanding line of Kolpin archery products. They have kept abreast of the growing demands and increasing numbers of bowhunters and tournament archers, and they offer a line of top-quality accessories.

Some of the Kolpin archery products are subject to the 11 percent Federal Excise Tax (FET) on archery tackle. The prices below include that tax where it applies.

#T-9 Super Deluxe Tournament Quiver—This outstanding quiver is made of oiled tan leather and features three separate arrow compartments, sculptured scorecard holder compartment, belt loop that fits any belt, hang-up loop, built-in pencil holder, two large YKK nylon zippered pockets and Western saddle color. It is equipped with three brass-plated

#T-9 Quiver

rings for attaching accessories such as powder pouch, yarn, arrow cleaners, gloves, etc. Price: $35.52 (includes FET).

#T-5 Deluxe Tournament Quiver—This quiver has the same features as the T-9, but features two arrow compartments and one pocket. Price: $31.08 (includes FET).

#800 Quiver—This unique quiver fits all compound and conventional bows and can be used with any bow sight, including Check-it or Killian. The quiver frame and broadhead shield are molded from fiberglass reinforced polycarbonate—the same material used in football helmets. Practically indestructible, it won't crack or break, even under the hardest impact. Comes complete with wood and metal screws. The entire assembly is precoated with a forest green finish. Price: $16.65 (includes FET).

#P-33 Powder Pouch—Genuine leather with clear vinyl flap that protects powder from rain and dampness. Features include cloth dispenser, scorecard clip, pencil holder, and clip for belt or quiver pocket. Tournament archers rub fingers in powder puff to achieve smooth release. Price: $2.75.

#A1C Camp Hip Quiver—Green camo pattern on expanded vinyl. Belt loops attach to either side with snaps. Ties down firmly to leg. Six molded rubber arrow holders and Styrofoam insert in molded rubber bottom hold broadheads firmly and silently. Snap fastener on belt strap for easy attachment. Price: $14.99 (includes FET).

#K2C Camo Shoulder Quiver—Green camo pattern on heavy-duty expanded vinyl with Styrofoam insert in rubber base. Adjustable leather shoulder strap. Holds eighteen arrows. Price $11.10 (includes FET).

#CH53C Compound Bow Case—This lightweight, green camouflage, cotton case has a full length YKK nylon coil zipper and permits compound bows to be carried without loosening tension on the limbs. Fold it up and carry it in your pocket, or unzip it and use it as a blind, scarf, or seat. Length: 53 inches. Price: $10.50.

MICRO MOTION, INC.

This company manufactures the Arrometer—a digital readout chronograph for serious archers. The company also offers three accessories for the Arrometer: an adjustable tripod stand, an automotive power adapter, and a synthetic leather carrying case.

If you're interested in testing bows and arrows, you might want to send for the latest flyer on the Arrometer.

Arrometer—This unique new device measures arrow velocity to within ± 1 foot/second, using opti-electronic techniques. It operates on either 12V DC or 115V AC. To operate the Arrometer, dial arrow length on switch provided and reset display using reset button. Shoot arrow through 10×14-inch opening. Arrow speed in feet per second will immediately appear on digital display and remain until next reset. With this instrument you can compare stainless steel, fiberglass, aluminum, graphite, and wooden arrows; compound bows and conventional bows; short bows with long bows. Measure the effect of different draw lengths or the effect of brace height. Price: $329.95.

Arrometer

NATIONAL ARCHERY CO.

National Archery produces the Kantpinch line of finger tabs as well as several other accessories for the archer, including an economically priced bow quiver.

Kantpinch Tab #300—The famous Kantpinch Tab has proven to be the answer to better shooting. The patented finger separator helps prevent pinching. These tabs are used by thousands of bowhunters, field shooters, and target archers the world over. The #300 features a calfskin back with exclusive, replaceable, snap-on calf-hair face. Price: $3.

National Bow Quiver—This quiver holds five arrows securely and allows instant, silent finger release. Fits all bows securely without cutting or

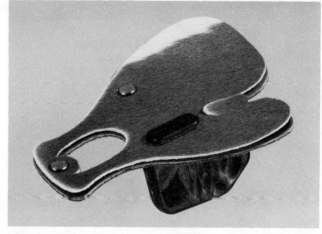

Kantpinch Tab 300

drilling. Constructed of 100-percent specially compounded rubber. Price: $4.50.

Bowhunter's Arrow Rest and Arrow Plate—The rest is formed from foamed PVC, covered with nylon hair. The plate is formed with nylon sheet backing on nylon hair. The combination produces silent, accurate, full-speed arrow flight. Specially designed for bowhunting and field shooting. Both arrow plate and rest have self-adhesive backing for easy, permanent installation. Price: $1.

NOCK-RITE CO.

From Nock-Rite comes a neat bowstring attachment by the same name. It is marketed nationally through archery and sporting-goods dealers.

Nock-Rite Bowstring Attachment—This device is made of weather-resistant, high-quality, flexible Neoprene. It flexes with the bowstring and assures smooth arrow release with no finger protecion necessary. Its comfortable fit provides a balanced three-finger action. Nock, draw, aim, and shoot with greater speed and accuracy. Nock-Rite's ability to provide lightning-fast perfect nocking of the arrow makes it ideal for hunting. Bow fishermen like it for its speed and convenience, and many archers use it for target shooting. Prices will vary from dealer to dealer, but will probably be less than $2.

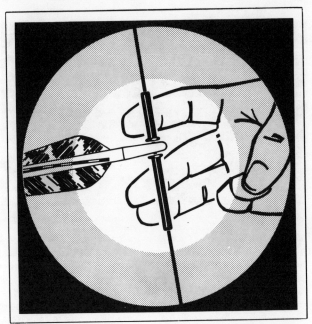

Bowstring Attachment

BEN PEARSON

A name long known in the world of archery, this Division of Brunswick Corporation offers an extensive line of archery tackle, including compound and conventional bows, arrows, sights, quivers, bowfishing reels, and other tackle and accessories.

Ben Pearson tackle is marketed nationally through archery and sporting-goods dealers and mail-order companies.

Shadow 600 Bow—This adjustable six-wheeler combines two-wheel simplicity with four-wheel performance for greater stability and speed. It features choice of adjustable peak weights with no fine tuning required. Self-compensating design keeps bow in perfect balance. Precision die-cast magnesium riser graces interchangeable, laminated "Hyper-Flex" limbs, tapped for three stabilizers, bow quiver, bow sight, and cushion

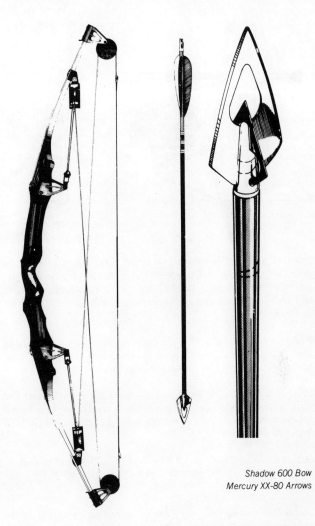

*Shadow 600 Bow
Mercury XX-80 Arrows*

plunger. Length: 44 inches axle to axle. Draw lengths: 28 to 29 inches, and 30 to 31 inches. Draw weights: 45 to 50 pounds, and 55 to 65 pounds. Let-off: 30 percent.

Shadow 100 Bow—This adjustable, economy two-wheeler requires no fine tuning. Self-compensating design keeps bow in perfect balance. Riser is precision, die-cast magnesium and interchangeable limbs are of reinforced poly-fiberglass. Drilled and tapped for stabilizer and cushion plunger. Length: 41¾ inches axle to axle. Draw lengths: 28 to 29 inches, 30 to 31 inches. Draw weights: 50 to 60 pounds. Let-off: 45 percent.

Hunter II Set—Everything you need to take to the field for plenty of hunting fun. For right-handed archers only. Contains 58-inch Hunter II bow, four 29-inch cedar hunting arrows with color band and crest, bow quiver, armguard, leather finger tab, 16-inch leopard target face, and the Ben Pearson booklet, "Secrets of Successful Bow Hunting."

Ben Pearson Collegian Target Set—The target set most recommended for schools, camps, and youth groups. Contains all the equipment necessary to put an archer on the line or in the field: 64-inch Collegian bow for right-handed shooters, four 28-inch cedar target arrows, belt quiver, armguard, leather finger tab, 16-inch target face, and "How To Shoot" booklet.

Mercury XX-80 Pearson-Easton Aluminum Arrows—For trophy hunters who demand a superior arrow. Matched to precision in weight and spine, with Pearson Switchblade broadheads. Anodized green hunting finish, parabolic fletching, distinctive hand cresting. Uniformly perfect performance, shot after shot.

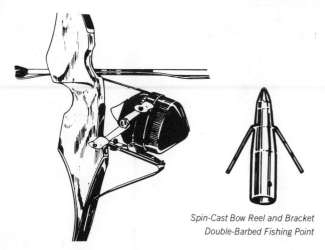

Spin-Cast Bow Reel and Bracket
Double-Barbed Fishing Point

Spin-Cast Bow Reel and Bracket—Famous Zebco 808 is a heavy-duty bow reel that comes loaded with 60 feet of 80-pound nylon line. Has precision, self-lubricating stainless steel gears, bronze bearings, and disk drag system, and durable Lexan body. Bracket tapes to any bow. Salt water resistant.

Bow Reel #9990-0—Efficient, one-piece aluminum reel, equipped with spring wire line clip. Sturdy, yet lightweight. Tapes easily to any bow. Loaded with 50 feet of 80-pound-test nylon line.

Shoot-Thru Bow Reel #9995-0—This reel is 7 inches in diameter and mounts easily to your bow. Has line holder to prevent line from paying out too soon when shooting at sharp downward angles. Loaded with 75 feet of 72-pound line.

Double-Barbed Fishing Point #9870-0—Fishing line attaches to lower section of point, which unscrews from the harpoon head. For ⁵/₁₆-inch shaft.

Sting-A-Ree Fishing Point #9825-0—Designed for bowfishing for the big ones. Ideal for gar, sharks, and large rough fish. Long, extra-strength design for deep penetration. Large double barb holds the big ones. Retractable design, for ⁵/₁₆-inch shaft.

PLAS/STEEL PRODUCTS, INC.

From Plas/Steel comes the Glas-Lite line of archery products, including the economically priced Bushwhacker and Stinger bows, as well as a variety of Glas-Lite arrows.

For the Glas-Lite line of fishing rods, see Chapter 2.

Bushwhacker I Bow—This sensational takedown bow with interchangeable limbs of perfected Laminaglass give the performance you'd expect from custom conventionally laminated bows. Thanks to a creative design that combines high-tensile aluminum alloy with extra-wide limbs of prestressed fiberglass, it's packed with custom tournament features. Takes down to 24 inches for easy packing. The center section is finished in lustrous, nonreflecting black. The limbs have an integral woodgrained finish. Features include full-working recurve, extra-wide limbs; sure-grip takedown system; long, slim sight window; bi-radial arrow

Stinger Bow

shelf; comfortable pistol-grip handle; and integral stabilizer points to dissipate vibration. Length: 60 inches. Draw length: 30 inches. Draw weights: 25 to 65 pounds. Price: $29.95.

Stinger Bow—Here's a bow that's smooth as silk and fast as lightning. The Laminaglass powered limbs give it performance like custom bows. Form-fitted, high-tensile aluminum alloy handle in lustrous nonreflecting black. Wide, gracefully recurved limbs with integral woodgrained look. Good looking and a compact 50 inches overall, the Stinger has three-piece takedown for handy packing to camp or on hikes. Like the larger Bushwhacker, the Stinger comes complete in its own combination shipping carton and handled carrying case with fitted insert. Draw length: 28 inches. Draw weights: 15 to 40 pounds. Price: $18.50.

Glas-Lite Deluxe Matched Tubular Fiberglass Arrows—Exclusive filament-woven fiberglass shafts assure strength and accuracy. No seam or overlap to reduce concentricity. Available with a variety of head options for hunting, field, and target. Prices: from $23.34/dozen to $29.81/dozen.

RORCO

This firm offers a unique product for the bowhunter—an ingenious device called the Shaft Spider, which is a tracking arrow that will lead you to your downed game, or, in the event of a miss, to your expensive arrow.

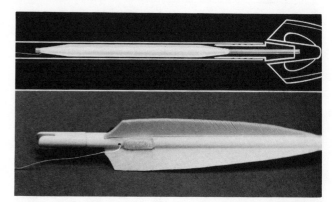

Detail of Shaft Spider Installation

The Shaft Spider Tracking Arrow Kit—The tracking arrow leaves a continuous web trail for you to follow easily. After you've shot that big buck, the trail begins right at your fingertips and will be obvious regardless of weather, time, or terrain. And if you missed, the Shaft Spider solves your lost-arrow problem. Simply follow the trail, retrieve your arrow, and be ready for another shot. Shaft Spider kits come with parts to fit three of your own hollow shafts—either aluminum or fiberglass. A lightweight, precisely wound bobbin attached to the broadhead insert and fitted inside a hollow shaft lays 1,800 feet of trail through a small hole near the nock as the arrow accelerates. The web end catches on a small Velcro bow piece to mark the beginning of the trail. The Shaft Spider trail is laid, not dragged by the arrow, and therefore will not break while unraveling through even the heaviest brush, will not impede game, and will not affect arrow flight. Kit comes with complete, easy-to-use instructions. Price: $4.95.

SAUNDERS ARCHERY CO.

This company's product line is made up of a variety of tackle and accessories for bowhunting, bowfishing, and target archery.

Scoremore Sight—For target archers who need a short bar sight, Saunders offers this new, inexpensive sight. It features pressure-sensitive coated copper attachment brackets, which eliminate the need for drilling holes in the bow. Adjustment screws on the sight are self-locking, and a special patented expanding Lexan V-bar locks the head with absolute zero play. The complete bar and head can be removed for transport. All parts are guaranteed against breakage, except the sight pin, which is replaceable. Price: $6. Extra pins: 50¢.

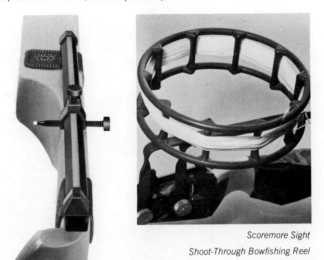

Scoremore Sight
Shoot-Through Bowfishing Reel

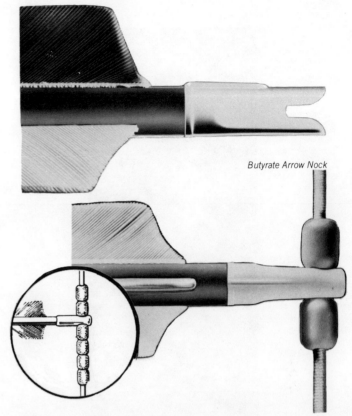

Butyrate Arrow Nock

Nock Locks

Shoot-Through Bowfishing Reel—Bow fishermen will appreciate the new„ open-design reel offered by Saunders. The reel is available in three styles: a tape-on model, Kwik Mount Bracket, and side mount. A magic finger line holder holds the line until the shot is made and then releases it. The outside rim allows a smooth, low-friction line payout during the shot. The 7-inch diameter allows fast rewind and the open construction allows line to dry fast. The reel comes with 50 feet of 80-pound line. Price: $8.

Reel Holder—Shooting gar, carp, and other rough fish with a bow and special fishing arrow is thrilling sport as well as a tough challenge. An economical way to begin is with Saunders' Reel Holder, which is easy to install and use. It quickly adapts a closed-face spin-casting reel to any bow with a standard stabilizer hole. Price: $3.

Ventilated Armguard—Warm weather is the best time for enjoying archery outdoors, but short sleeve climate conditions also emphasize the need for an armguard. Armguards can be uncomfortable in hot weather, unless they are ventilated. This new armguard solves the comfort problem and is priced economically, too. It is made of tough polyurethane that will not crack or curl. It features two elastic bands that adjust easily and quickly. Price: $3.

WILSON-ALLEN CORP.

Wilson-Allen's archery products include Butyrate arrow nocks, Nock Locks, Brush Knocks, and Bow-Tip Protectors. The company has no catalog, but descriptive literature is available.

Butyrate Arrow Nocks—These nocks, made of tough, resilient Butyrate, have high-impact strength that lessens breakage. They are easy to draw, easy to release, comfortable to grip, and are excellent for hunters and target shooters. Sizes: 11/32, 5/16, 9/32, and ¼ inch. Colors: white, red, blue, green, yellow, black, and orange. Price: 50¢/dozen.

Arrow Nock Locks—These bowstring attachments help to increase accuracy, as the arrow is nocked in the same position for every shot. Arrows nock instantly and stay nocked. Reduced finger tension eliminates scrape of string on fingers or guard. By using four Nock Locks below the nock and two above, there's no need to use a glove or tab, as the Nock Locks will protect and cushion fingertips. Price: 60¢/pair.

Brush Knock—Use Brush Knocks at each end of the bow to protect bow from snagging brush and grass between string and bow. Made of pure gum rubber, Brush Knocks will not mar bow and will serve as silencers, too. Fit all bows. Price: $1/pair.

Bow-Tip Protector—This little device, made of soft and pliable rubber, protects bow while stringing, holds string in place, keeps bow tip in new condition, and fits all bows. Use one on each end of bow. Price: 60¢ each.

YORK ARCHERY

While York currently offers only one compound bow, their line of recurve bows includes nine models. They also carry a wide variety of arrows and other tackle for target shooting, bowhunting, and bowfishing.

Coronet Compound—This two-wheeler features an aluminum alloy handle and solid epoxy fiberglass limbs. It is available in a right-handed model only. Length: 43 inches axle to axle. Draw lengths: 26 to 27, 28 to 29, and 30 to 31 inches. Draw weights: 50, 55, and 60 pounds. Let-off: 50 percent. Price: $88.80.

Trophy Recurve Bow—Classic beauty with unsurpassed shooting stability. Available in right- or left-handed models. Comes with stabilizer bushing. Length: 60 inches. Draw length: unlimited. Draw weights: 40, 45, 50, and 55 pounds. Price: $75.50.

Thunderbolt Recurve Bow—Short and powerful for deep woods hunting, this bow is available in right- or left-handed models. Length: 54 inches. Draw length: unlimited. Draw weights: 40, 45, 50, and 55 pounds. Price: $62.

Tracker Recurve Bow—This is the perfect bow for the beginning bowhunter. It is available in right- or left-handed models. Length: 58 inches. Draw length: unlimited. Draw weights: 40, 45, 50, and 55 pounds. Price: $57.70

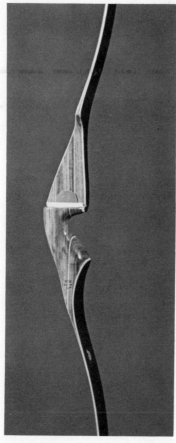

Thunderbolt Bow

Crest Recurve Bow—With superb craftsmanship and design, this bow is for the advanced archer. Available in right- or left-handed models. Comes with stabilizer bushing installed. Length: 68 inches. Draw length: unlimited. Draw weights: 20, 25, 30, 35, and 40 pounds. Price: $71.

Matched Aluminum Target Arrows—These tournament-quality target arrows are made from Easton/Swift aluminum tubing, matched to precise weight and spine tolerance. Colored white with multicolored hand cresting. For 25- to 45-pound bows. Lengths: 26, 28, 29, and 30 inches. Price: $43.30/dozen.

Matched Fiberglass Target Arrows—These high-quality arrows are made from Gordon shafts, matched in weight and spine for precision shooting. Shafts are yellow with multicolored hand cresting. For 25- to 45-pound bows. Lengths: 26, 28, 29, and 30 inches. Price: $37.70/dozen.

Matched Cedar Target Arrows—These deluxe arrows are made of choice Port Orford cedar shafts and are matched for accurate shooting. They are equipped with parallel target points, plastic nocks, and parabolic-shaped fletching. Colored white and crested in six standard color combinations. For 20- to 40-pound bows. Lengths: 24, 26, 28, and 30 inches. Price: $13.80/dozen.

Beginner's Practice Arrows—These arrows are made of brightly colored Port Orford cedar shafts with contrasting crest, bullet points, and plastic nocks. Not recommended for bows over 40 pounds. Lengths: 26 and 28 inches. Price: $8/dozen.

Flu Flu Arrows—These arrows are made of Port Orford cedar shafts with six-feather fletchings for proper breaking action. Full-color shafts with multicolor cresting and nonskid point. Length: 29 inches. Packed four to a box. Price: $11.10/box.

CHAPTER SEVEN

CAMPING AND BACKPACKING EQUIPMENT AND ACCESSORIES

The term "camping" encompasses a vast array of outdoor recreational activities. To one person, camping means climbing aboard a self-contained motor home—complete with carpeting, air conditioning, shower, stereo, and color TV—and driving off to a campground where the rig can be plugged into the 110V outlet and hooked up to water and sewer systems.

To another, camping means donning oiled leather boots with Vibram soles, and carefully filling and balancing a lightweight backpack with freeze-dried foods, clothing, down bag, 5-pound tent, and other essentials and trekking off to the high country where convenience means a nearby stream for drinking water and a fairly level spot for pitching the tent.

To still another, camping means loading waterproof bags of duffel into a sleek 17-foot canoe and paddling off into a watery wilderness.

For some, camping is a part of another outdoor activity, such as fishing, hunting, or outdoor photography, while others just enjoy camping for its own sake.

It's no wonder, then, that it takes such a broad selection of equipment and accessories to satisfy the diverse requirements of "campers." No matter what sort of camping suits you, we're sure you will find some gear and gadgets in the following pages to fit your particular needs.

ALTRA, INC.

For the cost-conscious do-it-yourselfer, Altra offers kits for making your own tents, day packs, cargo bags, and sleeping bags. Their clothing kits are described in Chapter 8.

Two-Person Tent

Two-Person Tent Kit—This new design features an airy, light, livable interior with 360-degree visibility. The tent is free-standing, compact, and easy to pitch. The extra-wide pole sleeves provide a 3-inch clearance between the tent walls and the rain fly to increase breathability and prevent condensation. The optional vestibule gives more space for storing your gear and allows a dry entrance in foul weather. There are four storage pockets sewn into the 1.9-ounce ripstop nylon canopy and the floor fabric is a tough, coated taffeta. The entire tent is fire-retardant. Floor size: 7 feet 2 inches by 4½ feet. Tent weight: 6 pounds 10 ounces (add 1 pound for vestibule). Prices: $99.50 (tent and fly), $115 (with vestibule).

Day Pack Kit—This is a functional, dual-compartment carrying pack that can be used for extended day hikes or for an everyday tote bag. Its inner compartment is designed to handle many items and accessories, including parka or rain gear. Made of heavy Cordura nylon, this pack is rugged, lightweight, and comfortable to carry. Even though the material is tough, this pack can be sewn on a home machine. Color: green. Price: $12.50.

EDDIE BAUER

This company is a major mail-order supplier of fine camping and backpacking equipment and outdoor clothing. Their catalogs are mailed free on request in the spring and fall.

See Chapter 8 for other Eddie Bauer products.

Heavy-Duty Sleeping Bag

Expedition Mummy Bag

Heavy-Duty Sleeping Bag—If you're traveling by pack train or Jeep to set up a high-country big-game camp, driving a long-haul rig to Alaska via the Alcan Highway, spending the winter north of the Arctic Circle, or if you just want the peace of mind that comes with owning a fine sleeping bag, this is the one for you. These bags aren't for the backpacker or hike-in camper. They are big, full-size, heavy-duty heavyweights, built to do a man-sized job of keeping you comfortably warm when the weather is downright miserable. These bags are available in three models. Model 0485 is a regular-length bag insulated with 2 pounds 8 ounces of goose down for a comfort range of +15° to +60° F. Model 0486 is a regular-length bag with 3 pounds 8 ounces of goose down insulation for a comfort range of −10° to +55° F. Model 0487 is a large and long bag, insulated with 5 pounds of goose down for a comfort range of −30° to +50° F. Prices: $145 (#0485), $165 (#0486), $195 (#0487).

Kara Koram Expedition Mummy Sleeping Bag—This bag is engineered to keep you warm and safe in −30° F. temperatures and comfortable at +50° F. with two-way zipper adjusted for maximum ventilation. Four models in this comfort range are insulated with premium-quality goose down. Prices: from $149 to $159.

L. L. BEAN

It all started back in 1912 when L. L. Bean, weary of wandering through the woods with wet feet, decided to design a better hunting boot. What he came up with was the legendary Maine Hunting Shoe with premium leather uppers stitched to waterproof rubber bottoms. This boot was an immediate success, and L. L. Bean was in business. Mr. Bean borrowed $400 to start his business. Today, L. L. Bean's annual sales exceed $40 million.

The company is one of the largest mail-order firms in the world. So great is their volume of mail, in fact, that they have their own zip code. With two million catalogs being sent out four times a year, their postal bill alone is $2½ million a year.

Bean offers a large line of top-quality camping and backpacking gear, as well as superior clothing for outdoorsmen. Check Chapter 8 for the L. L. Bean clothing line.

Timberline Tents—Compact and lightweight backpacking tents that are easy to set up and efficient in all kinds of weather. Self-supporting and suspended from an external frame with shock cords that absorb stress from wind and rain and keep tent trim. Usable on almost any site all year round. A-type storm door opens completely to the side for easy entry. Nylon netting inner door and rear window for cross ventilation. Nylon-coil zippers are freeze resistant and self-healing. Wraparound floor of 1.9-ounce coated ripstop nylon extends up the sides of the tent. Two-man and four-man models available. Storm flies available for both models. Dimensions: 5 feet 3 inches by 7 feet 2 inches by 42 inches (two-man), 7 feet 2 inches by 8 feet 9 inches by 58 inches (four-man). Weights: 7 pounds 14 ounces (two-man), 9 pounds 14 ounces (four-man). Prices: $83 (two-man), $118 (four-man), $59 (two-man fly), $76 (four-man fly), all postpaid.

Bean's Zipper Duffel Bags—Rugged 12-ounce army duck is water repellent and mildew resistant. Lock-stitched seams and sides reinforced with 1½-inch webbing straps. Ends piped with leather for strength and rigidity. Comfortable leather handles, and bottom reinforced with sturdy vinyl-coated fabric. Heavy-duty zipper runs full length of bag. Two sizes: 21×11 inches and 27×16½ inches. Prices: $16, $22, postpaid.

Snow Lion Limited Edition Light Goose Down Bag—The ideal three-season backpacking and bicycle touring bag, it combines minimum weight (under 3 pounds) with exceptional compactness (will fit in rucksack), and is comfortable over a wide temperature range (+5° F. minimum). Available in regular or long lengths. Prices: $97, $104, postpaid.

Timberline Tent

Duffel Bags

Hudson's Bay Point Blankets—Famous the world over for lifetime comfort and wear. These genuine four-point Hudson's Bay Blankets are made of the very finest pure virgin wool, tightly woven for extra thickness and warmth. The Hudson's Bay Company started making these blankets in 1779, and the four points shown on the blanket indicate the price paid by Indian fur traders—four large beaver skins. Regular size: 72×90 inches. Queen size: 90×100 inches. Colors: white with candy stripes, red with black stripe, gold with dark gold stripe, green with black stripe (green not available in queen size). Prices: $65, $85, postpaid.

Boat and Tote Bags—Handy tote bags for boaters and campers. Sturdily constructed from extra-heavy white duck. Sizes: 6×13½ inches by 12 inches high, 8×17 inches by 16 inches high. Prices: $7.75, $8.75, postpaid.

BECKEL CANVAS PRODUCTS

Bob Beckel sends out a catalog that is both fun to browse through and interesting to read. It contains tenting products and camping equipment, as well as some items not likely to be found elsewhere.

Eena Wall Tents—These tents were originally built to meet the needs of Oregon elk hunters who often encounter severe weather and heavy

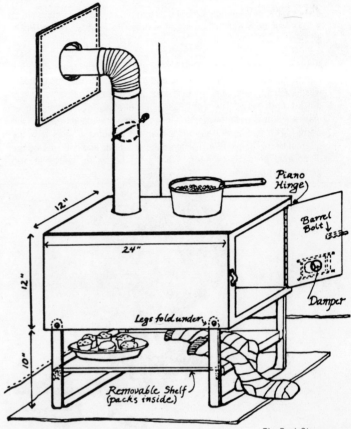

The Pack Stove

snow loads. All Eena tents are made of heavy-duty 10-ounces-per-square-yard, breathable, marine-grade cotton canvas. It is extremely water repellent and mildew resistant. It is preshrunk and tightly woven for good heat retention and has a high strength to weight ratio. Cut sizes: from 9×9 feet to 15×21 feet. Prices: from $119.95 to $310.95.

The Pack Stove—This stove has fold-up legs, a biscuit-warming and sock-drying shelf, an easy-to-use draft, and a sturdy latch that works. There's also room to pack the pipe and pots and pans inside. It weighs about 30 pounds, complete with 60 inches of 3-inch-diameter pipe, damper, one elbow and a T for the end of the pipe. It is made of 22-gauge black iron and stands 22 inches high with legs extended, 12 inches without. It is 12 inches wide and 24 inches long and will burn 20-inch wood with ease. Price: $74.95 postpaid.

BERNZOMATIC CORP.

This company produces a number of propane-fueled camping accessories, such as stoves, lanterns, and catalytic heaters. They utilize convenient, safe, and clean-burning propane cylinders that are easy to pack along and can be replaced in seconds.

Propane Catalytic Heater Model HT-5000—Campers, hunters, fishermen, and outdoors people everywhere enjoy the flameless comfort of these heaters, which light instantly without priming or pumping. This economy model comes with regulator valve. The unit includes a tipproof cylinder stand that will accommodate either a 14.1-ounce or 16-ounce BernzOmatic disposable cylinder. One 16-ounce cylinder included. Heat range: 1,000 to 5,000 BTUs per hour. Price: $32.20.

Propane Lantern Model TX007—In the woods, at the campsite, or in a power shortage, the convenience of a BernzOmatic propane lantern is unsurpassed. This single-mantle model with tipproof cylinder stand accommodates both 14.1-ounce and 16-ounce disposable cylinders and comes with the 16-ounce size. The lantern provides a light equivalent to a 100 watt bulb with a burning time of ten to fourteen hours. Price: $17.50.

Propane Thermo Fogger—This lightweight, cordless propane-powered thermo fogger clears picnic areas and campsites of flies, mosquitoes, wasps, bees, gnats, ants, moths, ticks, and other troublesome insects quickly and easily. The nonstaining, penetrating fog reaches under leaves and bushes far beyond the reach of wet sprays to kill insects. One filling fogs a half-acre area in less than ten minutes. Comes with one quart of BernzOmatic EPA-registered Super Jet Fog and one 14.1-ounce disposable propane cylinder. Available at hardware, camping, and garden-supply stores.

Catalytic Heater Model HT-5000

Thermo Fogger

BROWNING

Browning's long list of top-quality products for the outdoorsman includes five different models of sleeping bags and a backpacker's tent. For other Browning products, see Chapters 4, 6, 8, and 9.

Wind River Sleeping Bag—You won't get cold feet in this mummy bag. It has a side center stopper. Its lining is cut smaller than the cover to keep the cover from compressing the down plumules. The baffles take the stress off the seams and keep the down evenly distributed. Add its heat-conserving slant-wall baffles and offset seams, full-length insulated weather seal, zipper guard, snug draw collar, ultralight weight, and you have the ultimate mummy bag. To pair two together, simply buy one with a right pull zipper and one with a left pull zipper. Insulation: 32 ounces of prime northern goose down, 550 loft. Weight: 3 pounds 9 ounces. Minimum temperature range: −10° F. Price: $128.50.

Sawtooth II Backpacker Tent

Eldorado Expedition Bag—If you're a sprawling sleeper, here's a bag that will give you plenty of room without sacrificing warmth. Its full rectangular style measures 82×32 inches. The secret of its warmth is its unique z tube baffle construction, formed by crossing the diagonal in a box baffle to actually create twice as many baffles. The small z tube baffles better confine and concentrate the down to prevent shifting and to eliminate cold voids. The Eldorado has a side center stopper so the down can't shift from over you to under you. A zipper guard keeps the zipper from snagging in the lining and helps the down-filled weather strip to keep cold air out and body heat in. Insulation: 48 ounces of prime northern goose down, 550 loft. Weight: 5 pounds 4 ounces. Minimum temperature range: −10° F. Price: $159.50.

Sawtooth II Backpacker Tent—This tent is easy to set up. Aluminum poles and stakes are included, and special shock cord pullouts act to let the tent give in the wind, not blow over. The inside has a heavy urethane-coated nylon floor that extends 8 inches up the walls. The top is 2.5-ounce nylon that breathes to reduce condensation, but just to make sure, a 10×48-inch nylon mesh panel is installed in the ridge. The rain fly is made of 2.75-ounce urethane-coated nylon that shrugs off rain and snow. The Sawtooth II is a roomy, two-man tent that's 5×7 feet at the base and 40 inches tall in the center. It is treated with the best fire retardant available. Weight: 5 pounds. Color: blue and white. Price: $74.95.

CENTURY TOOL & MANUFACTURING CO.

From this company comes the popular line of Primus Propane camping equipment. They offer a wide variety of stoves, lanterns, and heaters. They have large models for use in base camps and small, compact, lightweight models suitable for spike camps and backpacking. Primus propane is available in 10-ounce cartridges, 14.1-ounce and 16.4-ounce disposable cylinders, and 4¼-pound and 11-pound refillable cylinders.

#2500 "Ulti-Mate" Camp Kitchen—Cooking convenience for the entire family starts off with the super-deluxe Primus "Ultima" three-burner propane stove that can accommodate a 10-inch fry pan, a 7-inch saucepan, and a 6-inch coffee pot on its extra-large cooking area; plus the "Classic" double-mantle propane lantern set with stand and cylinder, and the Primus 30-inch Tri-Outlet Safety Post that makes it possible to operate three appliances from the same cylinder. The whole Camp Kitchen is safely powered by the lasting Primus 11-pound refillable propane cylinder—large enough for an entire camping vacation. Weight: 55 pounds.

#2361 "Grasshopper" Single-Burner Stove—Nickel-plated steel. Lightweight, compact, and portable. Sturdy tripod stand. Eight to ten hours

average cooking time. Accommodates soup can to 11-inch fry pan. Fits any 14-ounce or 16-ounce disposable cylinder, and comes with Primus 14-ounce cylinder. Nickel-plated, 4,800-BTU, anticlog burner. Ideal for fishermen, hunters, and backpackers. Size: 8 inches high by 17 inches long standing on cylinder. Weight: 2½ pounds.

#2395 "Streamliner II" Two-Burner Propane Stove—Full five-year warranty. Fits standard disposable cylinders. Pots cannot tip on hinged nickel-plated heavy-duty grid. Anticlog, 8,000-BTU, nickel-plated burners. Each individually regulated burner gives hours of cooking time per cylinder. Windshield prevents flame-outs. Size open: 20¼×13½×13¼ inches. Size closed: 19×11×3⅞ inches. Weight: 8 pounds.

"Streamliner II" Stove

#2220 "Explorer" Minilantern—Soft, pleasant light, equivalent to a 75 watt bulb, regulates bright to dim. Attractive, sturdy base—exclusive carrying case stands or hangs and protects lantern during transport. Windproof. Five-year warranty on stainless steel burner. Frosted, glare-free glass globe. Cartridge lasts an average of eight hours. Height: 11 inches. Weight: 1 pound 9 ounces with cartridge. Cartridge not included.

"Pioneer" Miniheater

#2228 "Pioneer" Miniheater—Infrared radiation heater provides instant heat indoors or outdoors. Compact, efficient, and practical. Two-year warranty on heating element. Adjustable wire-guard heat reflector. Precision valve provides controlled heat between 500 and 2,000 BTUs. Cartridge lasts average of seven hours.

#2255 "Ranger" Ministove—The perfect stove for the backpacker. Average cooking time is four hours per cartridge. Nickel-plated, anticlog, 4,800-BTU burner with five-year warranty. Easy to pack—folds to 12½×3×3 inches. Sturdy tripod stand rests firmly, even on rough ground. Weight: 13 ounces without cartridge. Cartridge not included.

COGHLAN'S, LTD.

This Canadian firm produces a wide variety of camping and backpacking accessories, many of which we have used for years. Most are quite inexpensive and are available at camping centers and sporting-goods stores nationwide.

Camping Mirror—Quality 5×7-inch mirror in sturdy, colorful plastic frame. Unique metal hook on back enables mirror to stand, clamp on pole, or hang. Handy for tents, trailers, campers, summer cottage, or home.

Camp Stove Toaster

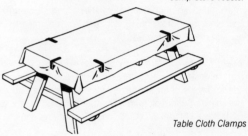

Table Cloth Clamps

Camp Stove Toaster—Has exclusive new sure-grip toast holders. Toast the way you like it outdoors. Folds to dinner plate size. Toasts up to four slices at one time. Folds flat for easy packing. Coated wires won't rust. Heavy steel construction—won't warp.

Aluminum Camp Stove Griddle—The ideal way to prepare outdoor meals for hungry campers. Heavy-gauge aluminum. Covers grate area of popular two-burner camp stoves—ideal for three-burner stoves, too. Size: 16½×10 inches.

Picnic Table Cloth Clamps—Six rust-resistant, spring steel clamps fit most table thicknesses, hold tablecloth tight so it lays flat. Ideal for all outdoor activities.

Plus 50 Sportsman's Soap—Mild, biodegradable, coconut oil concentrated liquid soap for hands and face. Packaged two tubes per card. Get fifty or more washings per tube. Sanitary, leakproof, lightweight, easy to dispense, mild, and fragrant. Will not pollute lakes and streams.

Camp Stove Lighter—Now light a stove in wind or rain with no stove flareup. Automatic press release action. Spark ignites main burner. Uses ordinary lighter flints. Unconditionally guaranteed for one year. Length: 9½ inches.

Automatic Lantern Lighter—Attaches to most popular makes of gas lanterns. Uses ordinary lighter flints. No special tools needed to install. Unconditionally guaranteed for one year. Comes with simple instructions.

Tent Peg Remover—Removes all types of tent pegs in a jiffy. Hardened steel construction. Soft rubber handle. Easy to use.

Dripless, Smokeless Candles—Original Pink Lady candles. Burning time is approximately five to six hours. Fits many popular candle lanterns. Size: ¾×5 inches. Five candles per package.

Rope Tips—End frayed ropes forever. By placing tip on end of rope and applying heat from a match, the tube will shrink to form a permanent end. Two sizes available for rope from ³/₁₆ to ⁵/₁₆ inch and from ⅜ to ⅝ inch.

Aluminum Pot Holder—A must on all camping trips. Strong, lightweight, and dependable. Helps prevent burned fingers and spills. Opens like pliers and clamps on any size pot, cake pan, or tin can.

COLEMAN CO., INC.

A name well known among outdoors people everywhere, Coleman manufactures a large line of camping equipment and accessories and markets their products nationally through mass-merchandising outlets, sporting-goods stores, and camping centers.

In addition to the many familiar and famous Coleman products, there have been some recent additions, including a new deluxe lantern, some new coolers and insulated jugs, and the new Peak I line of lightweight backpacking gear.

Model 275-710 Double-Mantle Lantern—The latest advance in Coleman's gasoline lantern line, this model will operate for eight or more hours on a single filling of fuel. It features an Easy-Lite valve with automatic tip cleaner, contemporary styling, and stripe-frosted globe. Fuel capacity: 1 quart. Height: 13½ inches. Base diameter: 6¾ inches. Ventilator diameter: 8¼ inches.

Model 275-764 Lantern Carrying Case—Protect your Coleman lantern in this new carrying case. Prevents dents, scratches, broken globes, and adds to the life of the mantles. Molded from tough polyethylene. Won't rust. There's built-in storage for funnel, spare generator, and extra mantles. Holds all Model 275, 220, and 228 lanterns and can be adapted to hold Models 200 and 201.

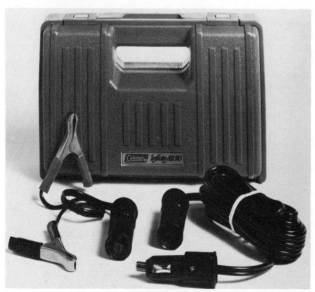

Inflate-All 90

Charger SP Electric Lantern—New sealed power battery for carefree light. Rugged, high-impact outer case. Large, easy-grip handle; tote it anywhere. Dial adjusts for low intensity, high intensity. Recharge on–off position. Tough, transparent lens. High-gloss white reflector. Snap-off lens cover. Standard 8 watt fluorescent bulb. AC and DC plugs are attached and tuck away neatly in storage compartment. Recharge up to

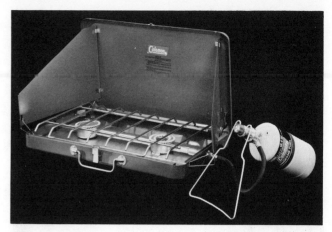

Standard Propane Stove

150 times from auto cigarette lighter or 115-volt household current. Costs one tenth as much to own as dry cell lanterns.

Double-Mantle Propane Lantern—Use with 16.4-ounce or 14.1-ounce disposable bottles. Hooks up to bulk tank, too. Adjustable for high or low light levels. One 16.4-ounce bottle will burn seven hours on high, up to twenty hours on low.

Coleman Standard Propane Stove—Two famous Band-A-Blu Burners with plated grate. Operates from disposable cylinders or bulk tanks. Size folded: 20½×12×4 inches.

Coleman Deluxe Two-Burner Stove—Fully adjustable flame, famous Band-A-Blu burners, and steel case with nickel-chrome grate are features on this popular gasoline stove. Fuel capacity: 3½ pints. Burning time with both burners on high is about two hours. Size folded: 22×13¾×6¼ inches.

Coleman Fall Cat Heater—The catalytic heater with lots of portable comfort with a safe, platinum catalyst. Exclusive Dial-Temp adjusts the warmth. Approximate input: 3,000 to 5,000 BTUs. Height: 10⅞ inches. Diameter: 9⅞ inches. Fuel capacity: 3 quarts.

Villa Del Mar Tent—Here's unique styling in America's favorite tent size. Side entrance zippered door provides ease of entry and greater ventilation. Door flap can be partly or fully closed. Light color top provides weather resistance, reduces heat, and improves lighting inside the tent. Large Mediterranean-type side windows offer style plus ventilation. Welded-seam double vinyl-coated nylon floor so water can't get in. Flame resistant. Size: 12×9 feet with 8-foot ridge and 5-foot 9-inch sidewall. Self-supporting outside frame.

Inflate-All 90—This new portable inflator plugs into car or boat cigarette lighter and inflates almost anything. It is a compact machine in a snap-open plastic case. Inside is a 12-volt motor, air compressor, 10-foot electrical cord, and 2-foot air hose. It is available through automotive stores. Accessories include an optional 15-foot extension cord and handy clamp-on battery clips for even more versatility.

Oscar—This is Coleman's new four-gallon-capacity cooler that goes anywhere. It is strong enough to sit on and has built-in drink holders on the flip side of the lid. Oscar easily holds twelve cans plus a 10-pound bag of ice. Its two-position locking handle goes up or down to one side. Color: white with green lid.

The Runabout—This is a cooler that's a jug that's a cooler. It has a two-position handle, food tray, and Fast Flo faucet. It comes in two sizes: three or four gallon. It is highly insulated, and its all-plastic construction makes it rustproof and easy to clean with water and a mild detergent. It is an all-in-one cooler with separate compartments for food and beverages.

Peak I Model 770 Pack and Frame—New for 1977, this is the top-of-the-line model pack of rugged Cordura nylon, with double compartments and five pockets as extra features. In addition, it has a top compartment that removes quickly and attaches to the hip strap for use as a fanny pack on side trips from camp. Lift straps on the shoulder straps are another feature of this backpack to help transfer the load and absorb shock. Peak I frame is foamed polypropylene, unlike the familiar tubular aluminum frame that has dominated the market until now. Frame weighs 33 ounces and has built-in adjustability. The Peak I line will be marketed exclusively through specialty camping and backpacking stores. Price: $57.50.

EARLY WINTERS, LTD.

A selection of fine outdoor equipment comes from this company, which offers a complete line of Gore-Tex gear. Gore-Tex is a new laminated fabric that allows water vapor to pass through it but repels liquid, making it ideally suited for use in small tents, sleeping bag covers, rain wear, and the like.

Light Dimension Tent

Light Dimension Tent—Amazing as it sounds, you can set up your Light Dimension tent in about a minute—even less if you hurry. Furthermore, it all folds into a compact 7×16-inch bag and weighs a scant 3½ pounds. Features include a big, adjustable window vent in the rear that gives you flow-through ventilation on hot days; shock loaded poles that feed from the front for quick pitching; weather hood that acts as an eave and lets you see out and have fresh air even when it rains; large door for easy access; bathtub floor that keeps ground water out; unique double zippers to keep you snug and dry in the worst weather; and fully zippered mosquito netting (inside) to cover the door. Price: $195 postpaid.

Marmot Sleeping Bag

Marmot Sleeping Bags—Here are bags so warm and light that they've rapidly become favored by serious mountaineers. Yet, they're so comfortable and inviting that you'll sleep in them every chance you get. A

Marmot bag cannot be mass produced. Every piece of fabric must be hand hot-cut one at a time. After hot-cutting, your bag is carefully sewn and fitted. Three sizes of Marmot bags are available, ranging in weight from 3 pounds 4 ounces to 5 pounds. Insulated with the finest down, fill weights range from 1 pound 12 ounces to 3 pounds 2 ounces. Prices: from $158.95 to $302.95, all postpaid.

EDMUND SCIENTIFIC CO.

Among the thousands of items in the big Edmund catalog are several of potential interest to campers and backpackers. For other Edmund products, see Chapters 2, 3, 4, 5, and 11.

Flywheel Flashlight—This flashlight generator uses flywheel energy. Each time you squeeze the easy-press handle the alternator generator spins, the flywheel disengages from the clutch and the flashlight lights for about two seconds. By continuously squeezing the handle you generate a soft hum and the light remains bright. Length: 5½ inches. Weight: 6 ounces. Never needs batteries. Price: $14.95 postpaid.

Digital Pedometer—Now you can measure the distance you walk, precisely to the tenth of a mile, with this digital pedometer. Has three-digit display and registers up to 99.9 miles. Adjusts for your stride. Great for hikers, backpackers and campers, hunters, and hike-in fishermen. Compact black plastic case. Weight: 1¾ ounces. Size: 1¾ inches square. Features belt clip, loop chain, and ring. Price: $14.75 postpaid.

Portable Solar Cooker—No mess, smoke, fuel, or flame. All you need is a sunny day. Put food on skewer, wrap with solar foil, insert in cooker. In high sun the focused rays normally cook food in just ten to fifteen minutes. Comes with sun-tracking device, skewer lock, reflector, and adjustable stand. Dimensions: 13×13×4 inches. Weight: less than 1 pound. Price: $13.95 postpaid. Forty extra sheets of Solar Foil: $3.95 postpaid.

Flywheel Flashlight

GANDER MOUNTAIN, INC.

For campers and backpackers, Gander Mountain offers cookware, tents, backpacks, sleeping bags, camp stoves, and numerous accessories.

Other Gander Mountain products can be found in Chapters 2, 3, 4, 5, 6, 8, and 9.

Palco Aluminum Cooking Kit—Set for four nests into compact, easy-to-carry unit. Consists of 6-quart bucket and cover, 4-quart pot, 2-quart pot, coffee pot and cover, 9¼-inch fry pan, 7⅞-inch fry pan, four plates, and four cups. G.M. price: $18.97.

Palco Aluminum Five-Piece Mess Kit—The favorite of campers and scouters for years. Made of durable, easy-to-clean aluminum. Consists of fry pan, deep plate, pot with lid, and plastic cup. Entire set nests into durable cloth cover with adjustable shoulder strap. G.M. price: $5.97.

Eureka Timberline Draw-Tite Tent

Eureka Riverside Lodge Family Camping Tent—A deluxe-quality tent built to give rugged service for many years. Plenty of room for all family activities in carefree comfort. Has strong, pearl gray, high-count, 6½-ounce poplin body and roof, treated to repel water, plus an 8-ounce vinyl-coated nylon floor and splash cloth. With heavy-duty aluminum poles and ridges, three large triangular zippered windows, large nylon net zippered door, and shock cord loops on eaves for a trim look in all weather. Finished floor size: 10×8 feet. Complete with frame and tent bag, stakes, and instructions. G.M. price: $174.97.

Eureka Timberline Draw-Tite Tent—The most compact and lightweight of the Draw-Tite design tents, featuring simplicity of design and quick, easy erection of the strong aluminum frame from which tent is suspended. Roof is 1.9-ounce golden ripstop breathable nylon. Ripstop nylon is also used for the fly and wraparound floor that extends up the sides of the tent. Large rear window and A-type door provide controlled cross ventilation. Fly is hooded front and rear and secured to frame by shock cords. Zippers are nylon coil. Seams are double-stitched. Carrying bag included. Floor size: 5 feet 3 inches by 7 feet 2 inches. Weight: 7 pounds 8 ounces. G.M. price: $79.97.

Camp Trails Nylon Day Hiker

Camp Trails Astral Combination—Two of the most popular items in the Gander line—515 Astral Cruiser Frame and Astral bag. Bag is tapered in four directions to give wearer a snug load that can't shift. Made of special waterproof urethane-coated oxford-weave nylon. Five large outside pockets. Divided bag. Map pocket. Extendable top with drawstring and cord lock. Spreader bar. Pin-mounted to frame. Protective storm flaps with cord lock closure. G.M. price: $59.97.

Camp Trails Nylon Day Hiker—Rugged, waterproof, 8-ounce urethane-coated nylon. Roomy main compartment has nylon drawstring closure with weatherproof tie-down flap. Separate "kangaroo" pouch has full-width covered zipper. Adjustable, padded nylon shoulder straps. Dimensions: 16×12×5 inches. Weight: 12 ounces. G.M. price: $11.87.

Camp Trails Belt (Fanny) Pack—A large, contour-fitted accessory bag. Wear in any position—front, rear, or side. Waterproof, snagproof, and abrasion-resistant nylon fabric. Inside elastic pocket, flap-covered double zipper, nylon belt with quick-release buckle. Size: 17×8×5 inches. Weight: 9 ounces. G.M. price: $9.97.

GERRY

The Gerry catalog has always been one of our favorites. Not only does it contain descriptions and photographs of the superb line of Gerry camping and backpacking gear, but it is also full of helpful information that any active outdoorsman should find useful.

Series 70 Pack Frame—Crafted from 7001 aluminum alloy. Joints are epoxied to form a bond as strong as the aluminum itself. New padded hip belt with sliding ring feature fits any size hips. Sliding ring also exerts continuous pull on the side of the frame, preventing any side-to-side sway. Features breathable mesh backbands and an adjustable neck opening between shoulder straps. Available in four sizes, from small to extra large, in weights from 2 pounds 4 ounces to 2 pounds 7 ounces. Price: $45.

Horse Pack—Five big compartments for controlled weight distribution. Features weatherproof zippers and is available in various colors. Size: each side is 24×16×9 inches. Weight: 1 pound 15 ounces. Price: $50.

Doggie Pack—Let Fido carry his own food with this sturdy, lightweight pack of durable nylon with leather reinforced corners and waterproof zippers. Size: each side 9×10×4 inches. Weight: 1 pound. Price: $26.

Bicycle Pannier—Takes any Gerry sleeping system, plus other gear. Compartments are protected by covered zippers. Color: red. Size: 28×17×5½ inches. Weight: 2 pounds 4 ounces. Price: $22.

Air Bags—Available in two sizes, these nylon bags are padded with urethane foam for protection and feature flap-covered zippers and leather handles. Sizes: 25×16×9 inches (regular), 32½×15½×11½ inches (large). Weights: 1 pound 12 ounces (regular), 2 pounds 10 ounces (large). Prices: $37, $42.50.

Camponaire II Tent—This popular three-man backpacking tent is a cross-ridge series tent made to keep you cozy at all times for about 3 pounds per man. Its high center and 12-inch vertical sidewalls make it

Doggie Pack

the roomiest tent in its class. In addition, it has two inside pockets and clothesline loops for drying. All stress points are reinforced. Includes poles, fly, and stakes. Dimensions: 7×6½ feet with center height of 5¼ feet. Weight: 9 pounds 8 ounces. Colors: blue floor, gold canopy, blue fly; or brown floor, gold canopy, khaki fly. Price: $189.

Bicycle Pannier

HINE/SNOWBRIDGE, INC.

Here's a company that produces a wide variety of packs for hiking, camping, backpacking, ski touring, and bicycle touring. They have two full-color catalogs available that are quite interesting and informative: one for their line of backpacks, the other for their Kirtland Tour Paks.

H/S Basic—This is an excellent inexpensive pack featuring drawstring closure with cord lock, top flap pocket, kangaroo pocket on the front, strong nylon web shoulder straps, hang loop, double-sewn zipper, reinforced stitching at points of high stress, and D rings for attachment of a waist belt. The pack is constructed of 8-ounce nylon pack cloth and is available in four colors. Size: 14×5½×10 inches. Weight: 11 ounces.

Serex—This is an expedition-grade pack, ideally suited for summer/winter mountaineering, hiking into almost inaccessible climbs, high-country extended ski tours, and many other applications where the user does not want the rigid back and shoulder constrictions of a standard-frame pack. Features include drawstring closure, optional pockets, top flap tie-downs, contour cut bottom, accessory strap holders, aluminum stays, adjustable chest strap, adjustable yoke suspension, fully padded shoulder straps and waist belt, and compressor straps. Constructed of tough and durable Cordura, this pack is available in navy blue or bright red. Size: 26×8×16 inches. Weight: 63 ounces.

Powell Pack—Worn around the waist, this pack frees the user's shoulders, making it ideal for ski touring, day hiking, climbing, fishing, and hunting. It has a double-slide zipper for easy access with two accessory strap holders on top for tying on gear. The 2-inch-wide waist belt adds carrying comfort. Made of 11-ounce Cordura cloth, the Powell Pack comes in navy blue and bright red. Price: $13.50.

Belt Pack—This is a versatile little organizer. It can be carried on a belt, inside another back as a sorter, or as a seat bag on bicycles. It is made of 8-ounce waterproofed nylon pack cloth and comes in navy blue, forest green, bright red, or orange. Price: $3.50.

Serex Pack

H/S Cargo Bags—Versatile, practical, and tough, these cargo bags are great for any outdoorsman's traveling needs. They feature #10 zippers with two sliders that can be locked together, 11-ounce Cordura cloth construction, midline and end carrying handles, and an extra zipper pocket in one end. Available in two sizes: 11×20 inches and 13×26 inches. Weights: 18 ounces, 24 ounces. Colors: navy blue or bright red.

Century 600 Handlebar Bag—This bag incorporates the stable K/T Front Bag Support, and the Elite quick-mounting features into an economy-priced bag. It has the integrated vinyl-covered map compartment in the top, a separate zippered envelope pocket on the front, and can be used as a handbag with the K/T shoulder strap (optional). It has aluminum stiffeners to prevent overloading. Colors: navy blue, red, and bright yellow. Size: 7½×9¼×5½ inches. Weight: 20 ounces. Price: $38.

Century 100 Seat Bag—This is the perfect companion for the cyclist's day rides where a few tools, wallet, sew-up tire, and other small necessities are all he needs to take along. It has two-point suspension, a sturdy foam stiffener, and hangs conveniently under the seat. Colors: navy blue, red, or bright yellow. Size: 6×9×5 inches. Weight: 4 ounces. Price: $9.50.

Stag "Bright Bags"

HIRSCH-WEIS

From this company comes the very popular Stag brand of sleeping bags and tents. Their line includes more than twenty different sleeping bags and twenty-three different tents with models for everything from backpacking to family camping. They also offer a number of camping accessories and a line of outdoor clothing.

Stag Brand clothing is described in Chapter 8.

Stag "Bright Bags"—For campers who have decided that fashion has a place inside the tent or recreational vehicle, Hirsch-Weis has come up with a series of new sleeping bags that combine stripes, paisleys, tiki prints, denims, and solids for a colorful array that can be used either as regular camping sleeping bags or, when zipped open, full-size comforters. All are 33×75 inches and each contains 3 pounds of Thermofluff polyester insulation for cool-weather camping. Prices: from $22 to $27.

Mountain High Tent—A new mountain tent with a snow tunnel entry in one end for use in the high country, plus a "Man-Sized" door in the other end for regular camping. The snow tunnel has a fabric door that can be closed off, plus a round section of polyester netting with a nylon zipper. Above the door is a tube-type vent that can be tied shut. The tent is made of breathable ripstop nylon, and the fly of waterproof ripstop nylon. The waterproof floor extends several inches up the sidewalls to prevent water entry. The entire tent is treated for flame retardancy. Size: 5×7½ feet, with 3½-foot center height. Weight: 6 pounds. Price: $150.

High Country Tents—These two-man and four-man tents are suspended from a frame system that incorporates A-frames at either end with a ridge pole connecting the A-frames. A section of frame that overhangs the front supports the front of the fly to form a canopy to protect the entry and reduce air flow past the tent. Made of ripstop nylon, chemically treated for flame retardancy, these tents are breathable, while the flies are completely waterproof. The fly is attached by shock cords, with Velcro tabs boxing out the tent for more room inside. Features include a "Man-Sized" door with nylon zippers, zippered rear window, waterproof floor that extends several inches up the sidewalls, inside clothesline loops, a storage pocket, complete guy lines with tighteners, aluminum skewer stakes, and a waterproof carry bag. Sizes: 5 feet 6 inches by 7 feet 5 inches, with 3½-foot center height (two-man), 7½×9½ feet, with a 5-foot 2-inch center height (four-man). Weights: 6 pounds 9 ounces, and 10 pounds 7 ounces. Prices: $115, $180.

High Country Tent

IGLOO CORP.

Igloo is the brand name of a popular line of insulated coolers and jugs that have found favor among many campers, hunters, and fishermen. There's something in the Igloo selection to fit everyone's needs.

Two-Gallon Seat-Top Beverage Cooler—This cooler is made of tough, high-impact plastic outside and easy-to-clean, sanitary white plastic inside. It won't rust, corrode, chip, or dent. A hidden metal backplate gives added support to the bail-type handle. A removable food tray adds extra top-side storage. The recessed spigot is dripproof and stays out of the way. Sit on it—this one supports 300 pounds. Colors: white with either red, blue, green, or yellow. Dimensions: 11×13½ inches. Price: $14.78.

Igloo Playmate—This cooler keeps eighteen cans of beverage icy cold all day long. A pushbutton release allows the lid to swing to either side, yet locks shut for easy carrying. The Playmate is made of tough, high-impact plastic that will take rough punishment. The interior is stain and odor resistant and easy to clean. Available in four fashionable Igloo colors. Dimensions: 14½×13⅞×11 inches. Price: $19.05.

Igloo Giant Sea Chest—This is a sailor's pride and joy. It will support 500 pounds as an extra seat and will hold 300 pounds of provisions or freshly caught fish on the inside. Its tough, high-impact plastic construction is ideal for saltwater living. It won't rust, corrode, chip, or dent. The plastic inside is easy to clean and won't absorb odors. Two snap-locks keep contents safe and secure. Jaunty rope and wood handles make for easy carrying and add a nautical touch. An optional seat cushion snaps onto the sturdy seat-top lid. Available in all red or all white. Dimensions: 43½×18½×19⅝ inches. Capacity: 151 quarts. Price: $186.16.

Igloo 68-Quart Ice Chest—This new chest is the perfect size for those who have wanted something in between Igloo's 48-quart and 86-quart ice chests. It has the same durable, high-impact plastic construction that won't rust, chip, or dent. It comes with a removable food tray and the white plastic interior is easy to clean. It's sturdy enough to support 300 pounds when used as an extra seat. It has swing-up handles with tie-down loops, a snap-lock lid, and recessed drain plug. Dimensions: 28¾×16⅛×15¼ inches. Price: $52.

Two-Gallon Seat-Top Beverage Cooler

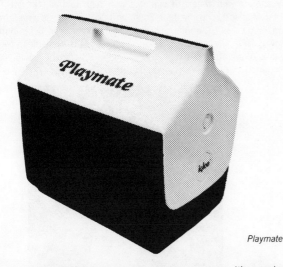

Playmate

Hunt'n Seat Cooler—This is the perfect hunting accessory. It's a cooler, seat, and storage container all in one. The big three-gallon cooler holds enough icy-cold liquid to keep the thirstiest hunter satisfied all day long. A recessed, dripproof spigot stays clean and out of the way. A deep, top-side tray is a great place to store sandwiches or extra shells. And a reinforced, bail-type handle makes for easy carrying. The cooler's olive drab color blends well with surroundings. It will hold 300 pounds as a seat and you can stash your game in the cooler to keep it fresh on the trip home. Dimensions: 12¾×13½ inches. Price: $22.14.

KELTY PACK, INC.

Kelty makes some of the finest packs and frames to be found for day tripping, camping, mountaineering, or expeditions of any sort.

Sonora Pack

Sonora Pack—This is a new front- and top-loading, large-capacity backpack for long-distance hiking and expeditionary-type large-load carrying. Easy access from the front double-slider opening and the quick-entry top opening make this a unique but practical pack. Four inside pockets provide added area for accessories, food, or clothing. The voluminous center pocket is an excellent compartment for quick access items—gloves, hats, sunglasses, etc. The Sonora is fitted with a Massif frame and padded sectional suspension system that encircles the hips with firm, comfortable, foam padding. The rear section is attached directly to the packframe with 5-inch wide, tough, nylon webbing, and the front sections are angled to curve naturally around the hips. Features include four outside pockets, extra-long accessory strap holders, Cordura nylon crampon patch, zippers of nickel steel or polyester, and ice axe loop. The Sonora is available in small, medium large, and extra-large sizes. Colors: Kelty Red, olive green, and blue.

Tioga Pack—Meeting the demand for larger capacities than those normally offered is the Tioga Pack. It has a two-compartment packbag—the most popular style—with a large upper section for bulky items and a lower one for smaller gear. Features include a padded suspension system and adjustable frame extension, five large pockets for convenient access, extra-long accessory strap holders for no-bounce carrying of foam pads or crampons, Cordura nylon crampon patch, all-nickel zippers, and an ice axe loop. A coated fabric panel against the frame provides extra rain protection to pack contents when the Super Raincover is used. Available in small, medium, large, and extra-large sizes. Colors: Kelty Red, royal blue, and olive green.

Condor Day Pack—This new pack is designed for the person who needs a day pack and more. Whether you're a backpacker, tennis player, or student, the Condor's features will provide you with maximum versatility and a comfortable ride. With a zippered interior divider the Condor transforms from a two-compartment pack to a single, large-compartment day pack. This unique feature allows carrying of long items when the interior divider is unzipped, and maximum load control when the divider is zipped closed. Special features include an upper compartment opening with double-slider zipper and a lower compartment opening with single-slider zipper. For ease of opening, the Condor has zipper pull tabs. Other features include padded shoulder straps, ice axe loop, three leather accessory patches, haul strap, and D-rings for accessory waist strap. Dimensions: 19½×13×5 inches. Weight: 15.8 ounces. Color: tan.

MIRRO ALUMINUM CO.

The Mirro catalog is one of the most enjoyable that we have come across. Not only does it contain descriptions and photographs of all their fine camping cookware and accessories, but it also has a mini-history of outdoor Wisconsin, complete with some fine old photographs of outdoor activities and scenes.

Holiday Cook Kit—Rugged, lightweight, compact, and complete, this cook kit matches the cooking requirements of a party of six. Pots and pans are practically designed of durable, lightweight aluminum. Fry pan features no-stick Teflon II interior. Cups and compartment plates are unbreakable thermo plastic. For easy traveling, all components pack into 10-quart kettle. Kit also contains a 4-quart kettle with cover, 2-quart kettle with cover, 6-cup Camp Perk (including basket assembly and glass top), six 8-ounce polyethylene cups, six 9-inch polypropylene plates, 10-inch fry pan (Teflon II), and 9-inch fry pan (Teflon II).

The Backpacker

The Backpacker—This cook kit was designed by outdoors people for rugged use. Eight essential cooking tools are packed tightly and compactly by a laminated fabric strap. Clamp handle works with all pans. Long-wearing aluminum pans and dishes and polyethylene cups are included. Kit contains 1¼-quart kettle, two 8-ounce polyethylene cups, two 6¼-inch dishes, 7-inch fry pan, 5½-inch clamp handle, and 24-inch fabric strap.

Campfire Grids—Each size is heavy-gauge, spot-welded steel for strength and durability. The M-4742 and M-4743 have permanently attached, foldaway legs. The M-4740 adjusts to a variety of heights on an 11-inch steel stake. M-4743 Camper's Heavy-Duty Grid measures

23½×12¼ inches. M-4740 Camper's Adjustable Grid measures 13×9¼ inches. M-4742 Explorer Grid is 12×6½ inches. M-4741 Backpacker's Grid measures 15½×16½ inches.

Wash Basins—Two sizes of lightweight, long-lasting aluminum wash basins are available from Mirro. They feature extra-wide, easy-to-grip rims, and are essential in any camp. Sizes: 16 inches in diameter and 9¾ inches deep (10 quart), 13¾ inches in diameter and 5½ inches deep (5 quart).

Salt and Pepper Shakers—They're Mirro, and they're rugged. Handy in any camp kitchen. Dimensions: 3⅞×2⅝ inches. They hold plenty of salt and pepper for entire camping trip.

Canteens—A Mirro Canteen is your first friend in desert, forest, or while simply hiking down the road. These canteens are made in America of welded aluminum for lightweight, leakproof performance. Screw-on polypropylene cap is anchored with chain. Nylon, snap-on cover with adjustable strap is available in red or green. Canteen sizes: 1 quart, 2 quart.

NORTH FACE

From this company comes the North Face brand of camping and backpacking gear that includes backpacks, sleeping bags with either down or PolarGuard insulation, and lightweight backpacking tents.
North Face parkas are described in Chapter 8.

Cat's Meow—This sleeping bag was designed to provide the advantages of PolarGuard in an efficient, backpackable package with minimum weight. It weighs in at 4 pounds 2 ounces and offers superior performance in areas of high humidity since the loft is not significantly reduced by contact with water. In climates with high rainfall, like the Pacific Northwest and portions of the South and Southwest, it is a preferred design. Fabric is 1.9-ounce ripstop nylon, finished with Zepel and Ken-Down. This symmetrical modified mummy bag is available in two sizes with a temperature range to 20° F. Lengths: 83 and 89 inches. Weights: 3 pounds 10 ounces, 4 pounds 2 ounces. Prices: $63.50, $67.50.

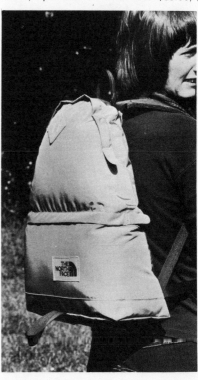

Day Pack

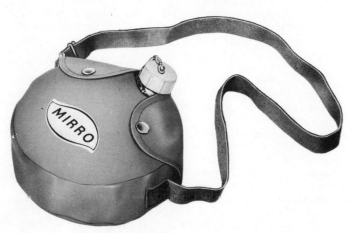

Two-Quart Canteen

Day Pack—The Northface Teardrop Day Packs are overengineered for strength and durability. Two compartments are separated by a horizontal divider; both compartments open via covered coil zippers with leather grab tabs. The 8-ounce waterproof Super K-Koted pack cloth is abrasion resistant and durable; the padded harness straps are mounted in a reinforced leather plate, which also sports a hauling loop. An ice axe loop with leather accessory patch is mounted in the back. The Day Pack is available with a double nylon bottom, or with a full-grain leather bottom. Volume: 19 liters (1,160 cubic inches). Colors: orange, navy, and forest green. Weights: 16 ounces (nylon), 20 ounces (leather). Prices: $23.50, $27.50.

Sierra Tent—This is a comfortable shelter for two persons and gear, with double A-pole stability and strength. It's roomy and well ventilated, with a mosquito-netted, zipper-adjusted window at the rear and a zippered door in front. Perhaps the best feature of the Sierra is its taut, wrinkle-free pitch; it resists wind and snow loading, and creates a calm environment within. Features include a tub floor design, with waterproof fabric extending up to the apexes on the ends, for protection from storm-driven rain; sewn-in pockets for easily mislaid items; lap-felled, double-needle seams throughout; oversized, waterproof-coated fly sheet. Floor dimensions: 56×89 inches. Colors: gold/taupe, gold/navy. Weight: 6 pounds 15 ounces. Price: $165.

Sierra Tent

OREGON FREEZE DRY FOODS, INC.

From this company comes the Mountain House brand of ultralight, freeze-dried backpacking vittles—everything from beef dinners to ice cream milk shakes. Mrs. Mickey Lancer told us that anyone desiring information about their products and the names of the dealers nearest them should send a self-addressed stamped envelope and a request for their Customer Catalog.

Beef Stew Main Course Entree for Two—This package contains two 8-ounce servings. Dry weight: 3.75 ounces. Price: $2.20.

Chili and Beans for Two—This main-course entree contains enough for two 8-ounce servings. Dry weight: 5.5 ounces. Price: $2.10.

Rice and Chicken for Four—This main-course entree contains enough for four 10-ounce servings. Dry weight: 12.8 ounces. Price: $5.

Precooked Eggs with Real Bacon—This package contains enough for four 10-ounce servings. Dry weight: 4.2 ounces. Price: $3.50.

Green Beans—There's enough in this package for five ½-cup servings. Dry weight: 1.6 ounces. Price: $2.60.

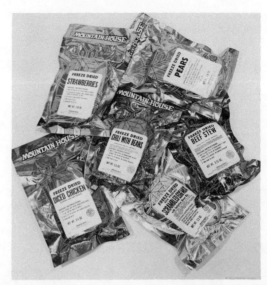

Mountain House Freeze-Dried Foods

Corn—This package contains five ½-cup servings. Dry weight: 4.9 ounces. Price: $2.60.

Applesauce—There's enough in this package for four 4-ounce servings. Dry weight: 4 ounces. Price: $1.15.

Ice Cream Shakes—Available in vanilla, chocolate, or strawberry flavors. Enough in each package for two 8-ounce servings. Dry weight: 4.8 ounces. Price: $1.65.

Lurps—This package of trail snacks includes chocolates, cashews, peanuts, and freeze-dried raisins. Weight: 3 ounces. Price: 80¢.

Fruit-Nut Lurps—Contains peanuts, banana chips, freeze-dried raisins, cashews, apples, freeze-dried plums. Weight: 2 ounces. Price: 80¢.

Natural Fruit Lurps—A blend of freeze-dried natural fruits including plums, blueberries, pineapple, and strawberries. Dry weight: 7 ounces. Price: 80¢.

Instant Pudding—Available in butterscotch, chocolate, or banana cream flavors. Each package serves four. Dry weight: 5 ounces. Price: 85¢.

Freeze-Dried Coffee—Ten packs of single-cup foil packets for ten single-cup servings. Dry weight: 10/.4 ounce. Price: $1.

P. & S. SALES

This mail-order company offers quite a number of camping and backpacking items, including packs, sleeping bags, tents, and numerous accessories.

For other P. & S. products, see Chapters 2, 8, and 9.

Vinyl Ground Cloths—Available in three sizes, these cloths are made of heavy olive drab plastic. All edges are heat-sealed and have reinforced metal grommets. Sizes: 4×6 feet, 5×7 feet, 8×10 feet. Prices: $2.95, $3.25, $6.50.

Camp Blankets—These blankets are excellent for camping, cabin and general use. They are made of new wool with 10 percent acrylic and nylon added for strength and durability. Ends are securely whip-stitched. Colors: gray, blue, forest green, and maroon. Weight: 3¼ pounds. Size: 60×80 inches. Price: $9.95.

Aluminum Canteen Cup—Made to fit over the army canteen of heavy-gauge aluminum with folding metal handle. Capacity: 32 ounces. Price: $1.25.

Army Style Canteen—Made of aluminum and holds 1 quart. Canteen covers are made of heavy-duty duck, are olive drab and have belt hooks. Prices: $1.95 (canteen), $1.50 (cover), $3.25 (canteen and cover).

Army Style Duffel Bag—Made to give rugged service. Olive drab heavy-duty canvas has reinforced carrying handle, and shoulder strap with snap fastener on end. Dimensions: 36 inches long by 21 inches in diameter. Price: $9.25.

Army Mess Kit—Consists of oval frying pan and two-compartment plate. Made of heavy-gauge aluminum and in excellent condition. Price: $2.95.

RECREATIONAL EQUIPMENT, INC.

To our knowledge, R.E.I. is unique among mail-order companies. It is a co-op membership corporation that can save the serious outdoors person a lot of money over the years. The co-op was organized in 1938 and incorporated in 1956.

Membership is open to anyone who completes the application and submits it with a $2 fee. You need only buy $5 worth of equipment a year to remain on active status. If you buy nothing for five years your membership will be terminated, but can be renewed by paying another $2 fee. Active members receive catalogs twice a year and dividends annually.

According to R.E.I., "For purchases made from 1970 through 1976, the Co-op returned over $7½ million in dividends to its members."

Their hefty catalog contains a full range of camping and backpacking equipment as well as outdoor clothing described in Chapter 8.

Pannier II

R.E.I. Basic Cruisers—The Basic Cruiser frames are made of tubular aluminum with padded shoulder straps, nylon backbands, and a 1½-inch-wide waist belt. The bags are made of 6-ounce coated nylon pack cloth and are attached to the frames with clevis pins and lock rings. The Large Cruiser frame is 14½ inches by 31½ inches high and fits most adults. The single-compartment bag is 6×14½ inches by 20½ inches high with a cover flap and tie cords. Two side pockets with covered zippers and a center pocket are featured. The Small Cruiser features an

aluminum frame that is 14½ inches by 28 inches high and fits small adults and youths. The single-compartment bag is 6×14½ inches by 18 inches high and features two side pockets with zippers and a center pocket. Color: light blue. Weights: 3 pounds 2 ounces, and 3 pounds. Capacities: 2,073 cubic inches, 1,821 cubic inches. Price: $25.95.

R.E.I. Pannier II—Tapered side bags are made of coated nylon pack cloth with fiberboard inserts and drawstring top. Bags are 18 inches high by 6×13½ inches at the top and 6×7½ inches at the bottom. Pockets are 2×5 inches by 11½ inches high. Features covered zippers, carrying handle, and four accessory strap holders. Colors: red or blue. Capacity: 2,268 cubic inches. Price: $29.95.

Nesting Billies—Lightweight 1-quart, 2-quart, and 3-quart aluminum pails with wire handles and lids that serve as plates or fry pans. The 1-quart size will hold Svea 123R stove. Dimensions: 6⅛ inches high by 7 inches in diameter. Weight: 1 pound 13 ounces. Price: $9.10.

R.E.I. McKinley II Tent—A large, four-person tent for winter or expedition use. It is 88 inches high at the peak for standing upright to dress or relieve tent fatigue during bad weather. The 78×96-inch floor with a zippered cook hole is made of lightweight, strong, coated nylon taffeta. The coated, ripstop nylon sidewalls are 17 inches high at the corners and 32 inches high at the tent midpoints. U-shaped entrance, backed by mosquito netting, has a two-way, double-pull zipper that can be opened at any point on the curve. The other end has a 30×32×26-inch tunnel entrance of coated nylon. The two triangular side windows of mosquito netting have zippered panels. A tunnel vent in the upper front wall is above the cook hole for ventilation. Snow-sod flaps are attached around the tent base. An 88-inch long center pole nests to 25 inches for packing. Tent comes with pole, earth stakes, cord, and carrying bag. For winter use, snow stakes are available at extra cost. Color: yellow with sand sidewalls. Prices: $175.95 (tent without rainfly), $55.95 (fitted, coated ripstop nylon rainfly with zippered entrance), $6.95 (snow stakes, pack of twenty).

RELIANCE PRODUCTS, LTD.

This Canadian firm offers a line of innovative products for the camper. We have been using one of their Port-A-Sinks for years and wonder how we ever got along without it.

Reliance products are marketed in the United States through sporting-goods stores and camping centers.

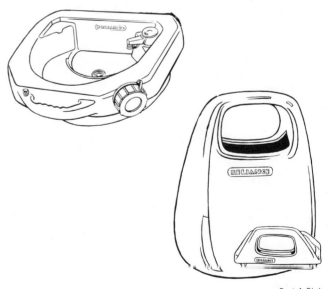

Port-A-Sink
Fold-A-Bucket

Port-A-Sink—Convenient size fits almost any table or counter; or it can be recess-mounted in any trailer, boat, or cabin. This neat, "sink away from home" holds its own 5-gallon water supply and features a double-acting pump with lock-down faucet to prevent accidental spillage. Made of tough, long-wearing polyethylene, it does not leak, crack, or break. Plus there's a built-in drain with plug and detachable plastic hose to carry wash water to safe drainage area or bucket. Other features include an extra-strong handle and jumbo filler cap. Dimensions: 21×17×6½ inches. Color: orange.

Portable Chemical Toilet—"Indoor plumbing" for all sports and seasons. This portable comfort station goes anywhere you do. It's packed with features designed to give you all the comforts of home—a molded hassock-style seat; a holder for toilet paper in inner lid; a removable interior container for waste disposal, plus a generous supply of new, improved Reliance Septic Blue chemical. Dimensions: 14 inches high by 14 inches in diameter. Color: forest green.

Fold-A-Bucket—This handy bucket has an infinite number of uses around camp. Its generous 3-gallon capacity and unique tapered design helps eliminate water splash and loss. Made of sturdy polyethylene. Folds flat for easy storage and packing.

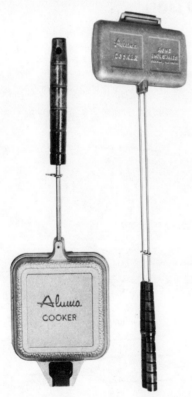

Snack'n Sandwich Cooker
Double Sandwich and Steak Cooker

ROME INDUSTRIES, INC.

From this company comes the Aluma brand of outdoor cooking accessories. In addition to the items described below, they offer a selection of cast-aluminum cookware and giant wienie forks for cooking hotdogs over the campfire.

Snack'n Sandwich Cooker—So simple almost anyone can use it to make almost any kind of hot sandwich almost anyplace. Everything from pizzaburgers to desserts, all in minutes. It can do absolutely anything its electric counterparts can do. It's constructed of cast aluminum and can be used anywhere from your kitchen stove to a campfire in the middle of the woods. It works well over any camp stove, too. Hinges come apart for

easy cleaning, and you can even use the two halves as frying pans. Comes fully guaranteed and with a book of recipes. Regular and nonstick models available, each with 14-inch square grills. Prices: $6.66 (regular), $7.66 (nonstick).

Double Sandwich and Steak Cooker—Makes your instant sandwiches twice as fast. This model has room for two sandwiches at once with no hot spots. All Aluma cookers come apart for easy cleaning and are available with Teflon coating. This unit can also cook steaks and chops. Can be used as two skillets when taken apart. Prices: $12.99 (regular), $14.99 (Teflon).

Aluma Shishkebab Skewers—They'll never rust and their aluminum construction helps assure fast cooking by spreading the heat to the center of the food. Great for any kind of skewer cooking. Packed four to a bag. Length: 18 inches. Price: $4/set of four.

Aluma Bar-B-Q Skewers—Safe for the entire family, these 24-inch-long skewers have wooden handles and are formed of aluminum for all types of skewer cooking. Great for campfire cookery and for wienie roasts. Price: $4/set of three.

SEAWAY IMPORTING CO.

Seaway offers a broad line of camping and backpacking equipment and accessories, most of which are quite economically priced.

For other Seaway products, take a look at Chapters 2, 4, and 8.

Model 3000 "Packmaster" Backpack—Coated dampproof oxford nylon bag with two main storage compartments, four large outside pockets, plus map pocket. Covered rustproof zippers, extra stitching at stress points. Anodized aluminum alloy H frame with hand-welded joints, nylon frame bands, adjustable turnbuckles, webbed nylon waist strap, and padded shoulder straps. Colors: orange, blue, and green. Price: $23.20.

Model 170 Nylon Tear-Drop Pack—This day pack features two-zipper compartment construction. Size: 12×16 inches. Colors: yellow, green, blue, and orange. Price: $7.60.

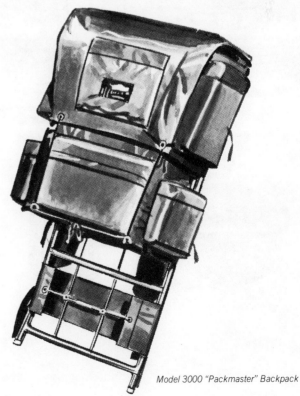

Model 3000 "Packmaster" Backpack

Model 170 Tear-Drop Pack
Model N440 Musette Bag

Model N440 Nylon Musette Bag—Heavy-duty water-repellent oxford nylon fabric. Divided front pocket with snap. Adjustable straps, extra side pocket. Size: 12×12×7 inches. Colors: blue/red, green/yellow, and orange/black. Price: $5.60.

Model L100 Foot Pump
Model OAS Desert Canteen
Blanket Canteen
Model RK12 Kerosene Lantern

Model P600 Deluxe Vinyl Air Mattress with Pillow—Heavy-gauge vinyl. Size: 30×74 inches. Multicolor design. Price: $4.40.

Model 3072 Fabric/Vinyl Air Mattress—"Floating Tufts" construction features vinylized fabric upper, self-locking safety valve, heavy-gauge vinyl bottom. Size: 30×72 inches. Colors: blue and orange. Price: $9.60.

Model L100 Foot Pump—This deluxe pump comes complete with long, flexible hose. Heavy-duty vinyl construction. Inflates and deflates with ease. Price: $2.96.

Model OAS Plastic Desert Canteen—This canteen features lightweight plastic construction with metal belt clip. Capacity: 1 quart. Price: $1.23.

Blanket Canteens—High-pressure molded plastic interiors, built-in blanket insulators, and permanently attached screw-on caps are features of these canteens with adjustable webbed cotton shoulder straps. Available in 2-quart and 4-quart models. Prices: $4.16, $4.80.

Model RK12 Kerosene Lantern—Inexpensive to own and to operate, this red lantern stands 12¾ inches high. Price: $3.60.

SNOW LION

Products from this company include sleeping bags and garments insulated either with down or with PolarGuard—a continuous filament polyester fiber. Their 48-page catalog is a good one for browsing and for learning. In addition to giving complete descriptions and illustrations of their products, it explains every step of construction and the characteristics of all materials used.

For other Snow Lion products, see Chapter 8.

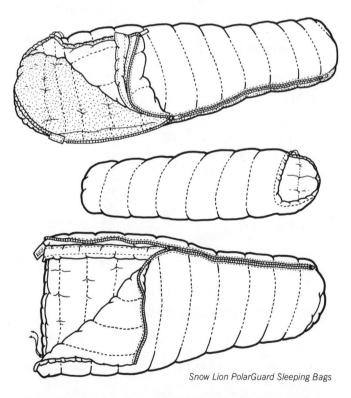

Snow Lion PolarGuard Sleeping Bags

Snow Fox—This PolarGuard-insulated bag defies the skeptics who contend that all synthetic bags are heavy and bulky. The design and development of the Snow Fox represents a major achievement in the production of PolarGuard-filled sleeping bags. Construction is offset double quilt throughout—two layers of PolarGuard on the top and two layers on the bottom. All quilted sections are individually cut, overlock stitched, and reinforced before being joined to adjacent sections. The Fox's two-way #5 Vislon zipper is backed by an exclusive PolarGuard-filled draft flap and can be paired with any Snow Lion mummy except the Small Sack and Small Sack Super. Average minimum temperature: 35° F. Regular and long models available. Weights: 3 pounds 3 ounces (regular), 3 pounds 8 ounces (long). Prices: $52.50, $56.

Footsack—Specially designed for use in tentless bivouacs, Snow Lion's PolarGuard Footsack is virtually replacing down-filled versions among serious climbers across the country. Unlike down footsacks, the Polar-Guard Footsack provides crucial protection from the rain and snow that constantly plague vertical bivouacs and gives excellent insulation underneath—where the luxury of a pad is rarely enjoyed. The Footsack features a wide, arc-shaped hood with drawcord to insulate the kidneys and lower back. The construction is offset double-quilt top, bottom, and foot. Average minimum temperature: 20° F. Weight: 2 pounds 2 ounces. Price: $41.50.

Overbag—This is a giant, hoodless mummy with a large foot section and an around-the-foot #5 Vislon zipper. It is designed to combine with down or PolarGuard mummy-shaped bags to provide the ultimate in comfort and protection during prolonged exposure to cold or cold-wet conditions. This versatile bag can be opened to form a comforter, or two can be zipped together to provide extra-spacious sleeping accommodations. Weight: 5 pounds 4 ounces. Price: $67.50.

Single-Burner Stove/Sterno Combo

STERNO

From this company comes that famous solid fuel by the same name, as well as several styles of Sterno stoves that are ideal for camping and backpacking.

Sterno Canned Heat—This is a solid, nonmelting, portable fuel. It ignites readily and burns steadily and intensely until consumed. It can be extinguished and relit as many times as desired until entire contents of the can have been consumed. Packed in seamless metal cans, Sterno is absolutely safe, odorless, and nonexplosive. Two can sizes are available:

Double-Burner Stove

2⅝ ounces and 7 ounces. Small cans come three to a sleeve-pack; large cans come two per sleeve-pack. Prices: $1.35, $1.80.

Single-Burner Stove—This is an ideal stove for light camping and backpacking. It will boil 1 quart of cold water at sea level in eighteen minutes, and is efficient enough to perc coffee, scramble eggs, or cook hamburgers. Comes with four 7-ounce cans of Sterno that will burn for a total of six hours. Price: $6.67.

Double-Burner Stove—For the camper or backpacker who wants the versatility of a two-burner stove. This one folds flat for easy packing or storage. Price: $5.20.

NORM THOMPSON OUTFITTERS

This Portland, Oregon, company puts out a catalog that is certainly a "dream book." In it are a few camping items, but primarily the catalog is full of top-quality clothing items for active outdoor folks.

Some of their popular clothing will be described in Chapter 8. For now, here are two items that might catch your fancy.

"Executive" Backpack

Shikari Grill

"Executive" Backpack—Popular in Europe as a wear-on travel bag as well as for hiking, this leather backpack is now available in the United States exclusively from Norm Thompson Outfitters. The supple leather is bark-tanned steerhide, specially softened. The entire back, bottom, and top flap is one continuous piece of leather with no seams to pull out, and the shoulder straps are faced with shearling for extra softness. The back is braced with lightweight, high-tensile steel with adjustable nylon webbing to allow air circulation. Zipper is extra-heavy-duty brass. Price: $57.50, plus $1.25 shipping.

Shikari Grill—Four pages from the newspaper can cook a steak to perfection in less than six minutes. This thing really does work! No need for wood or charcoal, forks, or spatulas, because entire grid turns over. Comes packed in a box that serves as a carrying case—easy to stick in the car and take along for a fast meal. Price: $15, plus 75¢ postage.

Rec-Pac Backpack

WEST FORK, INC.

This company sends out a small catalog with some big values in it. They guarantee every item in their product line, and if you are not satisfied you can return your purchase for replacement or full refund. The catalog is free, and we think you'll find it useful.

Rec-Pac Rigid Waterproof Backpack—This tough, rigid pack of high-density polyethylene is waterproof with a gasket inside the top lid.

Trois Riviers Tent

Molded-in handles, 3,000-cubic inch volume, and padded adjustable shoulder straps are only a few of the features in this unique pack. It makes an ideal food carrier because it eliminates worry over weather, rodents, and insects. It also floats, so it is ideally suited to boat or canoe camping. Dimensions: 22 inches high by 15 inches wide by 9 inches deep. Weight: 5 pounds 8 ounces. Price: $29.00 postpaid.

Model Trois Riviers Three-Man Tent—A roomy, comfortable tent with 7×7-foot floor area, 5-foot center height, 18-inch sidewall, vinyl-coated floor, mosquito front and storm flap with three-way zippers, four-piece aluminum poles, nylon guy ropes, ABS plastic stakes. Comes complete with nylon carrying bag. Weight: 8 pounds 14 ounces. A high-quality tent—easy to pack, easy to erect. Price: $54.00 postpaid.

Combination Pick and Shovel—Pick and shovel blade secures instantly with snap lock. Hardened steel blade and pick. Hardwood handle. An important tool for any camper. Price: $5.50 postpaid.

Mini Rucksack—Tough nylon 24-inch rucksack folds into its own 5×9-inch zippered carrying pouch when not in use. Carrying pouch has belt loops for easy carrying. Adjustable shoulder straps. Drawstring closure with flap cover. Price: $3.95 postpaid.

Combination Pick and Shovel

Mini Rucksack

CHAPTER EIGHT

CLOTHING FOR THE OUTDOORSMAN

To paraphrase an old adage, perhaps clothes don't make the outdoorsman, but the right clothes can certainly make him more comfortable. And in the case of some specialized clothing items, they can even help to keep him alive in a harsh environment. The ultimate value in any outdoor garment, therefore, is in its utility.

In the pages that follow are some of the toughest, most durable, and functional garments available to today's demanding and active outdoorsmen.

ALTRA, INC.

Sewing kits for active outdoors people are available from Altra. They offer kits for down-filled and PolarGuard-insulated garments as well as kits for making your own camping gear.

For the Altra camping line, see Chapter 7.

PolarGuard Parka Kit

Altra PolarGuard Parka—This parka keeps you insulated against the cold even when it's wet. The raglan shoulder construction gives a better fit and minimizes heat loss through the shoulders. A large self-repairing coil zipper and Velcro fasteners offer double protection from cold drafts. The double handwarmer pockets are also fully insulated and two roomy cargo pockets have Velcro-fastened flaps for easy access and secure storage. Available in nylon taffeta or rugged polyester-cotton blend. Sizes: from extra small to extra large. Prices: $31 (taffeta), $37.50 (polyester-cotton), $7 (taffeta hood), $8 (polyester-cotton hood).

Altra PolarGuard Reversible Vest—It's like two vests in one. With a rugged, quilted mountain-man look on one side, and a smooth, nylon fashion look on the other, the PolarGuard vest is an excellent starter kit. For all-around spring and fall wear the vest is a natural. Available in rugged, water-repellent polyester-cotton or long-lasting nylon taffeta. Prices: $18.50 (taffeta), $23.50 (polyester-cotton).

Altra Down and PolarGuard Booties—These booties have durable, waterproof Cordura nylon bottoms and Ensolite soles. A top drawstring and built-in elastic cross bands over the instep and around the ankle keep your feet snug and secure. Men's sizes: from 4 to 13. Women's sizes: from 5 to 12. Prices: $12.50 (down), $10.50 (PolarGuard).

EDDIE BAUER

A major mail-order supplier of outdoor gear, Eddie Bauer's clothing line is extensive. This company can outfit you for any outdoor activity, from a stroll through the woods to a polar expedition.

Bauer's down clothing is favored by many outdoorsmen who enjoy their sports in colder climates. Before you buy your next sport garment, you'll want to send for the Eddie Bauer catalog.

For other Bauer products, see Chapter 7.

Heavy-Duty Kara Koram Parka—Every feature of this parka is designed to give outdoors people warmth, protection, and action-free comfort through a broad spectrum of extremes in temperature and critical wind-chill factors. The outer fabric is a tightly woven, windproof, water-repellent blend of nylon and cotton. Inner lining is tough, long-wearing expedition ripstop nylon. The entire parka is insulated with Bauer goose down. Heavy-duty zipper closure is protected full length by a goose down insulated storm flap that overlaps and secures with heavy-duty brass snaps. Foul-weather parka hood, which folds back to form a wide collar when not in use, has a back strap to adjust height of face opening. Goose down inner collar makes an effective weather seal around the neck. Sleeves are fitted with stretch-knit nylon storm cuffs. Large, flap-protected cargo pockets conceal handwarmer pockets. Drawstrings at waist and lower hem keep warmth in and cold out. Though designed for temperatures as frigid as those at the South Pole, this parka meets the needs of anyone who wants maximum protection. Sizes: extra small to extra large. Colors: red, autumn tan, and olive. Comfort Range: −40° to +50° F. Price: $82.50.

Kara Koram Parka and Pants

Kara Koram Heavy-Duty Pants—These pants match the parka in design, construction, and comfort range. They provide the protection needed for outdoor activities in extreme temperatures. For people who find the active outdoor life a challenge, there is a need for pants that move with the wearer. "Action Knees" of the Kara Koram pants give greatest possible freedom for hiking, climbing, bending, sitting, and getting around in deep snow. Goose down insulation protects lower back and kidney area. Two large cargo pockets are flap protected. Stretch-knit cuffs hug ankles, fit comfortably inside boots. Fabric is Ramar cloth of 60 percent cotton and 40 percent nylon. Sizes: from small to extra large. Colors: red, autumn tan, and olive. Price: $69.50.

Yukon Down Jacket—This is Bauer's most popular jacket, expertly tailored and beautifully styled. Handsomely constructed for full freedom of action, the Yukon is protectively warm in subzero temperatures and because of the unequaled thermal efficiency of Bauer goose down it is completely comfortable in moderate weather. The outer fabric is a blend of cotton and nylon for maximum durability, a high degree of water repellency and superior protection against heat-robbing winds that can push the chill factor into critical ranges. The soft, warm, dyed mouton lamb collar is both face-flattering and practical; turn it up and button it in front for maximum protection of neck and throat when chill winds blow. Large bellows pockets are fitted with button-down flaps to keep snow out and protect valuables from loss. For an added touch of comfort, there's a pair of pockets under the bellows pockets, lined with soft nylon fleece to serve as handwarmers. There is another pocket inside the Yukon to safely carry your smokes, sunglasses, or wallet. Sleeves have button cuffs that conceal inner knit wristlets of stretch-knit nylon to keep cold out and warmth in. Available in women's sizes and men's regular and long sizes. Colors: autumn tan, olive, and red (men); autumn tan, spur green, and red (women). Comfort range: −20° to +50° F. Prices: $84.50 (women's and men's regular), $86.50 (men's long).

Downlight Canadian Vests—Weighs less than 12 ounces yet is so warm it takes the place of heavy and bulky outdoor garments. Worn over a wool shirt, it leaves arms free for action—very comfortable worn under a windbreaker or rain jacket. Tailored extra long in back to protect the sensitive kidney area. Rolls to tote in a compact bundle no larger than a can of beans. Insulation is Bauer goose down quilted in long-wearing ripstop nylon. Vest front is fitted with a zipper closure. Roomy slash pockets are handwarmer lined with soft nylon fleece. Elastic-knit nylon collar hugs the neck protectively. Men's sizes: 36 to 48 even. Women's sizes: 8 (bust 32) to 20 (bust 41). Colors: red, Scotch mist green, and beige (men's); red, avocado, and blue (women's). Price: $27.50.

L. L. BEAN

Just about any sort of outdoor clothing you could want can be found in the L. L. Bean catalog. Our sampling begins the same way the company did sixty-five years ago—with the famous Maine Hunting Shoe.

For other Bean products, see Chapter 7.

Maine Hunting Shoe—Mr. Bean first developed this boot in 1912. He combined the lightweight, snug fit of custom-made leather tops with the protective, waterproof features of rubber bottoms. The practical advantages of this design made his Maine Hunting Shoe an immediate success. Continuous improvements in material and construction have been added. But the basic design has yet to be improved for all-weather and all-purpose outdoors comfort. Uppers are of supple, long-wearing top-grain cowhide, organically treated in the tanning process to resist water. Bottoms of tough, ozone-resistant rubber with cushioned innersole. Outersole of durable crepe is permanently vulcanized to the vamp and features Bean's famous nonslip chain tread. Sizes: 3 to 14D (narrow) and EE (medium), 5 to 14FF (wide), whole sizes only. Heights: 6, 8, 10, 12, 14, and 16 inches. Prices: $24 to $40, all postpaid.

Maine Hunting Shoe

Bean's Blucher Moccasins—Oil-tanned, brown ski-grain uppers. True moccasin construction with hand-sewed toe piece. Blucher-style lacing for snug fit at heel and arch. Durable, nonslip rubber sole with molded arch support for walking comfort. Women's sizes: 5 to 9, whole and half sizes, medium width. Men's sizes: 6½ to 13D, 3 to 13EE, whole and half sizes. Prices: $18 (women's), $21.50 (men's), postpaid.

Bean's Pork Pie Hat—A very well-made hat of fine preshrunk polyester and cotton gabardine with taped seams, lined crown to prevent stain, and stitched flexible brim. Water repellent. Fine for fishing, camping, or everyday use. Color: light tan with red tartan band. Sizes: 6¾ to 7¾. Price: $6.25 postpaid.

Chamois Cloth Shirt—Made on extra-full shirt patterns, with two large breast pockets with button flaps, long sleeves, and long, tuck-in tails (women's model has squared tails). Fabric is finest grade cotton flannel, thickly napped on both sides. As warm and durable as wool and machine washable. Colors: navy, bright red, tan, and forest green. Men's sizes: 14½ to 20 (regular), 15 to 19 (long). Women's sizes: 10 to 20. Prices: $13 (men's regular), $14 (men's long), $12.50 (women's), all postpaid.

Maine Guide Shirt—A practical, mediumweight garment, cut roomy. Made of 85 percent pure wool with 15 percent nylon added for strength. Two button-flap pockets. Long tails. Men's colors: four plaids, brown, tan, and natural. Women's colors: two plaids, brown, tan, and natural. Men's sizes: 14 to 19. Women's sizes: 10 to 18. Prices: $18 (men's sizes 14 to 17), $19.50 (men's sizes 18 and 19), $18 (women's), all postpaid.

Bean's Country Slacks—Wide-wale corduroy is thickly napped for a rich, handsome appearance. Soft and comfortable, these pants will give long and satisfying service for casual wear. Men's sizes: 30 to 42. Colors: hunter green, redwood, light brown, and blueberry. Price: $22.50 postpaid.

BROWNING

Browning's line of outdoor clothing includes coats, vests, rain wear, underwear, hats, gloves, belts, and boots. We have found Browning clothing to be extremely tough and comfortable. Their boots almost refuse to wear out.

For other Browning products, see Chapters 4, 6, 7, and 9.

Fiberfill II Reversible Vest—Wear the brilliant blaze orange side out when you're hunting big game and upland birds. And when duck season rolls in, reverse it to the mesa tan side and stay snug and warm in the blind all day. It's the perfect vest for wet, rainy climates, because Fiberfill II won't absorb moisture; it retains its loft and insulates even when wet. The 3-inch back extension below the waist and large pockets on both sides make it warm and convenient. Sizes: small to extra large. Price: $28.95.

Fiberfill II Reversible Vest

Featherweight Boots—This boot's extreme light weight and the comfort of soft, pliable leather make walking a new, exhilarating experience. Adaptable to hunting almost any upland species, this fine boot is crafted from "Tundra" cowhide, a recently developed ultralight tannage that will take rough treatment. Tough cushion crepe soles provide exceptional protection on rough terrain and give good traction when combing ditch banks for pheasants, or working the rolling hills in search of sharptails. Fully lined with soft glove leather, the boot has cushioned leather insoles for added comfort. Decayproof Dacron thread, tempered steel shanks, nailless construction, and Taslan laces are other quality features. Men's sizes: 9 to 14 (B widths), 7 to 14 (D & EE widths). Women's and Juniors' sizes: 5 to 10, A and C widths. Prices: $61.95 (men's), $52.95 (women's and juniors').

Boulder Vibram Insulated Boots—Heavily insulated to keep your feet warm in snow and winter cold, this boot is specially designed to meet the most rugged type of terrain. Best of all you'll experience foot comfort you never believed possible in a tough, rugged boot. The basic construction of this "go anywhere" 9-inch boot is a combination of heavy-duty, water-repellent, oil-tanned leather and the famous cleated Vibram heel and sole for sure footing. The Boulder Vibram is resistant to water penetration from top to bottom. Other features include lightweight nailless construction, comfortable Goodyear moccasin toe, and spring steel shanks that give added support to the Boulder Vibram. All seams are stitched with decayproof Dacron thread. You'll appreciate the convenient German speed lacing, too. Sizes: 9 to 14 (B widths), 7 to 14 (D and EE widths). Price: $66.95.

DANNER SHOE MANUFACTURING CO.

Danner manufactures a superb line of boots for a wide variety of outdoor activities, from hiking to mountain climbing, and they have several models that should be of particular interest to hunters.

Swale and Tule Hunter Boots—At last, a hunting boot designed for solid comfort as well as service. Cushioned insoles and padded ankles and

tongues. Tendon pads and scree guards. Durable brass hooks and Vibram soles. A classic hunting style. Fully lined. Weight: 5 pounds. Sizes: 8½ to 12, 13, and 14 (B width), 7 to 12, 13, and 14 (D width), 6 to 12 and 13 (EE width). Price: $82.50, plus $1.50 delivery charge.

Trail Boots—Double-riveted lacing hooks and larger D-rings with special washers. Fully leather lined. Padded tongue and ankle. One-piece upper and Vibram heel and sole. Danner's finest trail boot. Weight: 3½ pounds. Men's sizes: 8 to 12, 13, 14 (B width), 6 to 12, 13 (D width), 6 to 12 (EE width). Women's sizes: 5 to 10 (A, B, C widths). Price: $54.50, plus $1.25 delivery charge.

Trail Boots

Canoe Moc—Walk softly on a leather-covered cushion a half-inch thick. Danner's hand-stitched moccasin style is cut from Shasta tan leather upper stock that will mold itself to the shape of your foot for flexible comfort plus protection. Excellent for around home or in camp. Weight: ¾ pound. Men's sizes: 6 to 12, 13, 14 (D and EE widths). Women's sizes: 6 to 10 (B width). Price: $25 postpaid.

EARLY WINTERS, LTD.

The Early Winters clothing line includes Gore-Tex rain wear and several down-filled vests, sweaters, and parkas.

Other Early Winters products appear in Chapters 7 and 11.

Gore-Tex Rain Wear—Your Early Winters Gore-Tex Parka or pullover Anorak is like several garments in one. They're both waterproof to keep you dry from the rain, yet breathable to help keep you dry from yourself. And at the same time, each garment functions as a windbreaker. Spe-

Gore-Tex Parka and Anorak

cial patterns give you good-looking, high-performance outdoor wear. They're designed for action with adjustable underarm vents for easy temperature control and contour-fitted three-piece hoods that give you full head protection without loss of peripheral vision. Velcro cuffs adjust to fit your wrists to keep the wind from coming up your arms. The Parka has two 7×10-inch cargo pockets with built-in bellows that expand to hold plenty, and Velcro fasteners on the flaps. The Anorak features a 9×13-inch kangaroo pocket at chest height. Colors: royal blue/navy, and gold/orange. Sizes: 6 to 18 (women's), 30 to 48 (men's). Prices: $79.95 postpaid (Parka), $62.95 postpaid (Anorak).

The Marmot Shirt—This down shirt will give you the warmth of ordinary down sweaters, with a total weight of only 15 ounces. It is designed to give you full, unrestricted arm and body action for all your cold-weather activities. It closes with a YKK coil zipper, backed with a full-length down-filled draft tube to stop all wind from reaching you. The waist seals with a nylon/elastic storm skirt, and the cuffs are hidden 100 percent nylon stretch-knit. A down-filled collar comforts your neck. As with all Marmot gear, every piece of fabric is individually hot-cut to assure you of many years of good use. The Marmot Shirt features two insulated pockets to warm your hands and a roomy, Velcro-sealed stash pocket for small items and valuables. Sizes: extra small to extra large. Prices: $52.95 (regular), $72.95 (Gore-Tex), both postpaid.

BOB HINMAN OUTFITTERS

In his catalog, Bob offers a fine selection of clothing for hunters, fishermen, and campers. His company specializes in cold-weather clothing and ultra-lightweight outdoor equipment.

In addition to being long-time shotgun editor of *Shooting Times* and the author of *The Duck Hunter's Handbook* and *The Golden Age of Shotgunning*—both books published by Winchester Press—Bob has done outdoor clothing design for the U.S. Army and many clothing makers.

His annual catalog is free. So be sure to send for one.

Polar Hunting Gloves—The problem in the past has been to find an insulated glove thin enough to shoot with—this glove is. It offers little more warmth than regular gloves at mild temperatures, but retains natural heat in very cold weather to keep your hands warmer with less weight and bulk than other designs. Made of lightweight, seamless capeskin leather insulated with closed-cell foam. A soft, beautiful glove in a rich patina brown or black. Sizes: S, M, ML, L, and XL. Price: $14.95.

Polar Gloves

Cotton "Sun" Shirt—A very lightweight, all-cotton fishing shirt made in Guatemala. The special weave and long sleeves give coolest possible protection from intense all-day sun in such areas as the Florida Keys. Zipper closure, four large front pockets, and one pocket on arm. Wide collar turns up to shield neck. Hand washable. Color: sand tan. Sizes: S, M, L, and XL. Price: $19.50.

The Duck Hunter—A prime down-insulated cold-weather jacket of just the right length for wear with hip boots or waders. Action-free raglan shoulders and ripstop nylon inner lining. Outer shell is 60/40 Ramar cloth in a highly water-resistant, tough twill that will stand up to heaviest use in brush. The predominantly brown and tan camouflage blends perfectly with most marsh backgrounds. A knit insert in the collar adds warmth as well as lessens wear and grime in this area. The knit bottom gives protection from cold and wind. There are two large, flapped cargo pockets, each bar-tacked to carry heavy shell loads. Other features include slash handwarmer pockets, knit wristlets, heavy-duty zipper, and detachable insulated hood. Sizes: S, M, L, XL, and XXL. Prices: $67.50 (S to XL), $77.50 (XXL).

The Duck Hunter

HIRSCH-WEIS

The Stag line of clothing manufactured by this company includes down-filled and PolarGuard-insulated cold-weather garments, rain wear, and a variety of jackets and vests for hunters, fishermen, campers, and backpackers.

For other Stag brand outdoor products, see Chapter 7.

Klamath Fishing Vest—One of the most rugged and durable vests ever constructed. Made of heavy-duty Aquaduck, the Klamath has ten front pockets, including one that's zippered, two inside pockets, and a large rear-zippered cargo or fish pocket. Velcro tabs protect the inside and front pocket flaps. Other features include a sheepskin flyholder, clear plastic license holder, two D-rings, a dog-leash snap, and rod holders. Sizes: small to extra large. Color: tan.

Woodsman Wool Cruiser Coat—Made of 25/26-ounce 100 percent wool, the Woodsman has double layers of fabric over the shoulders, front, and back for extra warmth and rain protection. There is a total of six button-down pockets on the front, plus a large rear cargo pocket secured by button flaps on both sides. Buffalo plaid pattern. Sizes: small to extra extra large. Colors: blue/black and red/black.

Klamath Fishing Vest
Woodsman Cruiser Coat

KOLPIN MANUFACTURING, INC.

In addition to their line of gun cases and archery accessories found in Chapters 4 and 6, Kolpin offers a line of knitwear and thermal parkas for hunters.

All-Seasons Camo Sweaters—Kolpin's line of camo knitwear is available in colors for all seasons. Using a genuine three-color jacquard stitch, Kolpin has designed their knitwear so the pattern and color become an integral part of the garment. Features include overlocking seams, tapered shoulders, and 100 percent acrylic yarn. These sweaters are preshrunk and they never itch. Available in orange, green, and brown camouflage patterns. Sizes: small to extra large. Price: $31.

All-Seasons Camo Caps—Wear a cap with your sweater for the total matched look. Caps can be worn over face mask in cold weather or used alone. Comfortable 100 percent acrylic yarn stretches so one size fits all. Same colors as sweaters. Price: $8.75.

All-Seasons Camo Sweater and Cap

Lightweight Thermal Parkas—These brand-new Kolpin parkas are filled with polyester foam. They retain heat by using a fully lined thermo cloth. They're water repellent and warm, yet provide super-lightweight comfort. They come with hood, drawstring closure, stretch waist band and cuffs, and heavy-duty YKK zipper. Colors: safety orange and camouflage. Sizes: small to extra large. Prices: from $26 to $30.80.

S. D. MYRES SADDLE CO.

This company manufactures fine leather goods, and they offer the outdoorsman a wide selection of exquisite hand-carved belts. They also carry a line of belt buckles—commercial models as well as hand-made sterling silver ones.

Myres holsters appear in Chapter 4.

Myres No. 4 Rosebud—This belt features closed flower and leaf pattern with a border edge. A beautiful belt with optional dyed background available. Price: $25.

Myres No. 15 Wild Flower—This belt features a very intricate flower and leaf pattern, with two-tone finish. This is the best of the Myres belts, 1½ inches or wider. Hand-engraved solid sterling silver letters are optional. Price: $50.

Myres Belts

NORTH FACE

The popular North Face line of outdoor clothing includes parkas, vests, and rain wear in sizes for men, women, and children, all of which are described in a full-color, 44-page catalog that's free for the asking.

North Face camping and backpacking gear can be found in Chapter 7.

Serow Parka—The Serow is a heavy-duty low-temperature parka combining the insulation of goose down and a wind-resistant 60/40 cloth shell. An average of 290 grams of down is quilted between two layers of 2.5-ounce nylon taffeta, creating an ample layer of insulation. The Serow is popular with people who work outdoors in winter conditions in Alaska, Canada, and the northern United States. It is most efficient and practical in subfreezing temperatures. Features include high, overstuffed snap-closed collar; insulated flap over the zipper for stopping wind penetration; Velcro-closed cuffs, large enough to slip over bulky gloves; and a waist drawcord. Pockets are down insulated, with handwarmers opening from the side and flap-closed cargo pockets opening from the top. There are six pockets in all. A down-insulated hood is sold separately. Colors: navy and tan. Sizes: extra small to extra large. Price: $82.50 (parka), $12.50 (hood).

Serow Parka

Sierra Parka—This parka is insulated with an average of 270 grams (10 ounces) of prime goose down. Two shell fabrics are available: 1.9-ounce ripstop nylon, finished with Kendown and Zepel; and 5-ounce high thread count 65/35 polyester/cotton. Both fabrics are breathable, resistant to abrasion, and very durable. The 65/35 outer, though heavier, is excellent for use in brush. Hoods are available for both styles. Features include a high, overstuffed, snap-closed collar; a double-slider coil zipper with a down-insulated, snap-over flap; double handwarmer/cargo pockets; and hip drawcord. Cuffs close with elastic and snaps. Detail in sewing and finishing is superb. Colors: green, brown, red, and navy (ripstop); navy (65/35). Sizes: extra extra small to extra large. Prices: $59.50 (ripstop parka), $11.50 (ripstop hood), $65 (65/35 parka), $12.50 (65/35 hood).

ORVIS

Orvis offers a broad line of apparel for hunters and fishermen, including fine coats, vests, shirts, slacks, and hats. We have been using a number of Orvis garments for years and have found them to be tough, comfortable, and always stylish.

For more Orvis products, check Chapters 2, 4, and 11.

Orvis Shortie Wader Vest—Rides high to keep your fly boxes dry in deep wading. This little vest really stores all your equipment—everything neatly in place and easy to reach, but well above high water. The non-corrosive nylon zippers and Velcro fasteners are one-hand operable.

Front vertical opening makes it very easy to get at fly boxes. The two small back pockets for extra reel or reel spools are an especial improvement. Large cargo compartment, and detachable fleece patch are other features. There are eight pockets in all. Color: olive. Sizes: small to extra large. Price: $27.50.

Orvis Flotation Fishing Vest—A real life jacket, floats a man safely and is completely practical as a fishing vest. Two upper pockets, two lower fly box pockets, all with Velcro closure for one-hand access. There is a huge all-across-the-back cargo pocket, two fleece fly patches top front, a net ring top back. Flotation comes from a buoyant foam in the vest, so there are no cords to pull, no bulky air bags in the vest. Men's sizes: small to extra large. Price: $32.50.

Flotation Fishing Vest

New Ladies' Orvis Waders—Full-cut wader for free and active movement in the stream or the surf. Three-ply construction for durability and comfort. Nylon satin cloth inside and outside with rubber in between to ensure waterproofness. Waders have drawstring top, belt loops, and roomy inside pocket for fly boxes. Absorptive fabric lining in boot legs to limit condensation and for easy on and off. Seams are fully vulcanized. Other features include inside leg chafe guard, semihard toe, and steel shank for support. Available with felt sole in sizes 6, 7, 8, and 9. Price: $58.75.

Ladies' Waders

New Orvis Hippers—Available with studded or plain felt sole or rubber sole. Three-ply construction. Nylon satin cloth both inside and out with rubber between plies. They have adjustable knee harness and generous belt straps to keep them taut at the thigh. Semihard toe cap to prevent stone bruises. Steel shank for support. Men's sizes: 7 through 13. Women's sizes: 6 through 9. Prices: $49.75 (men's and women's felt soled), $59.75 (men's felt soled with aluminum studs), $42.75 (men's rubber soled).

Duck Hunter's Hat—All the right features—brown camouflage; big, wide, stiff brim; oversize weather flap; folding ear flap; quilted insulation. This hat completes your cover and keeps you warm. Sizes: 6¾ through 8. Price: $7.95.

Duck Hunter's Hat

Camouflage Chamois Shirt—Warm, comfortable, 100 percent cotton with brushed silky feel, rugged wear, and incredible durability. The Orvis chamois cloth is marvelous material and the tailoring is sturdy and careful, with comfortably rounded tails. A good working shirt for hunting. Men's sizes: small to extra large. Price: $22.95.

Duck Hunter's Mitt—Brown leather, fleece lined in both the glove hand that supports the gun and in the "muff pocket" for the trigger hand. You can draw out this bare hand and shoot like a flash. The President of Ducks Unlimited was instrumental in its design. This is an Orvis exclusive and enthusiastically approved by every hunter who has tried one on. It keeps your hands really warm and very much improves your shooting. There is a hand warmer compartment for bitter cold weather. It can make all the difference in your comfort and your score. One size fits everyone. Price: $21.50.

P. & S. SALES

This company has a large line of outdoor clothing available by mail. Their catalog includes garments and footwear for hunters, fishermen, campers, and backpackers.

For other P. & S. products, see Chapters 2, 7, and 9.

Fringed Rawhide Westerner Coat—This coat has the authentic look of the Western frontier. It's a warm, comfortable coat, perfect on any outing. Made of carefully selected split-cowhide skins, it comes in sizes for both men and women. Has long fringe on the sleeves, shoulders, and front and back yokes, as well as on the large patch pockets and around the bottom. Leather button front. Body and sleeve lining made of rich rayon-acetate material. Honey-brown color. This practical, colorful coat will give you years of satisfaction and pleasure. Men's sizes: 36 through 46. Women's sizes: 8 through 18. Prices: $67.50 (men's), $63.95 (women's).

Horseman's Riding Slicker—Rubber slicker has a split tail and a built-in back piece that covers the cantle of the saddle. Made of heavy rubber sheeting on cotton backing. Stand-up collar is corduroy lined. Button storm fly front. Double-stitched and taped seams. Color: yellow. Sizes: small to extra large. Price: $16.95.

Fringed Rawhide Westerner Coat
Horseman's Riding Slicker

Sierra Backpacker Shoe—This boot was designed for hiking. Tops are 6 inches high, made of fine oil tan leather. Features Chippewa's no-bind, no-chafe patented Kush-N-Kollar design. All leather lined with padded quarter. Cushioned insole. Box toe. Rugged, nonslip Vibram sole and heel. Speed lacing with padded gusset. Sizes: 7 through 12, whole and half sizes, D width. Price: $39.95.

Army Surplus Canvas Leggins—These will save your legs (and trousers, too) when you're walking through rough brush and brambles. Made of heavy, rugged canvas, they'll take a lot of punishment. Lacing strings included with each pair. Price: $1.50.

RECREATIONAL EQUIPMENT, INC.

R.E.I. carries a complete line of clothing for outdoorsmen, and their prices are some of the best to be found. For a complete description of how this membership co-op works and a sampling of some of their camping and backpacking gear, turn to Chapter 7.

Ventile Mountain Parka—A fine quality parka that is a good choice for strenuous activities. Made of Ventile cotton fabric, a very tightly woven 100 percent cotton material that is water repellent yet breathes to reduce condensation inside the garment. Fully lined in the body, sleeves, and hood for added warmth. Features include a two-way YKK Vislon

Ventile Mountain Parka

zipper with snap-over storm front, an inner drawstring at waist and hem, two large cargo pockets with Velcro closures, an upper map pocket with vertical zipper, and an inner pocket. Cuffs have gussets and adjustable tabs with Velcro closures. The hood with drawstring has a snap system at the back to hold the sides of the hood back for unrestricted vision. Men's sizes: small to extra large. Women's sizes: small to large. Colors: blue and tan. Price: $59.95.

Fashion Vest—Stylish, fitted, two-tone vest with contrasting yoke top and piping trim. Made of tough Taslan nylon with nylon taffeta lining and sewn-through in horizontal bands filled with Prime Northern Silvergrey goose down to an average loft of 2½ inches. Features include stand-up collar with snaps, YKK Vislon-zippered front with snap-over flap, and two patch pockets with handwarmers behind them. Men's sizes: extra small to extra large. Extra small and small will fit women. Colors: blue/powder yoke/navy piping, and brown/beige yoke/dark brown piping. Price: $36.95.

Fashion Vests

Pullover Sweater—All-purpose, lightweight pullover with zippered placket front and knit collar, cuffs, and hem band accented with double white stripes. Made of nylsilk, a lightweight nylon taffeta sewn-through in horizontal bands filled with Prime Northern Silvergrey goose down to an average loft of 2 inches. It features a YKK coil zipper placket and a zippered kangaroo pocket with a down-insulated, pass-through handwarmer behind it. Men's sizes: extra extra small to extra large. Sizes XXS, XS, and S will fit women. Colors: blue, yellow, rust, and green. Price: $34.95.

HANK ROBERTS

The same company that produces those fine Hank Roberts flies and fly-tying materials also offers jackets and vests for the fisherman.

Other Hank Roberts products are described in Chapter 2.

No. RJ Rain Jacket—Unique, practical combination rain jacket and vest all in one garment. Plenty of pockets to store your tackle, but this jacket is lightweight and rainproof. Made of urethane-coated nylon taffeta. Features include Velcro and zipper closures for pockets, snap-off Velcro fly patch, Velcro adjustable cuffs, and D-ring for accessories. Sizes: small to extra large. Color: green. Price: $24.95.

No. PV Personal Vest—Crafted of a soft green, lightweight polyester and cotton combination material that is machine washable, durable, and water repellent and with a total of twenty pockets, this vest is a fisherman's dream. Other features include Velcro-fastened fly patches, upper bellows pockets with Velcro fasteners, zippered lower pockets, D-ring for attaching clippers or scissors, and more. Sizes: small to extra large. Price: $39.50.

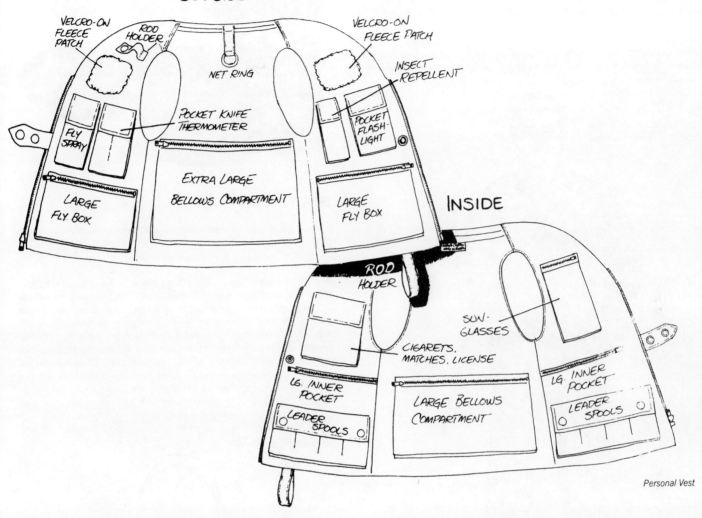

OUTSIDE

VELCRO-ON FLEECE PATCH
ROD HOLDER
NET RING
VELCRO-ON FLEECE PATCH
INSECT REPELLENT
POCKET KNIFE THERMOMETER
POCKET FLASH-LIGHT
FLY SPRAY
EXTRA LARGE BELLOWS COMPARTMENT
LARGE FLY BOX
LARGE FLY BOX

INSIDE

ROD HOLDER
SUN-GLASSES
CIGARETS, MATCHES, LICENSE
LG. INNER POCKET
LG. INNER POCKET
LEADER SPOOLS
LARGE BELLOWS COMPARTMENT
LEADER SPOOLS

Personal Vest

THE SCOTTISH PEDLAR, LTD.

From this company comes one garment that should be of interest to many active outdoors families—the British Regimental Sweater in sizes to fit everyone. Be sure to write for descriptive literature and order blanks.

Original British Regimental Sweater—Direct from England and available only from the Scottish Pedlar, these sweaters are ideal for the whole family. They're made of 100 percent pure new wool in heavy rib knit for incredible warmth and are styled with long-wearing patches at the shoulders and elbows. These stylish and rugged sweaters are perfect for all outdoor activities. Colors: navy and olive. Prices: $21.50 (children's sizes), $31.50 (adult sizes). No charge for postage and handling. Buy two or more and knock $1.50 off the price of each.

SEAWAY IMPORTING CO.

Seaway's line of outdoor clothing includes a variety of vests, jackets, coats, rain wear, and boots for all outdoor activities. They are economically priced and are marketed nationally.

Other Seaway products can be found in Chapters 2, 4, and 7.

Fluorescent Orange Safety Vest—Vinyl construction with a minimum of 400 square inches of fluorescent material. Tie front. Sizes: medium to extra large. Price: $1.44.

Fluorescent Orange Safety Vest

Nylon Backpacker Poncho—Lightweight, water-repellent nylon, draw-string hood, tie-down webbing and grommets, snap-lock fasteners, double stitching at stress points, perma-sealed seams and extra snaps to form sleeves are features in this poncho. Size: 50×90 inches (one size fits all). Colors: orange, blue, and green. Price: $8.40.

Camouflage Coveralls—One-piece construction of heavy cotton twill fabric. Full cut. Full-length heavy-duty zipper. Two breast pockets, two slash pockets. Sewn-in tabs and buttons for snug ankle fit. Sizes: medium to extra large. Price: $12.40.

Snowmobile Boots

SNOW LION

Parkas, jackets, and vests, insulated with down or PolarGuard, are included in the Snow Lion catalog, as are shells, booties, and mittens.
For other Snow Lion products, see Chapter 7.

Western Mountain Parka—The exterior fabric of this versatile shell garment is a wind-tight, water-repellent blend of 65/35 percent polyester/cotton. Shoulders, hood, upper back, and upper chest are covered with a scalloped "Western style" yoke of waterproof, double-ply nylon taffeta. The inside upper body, hood, and shoulders are lined with 100 percent Ventile cotton. The inside lower body and sleeves are lined with the same polyester/cotton blend as the outer shell. Other features include six pockets—two lower cargo pockets with Velcro closures, two handwarmer pockets, vertical chest and rear pockets with Zip'on coil zippers—two-way front Vislon zipper with snap-down weather flap; large, integral hood with nylon drawcord; Velcro tabs on wrists; and more. Sizes: extra small to extra large. Colors: midnight blue, rust, and forest green. Price: $56.

Camouflage Coveralls

Men's Insulated Polar Boot—All rubber outer with removable felt liner, molded lug sole and heel, and steel shank make this a tough and comfortable boot for all cold-weather activities. Price: $12.40.

Men's Snowmobile Boot—Deluxe waterproof coated nylon upper with heavy-duty, no-snag zipper tie closure; heavy adjustable ankle and in-step strap; and removable 8mm felt liner make this an excellent boot for many winter sports. Colors: black with red, white, and blue trim. Price: $10.40.

Stocking Foot Wader—These waders are full cut and made of heavy-gauge vinyl with all reinforced seams and attached suspenders. Sizes: small to extra large. Price: $3.60.

Western Mountain Parka

PolarGuard Mitts—These mitts average 13 inches in length, covering the hand as well as the forearm. The palm side of each is covered with rugged 11-ounce waterproof Cordura. The back side covering is 4-ounce oxford nylon, breathable and water repellent. Both sides are insulated with a single layer of 10-ounce PolarGuard. Fit is controlled by a strip of ¾-inch nylon webbing and an easy-to-adjust buckle located at the outer wrist. Available in assorted colors. Sizes: small, medium, and large. Price: $15.50.

NORM THOMPSON OUTFITTERS

The free, 86-page catalog from Norm Thompson is full of top-quality clothing for outdoors people. All their products are thoroughly tested before being offered to their customers, and their guarantee is one of the best we've seen.

Apollo Jacket—This is a 10-ounce reversible jacket that keeps you warm when it's cold and cool when it's hot. It was made possible by a fabric developed for use in space suits. A tough aluminum skin is bonded to durable 100 percent nylon. The result is a light, flexible fabric that reverses to either reflect or absorb warmth from the sun. Features include tuck-away hood in collar pouch, button cuffs that adjust to wearer, air circulation through nylon mesh under each arm, four pockets on both inside and outside, double-stitched seams, and drawstring at waist. An added bonus is that should you ever experience the misfortune of getting lost in the wilds, the silver side of the jacket can be picked up on radar. Colors: navy reversing to silver. Men's sizes: small to extra extra large. Women's sizes: small to large. Prices: $35 (men's XXL), $32 (all other sizes).

Apollo Jacket

Gamekeeper's Storm Coat—The special "waxed" fabric keeps you dry and is almost immune to snagging or tearing. Heavy-duty canvaslike fabric is tightly woven cotton, treated with a special wax dressing, so it's virtually waterproof, but it breathes. Lined with a soft, warm cotton fabric, and has an inner, extra-large nylon game pocket that is waterproof. Color: olive brown. Men's even sizes: 36 to 46. Price: $95, plus $1.50 handling and insured delivery charge.

Irish Country Hat—This classic for men or women is handmade in Ireland of rugged tweed. You can roll it up, sit on it, stuff it in your pocket and it keeps its style and character. It's lightweight, warm, and comfortable. Colors: brown or gray tweed. Price: $16.50, plus 75¢ postage and shipping.

Irish Country Hat

Big Horn Socks—Thick, heavy-duty footwarmers cushion your feet and absorb perspiration to keep your feet dry and comfortable. No seams to rub and cause irritation inside your boot. High tops provide protection against chafing, and they're completely washable and dryable. Price: $6.50, plus 75¢ shipping.

Rugged Chukka Boots—No boot is all-purpose, but this one comes close. It has the strength and durability of a rugged outdoors boot with the comfort of a casual chukka. Entire boot is foam padded, completely leather lined, and the stretch ankle collar adds comfort. Inside there's a thick pad of foam rubber in the sole that's completely covered with leather. An "S-tred" sole guards against slips and gives extra cushioning. Women's sizes: 5 to 10, narrow and medium widths. Men's sizes: 8 to 12, 13, 14 (narrow); 7 to 12, 13, 14 (medium and wide). Price: $47.50.

Rugged Chukka Boots

UNIROYAL, INC.

The Clothing and Footwear Divisions of this company produce the famous Royal Red Ball brand of rain wear, boots, waders, and fishing shoes.

We have tried a lot of different brands of rain wear and have found that nothing can beat Royal Red Ball for strength, comfort, and efficiency. Living in the Pacific Northwest, if we are to enjoy the outdoors at every opportunity, we have to count on getting rained on. So we've learned what to look for in quality rain wear. And what we expect is precisely what we get from Uniroyal—clothing that will keep us totally dry and a variety of styles and designs to fit the varied nature of our outdoor interests.

If you write for information, be sure to send 25¢ for the booklet "Professional Tips On Keeping Warm and Dry," by Homer Circle.

Flexnet GO Suits—These new rain suits are designed for all outdoor sports and feature "360 Batwing" shoulder construction, Therm-O-Rad seams, storm front, and attached drawcord hood with visor on the jacket. Match-up pants have shockcord waist and zipper fly. Women's jackets are correctly proportioned and pants are darted at the waist. These suits are 100 percent waterproof. Men's sizes: small to extra large. Women's sizes: small to large. Colors: royal blue, white, yellow, green, and red. Price: $45.

Flexnet Fishing Shirts—Two special items for the fisherman. The Troller Shirt is long and wide for comfortable sitting in boat or duck blind. Casting shirt is designed for wear with hip boots. Both feature Therm-O-Rad seams, front pocket with snaps, and attached drawcord hood. They're 100 percent waterproof. Sizes: small to extra large. Color: field tan. Prices: $29 (Troller Shirt), $24 (Casting Shirt).

"Professional Tips On Keeping Warm and Dry" booklet, by Homer Circle

GO Suits

Flexnet Upland Hunting Jacket—For protection against those chilly autumn rains, this jacket features the same quality materials, comfort, and durability of other Flexnet clothing, but also has a lined inside game pouch that can be dropped down for extra protection when seated. It is 100 percent waterproof. Color: field tan. Sizes: small to extra large. Price: $40.

Upland Hunting Jacket

Cahill Waders—These easy-on, easy-off waders feature three-ply Tuff-Guard tops, inside/outside pouch, extra suspender buttons, and inside belt loops for shorter men. They are 100 percent waterproof and Thermo-Ply insulated. Full sizes: 7 to 13. Price: $80.

Calhoun Bush Boot—Here's a durable and comfortable boot designed for all outdoor activities. It features a cleated, hobnail sole for good traction; Tuff-Guard three-ply nylon top; and snug ankle fit. Color: brown. Height: 10 inches. Full sizes: 7 to 13. Price: $25.

Sportster Boots—These are warm boots with quality features at an economical price. They feature open-cell sponge rubber insulation and are 100 percent waterproof. Two models are available: the full-lace Pathfinder, and the top-lace Explorer. Color: marsh brown. Heights: Men's 12 inches, Boy's 10½ inches, (Pathfinder); Men's 12 inches, Boy's 10½ inches, Youth's 9½ inches (Explorer). Men's sizes: 7 to 12. Boy's sizes: 3 to 6. Youth's sizes: 11 to 2. Prices: $23 (Pathfinder), $20 (Explorer).

Cayuga Boots—These favorite 16-inch pull-on boots are suitable for outdoors work and sports. They feature top strap and buckle for snug-up fit and are 100 percent waterproof. Color: marsh brown. Full sizes: 6 to 13. Price: $30.

The Lunker—This stylish casual is a super fishing shoe, made with breathable Dura-Kool polyester mesh uppers, rugged antislip cleated outsole, padded vinyl cuff, Sta-Kleen insole with sponge cushion, and foam and tricot lining. They are ideal over stocking-foot waders. Color: tan. Half sizes: 6½ to 12, 13. Price: $26.

The Lunker

UTICA DUXBAK CORP.

This company, in business since 1904, produces the well-known Duxbak line of hunting and fishing attire, trail wear, and cold-weather clothing. Their top-quality garments are marketed nationally through sporting-goods stores and mail-order companies.

Style 046 Deluxe Stream Fishing Vest—This 20-inch-long fishing vest with snap-tab front closure has ten fly box and spool pockets made to fit standard sizes and cut ¼ inch larger for ease in removing. It also features a sheepskin drying pad, rod holder straps, large Pakbak expanding lunch and raingear pocket, back D-ring for net, and reinforcements straps for pinned-on accessories. Sizes: small to extra large. Colors/Materials: dark blue Duxbak Denim, olive green Upland Poplin. Price: $36 (Denim), $34 (Poplin).

Deluxe Stream Fishing Vest

177

Style 052 Deluxe Hunting Vest—This 23-inch button-front vest features thirty-two closed cloth shell loops on front (for 12, 16, or 20 gauge), and a detachable Pakbak expansion game pocket. Sizes: small to extra large. Colors/Materials: forest brown Utica Duck, camouflage Featherweight Camo. Prices: $22 (brown) $22.50 (camouflage).

Deluxe Hunting Vest

Style 301 Men's Safari Shirt—This 31-inch button-front shirt with shoulder straps features two breast bellows pockets with button flaps, collar stays, and double back yoke. Sizes: small to extra large. Colors/Materials: tan Sahib Poplin, veldt green Sahib Poplin, tan Kamp-it Poplin. Prices: $23 (Sahib Poplin), $18 (Kamp-it Poplin).

Style 715 Cargo Pocket Pants—These rugged pants feature two front cargo pockets, top utility pocket with flaps, two hip pockets with button-down flaps and come in sizes 30 to 44 with inseams of 30 to 32. Colors/Materials: khaki Chino Gabardine, tan Kamp-it Twill, olive green Upland Poplin: Price: $19.

Style 150 Camouflage Jones Style Hat/Cap—This popular hat features a six-piece crown, multistitched front peak and turned-up, all-around brim. It has inside ear band and Kasha cloth lining. Made of Duxbak Cloth. Sizes: 6¾ to 7¾. $7.50.

CHAPTER NINE

CUTLERY FOR THE OUTDOORSMAN

No matter what your favorite outdoor activity is—hunting, fishing, camping, backpacking, boating, or canoeing—you need some kind of cutlery. Chances are, you will want several kinds of knives to adequately handle all the cutting jobs you will face. And if you're an all-around outdoorsman, your cutlery collection will be rather extensive.

Our own assortment of cutlery, for example, includes general-purpose knives for performing a variety of duties on any outing, hunting and skinning knives, filleting and boning knives of various sizes and designs, and several specialized knives that are handy for doing such jobs as clearing brush, building blinds, field dressing birds, or scaling fish. These tools are essential to maximum enjoyment of our outdoor activities.

In the pages that follow you will find samplings of the product lines of a number of cutlery manufacturers, as well as descriptions of fine knives offered by custom knifemakers.

BOWEN KNIFE CO.

The Bowen line of cutlery includes several sheath knives, folding knives, and a unique survival belt buckle knife. Their brochure is sent free on request.

Model R1306B Folding Hunter—This is a premium-quality lock-back knife, patterned after the classic Remington lock-backs. Lightweight and thin, yet strong, it is easy to carry for everyday use. Blade is 440 stainless steel and is 2½ inches long. The closed knife is 3½ inches. Handle is brown chip bark Delrin with bullet emblem. Price: $25.

Folding Hunter

Model 126 Bullet Hunter—This knife features a 440 stainless steel blade with stainless guard. The drop point blade measures 4 inches and has a full tang. Handle is brown chip bark Delrin with bullet emblem and hole for thong. Price: $25.

Models 209 and 205 Survivor Belt Knives—These revolutionary horizontal sheath knives fit in sheaths in the belts and double as buckles. They're not gadgets, but quality cutlery products crafted from 440 steel and suitable for skinning as well as heavy or light cutting. Buckles also work as bottle cap lifters. Each knife comes with a black or brown belt of 8-ounce top-grain cowhide in sizes from 30 to 48 inches, all 1¹¹/₁₆ inches wide. Model 209 is a single-edge blade; Model 205 is double-edged. Price: $30.

Survivor Belt Knives

BROWNING

Browning offers quite a selection of quality knives including seven fixed-blade models, ten folding knives, and ten pocketknives.

Other Browning products appear in Chapters 4, 6, 7, and 8.

Skinner I—For the hunter who skins his game, this knife's broad blade is deeply curved with serrations on the spine to hold your thumb in place on the back of the blade. It will make short work of dressing, skinning, and caping a trophy. Blade is crafted from the very finest 440C stainless

*Some of Browning's fixed-blade knives
(Fillet Knife is pictured at far left and Skinner I is in center)*

Some of Browning's folding knives (Folding Fish and Bird Knife is in center)

steel. Handle is of Stamina Wood, a hardwood laminate. Blade length: 4½ inches. Furnished with handmade, top-grain leather sheath. Price: $32.95.

Fillet Knife—This knife has just the correct flex for slicing next to the bone and rib cage on most fish. Its blade is rust resistant and the fine cork handle keeps it afloat in water. Blade length: 6 inches. Price: $10.95.

Outdoorsman Pocketknife—Here are ten tools in one: main blade, clip blade, survival match, scissors, saw blade, can opener, screwdriver, reamer, tweezers, and bottle opener. This knife has high-impact Lexan handles and is a perfect choice for an all-purpose knife. Closed length: 3½ inches. Price: $31.95.

Folding Fish and Bird Knife—This is the ideal knife for small varmints, birds, and fish. The 2¾-inch modified California clip blade is great for skinning small animals and cleaning fish, and it locks open. The 2-inch drop-point blade takes on any chore, especially dressing and skinning small game. Closed length: 3⅝ inches. Price: $16.95.

BUCK KNIVES

Buck offers a wide line of knives for outdoorsmen, including seventeen fixed-blade models, six styles of pocketknives, and four sheathed folding models. Additionally, they offer steels and stones for sharpening.

We have used Buck knives for years and have put them to rugged outdoor use in hunting, fishing, and camping situations. Their high-carbon blades hold an edge and won't rust. The handles are virtually indestructible. And Buck knives are guaranteed for life.

If you write for information about Buck's products, be sure to request a copy of Al Buck's booklet, "Knife Know-How."

Kalinga

Woodsman Model 102—This knife with a 4-inch straight blade and fine point is the perfect fish and small-game knife. Price: $15.

Skinner Model 103—This heavy knife with fine edge and wide 4-inch blade makes the toughest of skinning jobs simple. Price: $20.

Caper Model 116—This knife features a short 3¼-inch blade designed for saving the trophy. Best suited for working around the horns and ears. It is also a splendid knife for panfish, small game, and birds. Price: $16.

Folding Hunter Model 110—This is one of the handiest all-purpose knives around. The blade has a positive lock in open position, and the handle is of golden-grain ebony with solid brass bolsters and liner forged in one piece. Closed length: 4⅞ inches. Comes with sheath. Price: $22.

Kalinga Model 401—This beautiful knife has a 5-inch blade, brass guard, and Buckarta handle. It comes in a presentation case, complete with rugged sheath. Price: $50.

Empress Trio—Here's a set that is perfect for the motor home, cabin, or camp kitchen. It consists of one 9-inch carver, a 6-inch utility, and a 4-inch paring knife. The walnut case may be hung on a wall or used in a cabinet drawer. Price: $60.

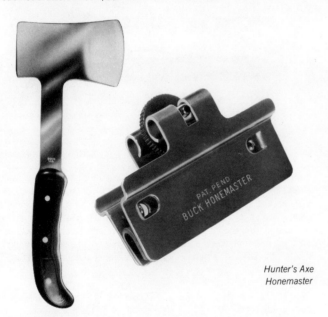

Hunter's Axe
Honemaster

Hunter's Axe Model 106—Here's the perfect companion for your Buck hunting knife. The axe has a 2½-inch cutting head and comes with sheath. Price: $32.

Buck Honing Kit Model 133—This kit combines a Washita Stone, Hard Arkansas Stone, and a can of Honing Oil in an attractive plastic case. A useful Buck Knife accessory. Price: $6.

Honemaster Model 136—This device attaches to any blade that is more than ⅝ inch wide to maintain the same angle while honing. Makes everyone a professional knife sharpener. Price: $5.

Steelmaster Model 137—This tool is comprised of a 5-inch steel and metal handle with cam lever to secure the steel when in use. It's a very aggressive sharpening device, and it comes with a sheath. Price: $12.

CAMILLUS CUTLERY CO.

The new Camillus catalog is 32 pages crammed with information on knives and contains helpful instructions and illustrations that show field

dressing of game birds and deer, how to bone out big game, and how to sharpen knives. It's yours for $1.

Their new American Wildlife series of knives should be of particular interest to most outdoors people.

No. 10 American Wildlife—This knife features etched blades of high-carbon stainless steel, solid nickel silver bolsters, and tough Delrin handle with sculptured pewter wildlife by Sid Bell embedded under acrylic into each handle. Available with buck deer, howling coyote, running deer, charging bear, bull moose, bugling elk, mountain sheep, or pronghorn antelope. Individually gift boxed with sharpening steel. Price: $25.

No. 10 American Wildlife

No. 17 American Wildlife—This bird hunter's knife features an etched stainless steel Turkish clip blade, gut hook, nickel silver bolsters, and Delrin handles with sculptured wildlife by Sid Bell embedded under acrylic and inset into the handle. Available with mallard duck, Canada goose, wild turkey, or ring-necked pheasant pewter sculpture. Individually gift boxed. Price: $15.

No. 32 American Wildlife—This fisherman's knife features an etched stainless steel sabre clip blade with serrated tip, a unique stainless fillet blade that locks in the open position, and hook disgorger. It has nickel silver bolsters and comes with sculptured pewter bass by Sid Bell embedded under acrylic and inset into ivory Delrin handle. Comes individually gift boxed. Closed length: 5 inches. Price: $15.

No. 1006 American Wildlife—This fillet knife with sculptured pewter bass in handle of ivory Delrin features an etched 6-inch flexible stainless steel blade and comes individually gift boxed with top-grain leather sheath. Price: $15.

No. 7 Sword Brand Deluxe—This single-bladed folding hunting knife with sliding lock action features a super cutting, stainless steel blade and hand-fitting Indian stag handles. It has solid nickel silver bolsters with stainless steel pin that resists corrosion. It comes with leather wrist loop and a genuine top-grain leather pouch. Closed length: 4¾ inches. Price: $19.95.

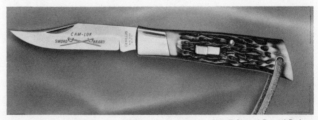

No. 7 Sword Brand Deluxe

DAN-D CUSTOM KNIVES

All of Dan Dennehy's knives are completely hand made by him. They never leave his shop for any processes. He does everything himself, including fitting and making the fine leather sheaths.

His informative catalog explains his knife-making processes and describes the knives he makes for sportsmen and collectors. If you're in the market for a fine custom knife, you should send for his catalog to see what he has to offer. Here's a sampling.

Yuma Skinner

Yuma Skinner Model 16—This is a specialized skinning tool for the man who does a lot of skinning and fleshing of stock or game. It will peel a hide off in no time flat. Blade length: 3¼ inches. Blade width: 1½ inches at widest point. Sambar stag handle with brass butt cap. Handle length: approximately 4½ inches. Price: $110.

Drop Point Model 3—This is the dropped-point hunter that has become so popular with hunters around the country in the past few years. The blade is made from ³⁄₁₆-inch stock. Blade length: 4 inches. Blade width: 1⅛ inches. Handle length: 4½ inches. Full tang slab. Micarta handle. No butt cap. Price: $115.

D'HOLDER CUSTOM KNIVES

Dalton Holder is another custom knifemaker who does every bit of the work on every knife he makes. He offers a variety of models of hunting and skinning knives and you will have a choice of several different top steels from which to select.

His knife handles are often of unusual materials and are some of the finest we've seen. His current delivery time is twelve to fourteen months.

A few of the D'Holder Knives available

Open Hilt—This new offering is a real brute in small size. The deeply hollow blade is cut from ⅜-inch stock and is of tapered tang construction with an integral guard. As the name implies, the hilt or handle area is completely hollow, being ringed by a perimeter of steel that has been fancy cross-cut file decorated. Don't let the thickness of the stock worry you. It weighs in at a light 5¼ ounces, less than many standard hunters of comparable size. This design has drawn praise from a number of well-known makers and collectors. Blade length: 4 inches. Price: $140.

Raised Blade Skinner—This skinner is of full tapered tang construction, ground from ³⁄₁₆-inch stock. It is designed for quick and easy skinning of any big game. It does a quick job on coyotes and javelina, too. A rugged knife with 4 inches of cutting edge. Price: $80.

EZE-LAP DIAMOND PRODUCTS

From this company comes the Eze-Lap Diamond Knife Sharpener and the Diamond Hone & Stone. These tools will sharpen just about anything and they do a quick and efficient job.

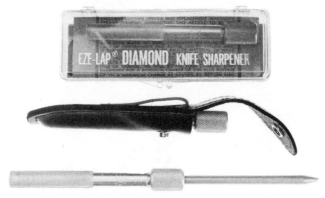

Diamond Knife Sharpener

Eze-Lap Diamond Knife Sharpener—Guaranteed to sharpen any knife in less than thirty seconds. Just lay the knife blade almost flat on the Eze-Lap and rub it with circular strokes. Ten million diamond cutting edges then go to work to put a razor edge on your knife. It will sharpen serrated knives, axes, fish hooks, razors, carving tools, chain saws, and anything else that needs a good cutting edge. Length extended: 8 inches. Length closed: 4½ inches. Comes with leather sheath with belt loop. Price: $19.95.

Eze-Lap Diamond Hone & Stone—This diamond stone has millions of cutting edges to sharpen your knives and tools. It is many times faster than dry stones or oil stones. Use it like a file or a stone—it cuts in all directions. Most users prefer the fine grade for all-purpose use, but it is also available in medium and coarse grades. Prices: $4.95 (fine), $7.95 (medium), $9.95 (coarse).

GANDER MOUNTAIN, INC.

Gander's knife selection includes cutlery from Buck, Gerber, Western, Normark, and Schrade, as well as some specialty knives that are Gander Mountain exclusives.

For other Gander Mountain products, see Chapters 2, 3, 4, 5, 6, 7, and 8.

Rapala Fish'n Fillet Knife—The knife that ushered in a new era of fish cleaning and preparation. The thin, curved, flexible blade stays sharp through long, hard use and inserts into the fish without effort, slicing cleanly along bone and skin. Birch handle. Tooled leather Laplander sheath. Blade lengths: 4, 6, and 9 inches. G.M. prices: $4.77, $4.97, $8.97.

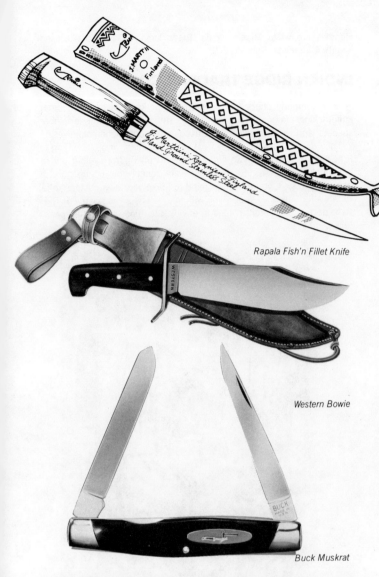

Rapala Fish'n Fillet Knife

Western Bowie

Buck Muskrat

Western Authentic Bowie Knife—American made of finest high-carbon chrome vanadium steel. Massive heavy-gauge blade with clip point sharpened on both edges. Blade steel extends full length of walnut-finished hardwood handles. Heavy solid brass guard. Genuine molded cowhide swing sheath with new D-ring attachment and leather leg thong for comfortable sitting and walking. Blade length: 9½ inches. Overall: almost 15 inches. G.M. price: $25.97.

Buck Trail Blazer—This folding knife features contoured handle for firm grip and two 4-inch precision-ground blades that will penetrate and disgorge fish or game instantly. Closed length: 5¼ inches. Comes with belt sheath. G.M. price: $24.

Buck Muskrat—This knife features two 2⅞-inch blades—one slim and tapered with a razor-sharp beveled point, the other an excellent skinning blade. Closed length: 3⅞ inches. G.M. price: $13.

Buck Trapper—Here's a knife with two beautifully honed blades, each 3¼ inches long. One is curved and pointed for slitting and disgorging fish and game. The other is well suited to skinning tasks. Closed length: 4 inches. G.M. price: $13.

Crock Stick—The foolproof way to correctly obtain a sharp blade. The angle of the rods provides the optimum sharpening angle for all types of knives. To use, simply cut down on the rods, drawing the blade toward you. The rods are of alumina ceramic and will not wear out from con-

tinuous use. Rods are detachable from base for storage. Will even sharpen serrated blades. Vinyl protective carrying case is included. G.M. price: $7.97.

GERBER LEGENDARY BLADES

Here is a manufacturer of top-quality knives that have found favor among hunters, fishermen, and campers throughout the country. Their line includes a wide selection of fixed-blade and folding knives, survival knives, and a number of fine filleting knives, as well as sharpening steels.

#A-324 Game & Fish—This is a fine little knife for cleaning small game or fish. It features the famous Armorhide nonslip handle and blade of high-speed tool steel with a special chrome plating that remains permanently bright and stainless. It comes with its own custom leather belt scabbard. Blade thickness: .062 inch. Blade length: 3¼ inches. Overall: 7½ inches. Price: $17.50.

#C 475 Custom Ebony Drop Point Blade—This new knife features a handle crafted of rich ebony, a rare tropical hardwood that makes this knife just as beautiful as it is rugged. It is fitted with a distinctive brass guard and has an extra-strong blade, precision ground to razor-sharp, double-wedge shape. Special industrial hard-chrome plating keeps the blade stainless through the demanding use for which it was designed. Patented front break-away scabbard design allows easy, one-handed withdrawal in a smooth, continuous motion. Blade thickness: .125 inch. Blade length: 4¾ inches. Overall: 9¼ inches. Price: $36.50.

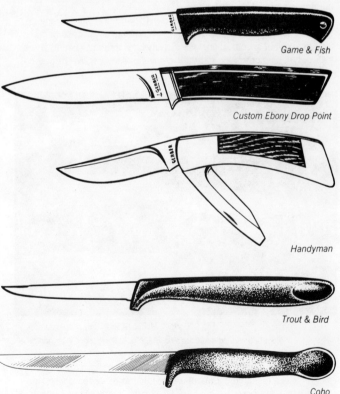

Game & Fish

Custom Ebony Drop Point

Handyman

Trout & Bird

Coho

#Pk-3 Handyman—This folder affords the versatility of an all-purpose knife, both in the field and around the house. It features a 3-inch trailing point blade of 440-C surgical stainless steel. Screwdriver blade locks in open position and doubles as a wire stripper. Handle is of stainless steel and brass with inlays of impregnated tropical hardwood. Screwdriver blade length: 2¾ inches. Length closed: 4 inches. Handle thickness: .410 inch. Scabbard optional. Price: $32.50.

#Tb Trout & Bird—This knife features a stripping spoon on the butt of the all-aluminum Armorhide handle that is coated for firm, nonslip control when hands are wet and slippery. Blade is surgical stainless steel. Comes with belt scabbard. Blade thickness: .050 inch. Blade length: 3¼ inches. Overall: 8 inches. Price: $13.

#Co Coho—This is the ideal knife for cleaning and filleting larger fish and features a stripping spoon on the butt of the all-aluminum Armorhide coated handle. Comes with scabbard. Blade thickness: .062 inch. Blade length: 6 inches. Overall: 11¾ inches. Price: $18.50.

Gerber Sportsman's Steel—This steel has chromium carbide diffused into the surface to make it hard enough to dress the edge of any cutting instrument. And further, it leaves an edge that is clean of any burr or feather. But its use isn't limited to sharpening knives. The tempered chisel point makes it a useful tool for hacking, prying, splitting—any job not suitable for a knife. It is available in either 5- or 8-inch length with a choice between a leather handle with a tie thong or conventional leather scabbard. Prices: from $11.50 to $14.50.

GEORGE HERRON

George is a custom knifemaker, specializing in working knives for rugged outdoor use. All of his blades are made of 154CM steel because of its many desirable features, such as hardness, corrosion resistance, and its extremely tough and fine finish. Standard handle material is wood Micarta, but black or brown linen Micarta, white Micarta, or coco-bolo wood are available at no extra charge. A number of optional handle materials, such as ivory, stag, rosewood, ebony, and fancy maples, are available at extra cost.

All of his knives are completely hand made and are fully guaranteed. He offers sixteen different models of his own design or will custom make the knife to your specifications. His delivery time is running twenty-three to twenty-four months for standard models and twenty-five to twenty-seven months for custom work.

Top to Bottom: *Model 14 with curly maple handle, Model 16 with white Micarta handle, Model 8 with coco-bolo handle*

Model 8—This is the most useful knife that Herron makes. He recommends it as a first knife for about any use. It comes standard with sambar stag handles, brass hilt, and 4½-inch blade. It is also available with a 4-inch blade. Price: $90.

Model 14—This is the very handy "Little Dude" knife that will take care of about 90 percent of the average hunter's knife work. Blade length: 2¾ inches. Blade width: about 1 inch. Overall: 7 inches. Price: $80.

Model 16—Known as "The Folder," this knife features liners, bolsters, spring, and pins of stainless steel, blade and locking bar of 154CM steel.

Handles are white Micarta scale. Blade length: 3¼ inches. Closed length: 4¼ inches. Price: $200.

INDIAN RIDGE TRADERS CO.

This company offers a wide selection of knife blades and other knifemaking materials such as cutler's rivets, handle materials, fiber spacers, and various brass pieces used in the construction of knives.

They do not offer kits. They deal with craftsmen, and, according to President Dick Blasius, "we find customers ranging from youngsters in industrial arts classes, to adults in every conceivable occupation, to many retirees." If you have it in mind to make your own custom knife, here's a firm that can supply you with the materials you will need. They have dozens of different blades from which to choose, and their prices look good to us.

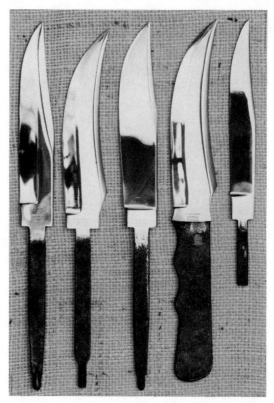

Sheffield Blades: HU-050, RT-050, SB-050, SK-050, ST-050

Sheffield HU-050 Blade—This is a high-carbon, heat-treated steel hunter pattern blade. Dimensions: 5×⅞×³/₁₆ inches. Weight: 3 ounces. Price: $5.80.

Sheffield RT-050 Blade—This is a round-tang skinner blade of high-carbon, heat-treated steel. Dimensions: 5×1×³/₁₆ inches. Weight: 3½ ounces. Price: $6.75.

Sheffield SB-050 Blade—This skinny broad blade is a very old pattern that has stood the test of time. Dimensions: 5×1×³/₁₆ inches. Weight: 3 ounces. Price: $5.60.

Sheffield SK-050 Blade—This blade is the same as RT-050, but with a full tang. Dimensions: 5×1×³/₁₆ inches. Weight: 4½ ounces. Price: $6.95.

Sheffield ST-050 Blade—This slim, short-tang model is easy to handle and makes a fine field-dressing knife. Dimensions: 5×¾×⅛ inches. Weight: 1½ ounces. Price: $4.25.

Dale's Broad Blade DBR-045—This is the old broad pattern updated with a dropped point. It skins nearly as well as the original pattern and performs field-dressing chores much better, so is a bit more useful to most hunters. The hollow grind is possible with the very tough 440 stainless steel and makes slicing almost a pleasure. Length: 4½ inches. Price: $21.85.

Dale's Slim Blade DSL-045—The slim pattern has always been the favorite of hunters who only field dress game at the kill site, leaving skinning, caping, and other work for camp or home. If this is your pattern, the 440 stainless steel Dale's Slim will serve you well. Length: 4½ inches. Price: $18.35.

Dale's Hunter Blade DHU-050—This is a clean-up of the old hunter pattern with a dropped point and a hollow grind. The revised version has a better skinning curve up front, a stronger point, improved slicing, but it loses some of its ability to take abuse because of the hollow grind. Made of 440 stainless steel. Length: 5 inches. Price: $19.25.

Dale's Skinner Blade DSK-055—A modification of the world's most popular skinning knife with the handle set back a bit to allow for a finger notch and thumb grip directly on the blade to improve control. The hollow grind holds down the weight and helps you get a keen edge quickly. This is a great skinner, made of 440 stainless steel. Length: 5½ inches. Price: $22.60.

JET-AER CORP.

The G-96 brand of cutlery comprises one of the broadest lines of knives for outdoors people that any manufacturer has to offer. There are dozens of fixed-blade and folding knives, ranging from general and utility designs to highly specialized knives. No matter what your cutlery need happens to be, chances are there's a G-96 knife to fit that need.

For other Jet-Aer products, see Chapters 2, 4, 5, 8, and 11.

Model #4040 Folding Rancher—This knife has a long, slender, heavy-duty blade that is excellent for slicing meat, cutting kindling, tent stakes, and the like. It is ideal for the person who needs an all-purpose knife and wants the compactness of a folding knife. It opens smoothly and locks firmly in the open position. Its blade is rustproof and Teflon coated for nonstick convenience. Nonslip handles are permanently bonded. Comes with heavy-duty molded plastic sheath. Blade length: 3¾ inches. Closed length: 5¼ inches. Price: $17.

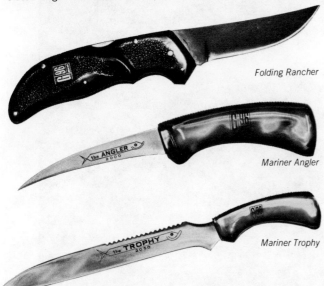

Folding Rancher

Mariner Angler

Mariner Trophy

Model #4020 African Hunter—This knife combines the long heavy-duty curved blade of a skinning knife with the tapered curve back of a field knife. Its design makes it ideal as an all-purpose big-game and survival knife. Its unique, nonstick Teflon-coated blade makes the most difficult cutting job simple. Blade length: 5⅛ inches. Handle length: 5 inches. Comes with heavy-duty molded plastic sheath. Price: $12.

Model #950 Classic Skinner—This knife has a broad, high-carbon, rustproof steel blade with a sweeping curved edge to make skinning fast and clean. This is all you need to skin any game. Handle is molded of phenolic resins and is impervious to heat, cold, and shock. Comes with custom-made Western cowhide sheath. Blade length: 4 inches. Handle length: 4¼ inches. Price: $18.

Model #2000 G-96 Mariner Angler—A unique filleting and gutting knife that features a reverse curved back that is designed to be drawn through the fish rather than pushed through in the conventional method. This makes gutting quick, clean, and effortless. One quick stroke from the vent forward will cleanly gut the fish. This method is especially important if you are preparing the fish for gourmet cooking and wish to leave on the head and tail. Comes with lightweight and waterproof plastic sheath. Blade length: 4¾ inches. Handle length: 4¾ inches. Price: $8.95.

Model #2020 G-96 Mariner Flex-Fillet—A slightly broader version of the Classic Fillet Knife, the Flex-Fillet combines the flexible action of a narrow filleting knife with the versatility of a slightly broader blade. Designed for heavy-duty use. Comes with plastic sheath, and has a rustproof blade. Blade length: 6¾ inches. Handle length: 4¾ inches. Price: $9.50.

Model #2050 G-96 Mariner Trophy—The real big ones need a big knife. The 11¼-inch blade makes long, clean cuts and is ideal for slicing fish steaks. The difficult job of filleting large fish is made easy and the heavy-duty scaler makes it the complete knife tool for the real lunkers. Handle length: 5 inches. Price: $13.95.

Model #2060 G-96 Mariner Cleaver, Knife & Scaler—This is a triple-purpose fishing tool. Ideal for de-tailing, deheading, and quickly getting through the heavy backbones. It saves time and effort when large quantities of cut bait are needed. A deep scaler on the husky blade makes scaling a simple chore. A must for those who have a lot of cleaning to do. This is a practical tool for use on both small and large fish. Blade length: 7¼ inches. Handle length: 5 inches. Price: $16 95.

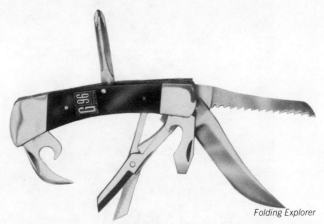

Folding Explorer

Model #965 Folding Explorer—This beautifully engineered knife is modeled after the classic European Army knife. The handle is made of solid brass with exotic Pacca wood inset. The knife contains the following features: screwdriver-cap lifter, scissors, 3⅛-inch blade, saw, Phillips screwdriver, and can opener. The holster-type sheath is made of cowhide and carefully contoured and formed to fit the knife. Price: $33.

Model #2070 Folding Fisherman—This beautifully balanced fishing knife contains a grooved hook sharpening stone imbedded in the wooden handle. The handle is made of solid brass and inset with exotic wood. The blade is carefully fitted into the handle and locks firmly open. It also has a hook remover and cap lifter. Blade length: 4 inches. Hook remover length: 3⅝ inches. Handle length: 4⅞ inches. Sheath included. Price: $23.

Model #3020 American Wildcat—This knife, from the Customline Series, is a classic multipurpose hunting and camping knife. Its tapered point and broad sweeping curved edge will enable you to slice meat as well as skin small game. The blade is made of a new steel alloy and is hand ground and shaped. This unique steel combines the rustproof properties of stainless with the edge-holding ability of high carbon steel. Handle is brass and is carefully fitted with rare wood inserts. The sheath is made of heavy-grade saddle leather and is carefully contoured to fit the shape of the knife. Blade length: 4⅞ inches. Overall: 9⅝ inches. Price: $45.

JIMMY LILE

So prominent and highly regarded is Jimmy Lile's reputation for superb craftsmanship that February 14 has been set aside, by executive proclamation, as Jimmy Lile Day in his home state of Arkansas. Jimmy's knives have been presented to two American presidents, to congressmen, kings, and other dignitaries, and are used by many average outdoorsmen as well.

Lile knife blades are generally made of D2 steel, which contains 1.55 percent carbon and 12 percent chromium, which, after being properly heat-treated in his shop, provides a combination of edge-holding ability, toughness, and rust resistance. He will also use 440C steel on request at no additional cost. He offers a wide range of knife styles with a number of options available at extra cost. Additionally, he accepts a limited number of commissions each year on collector-grade work.

Jimmy Lile Knives

Model #2—This is a Lile best seller and a very popular hunting knife. It is available with blades of 5, 6, and 7 inches. The blade is made from 3/16-inch stock and brass fittings are standard. Engraving is quoted on an individual basis and is not standard. Handles are of stag, Micarta, or wood and are available plain or with grooves. Prices: $115 (stag or Micarta), $105 (wood). Add $10 for grooves.

Model #3—A very popular design because of its weight, shape, and size. Blade is made from 3/16-inch stock. Handles are of stag, Micarta, or wood. Blade length: 5 inches. Prices: $65 (stag or Micarta), $60 (wood).

Regular #7—An original Jimmy Lile design, this is the knifemaker's personal favorite and the one he has been making the longest. Blade is made from 1/8-inch stock, and knife features brass fittings. Blade length: 4 inches. Overall: 8¼ to 8½ inches. Prices: $65 (stag or Micarta), $50 (wood).

Model #8—This skinner and caper is the companion piece to the famous #7, and the two are available in one sheath as a pair if desired. Blade is made from 1/8-inch stock, and fittings are brass. Blade length: 3 inches. Overall: 7¼ to 7½ inches. Prices: $65 (stag or Micarta), $50 (wood).

Large Folder—All blades are D2 steel. Frames are nickel silver, and a variety of standard handle materials is available. Blade length: 3 inches. Closed length: 3⅞ inches. Prices: $60 (plain, nickel silver handle), $80 (Micarta inlay or wood inlay), $100 (stag inlay, ivory inlay, stag scales), $150 (ivory scales).

Lile Bowie—Here's a beautiful 12-inch Bowie with brass guard and butt and full tang. Blade is made from ¼-inch stock, and handle is rosewood. Price: $250.

Model #2

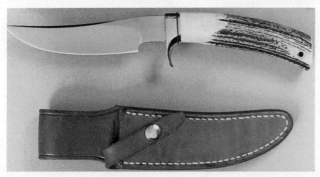

Model #3

Lile Bowie

HARVEY McBURNETTE

Not only does Harvey do his own heat treating and tempering, but he also does his own leather work, scrimshaw, etching, and engraving. And since his artwork is all done by freehand, no two knives are ever exactly alike. For most of his knives he uses D2 steel in the blades. For Bowies or show knives, however, he uses 440C steel because it takes a better finish. The D2 is a superior steel for holding an edge and is the better choice for any working knife. Other standard equipment in his knives are rosewood handles and brass trim. His brochure includes a long list of optional materials, and he will quote any custom features within reason.

Model FH-20

Model FH-20—This folding hunter features a front lock release and a blade made from 1/8-inch D2 steel. Blade length: 3¾ inches. Numerous options available. Price: $145 with any wood handle.

Model 2BF—This is a two-bladed, nonlocking folder. Rosewood handle and nickel silver trim are standard. Large blade: 3¼ inches. Small blade: 2½ inches. Blades made from 1/8-inch D2 steel. Price: $200.

NORMARK CORP.

The same company that produces the famous Rapala lures and Rapala knives also manufactures Normark Presentation Fillet Knives and Presentation Folding Knives and Hunting Knives.

For other Normark products, check Chapter 2.

Presentation Fillet Knife—Designed for filleting fish, but equally handy around the campsite, kitchen, or charter boat. This knife features progressively double-tapered stainless blade, ensuring flexibility toward the point for removing the skin of the fish, yet retaining the heft and strength at the base of the blade for heavier cutting of bones and flesh. The molded handle is a satin ebony color—guaranteed not to break or shatter for the life of the knife. Sheath is top-grain, tanned leather with traditional Laplander designs and plastic blade guard inside. Top belt loop gives the sheath the added safety feature of free swing. Three blade lengths available: 4, 6, and 7½ inches.

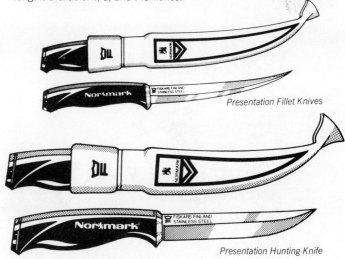

Presentation Fillet Knives

Presentation Hunting Knife

Presentation Hunting Knife—The ultimate in beauty and function. When you unsheath it, you can tell by the fine blade—a steel alloy of carbon, molybdenum, and chromium—that this knife is finely hand crafted. The blade gives you all the advantages of stainless steel and a longer lasting cutting edge, as well as ease of sharpening. Ideal for cutting the toughest hides, skinning through the thinnest membranes, performing routine camp and kitchen chores. Handle is a satin ebony

Presentation Big Swede

color—guaranteed not to break or shatter for the life of the knife. Sheath is top-grain, tanned leather with traditional Laplander designs and plastic blade guard inside. Blade length: 5 inches. Overall: 9¾ inches.

Presentation Big Swede—The rugged construction of this folding knife delivers when it really counts. Swedish stainless steel, solid brass fittings, and impact-resistant grips that are comfort molded are features that can be depended on. The Big Swede is designed to meet the demands of professional hunters, guides, and serious outdoorsmen. Blade length: 4 inches. Overall open: 8¼ inches. Handy sheath protects knife and adds ease for carrying.

P. & S. SALES

This mail-order company carries a large line of name-brand cutlery for the outdoors person—everything from pocketknives to machetes.

For other P. & S. products, check Chapters 2, 7, and 8.

Buck Special—This knife features a 6-inch Bowie-styled blade with groove. It has ebony phenolic handle and high-carbon steel blade that really holds an edge. Comes with genuine saddle leather sheath. Price: $22.

Buck Fisherman—The gently curving 5½-inch, high-carbon steel blade of this knife is perfect for filleting. Knife has ebony phenolic handle that is virtually indestructible. Comes with saddle leather sheath. Price: $16.

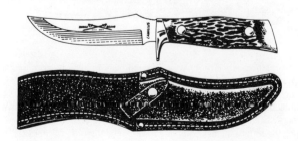

P&S Products

Buck Pathfinder—Here's the perfect all-purpose knife, well suited to hunting, fishing, and camping chores. Heavy-duty 5-inch blade is high-carbon steel that holds an edge and resists all rust and corrosion. Comes with fitted leather sheath. Price: $18.

Buck Stockman—Here's a rugged and nonrusting pocketknife featuring a 3-inch Barlow blade, plus two other blades, brass liners, and nonslip grips. Price: $15.

Buck Cadet—The same design and features as the Stockman, but smaller. Has a 2½-inch Barlow blade. Price: $14.

Buck Lancer—This pocketknife has all the rugged characteristics of its bigger brothers, but features a 2-inch Barlow blade and shorter coping blade. Price: $9.

Camillus Yellowstone Hunter—This tough and attractive hunting knife features a high-carbon steel blade, mirror polished and rust resistant. Comes with leather sheath. Blade length: 5 inches. Overall: 10 inches. Price: $14.50.

Camillus Trapper-Skinner—This deluxe, bench-made knife features solid nickel silver bolsters and two mirror polished skinning blades of carbon sword steel. Closed length: 3⅞ inches. Price: $9.25.

Woodsman's Saber Chopper—This handy tool will cut down trees 4 inches and more in diameter or clear heavy brush. Three-way blade has long axe-type edge, a sickle brush hook, and trenching edge. Made of oxidized manganese tool steel. Saber handle with leather grip and metal hand guard. Black oxidized metal carrying sheath included. Overall: 16 inches. Weight: 22 ounces. Price: $28.

Trail Blazer Machete—This one has saw teeth on the top of its blade for hacking heavy brush or dense vegetation. The 18-inch blade also has a sharp cutting edge. Plastic handle is fastened by five rivets. Price: $4.45.

RANDALL MADE KNIVES

Among the most famous and sought after knives in the world are those made by W. D. Randall, a Florida citrus grower, outdoorsman, and knifemaker. Randall Made Knives have won the favor of outdoorsmen from the Arctic to tropical jungles, and servicemen have carried these knives into all theatres of battle since World War II. The Project Mercury astronauts carried Randall Made Knives when they made their space flights and thought enough of them to mention them in their book, *We Seven*.

Randall blades are made of either the finest imported Swedish tool steel or high-carbon domestic stainless steel. And each blade is forged, ground, honed, and polished by hand by Randall craftsmen. Blades are perfectly balanced and handles are skillfully designed for the best grip.

The Randall catalog, with its dozens of knives and abundant information, is a must for anyone who is seriously considering the purchase of a fine handmade knife.

Model 3 Hunter—This is an ideal all-around heavy-duty sportsman's knife, scientifically designed for every outdoor use. It features a leather handle, brass hilt, and Duralumin butt cap. Blades are made from ¼-inch stock. Blade lengths: 5, 6, and 7 inches. Handle length: 4½ inches. Comes with sheath. Price: $70.

Model 7 Hunter-Fisherman—This knife is similar to the Model 3, except it is smaller and lighter—ideal for small game, creel, and tackle box. Blades are made from ³⁄₁₆-inch stock. Blade lengths: 4½ and 5 inches. Handle length: 4¼ inches. Comes with sheath. Price: $65.

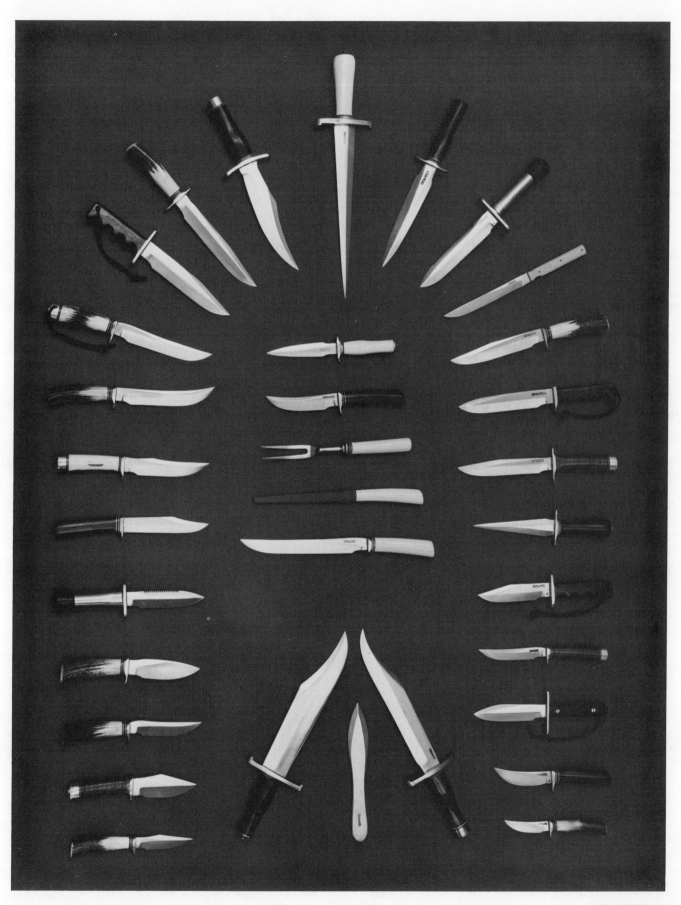

Randall Made Knives

Model 10 Salt Fisherman and Household Utility—This rustproof knife holds the keenest edge. Blade is not forged but is fully hand-ground from high-carbon stainless steel. Duralumin handle has comfortable slipproof grip, including notches for thumb placement where blade and handle join. It's available also with Micarta or rosewood handles at no extra cost. Available for delivery within five to six weeks. Blade lengths: 5 and 7 inches. Handle length: 4⅝ inches. Comes with sheath. Price: $35.

Model 11 Alaskan Skinner—The original drop-point blade, designed by Tommy Thompson, noted Alaskan guide, for big-game skinning, with point dropped below top of blade to prevent cutting too deeply through skins when used point first. Blade is made from ¼-inch stock and top is notched in front of hilt for thumb placement. Features include leather handle, brass hilt, and Duralumin butt cap. Blade lengths: 4, 4½, and 5 inches. Handle length: 4¼ inches. Comes with sheath. Price: $70.

SCHWARZ'S GUN SHOP

John Schwarz is a full-time gunsmith and cutler with more than thirty years of experience in making knives. His forged blades are made by hand and heat-treated in his shop.

His standard knives feature 01 steel blades, brass fittings, and brown Micarta handles, and all come with good quality, hand-sewn sheaths. He also offers blades of D2 and 440C steel, and for smaller forged blades he has Jessup No. 139B. Handle materials available include stag; leather; fancy woods; brown, black, and white Micarta; and wood Micarta in black or rosewood.

He will quote prices on large Bowies, folding knives, and custom knives. He charges $1 for this service. And for those who want to fit their own handles, he will furnish any of his blades for half the price of a completely finished knife.

All Schwarz knives come with a lifetime guarantee.

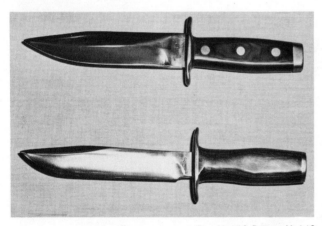

Top: *Model 6.* Bottom: *Model 3.*

Model 3—This is a heavy Bowie-style defense or survival knife, intended for rough work. Blade is made from ¼-inch stock and is 1¼ to 1½ inches wide. Blade lengths: 5 to 8 inches. Choice of steel and handle material. Price: $60 for 5-inch blade.

Model 4—This long blade hunter features a blade made from ³⁄₁₆-inch stock with 2 inches of the back sharpened, crown stag capped handle, with choice of steel and fittings. Blade lengths: 4 to 6 inches. Price: $55 with 4-inch blade.

Model 5—This skindiver's knife comes with a blade made from either D2 or 440C steel, ¼ inch thick and 1½ inches wide. The knife features brass or nickel silver fittings, Micarta handle, and waterproofing. Blade length: 6¾ inches. Price: $75.

Model 6—This dropped-point hunter is a mediumweight knife with epoxy-fitted leather handle, aluminum alloy cap, and brass fittings. Blade is made from ³⁄₁₆-inch stock. Blade lengths: 4 to 5 inches. Price: $50 with 4-inch blade.

SHAW-LEIBOWITZ

The wife-husband team of Sherrill Shaw and Leonard Leibowitz is certainly destined for legendary fame. The two artists do some of the finest custom etching of knives to be found anywhere. They also offer a number of custom-made knives—by such well-known knifemakers as George Herron, Jimmy Lile, and others—that feature beautifully etched blades. Even their catalog is a work of art, and certainly well worth the $2 price. Browsing through it is more like studying an artist's portfolio.

In their work, they make the original drawings and put all the artwork on the knives themselves. They use no photographic or other reproductive processes, so each design is an original work of art. Because of the varied nature of their work, they cannot list prices in their catalog. Instead, they request that the customer send them a tracing of the area to be etched, and they will provide an estimate. They have a minimum order of $100.

If you have a fine knife and would like to have the blade etched, we suggest that you order the Shaw-Leibowitz catalog and study some of the examples of their fine work. If you are having a custom knife made for you, you might discuss any plans you have for etching with your knifemaker. The artwork can be based on your own personal interests, and you can supply Shaw-Leibowitz with reference material if you wish. They also offer scrimshaw and painting on ivory handles and selective gold plating of etched blades. They have original floral patterns to cover small areas and will do scroll work on request.

The Polar Bear

The Polar Bear—This etching is on a custom-made knife by D'Holder of Arizona. The blade is 440C steel with a finger-grooved handle of polished Arizona desert ironwood. Butt cap and guard are nickel silver. The Polar Bear knife is an edition not to exceed fifteen and could be purchased plain or with the bear gold-plated, the seal silver, and the trickle of blood from the seal in copper over gold. Prices: $275 (plain), $325 (with multiplating).

JOHN T. SMITH

John's knives are completely hand made. His blades are ground from flat bars of high-carbon tool steel, and he uses the finest quality brass bar stock to make hilts and butt caps. Handles are made from the best quality India stag horn, exotic woods, and Micarta.

Model 18 Boot Knife—This knife features a bone Micarta handle that is very flat. Blade is ⅞ inch wide and ³⁄₁₆ inch thick and made of A2 or 440C steel. Standard handle materials are hardwood and Micarta. Blade length: 4 inches. Price: $120.

Model 19 Featherweight Hunter—This knife has a hollow ground blade with a tapered tang and rosewood Micarta handle. Blade is ⅞ inch wide and ⁵⁄₃₂ inch thick. Standard handle materials are stag horn, hardwood, and Micarta. This model is also available in ⅛-inch blade thickness without a tapered tang. Blade length: 4 inches. Weight: 4 ounces. Prices: $100 (⁵⁄₃₂ inch thick), $90 (⅛ inch thick without tapered tang).

Model 20 Featherweight Caper—This knife features a hollow ground blade ¾ inch wide and ⅛ inch thick, and a bone Micarta handle. Blade length: 3½ inches. Weight: 2½ ounces. Price: $75.

Left: Model 18, *Right:* Model 20, *Foreground:* Model 19 with new handle

TMD KNIVES

TMD Knives are the bench-made products of T. M. Dowell's craftsmanship. He offers blades of D2, 154CM, or 440C steels. He recommends the D2 steel for its edge-holding abilities for any working knife that will not be used on or near salt water. For a sea-going blade, he prefers one of the two stainless steels he offers. He also offers a variety of different handle materials and says that he has found linen base Micarta to be the most durable of knife handle materials.

Delivery time on a TMD Knife is currently running about three years, give or take six months.

Integral Hilt and Cap Knife—Once you've designed a knife with an integral hilt, the next logical step is to include an integral cap. Here it is: 2¼ pounds of steel reduced to a blade, hilt, tang, and cap, all in one piece and weighing 5 to 8 ounces. Grinding and tapering the tang are much more difficult than on a conventional full tang knife or on the regular integral hilt because of the cap. The fitting of grips is necessarily a slow and painstaking process on this model. The Integral Hilt and Cap Knife can be made to weigh anywhere from 5½ to 10 ounces, depending on the weight left in the blade and the tang, and on the handle material used. Price: $375.

Integral Hilt and Cap Knife

Standard folder—The TMD Standard Folder is available with or without bolsters. This redesigned folder has a heavy locking bar and blade (³⁄₁₆ inch) and operates with a coil spring rather than a leaf spring. The idea here was to produce a folder with strength approximating that of a fixed-blade knife. A specially made ¼-inch stainless steel bolt is used to secure the blade and provide a pivot. The locking bar has a deep notch and the overall result is a very snug, tight lock-up with no noticeable play. Liners are made of either stainless steel or brass, and bolsters are of either brass or nickel silver. Grips of hardwood are available only on the no-bolster model. Hardwood, Micarta, ivory, or sheep horn grips are

available on the bolster model. Stag is not available on either. Blades can be of D2, 440C, or 154CM steel. Prices: $300 (no bolsters), $375 (bolsters).

WESTERN CUTLERY CO.

Western is a major manufacturer of fine cutlery for outdoors people, and they offer an extensive line that includes many sizes and designs of fixed-blade, folding, and pocketknives for hunting, fishing, and camp chores. You can obtain a copy of their large, 32-page booklet called "Western Knives and Knife Nostalgia" by sending them $2.95. It has a good bit about the history of Western Cutlery and full-color photographs of the knife-making process between its color covers.

No. 932 Folding Hunting Knife-Saw—This handy folder features a 4½-inch knife blade with safety lock, 5-inch spring-tempered saw blade, and leather belt sheath. Closed length: 6 inches. Price: $19.95.

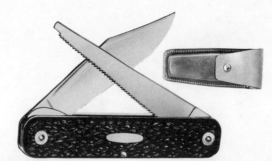

Folding Hunting Knife-Saw

W6610 Axe-Knife Combination

Super Fillet

No. W36 Hunting Knife—This rugged knife features an extra-strong flat ground blade and hardwood handle. It comes with a molded leather sheath. Blade length: 5½ inches. Overall: 10 inches. Price: $18.50.

No. W6610 Axe-Knife Combination—This lightweight combo features matched resin-impregnated hardwood handles. Knife has 4½-inch sabre ground blade. Axe has 2¾-inch cutting edge and overall length of 11 inches. Sheath is one-piece genuine cowhide and hangs on belt. Price: $29.50.

Western Fish Fillet Knives—Here's a complete line of knives for the fisherman. Blades are corrosion-resistant stainless steel, full bevel ground.

Handles are laminated hardwood that will not shrink, crack, or discolor under roughest use. Special wide tang and large rivets permanently secure the handles. Super Fillet model is perfect for filleting large fish with its 9-inch blade and 14-inch overall length. The Fish Fillet Knife features a 6-inch blade and is 11 inches overall. The Fish Camp Knife is a great multipurpose fish, bait, or camp knife with a 4½-inch blade and 9-inch overall length. All three models come with molded cowhide sheaths. Prices: $10.50, $9.50, $8.50.

W. C. WILBER

Bill Wilber's knives are completely hand made and finished in his one-man shop in the foothills of the Great Smoky Mountains. In addition to making his own fine models, he specializes in strictly custom knives, either by using information from the customer or by building his own interpretation of the customer's specific desires.

Example of Wilber's custom work, with scrimshaw by Michael Collins

Model D3 Drop Point Hunter—This knife features a hollow ground, mirror-finished blade of 440C steel and handles of bone Micarta. The guard is of stainless steel, and the knife comes with Wilber's own hand-made sheath of the wet-formed pouch design. The drop-point blade design is currently at the top of the popularity list and will do most any job the sportsman may tackle. The knife is guaranteed for life against workmanship and materials. Price: $155.

ZAK TACKLE MANUFACTURING CO.

One of Felix Zak's own patented inventions is the Zak Fish and Deer Knife, and it is included in his fishing tackle catalog.

For other Zak products, see Chapter 2.

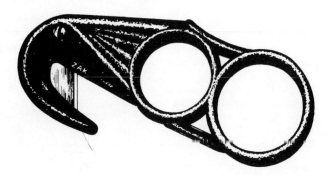

Zak Fish and Deer Knife

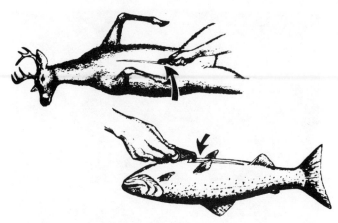

Zak Fish and Deer Knife—With this tool anyone can open a deer or any other big-game animal with a minimum of effort. And it's great for easy, fast, clean, and safe opening or field dressing of fish. It will help you do many other cutting jobs, such as cleaning small game and birds, cutting line, rubber, leather, or paper. The knife has two finger holes and a blunt hook with inset razor-sharp blade and is used draw fashion. An amateur can do a professional job in minutes with this knife. Comes with complete instructions. Price: $1.95.

CHAPTER TEN

PHOTOGRAPHIC EQUIPMENT AND ACCESSORIES

For the outdoors person, photography can be a rewarding adjunct to the pursuit of fish and game. It can eternalize adventurous canoe trips, or record the memorable moments of a high-country backpacking journey. For the serious outdoor photographer, it can be the reason for venturing into the wilds in the first place.

World wide, photography is the most popular pastime there is, and increasing numbers of outdoors people are toting cameras with them wherever they go. With a camera a hunter can extend his favorite sport into a year-round activity, and what he learns in the process of photographing his quarry will not only make him a better photographer, but a more skillful hunter as well. The fisherman who carries a camera has the ability to catch and release a lunker-size fish, yet still return home with a trophy to hang on the den wall. And the photographic trophy is far cheaper than any taxidermist's artwork.

Whether you're an occasional snapshooter, a serious shutterbug, or a professional outdoor photographer, we're sure you'll find some companies and products of interest in this chapter.

BRAUN NORTH AMERICA

This company is a major supplier of photographic equipment. In addition to the popular Braun line of electronic flash units (most computerized), other famous brand equipment offered by Braun are Hasselblad, Nizo, Paterson, and Ricoh.

Following is just a small sampling of the many photographic products they have to offer.

Braun F900 Professional—More than twenty years of experience and worldwide proving have gone into the current design of this professional "Super Flash." Radical rethinking and redesigning have produced the most powerful, most efficient, and sturdiest portable flash ever to carry the Braun name. The F900 Vario-Computer Flash measures light reflected back to the camera and disconnects the flash when the correct exposure has been achieved. Any unused power is stored for the next exposure, which will therefore be available more quickly and require less energy from the battery. By setting the convenient control on the flash head, the photographer can program the computer of the F900 to three lens openings at two-stop intervals. Recycling takes a maximum of three seconds, depending on flash-to-subject distance. Barix batteries supply well over a hundred flashes in manual operation, and several hundred in the computer mode. At close range, the output is increased again. In addition to the Barix unit, a nickel cadmium battery pack is also available.

F900 Professional Flash

Hasselblad 500C/M—This 2¼×2¼ single-lens reflex camera is the basic unit in the Hasselblad system. It features outstanding versatility and is capable of dealing with almost any photographic problems. The 80mm f/2.8 Zeiss Planar T lens has a fully synchronized leaf shutter, a manual and automatic diaphragm, automatic depth-of-field indicators, and an exposure value scale. The film magazine provides twelve 2¼-inch square exposures on 120 roll film. The focusing hood has a folding fine-focus magnifier to facilitate focusing on the focusing screen, whose Fresnel lens provide a sparkling image right out to the corners of the field. The film-winding knob simultaneously advances the film and cocks the shutter. The lens, magazine, focusing screen, focusing hood, and winding knob are all interchangeable, thereby adding to the camera's versatility. The 500C/M has an auxiliary shutter, a signal system to

prevent double exposures, a film counter, prerelease button and a quick-attachment shoe with ⅜- and ¼-inch tripod sockets. Dimensions: 6½×4¼×4 inches. Weight: 50.8 ounces. Available with chrome or black trim. Prices: $1,425 (chrome), $1,455 (black).

Hasselblad 500 C/M SLR Camera

Zeiss 300mm Tele-Tessar Telephoto Lens for the Hasselblad—This f/5.6 lens fits the Hasselblad Models 500C/M, 500C, 500EL/M, and 500EL. It contains a system of four multicoated elements and has a focusing range from 16½ feet to infinity. Diaphragm: f/5.6 to f/45. Length: 9 inches. Weight: 47½ ounces. Supplied in case with front lens cap, rear lens cap, and lens shade. Price: $1,575.

Zeiss 500mm and 300mm Tele-Tessar Lenses

Zeiss 500mm T Tele-Tessar Telephoto Lens for the Hasselblad—This f/8 telephoto lens fits the same models as the 350mm lens. It contains a system of five multicoated elements and has a focusing range from 28 feet to infinity. Diaphragm: f/8 to f/64. Length: 12½ inches. Weight: 74 ounces. Supplied in case with front lens cap, rear lens cap, lens shade, and focusing ring with movable index markers. Price: $1,785.

Hasselblad Underwater Housing—This housing is made of die-cast aluminum, and it consists of a front section plus a rear section for either the 500C/M or 500C or a rear section for the SWC. It has a blue enamel finish with yellow handgrips and black operating controls. The camera's shutter speed, diaphragm and focusing rings, film winding, shutter cocking, and shutter release are operated from the outside via knobs. Settings are facilitated by built-in scale illumination. A built-in battery unit makes it possible to use expendable flash with the housing. Prior to delivery, each underwater housing is tested at a pressure corresponding to a depth of 500 feet. Prices: $1,467 (for 500C/M or 500C), $1,275 (for SWC).

Hasselblad Underwater Housing

Ricoh Auto TLS EE—Ricoh's advanced technology brings you the "next step" in automatic EE SLR camera techniques. A super-sensitive, behind-the-lens meter measures only the light that the lens sees. Full shutter speed selection is maintained throughout the entire EE exposure-control range. The correct exposure is made automatically. Compact styling in a bold black professional finish. Absolute ease of operation. Many features to please the advanced amateur or the professional. Camera comes with Auto Rikenon EE 50mm f/1.4 or 50mm f/1.7 lens. Other EE interchangeable lenses are 28mm f/2.8, 35mm f/2.8, 135mm f/2.8, 200mm f/3.5, and 70mm–200mm f/4.5. Non-EE lenses may be used in manual mode.

Ricoh 500G—This is an exciting new pocket camera that invites feature comparison with any camera in its class. Just set the camera speed for the picture situation—up to ¹/₅₀₀ second for fast action, down to ⅛ second for very dim light situations. The proper light adjustment is made automatically. A highly sensitive CdS electronic light measurement system measures the light. All you do is shoot. The more advanced photographer will find no restrictions, because there is full manual override of the automatic exposure system. The brilliant f/2.8 lens and wide shutter speed range will handle shooting assignments comparable to cameras costing much more. Standard features include satin chrome metal-clad body, cordless flash-mounting shoe, folding rewind crank, rugged neck

strap support, smooth rangefinder focus ring, self-timer, automatic resetting film counter, single stroke film advance lever, and new "soft release" shutter button. Dimensions: 4.3×2.8×2.2 inches. Weight: 13.75 ounces.

Ricoh Auto TLS EE Camera

Ricoh Auto EE Lenses

Ricoh 500G

BUSHNELL OPTICAL CORP.

From Bushnell comes a series of photographic lenses sure to rouse the interest of the outdoor photographer. These lenses are designed to fit most popular single-lens reflex (SLR) cameras without the need for expensive adapters. And the lenses are priced economically, too.

For more Bushnell products, see Chapters 4 and 11.

35mm f/2.8 Wide Angle—This immensely versatile, lightweight lens requires a minimum of focusing. The 35mm is often used by photojournalists on their SLRs as a permanent, slightly wide angle, normal lens. It is particularly handy in close quarters and offers great depth of field. Aperture: f/2.8 to f/16. Minimum focus: 16 inches. Filter size: 52mm. Length: 2 inches. Weight: 7.8 ounces. Price: $92.

135mm f/2.8 Telephoto—This is considered the "standard" telephoto. It is just right for outdoor portraits, large images of sports at medium distance, and landscape shots. Image is magnified nearly three times. This fully automatic lens comes with retractable lens shade. Aperture: f/2.8 to f/22. Minimum focus: 6 feet. Filter size: 55mm. Length: 3½ inches. Weight: 14 ounces. Price: $104.

135mm Telephoto

200mm f/3.5 Telephoto—In spite of the long focal length (magnifies four times), the 200mm has high mobility and can be hand held. Excellent for small landscape or architectural details. A good wildlife lens. Shallow depth of field emphasizes special features. This automatic lens comes with retractable lens shade. Aperture: f/3.5 to f/22. Minimum focus: 7 feet. Filter size: 62mm. Length: 4½ inches. Weight: 19 ounces. Price: $132.

200mm Telephoto

400mm f/6.3 Telephoto—The 400 in the group of automatic lenses is the longest focal distance that can be used effectively for hand-held photography. It magnifies eight times and is excellent for wildlife photography, and is invaluable for photographing unapproachable subjects or to keep a safe distance from dangerous conditions. It comes with built-in tripod socket and retractable lens shade. Aperture: f/6.3 to f/22.

Minimum focus: 31 feet. Filter size: 72mm. Length: 13 inches. Weight: 37 ounces. Price: $178.

400mm Telephoto

35mm–105mm f/3.5 Macro and Zoom—The best of all worlds is yours with this multicoated macro-zoom. Unique lens enables you to start with a flower and end with the field—without moving. Extremely high light transmission and color saturation never before possible in a lens of this type. Gives you extreme close-up through wide angle to telephoto in a single lens. This automatic lens comes with hard case. Aperture: f/3.5 to f/16. Minimum focus: 5 feet, and with macro-range mechanism as close as 6¼ inches. Filter size: 72mm. Length: 4 inches. Weight: 24 ounces. Price: $410.

35–105mm Macro and Zoom

90mm–230mm f/4.5 Zoom—In one compact package a zoom range that provides medium telephoto at one end suitable for portraits and nearby candid shots, and a super telephoto at the other end for sport, action, and wildlife photography. Comes with built-in tripod socket and retractable lens shade. Aperture: f/4.5 to f/22. Minimum focus: 10 feet. Filter size: 58mm. Length: 7¼ inches. Weight: 32 ounces. Price: $240.

CANON U.S.A., INC.

Canon has long been a leader in photographic research and technology and produces some of the finest photographic equipment to be found anywhere. We have used Canon equipment for a number of years and find it to be rugged and trustworthy, even under the most adverse conditions.

Perhaps the hottest new item to come along in a good while is the new Canon AE-1 camera described below. It is part of a vast line of photographic products carrying the Canon brand, which includes something to meet any photographer's needs.

Canon AE-1—As completely as possible, formerly mechanical controls have been replaced by smaller, electronically automated ones, which render more reliable service and lightning-fast, precision performance. And all functions come under the governing brain of a Central Processing Unit (CPU) that coordinates the SLR system response to any shooting situation.

With priority given to shutter speed and the aperture set automatically, no action shot ever need be lost. Because the AE-1 meters within a split second and the aperture is set just before the shutter is actually released, the possibility of error due to sudden change in conditions is virtually eliminated.

The Canon family of photographic equipment

AE-1 with Power Winder A

Cutaway view of AE-1 and Power Winder A

The AE-1 is extremely compact and lightweight. The camera and its accessories have been designed with all controls centralized and within instant reach for maximum ease of handling. And all metering information is conveniently displayed in the viewfinder.

Main accessories are the Power Winder A for continuous shooting and the Speedlight 155A electronic flash. Both couple to the electronic circuitry of the AE-1 to increase its automatic shooting capabilities and expand the range of its photographic possibilities. Independent operating controls allow an easy switch over to manual control if so desired.

The AE-1 utilizes the full range of Canon FD lenses, and a great assortment of accessories and attachments are available to make the AE-1 an all-embracing system of photography. Prices: $496 (AE-1 with FD 50mm f/1.4 SSC lens in case), $293 (AE-1 body only), $125 (Power Winder A in case), $75 (Speedlite 155A Set with case).

Canon 110ED—Unique among pocket cameras, the Canon 110ED joins a bright f/2 lens with date imprinting capability and easy-to-use controls that add another dimension. This camera also features an aperture-priority shutter and high precision rangefinder-type functions, all of which render it top-notch photographic equipment in its own right. Canon 110ED kit includes Canonlite ED flash and extender for Canonlite. Price: $189.

Canon Super 8 Movie Equipment—As in all product areas, Canon's Super 8 movie equipment ranges from beginner to professional level with everything in between. New sound equipment rounds out Canon's impressive lineup.

Canon 110ED

Topping off the Super 8 silent group is the versatile Auto Zoom 1014 Electronic, which incorporates lap dissolve, single-frame capability, and extensive superimposition features. Other Canon Super 8 cameras are the Auto Zoom 814 Electronic, AZ 512XL Electronic, 514XL, and, for the novice filmmaker, the 310XL. All models combine Canon quality with an unusual degree of creative flexibility, enabling demonstrably superior low-light and zoom photography. The new Canon 514SL-S sound Super 8 camera combines with the PS-100 sound projector to form an ideal system for the critical Super 8 sound filmmaker. Prices: $240 to $875.

COMPETITIVE CAMERA CORP.

This company puts out a 50-page catalog that is crammed with top name brand photographic equipment of all sorts, and, as the name implies, their prices are competitive.

Here's a sample of what you'll find in their catalog, if you only mail off a buck for it.

Canon F-1 — When it comes to top-notch performance and quality, nothing can match the Canon F-1 system. The superbly built F-1 body can tackle any photographic task with ease and truly professional results, under the most difficult conditions. It is designed to operate with com-

Three of Canon's Super 8 Movie Cameras

plete smoothness, day in and day out, and sets a new standard in photographic excellence. Features include central spot metering, shutter speeds to 1/2,000 second, breech lock lens mount, ultrasophisticated film transport system, rugged, smooth construction, and superior handling. C.C.C. prices: $329.95 (F-1 body), $394.50 (F-1 w/50mm f/1.8 FD SC lens), $434.95 (F-1 w/50mm f/1.4 FD SSC lens), $494.50 (F-1 w/50mm f/1.2 FD SCC lens).

Canon F-1

Canon 514XL-S Sound Movie Camera

Canon Canonet G-III—There are few cameras more fun to use than the compact and fully automatic Canonet G-III 17. Even though it is small enough to take along almost anywhere, it packs a host of features that belie its moderate price tag. Its sharp f/1.7 lens is focused with a precise coincidence-type rangefinder—no more out of focus shots—and is fast enough to permit photography indoors without flash. Even with flash, operation is completely automatic, when used with the Canonlite D electronic flash unit. The Canonet G-III 17 is capable of outstanding results in the hands of the pro or novice. Features include built-in self timer, manual override of auto exposure system, and exclusive Canon QL (quick-loading) mechanism. C.C.C. prices: $99.95 (camera and case), $119.95 (camera, case, and flash).

Canon Canonet G-III

Hasselblad 500EL/M

Canon 514XL-S Sound Movie Camera—This is Canon's new sound-equipped Super 8 with tone control, 5X zoom, and 12 or 24 feet per second speeds. C.C.C. prices: $284.50 (camera), $64.95 (boom mike).

Hasselblad 500EL/M—This camera opens up new opportunities for a photographer. Exposure after exposure can be burned off at less than a frame a second without any need to touch the camera. It can be triggered by cable at distances up to 650 feet and by remote radio at distances up to several miles. This and a great deal more is possible, thanks to the built-in motor that automatically advances the film and cocks the shutter after each exposure. All accessories for the 500C/M fit the 500EL/M. C.C.C. prices: $649 (EL/M body only), $1,249.95 (EL/M with A-12 magazine and 80mm f/2.8 Planar T lens).

Nizo XL Series—This new series of cameras differs from one to the other only in the type of rangefinder focusing device in the viewfinder and in the Schneider Variogon lenses fitted. The Nizo 156XL uses a split-image rangefinder spot in the center of the viewfinder, while the 148XL and 136XL employ a full-screen coincidental or double-image rangefinder device. The 156XL is equipped with 7–56mm f/1.8 lens with zoom ratio of 8:1. The 148XL comes with an 8–48mm f/1.8 lens with a zoom ratio of 6:1. The 136XL's lens is a 9–36mm f/1.8 with a 4:1 zoom ratio. C.C.C. prices: $249.95 (136XL), $274.95 (148XL), $319.95 (156XL).

199

Nizo 156XL

EASTMAN KODAK CO.

It's probably safe to assume that there isn't a photographer in the country who hasn't heard of this company. Indeed, there are few non-photographers who are unfamiliar with Kodak—a company that is certainly a pioneer in its field. In addition to producing still and movie

cameras, slide projectors, movie projectors, still and movie films, chemicals and darkroom equipment, Kodak offers an extensive list of publications that deal with every phase of photography. You can get a copy of the current "Index to Kodak Information" by sending 10¢ with your request for publication L-5. In this index you will find publications ranging in price from free to several dollars.

You can build quite a library with Kodak publications, and you can buy Kodak binders in two sizes that will keep everything orderly and attractive.

AW-22 Kodak Photographic Notebook—Designed to hold 5¾×8½-inch publications, this binder makes possible a photographic handbook tailored to individual interests and needs. Includes backbone title strips and tabbed separator pages. Most of the photo books and customer service pamphlets from Kodak are punched to fit this notebook. Price: $3.25.

W-4 Binder for Kodak Technical Information—This deluxe binder is designed to hold 8½×11-inch technical publications. It contains pocketed blank separators, printed index strips to classify Kodak technical information, and twelve sheets of note paper. Price: $3.95.

Binder for Technical Information

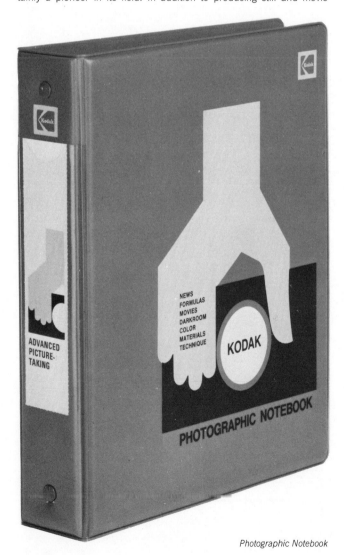

Photographic Notebook

Tele-Instamatic 708—This pocket-size camera uses 110 film cartridges and features drop-in loading and uses flipflash—shoot four flashes, flip, and shoot four more. It has "Soft-touch" shutter release, double-exposure prevention, and comes with monograms to personalize each camera. Other features include normal or telephoto at the flick of a finger, dual-magnification viewfinder that changes automatically, automatic exposure control, electronically controlled shutter speeds from 1/300 to 1/30 second, multielement f/5.6 lens, flashing low-light signal, battery tester, separate battery door, folding lens cover, focusing lens (3 feet to infinity), and a three-year warranty. The camera can be used with

Kodak Ektron electronic flash units. Comes supplied with wrist strap, K-size battery, pressure-sensitive monograms, and instruction book. Dimensions: 5⅞×2½×1¼ inches. Weight: 7½ ounces. Price: $95.50.

Tele-Instamatic 708

Clip-On Pouch Cases for Tele-Instamatic and Trimlite Instamatic— Convenient way to carry camera and one flipflash. Has attached clip for wearing on a belt and a detachable lanyard-type shoulder strap. A separate compartment holds the flipflash unit. Constructed of supple glove-soft brown vinyl with a lined interior and nylon zipper. Prices: $7.25 (for Tele-Instamatic 708), $5.75 (all other models).

Kodak Pocket Carousel 300—This projector accepts 30mm square plastic-mounted slides in 120-slide trays. It is compact for carrying and storing. It features automatic focusing; automatic timing at 5, 8, or 15 seconds; remote control change, forward and reverse; push-button forward and reverse; rear leveling foot; dust cover; and accessory outlet. Available with either Ektar 2½-inch f/2.8 lens or Ektar zoom (2 to 3 inches) f/2.8. Prices: $189.50 (2½-inch lens), $219.50 (2- to 3-inch zoom lens).

Pocket Carousel 300

Clip-On Pouch for Instamatics

Kodak Carousel 600H—This projector accepts 2×2-inch slides in 80- and 140-slide trays and features gentle gravity feed; quiet, dependable operation; preconditioning of slides; selective slide access for instant editing; dual-action "select" advance; manual knob focus; and projection elevation up to six degrees. Prices: $112.50 (with Ektanar C 102mm or 127mm f/2.8 lens), $142.50 (with Ektanar C Zoom 102mm to 152mm f/3.5 lens).

Kodak Carousel 860H—This top-of-the-line projector has all the Carousel features plus attractive wood-grain vinyl paneling with protective rubber molding and chrome edges; protective dust cover for out-in-the-open storage; sliding lens cover; automatic focusing; manual knob focus; remote focusing; automatic slide change at 5, 8, or 15 seconds; remote forward and reverse slide change; manual forward and reverse slide change; easy carrying with self-storing, retractable chrome carrying handle; easy access to lamp via rear compartment; attached power cord with wraparound storage; front storage compartment for remote control cord; accessory outlet; and four-position switch, including high and low brightness control for longer lamp life. Prices: $299.50 (with Ektanar C 102mm or 127mm f/2.8 lens), $329.50 (with Ekoanar C Zoom 102mm to 152mm f/3.5 lens).

Carousel 600H

Carousel 860H

caps. Prices: $299.95 (scope), $14.95 (telephoto adapter), $6.75 to $11.95 (camera adapters), all postpaid.

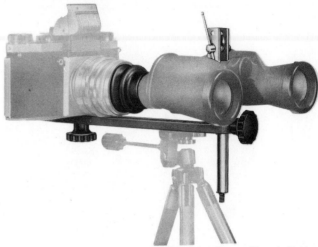

Camera-Binocular Holder

15X to 60X Zoom Telephoto Scope

EDMUND SCIENTIFIC CO.

The Edmund catalog carries several photographic products as well as a number of items that should interest experimental photographers.

Other Edmund products can be found in Chapters 2, 3, 4, 5, 7, and 11.

Camera Binocular Holder—Now take long-distance shots inexpensively with this sturdy, low-cost holder that screws onto standard ¼-inch by twenty-thread tripods. Rubber eyeguard couples binocular/monocular to camera lens. Gray- and chrome-finished metal holder includes ¼-inch by twenty-thread screw for use with threaded monoculars. Monoculars used with holder require either hinged lugs or threaded socket for mounting on tripods. Will not take binoculars without center pins. Can be used with still and movie cameras that have standard tripod sockets, adjustable apertures, and adjustable shutter speeds. Ideal for nature studies, sporting events, and candid shots. Price: $19.95 postpaid.

15X to 60X Zoom Telephoto Scope—Aim, focus, and zoom. All you need is an SLR camera, a T mount adapter, and telephoto adapter to use this scope as a 60X telephoto lens. Conventional 60X lenses cost over $1,000. This scope is priced far lower, yet it gives no noticeable vignetting even at 60X. Aperture: f/16 to f/64 equivalent. Focal length: 1,000mm to 4,000mm. Includes slide-out sun shade and screw-on

GAF CORP.

From GAF comes the familiar line of films for still and motion picture photography, as well as still and movie cameras, slide and movie projectors. Additionally, GAF has a large library of Pana-Vue Slides of scenes throughout the world. They also offer wildlife slides. For a complete listing and order blank, send 35¢ with your request for the "Scenic Slide Catalog."

GAF XL/2 Sound Camera—This new Sound Super 8 camera is designed for easy operation by the home moviemaker. The user can take normal views, or zoom in for closeups, with the added excitement of high-quality sound, perfectly synchronized with the colorful moving picture. The photographer only has to point, shoot, and zoom as desired. The camera automatically provides sharp focus, good exposure indoors or out, and sound volume control. It features a fast f/1.1 9.5mm to 19mm manual zoom lens and will accept sound or silent Super 8 film. The camera is supplied with an omnidirectional microphone.

GAF Compact 102A Movie Camera—This new movie camera for Super 8 silent moviemaking offers a 2X zoom lens and a unique design for one-hand operation. The camera nestles snugly in the palm of the hand, held securely in place with a wide, comfortable elastic hand strap that can be attached to either the right or left side of the camera, according to the user's preference. The pushbutton trigger release is conveniently located on top of the camera for fingertip operation. Exposure is fully automatic for ASA 25 to ASA 160 Type G Super 8 silent films. The camera has a prefocused f/1.8 12mm to 24mm manual zoom lens and is powered by four lightweight AAA 1.5V alkaline batteries.

XL/2 Sound Camera

Compact 102A Movie Camera

GAF 3100S Super 8 Sound Projector—Advanced recording and playback features make this projector ideal for home moviemaking, and for use in training seminars, club meetings, and other public presentations. Recording options for processed, sound-striped Super 8 or Single 8 movie film include a choice of automatic or manual record-level control, a recording level volume meter, erase and record feature, and a sound-on-sound system for adding new sound to an existing sound track or mixing sound from microphone and auxiliary sources. A unique built-in public address system allows the user to talk through the

speaker system while a movie is being shown. Other features are a powerful, four-watt built-in speaker output and eight-watt output for an auxiliary speaker, a sharp f/1.3 15mm to 30mm zoom lens, choice of eighteen or twenty-four frames-per-second running speed, and 600-foot reel capacity.

3100S Super 8 Sound Projector

GAF 2100R Slide Projector—This new projector is specifically designed for home slide projection and low cost. It's the latest addition to the popular line of GAF Hush-A-Matic slide projectors with whisper-quiet action and is made for remote-control operation using the built-in 7½-foot remote cord. The projector features a brilliant 4-inch f/3.5 coated lens for big, sharp pictures. A sliding cover protects the lens when the projector is not in use. Rototray circular slide trays, Easy-Edit straight trays, or GAF stack loader can all be used with the GAF 2100R slide projector.

2100R Slide Projector

GAF Compactible Camera 2020—This new 110-size pocket camera features a retractable camera body that simplifies film advance. One push-pull cycle of the camera body advances the film for the next exposure. The camera is designed for use with FlipFlash indoors or in low light and for use without flash in bright daylight. It is supplied with a wrist cord for carrying.

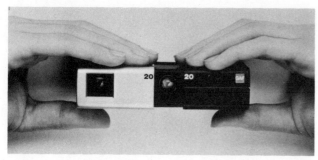

Compactible Camera 2020

GAF 64 Color Slide Film—An excellent general-purpose film. Medium speed, fine grain emulsion, balanced for daylight, electronic flash, blue flashbulbs, and flashcubes. The perfect color slide film for bright daylight situations requiring optimum image quality and color rendition. GAF 64 records colors accurately over a wide subject–brightness range, providing good detail in both the shadow and highlight areas of the image. Available in 126, 20-exposure cartridges, and 35mm in both 20-exposure and 36-exposure rolls.

GAF 500 Color Slide Film—This is the world's fastest consumer color slide film. This special-purpose film will record an image of virtually anything, any time, any place. If it can be seen, it can be photographed on GAF 500 film. Good image sharpness, brilliant color saturation, and the film's ability to record an image under low levels of illumination open up a new world for the creative photographer. GAF 500 is balanced for daylight, electronic flash, blue flashbulbs, and flashcubes. Available in 20-exposure and 36-exposure rolls for 35mm.

GRAPHIC IMPORTS

For those of you who prefer a large-format camera for your outdoor work, this company offers the Nagaoka 4×5-inch View Camera. This is a compact camera, sure to please the outdoor photographer because of its portability.

Nagaoka 4×5 View Camera—This lightweight and compact view camera meets the needs of the photographer who prefers the larger negative

Nagaoka 4 × 5 View Camera

and perspective controls of the view camera but would appreciate the portability of a 35mm. The Nagaoka 4×5 View Camera weighs only 2.6 pounds and folds easily to 7×8×2½ inches—small enough for shoulder bag or backpack. Standard 4×5 sheet film holders, film pack holders, Polaroid sheet film pack holders (500, 545, and 405), and Grafmatic sheet film holders are compatable with the Nagaoka. The camera is made of hardwood with natural lacquer finish, and hardware is chrome-plated brass. It uses Toyo-L or Linhoff Technika lens boards. Price: $295 (includes air postage). Add $7.50 for shipment to Canada.

Nagaoka 4 × 5 View Camera folded and compared to 35mm body

HANIMEX (U.S.A.), INC.

A large line of photographic products comes from this company. Included are the Hanimex 110 and 35mm still cameras and Hanimex movie cameras and projectors, as well as Praktica 35mm SLR cameras and lenses. The company also offers a number of photographic accessories.

Praktica LTL 3 SLR 35mm—In chrome or black with Pentacon multicoated f/1.8 lens, this camera features a steel-bladed shutter with speeds to 1/1,000 second, 1/125 second flash synch, built-in hot shoe, and universal Praktica thread mount. Focuses to 13 inches and has stop-down metering. Prices: $219.95 (chrome), $229.95 (black).

Praktica VLC 2—This camera has all the features of the LTL 3, plus a removable pentaprism for maximum SLR versatility. It's a complete system camera with wide-open metering and electric f/1.8 MC lens. Price: $279.95.

Hanimex Compact 35—Get big, full-frame 35mm slides and prints from the Hanimex compacts. These are easy-to-use automatics, with important features such as CdS meter, hot shoe, self-timer, parallax correction marks in viewfinder, coated lens, and settings from ASA 25 to ASA 400. The 35ZF features automatic operation with extended range electronic shutter from 10 seconds to 1/300 second. New f/2.8 Hanimar four-element coated lens with zone focusing from 3 feet to infinity. Lighted red arrows indicate proper exposure range. The 35RF has all the fine features of the 35ZF, plus coupled rangefinder from 3 feet to infinity and self-timer. Prices: $84.95 (35ZF), $94.95 (35RF).

Praktica LTL 3

Praktica VLC 2

Hanimex Compact 35

PF428 Pocket 110 Camera—Here's a handy little camera with auto exposure and electronic shutter with speeds from $1/30$ to $1/300$ second. It features zone focus, f/6.3 lens, and flip or electronic flash. Price: $61.95.

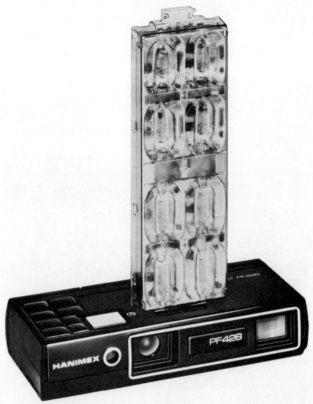

PF428 Pocket 110

IEF Pocket 110 Camera—This pocket camera comes with detachable electronic flash and a three-element f/8 lens. It features parallax correction and has a tripod socket. Price: $49.95.

ES Pocket 110 Camera—This is the top-of-the-line model featuring auto exposure, electronic shutter to $1/300$ second, f/5.6 lens, and three-position zone focus. It comes with a detachable electronic flash. Price: $84.95.

Model X130 Electronic Flash—This is a super-small, lightweight manual with hot shoe. Guide number is 30 with ASA 25 film. Gets up to 150 flashes from two #AA alkaline batteries. Price: $14.95.

Model X130 Electronic Flash

Model BX550 Electronic Flash—This thyristor computer flash has six-position internal bounce, two-position automatic and manual modes, flash tube and reflector covered with rolled diffusion screen, and guide number 50 with ASA 25. It will operate automatically up to 25 feet at f/4 and will recycle as fast as ½ second when shooting close to subject. It gets up to 1,500 flashes on auto with four #AA alkaline batteries. It comes with hot shoe and detachable PC cord. Price: $69.95.

Model XL25 Super 8 Movie Camera—This is a popular, low-light camera with 2½ to 1 power zoom. It features fresh new styling with quality all-metal body, automatic exposure control, and a super-fast f/1.2 lens. Price: $169.95.

Model XL25 Movie Camera

Model 800DST Instdual Movie Projector—This is the top Hanimex silent model projector with two-speed multimotion (6 feet per second on "slow" and 2 feet per second on "step"). Price: $189.95.

Model SR9000 Sound Projector

Model E310 Editor

Model SR9000 Sound Projector—This projector has complete control over sound editing with built-in auto recording-level control, auxiliary input and output for external speaker, plus mike and earphone. It features a 15mm to 25mm f/1.3 zoom lens, two speeds, and 600-foot reel capacity. Price: $319.95.

Model E310 Editor—This is a dual 8 editor with large 4×5-inch screen, Fresnel lens, geared rewind with 600-foot spool capacity. Sound attachments are available. Price: $73.95.

MINOX U.S.A.

This company offers Minox cameras and accessories. Their little Minox 35EL is no bigger than a pair of sunglasses and, according to Minox, is "the world's lightest 35mm camera." If you're looking for a real ultralight, you might check out the Minox C—the little 8×11mm subminiature camera. Minox also offers a complete range of film for this camera.

Literature is available on their entire product line.

Minox 35EL Automatic Compact Camera

Minox 35EL Automatic Compact Camera—This little beauty has a black matte finish and body made of Makrolon (fiberglass reinforced plastic) that is scratch resistant and impact resistant. It features a 35mm Minotar f/2.8 lens, electronically controlled shutter with selective aperture setting, bladed shutter with continuously variable controlled speeds (from 1 second to $1/500$ second at ASA 800, and from 30 seconds to $1/500$ second at ASA 25), and hot shoe for electronic flash. Front flap provides complete protection for the lens and viewfinder window and shuts off all meter systems when closed. The camera takes any 35mm film from ASA 25 to ASA 800, black and white or color, in standard cartridges. Viewfinder has vertical information scale with calibrations for $1/30$, $1/125$, $1/500$ second plus hatched areas to indicate speeds too fast for exposure control or too slow for hand-held exposures. Scale for focusing is from 3 feet to infinity. Weight: 6¾ ounces with battery. Price: $222.

Minox 110S Automatic Pocket Camera—This camera has rangefinder focusing and an automatic exposure system for daylight and flash. It features an electronic shutter with aperture selection from f/2.8 to f/16, shutter speeds continuously variable from 1/1,000 second to 4 seconds with arrows visible in the viewfinder to warn of camera shake or overexposure, split-image rangefinder focusing from 2 feet to infinity with automatic parallax compensation and automatic depth-of-field indicator, choice of meter or feet scale, and accommodations for Magi-cubes or the Minox F110 electronic flash. Front "doors" protect the lens and meter system when camera is not in use and also turn off the electronic system when closed. Body is made of lightweight, scratch-resistant Makrolon. Tripod socket and battery test located on bottom of camera. Lens is 25mm f/2.8. Comes with detachable wrist chain. Weight: 5 ounces. Price: $228.

Minox 110S Automatic Pocket Camera

NIKON, INC.

Nikon is one of the giants in the photography field. The Nikon 35mm single-lens reflex cameras and Nikon lenses have been preferred by serious amateur and professional photographers for years.

The list of Nikon lenses and accessories is seemingly endless, and every year new and exciting products are added to that list. Our primary system includes three Nikkormat cameras and five Nikkor lenses, plus accessories, all fitted into the fine Nikon FB-11A Compartment Case. This gear has seen a lot of rugged outdoor use—from bouncing across Alaska on a dog sled to wet-weather fishing trips in the Pacific Northwest, with two treks across North America in between. It has all held up remarkably well and continues to serve our demanding needs.

Nikon has plenty of literature available on their entire line.

Nikon F2 Camera

Nikon F2 Camera—Born of the Nikon heritage of surpassing quality, the F2 offers truly exceptional capabilities. However you judge this unique camera—for its quick, responsive handling, its wealth of built-in features, the magnificent sharpness and color fidelity of its renowned Nikkor optics, the incomparable versatility of its total system—here is your ultimate photographic system.

With the F2 you get foolproof exposure accuracy in a center-weighted system acclaimed by professionals for its reliable through-the-lens exposure control. Reliable viewing accuracy is another plus, because the viewing system is designed to show you what the film "sees." You can compose your photographs confident that unwanted subject matter will not disturb their effectiveness.

Nikkormat ELW with Auto Winder AW-1

The Nikon F2 shutter is a curtain of specially "quilted" titanium foil that is strong enough to maintain professional accuracy for more than 200,000 exposures and to withstand the pounding of electric motor drive operation and five frames per second. You can choose any shutter speed from 10 full seconds to 1/2,000 second, with continuously variable settings above $1/80$ second and below 1 second. The selected speed from B to 1/2,000 is indicated in the viewfinder.

Other features include full flash synchronization, independent mirror control, special film-flattening system, intentional multiple-exposure capability, threaded synch terminal, hinged back, and complete interchangeability with Nikon lenses and accessories. Prices: $495 (F2 chrome body only), $619.50 (chrome F2 w/50mm f/2), $711 (chrome F2 w/50mm f/1.4), $812.50 (chrome F2 w/55mm f/1.2). Add $20 for black body prices.

Nikkormat ELW—With this new camera, the instant you see a picture in the viewfinder you'll capture it on film. Just choose your lens opening, focus, and shoot; the Nikon center-weighted, through-the-lens meter relays its exposure command to the electronically controlled shutter for a perfectly exposed picture—automatically.

Suddenly, another picture appears. So quickly that there isn't time to wind the film. With the ELW and its accessory Auto Winder AW-1, there's no need to. The ingenious Auto Winder has already advanced the film and cocked the shutter for you. Shoot again and again, automatically, to capture the action as it occurs. And because the Nikkormat ELW is part of the Nikon system, you enjoy this automatic precision with any of more than fifty Nikkor lenses. With Nikon extension rings and bellows units, with filters, microscopes, and telescopes, the ELW will function perfectly. Or, if you prefer, override the automation for special effects.

Other features in this amazing camera include exposure "Memory Lock" and self timer, dual meter switches, depth-of-field preview, oversize automatic-return mirror, special film-flattening system, multiaid focusing screen, and full flash capabilities. Prices: $499.50 (ELW black body only), $169 (Auto Winder AW-1 only), $793 (ELW w/Auto Winder and 50mm f/2), $884.50 (ELW w/Auto Winder and 50mm f/1.4), $986 (ELW w/Auto Winder and 55mm f/1.2).

Nikonos III

Nikonos III—At first glance, the Nikonos III looks like any other fine 35mm camera—trim, compact, and obviously precision-built. But the similarity ends here, for no other camera can match its unique picture-taking capabilities. The Nikonos III is designed for underwater use. It is so effectively sealed that it needs no housing, even 160 feet below the surface. You simply grab the camera and dive in. There's no bulky, un-wieldy housing to impede your freedom of movement. In fact, the Nikonos III, with its slight negative buoyancy and simplified, oversize controls, handles more easily under water than many other cameras do on land.

Protected by its rugged exterior, the Nikonos III can be exposed to rain, snow, mud, and sand without ill effects. Nor is it fazed by extremes of temperature or humidity. And it is resistant to saltwater corrosion, mildew, fungus, and damp rot. To clean the camera, you simply rinse it with fresh water. Clearly, the Nikonos III can be used under conditions you'd never risk with another camera. For the active sportsman, it means pictures while boating, skiing, fishing, hunting, camping, or backpacking, with confidence in the camera's ability to take it.

Other features of the Nikonos III include automatic depth-of-field indicator, luminous-frame viewfinder, and synchro focal-plane shutter with speeds from $1/30$ to $1/500$ second plus B. Four lenses available are the ultrawide angle 15mm, 28mm, 35mm, and 80mm. A number of accessories are available, too. Prices: $289.50 (Nikonos III body only), $120 (35mm f/2.5 Nikkor IC lens), $1,050 (15mm f/2.8 U.W. Nikkor IC lens), $299.50 (28mm f/3.5 U.W. Nikkor lens), $299.50 (80mm f/4 Nikkor IC lens).

NORMAN CAMERA, INC.

Here's a mail-order company that we've dealt with for a number of years and have recommended to many folks. Their prices are some of the best to be found, and their service can't be beat. We've bought five cameras, five lenses, many accessories, and most of our darkroom equipment and supplies from them, and we generally buy our film from them, too. Not once have we had a complaint. They carry a good supply of name-brand cameras, lenses, and accessories, and their catalog is free. They're good folks to deal with and will answer your photographic questions by mail or over the phone.

Nikkormat FT2 Camera

Nikkormat FT2—Here's a great camera for amateur and professional alike. Some of the many features of this "workhorse" include fast and convenient handling, unique total-control viewfinder, foolproof exposure accuracy, built-in hot shoe and electronic flash capability, depth-of-field previewer, independent mirror control, film-flatness control, and inter-changeability with Nikkor lenses and accessories. Norman prices: $172 (chrome body only), $180 (black body only).

Auto-Nikkor 50mm f/2 Lens—This is a lens with superior optics and mechanical precision, accurate camera-lens fitting, and Nikon Total System Resolution. Norman price: $73.

Nikon FB-14 Compartment Case—Handsomely modern, semisoft shoulder bag with full-length zipper and outer pocket. Holds one camera and three lenses up to 80–200mm Nikkor Zoom. Made of fine black leather. Norman price: $103.

Nikon FB-11A Compartment Case—Extra-large pro-bag style, with carrying handle as well as detachable shoulder strap. Removable tray holds two cameras plus extra lens; additional lenses and accessories fit into bottom compartment, which has adjustable partitions. With partitions removed, there is room for an extra-long lens, up to 500mm Reflex Nikkor. Made of genuine cowhide. Norman price: $151.

Olympus 35RD Rangefinder Camera—This compact camera with fast f/1.7 Zuiko lens features shutter speeds from as slow as ½ to $1/500$ second as well as B and X flash synchronization. Coupled rangefinder/viewfinder has luminous bright frame with parallax correction marks, f-stop scale, and red zone for underexposure warning. Options for both fully automatic or manual operation. Norman price: $119.

Olympus 35RD Rangefinder Camera

Kodachrome 25 Film—This super fine-grain, warm color transparency film is available in 20- and 36-exposure canisters. It is the 35mm film preferred by many outdoor photographers for stunning landscape shots and other photographs that can be taken with the ASA 25 speed. Norman prices: $1.88 (20 exposure), $1.75 (20 exposure when ordering twenty or more rolls), $2.70 (36 exposure), $2.52 (36 exposure when ordering twenty or more rolls).

High Speed Ektachrome—This fast film is ideal for wildlife photography where low light levels or telephoto lenses might make other films unsatisfactory. It is rated for ASA 160, but can be "pushed" to ASA 400. It is a cool color, daylight transparency film. Norman Camera offers it in 20-exposure and 36-exposure 35mm canisters. Norman prices: $2.40 (20 exposure), $2.24 (20 exposure when ordering twenty or more rolls), $3.45 (36 exposure), $3.22 (36 exposure when ordering twenty or more rolls).

Kodak PK-20 Pre-Paid Mailers—Prepaid processing mailers for Kodak processing of Kodachrome and Ektachrome films, twenty exposures. Norman prices: $2.36, $2.20 (twenty or more).

Kodak PK-36 Pre-Paid Mailers—Prepaid processing mailers for 36-exposure Kodachrome and Ektachrome films. Norman prices: $3.86, $3.60 (twenty or more).

PONDER & BEST, INC.

The two important lines of photographic equipment supplied to the United States by this company are Olympus and Vivitar.

Olympus has long been a name associated with quality cameras and lenses, but won the widespread acclaim of professional and amateur photographers a few years ago when the OM system was introduced. The OM system includes 35mm SLR cameras and lenses and a full range of accessories, all designed to be compact and light in weight, but with all the features expected in a professional quality system.

The Vivitar line continues to grow each year and now includes some of the finest lenses (Series I) to be found anywhere and some of the most advanced electronic flash systems. The Vivitar name is on numerous accessories and cameras as well.

Olympus OM-2 Camera

Olympus OM-2 Camera—This is the smallest, lightest automatic electronic shutter 35mm SLR camera in the world. It accepts the entire range of precision Zuiko lenses, ranging from 8mm to 1,000mm, and other OM System accessories. The OM-2 Direct Light Measuring System features fast, sensitive SBC (Silicon Blue Cell) sensors that face the film plane and measure the light that actually reaches and is reflected from the film during exposure, providing instant responses to changes in light conditions while the picture is being taken. This is especially important for long exposures and in sequence photography with the motor drive.

Like its companion Olympus OM-1, the OM-2 has a viewfinder that is 30 percent larger and approximately 70 percent brighter than the average 35mm SLR and shows 97 percent of the actual picture field. The camera features a choice of either aperture-preferred fully automatic exposure control or manual exposure control by means of a single-touch selector switch. Other features include a progressive-type exposure counter with automatic reset, an optional Olympus accessory shoe, and a lever-type self-cocking manual advance with a 150-degree stroke angle for one long or several short strokes with double-advance and double-exposure prevention. Comes with black strap and pad. Prices: $499.95 (OM-2 chrome body only), $524.95 (OM-2 black body only), $100 (Zuiko 50mm f/1.8 Auto-S lens), $155 (Zuiko 50mm f/1.4 Auto-S lens), $255 (Zuiko 55mm f/1.2 Auto-S lens).

Olympus Winder 1

Olympus Winder 1—This winder provides automatic single-frame film advance for either the Olympus OM-1 MD or OM-2 35mm SLR cameras at speeds as fast as three frames per second. With four fresh #AA alkaline batteries, Winder 1 supplies automatic film-winding advance for about fifty rolls of 36-exposure film. Price: $179.98.

Vivitar Model 604 Pocket 110 Camera—Portrait photos from as close as 2 feet from the subject—with or without flash—are easy to take with the new Model 604 with built-in electronic flash. A single three-position switch controls the camera's operation for daylight, close-up flash, and normal flash pictures. A ready light for electronic flash, visible in the viewfinder, blinks on the close-up flash setting and built-in Vivitar electronic flash features 300 or more flashes per set of fresh batteries. "Point 'n Shoot" outfit comes with wrist strap, batteries, and film. Price: $79.95.

Vivitar Enduro Cases—Designed for active photographers, the Vivitar Enduro Case has a contoured molded high-impact outer shell that fits snugly to the body. Adjustable nylon web waist and shoulder straps hold the case securely to the photographer's back or side, leaving hands free for biking, hiking, fishing, hunting, and other sports. Colors: black, yellow, or orange. Price: $34.95.

Vivitar Model 604 Pocket 110 Camera

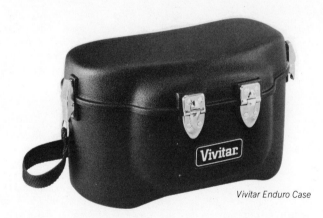

Vivitar Enduro Case

Model 865 Tele-Zoom Camera Case—Vivitar's upright Model 865 Compartment Case will accommodate a compact 35mm SLR camera mounted with a zoom lens as well as additional lenses and accessories, such as film, electronic flash, and filters. Lined in velveteen, the 865 features a convenient pocket in the inner lid for storing small accessories, a quick-release holding strap for secure equipment storage, and adjustable shoulder strap. Price: $49.95.

Vivitar Automatic 24mm Fixed Mount Lens—This new f/2.8 wide-angle lens yields an 84-degree angle of view with virtually no edge distortion. Shorter than most 28mm lenses, the computer-designed Vivitar 24mm lens is ideal for architectural photography, panoramic landscapes, or shooting in cramped quarters. The lens is made to fit Minolta SRT/SR Series, Canon FL/FD, Nikon F and Nikkormat, Konica Autoreflex, and Olympus OM Series, as well as cameras accepting universal thread mounts. Prices: $170 (universal thread and Minolta), $180 (all others).

Vivitar Model 865 Tele-Zoom Camera Case

Vivitar Automatic 24mm Fixed Mount Lens
Vivitar Automatic 35–105mm Fixed Mount Zoom Lens
Vivitar Automatic TX 100–300mm Zoom Lens

Vivitar 35–105mm Fixed Mount Zoom Lens—This f/3.5 zoom lens combines the features of a medium wide-angle 35mm lens with the capabilities of a medium-range telephoto. The close-up operation control is coupled to the zoom ring, eliminating any supplemental controls needed to switch from one mode to the other. In the zoom mode, the lens remains in focus throughout the entire range of focal lengths. It focuses as close as 4½ feet from the film plane in the telephoto position, and 11.4 inches from the film plane in the closest focusing position, which provides a reproduction ratio of 1:5. Made to fit same cameras as 24mm lens above. Prices: $385 (universal thread and Minolta), $395 (all other models).

Vivitar Automatic TX 100–300mm Zoom Lens—A compact, multicoated zoom lens with a 3:1 zoom ratio, the new 100–300mm f/4 Close Focusing TX Zoom also features a close-focusing mode with a reproduction ratio greater than one-fourth life size (1:3.5) at its closest focusing position. Switching from the normal zoom mode to the close-focusing position is accomplished quickly and easily by twisting the zoom ring to the left, in one single motion. In the zoom mode, the lens has a closest focus distance of 6.5 feet from the film plane. This lens is mounted to camera via a Vivitar TX Lens Mount Adapter, purchased separately, with prices running from $16 to $22.50, depending on camera make. Lens comes with retractable lens hood. Price: $285.

Vivitar Series 1 600mm Solid Catadioptric Lens—This f/8 lens is packaged complete with impact-resistant carrying case, screw-in lens hood, and four close-tolerance Series 1 VMC filters: UV (haze), 25A, K2, and 4X ND. Also included are front and rear lens caps and detachable tripod socket. This is an incredibly compact lens that utilizes a mirror system rather than the refractive optical system generally used in telephoto lenses. It employs a number of spherically shaped lens elements pieced together to virtually form a single solid element. The solid glass construction results in an extremely high resistance to both damage by shock and reaction to extreme temperature change. The short physical length of the lens reduces the horizontal and vertical travel of the front lens in

Vivitar Series 1 600mm Solid Catadioptric Lens

Vivitar Model 283 Auto Thyristor Electronic Flash

relation to the film plane, thereby increasing the sharpness of hand-held shots. Price: $799.

Vivitar Color Accent Filters—One of seven new groups of Vivitar special-effects filters, these are designed to create subtle differences in light intensity from one half of a photograph to the other half with no loss of highlight or shadow detail. The filters blend gradually at the center for smooth transition between the clear and tinted areas, and are available in blue, brown, yellow-green, and one- or two-stop neutral density. Other new Vivitar special effects filters are Cromo Blend, Thin Ring Polarizing, Dual Color, Multi-Image, Split Field, Cross Screen V, and Dual Cross filters.

Vivitar 283 Auto/Thyristor Electronic Flash—This powerful new flash features four auto f-stops, convenient 0–90-degree flash head tilt, unique Bounce Compensator Circuit to increase light output in 45-, 60-, or 75-degree bounce positions, fast recycle time (as short as ½ second in auto mode), built-in LED sensing circuit, and illuminated calculator dial with on/off switch. The 283 is equipped with a removable Remote Sensor that plugs into the front of the flash or mounts on a standard camera accessory shoe. The 283 comes complete with Remote Sensor, 1.2-meter Sensor Holder Cord, 12-inch PC-1 Shutter Cord, and Alkaline Battery Holder. Price: $124.95.

Film Identifier

PORTER'S CAMERA STORE, INC.

This is another mail-order company that we started dealing with a couple of years ago. Their giant tabloid catalog is crammed full of photographic equipment and supplies—some of which are not available anywhere else. Their prices are good, and their service is really fast.

Film Identifier—Stick it to the back of your camera or case with the self-adhesive strip. Then slide your film identifying box top in the slot and it stays. Box top is easy to remove when you change to another kind of film. With this identifier you will always know what kind of film is inside your camera. Prices: 99¢ each, $1.99 (set of three).

Shurfit Screw-In Front Lens Caps—For replacement of existing lens caps or those lost in the boondocks, these caps are made of aluminum and will fit 49, 52, 55, 58, 62, or 67mm threads. Prices: from $1.98 to $3.90.

Lens Reverse Adapters—These reversers simplify extreme close-up photography by permitting the standard camera lens to be put on the body in reverse position. The results are sharp, but the subject-to-lens distance covers a very small range. Available for most popular models of 35mm SLRs. Price: $6.50.

Lens Reverse Adapter
Filter Wrench

Wrench for Reluctant Filters—This handy squeeze wrench set solves an age-old problem—how to get a $7 filter off a $100 lens without a hacksaw. The Portertown Wrench Set squeezes firmly over 48, 49, 52, 55, and 58mm filters. It very easily screws off the most reluctant filters and other lens attachments. Price: $3.94.

Portertown Filter Wallet—This handy wallet holds six filters in easy view, each in an individual compartment. It is well padded for protection. White interior lining aids in filter color identification. Holds sizes 40.5, 43, 46, 48, 49, 52, 55, 58, and 62mm. Folds and snaps shut, protecting valuable filter surfaces from dust and scratching. Price: $5.60.

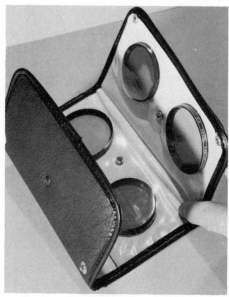

Filter Wallet

Zoom Duplicator—This is a complete zoom slide duplicator that fits directly into SLR bodies by using a T-mount adapter. It has its own highly corrected optical system. Zooms from 1:1 to 2:1 magnification of image. Adjustable slide holder allows for cropping. Requires no focusing. Comes with diffuser. Price: $57.95.

Photographer's Logbook—Spiral-bound 5½×10¾ inches, this log comes with complete instructions on how to best utilize the contents. It is a complete system of recording information about each roll of film, either during or after the exposure. This logbook also has many tables and charts on filter colors and factors, film ASA, etc. Price: $3.95.

Zoom Duplicator

Adapt-A-Case Model P-20E—This is the deluxe case for those who want a rigid, rugged aluminum case, suitable for both carrying and shipping. It comes equipped with a patented system of movable, interlocking partitions. Extra partitions can be purchased from Porter—either padded or unpadded. Shoulder strap also available. Size: 18×14×5 inches. Prices: $81.75 (case), $4.25 (heavy-duty shoulder strap), $3.58 (unpadded partition set).

Camera Belt "Holdster"—This handy item has a retaining screw to attach to the base of a 35mm camera. Perfect for holding your camera on your belt for a "fast draw." Made of highly polished silver spring steel—base is lined with soft black felt. For some cameras the Holdster does not have the wraparound end plate. Fits a variety of popular cameras. Price: $6.54.

Portertown Power Grip—This is a right-angle bracket made of one-piece ¼-inch metal with soft synthetic rubber camera protector, and is fitted with a standard, adjustable tripod screw and flash shoe on top of molded plastic handle grip. Strap assures positive handhold. Price: $7.75.

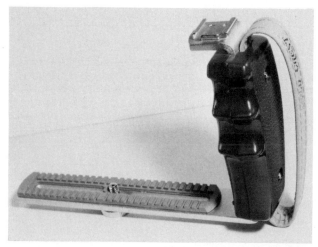

Power Grip

Deluxe Gun Stock—This stock is made of solid hardwood with a high degree of craftsmanship and finishing. The camera plate is designed to accommodate most telephoto lenses and SLR cameras or movie cameras. The "trigomatic" cable and push release can be removed. Comes with adjustable shoulder strap with shoulder pad and quick snap fasteners, and sturdy cable release that is plastic covered and 22 inches long. Price: $53.

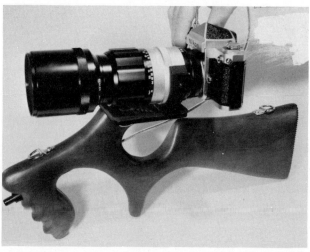

Deluxe Gun Stock

ROLLEI OF AMERICA, INC.

Rollei is a name long associated with superior quality in cameras, and their current lineup includes the tiny A110 pocket camera, the Rollei 35 S full-frame 35mm that fits in the palm of your hand, and the Rolleiflex SL35M 35mm SLR.

The Rollei 2¼×2¼ cameras are distributed in the United States by Erenreich Photo-Optical Industries, Inc., and for literature on these cameras you should write EPI at 101 Crossways Park West, Woodbury, N.Y. 11797.

A110 Pocket Camera

Rollei A110—Take this jewel in your hand. Fall in love with its fascinating photographic precision—and make pictures that all will envy. On bright or dull days, with lamplight or flash, the Rollei A110 gives automatically correct exposures. You set the distance and the camera automatically controls the exposure. You never worry over shutter speeds or apertures.

For the first time a pocket camera also controls flash cube exposure. In this minute, precision technology-packed camera a silicon photo diode electric eye instantly registers even a flash to regulate exposure.

Other features include a Carl Zeiss 23mm Tessar f/2.8 lens, combined meter/feet symbol scale, and shutter speeds from 4 seconds to ¹/₄₀₀ second. Camera comes with case, cube adapter, and carrying chain. Price: $300.

Rollei 35 S—A camera must be small, flat, and handy to take with you everywhere without being a burden. That is why in 1966 Rollei marketed the world's smallest 35mm camera: the Rollei 35. The Rollei 35 S has a top class 40mm Sonnar f/2.8 lens. Multicoating ensures better contrast, more brilliant colors, and improved color rendering. With the high speed of this lens, the Rollei 35 S becomes a camera for pin-sharp pictures every time—in poor light, too. Focusing range is from 3 feet to infinity. The camera is equipped with a special leaf shutter with speeds from ½ to ¹/₅₀₀ second and B. Exposure measurement is by CdS cell with follow-pointer system. Dimensions: 3.8×2.4×1.25 inches. Weight: 13 ounces. Price: $244 (chrome), $260 (black).

Rollei 35 S

Rolleiflex SL35M

Rolleiflex SL35M—This camera is certainly the true picture of an adventure. Without any fancies, without a range of silly features that are never used anyway, entirely developed for utility and with a finish designed to blend with it. Proven Rollei techniques such as open aperture metering, focal plane shutter from 1 to 1/1,000 second, film transport control, and rangefinder for rapid focusing. And all of this has been constructed into a body that secures a maximum of perfect handling by its handy design and rubber coating. Some of the many features include Rollei bayonet mount for interchangeable lenses, hot shoe with center contact, quick film loading system, double-exposure prevention device and film transport lock, aperture preview selection, delay action device, cable release socket, automatic setting frame counter with film speed indicator, ¼-inch tripod bushing, and carrying strap eyelets. The camera has a CdS system, through-the-lens center-weighted averaging meter visible in the viewfinder with open aperture or stop-down metering. A number of accessories are available, as well as a complete range of lenses from 15mm to 200mm. Comes with case, neck strap, battery, lens cap, and shoulder pad. Prices: $395 (SL35M w/50mm f/1.8 HFT lens), $449 (SL35M w/50mm f/1.4 HFT lens), $260 (SL35M body only).

Rolleiflex 2.8F—Truly the top of the twin-lens reflex (TLR) cameras, this model has 80mm Planar f/2.8 lenses with pinpoint definition to the very image edge and optimum optical correction. A coupled exposure meter steps up operation speed. The film feeder system eliminates laborious loading manipulations. The camera has a removable folding hood with 2.5X magnifier, built-in frame finder, and 4X fine-focusing magnifier. The focusing screen has square grid and wedge rangefinder. The built-in single-range exposure meter is coupled with shutter speeds and apertures. There are separate setting wheels for speeds and stops. Shutter: 1 to ¹/₅₀₀ second. Aperture: f/2.8 to f/22. Dimensions: 5⅞ inches high by 4⅜ inches wide by 4⅛ inches deep. Weight: 43 ounces. Uses 120 or 220 film for 2¼×2¼-inch negatives or transparencies. Price: $967.

Rolleiflex SL66—The 2¼×2¼-inch medium format of the Rolleiflex SL66 is the perfect compromise between the miniature and the large-format camera. It combines the easy handling of the miniature camera with a large image—four times the area of the 35mm picture. The SL66 body is the core of the huge Rolleiflex SL66 system of interchangeable units and accessories, and it has all the features you would expect from a functional and efficient, professional camera. It has a bellows to assure sharpness control, bayonet lenses for easy interchangeability, and stop-down key for depth of field previewing. The vertically running focal

Rolleiflex SL66

Rolleiflex 2.8F
Rolleiflex SLX

mirror; electronic compensation for extraneous light originating through the viewfinder; motorized film transport with automatic stop at first frame; motorized film transport after every exposure; frame sequencing time approximately 0.7 second (i.e., three frames every two seconds); automatic spooling off after the last exposure; power supply by interchangeable power pack incorporating rapid changing sinter ni-cad batteries, rechargeable in about one hour with rapid charger; high mirror; electric prerelease of mirror; and pneumatic mirror damper. Uses 120 film. Price: $3,038.50.

SPIRATONE, INC.

Anyone who reads the photography magazines has surely seen this company's advertisements. Spiratone offers a wide selection of economically priced photographic accessories. They carry a complete assortment of filters and many lenses that outdoor photographers will find useful. We have purchased a good bit of gear from Spiratone over the years and find their quality and service to be tops. Their catalog is free, and we suggest that you send for it. Meanwhile, here's a small sampling of what you will find in it.

Sun Multi-Coated Zoom Lenses—Sun Optical Company, one of the foremost manufacturers of zoom lenses, has designed three lenses that many consider the ultimate in quality, versatility, and workmanship: the 80–240mm Tele Zoom with macro focusing covering the most desirable of telephoto settings, including in its continuous zooming range such popular focal lengths as 85, 90, 135, and 200mm; the 38–90mm Wide Angle to Telephoto Zoom with macro focusing, the lens that comes closest to being a truly "Universal" lens; and now the 24–40mm Wide Angle Zoom. These lenses offer continuous, uninterrupted focusing from infinity to a 1:4 image ratio at the closest macro setting. Continuing the regular focusing into the macro range is as simple as pressing a button. The multiple coatings are an integral computed component of the lenses' optical design to achieve their optimum function: the control of flare and ghosting, and the achievement of maximum contrast, even under the most severe lighting conditions. All three lenses are fully automatic and meter coupled and are available for most popular SLRs. The 80–240mm has an aperture range of f/4 to f/22, normal focusing range from 8 feet to infinity, macro focusing from 14 inches to 8 feet, is 7½ inches long, weighs 42 ounces, and accepts 67mm filters. The 38–90mm has an aperture range of f/3.5 to f/22, normal focusing range of 5 feet to infinity, macro focusing from 5 inches to 5 feet, is 5 inches long, weighs 24 ounces, and accepts 67mm filters. The 24–40mm lens has an aperture range of f/3.5 to f/22, normal focusing range of 32 inches to infinity, macro focusing from 4 to 32 inches, is 3¼ inches long, weighs 20 ounces, and accepts 72mm filters. Price: $198 each.

plane shutter has speeds from 1 to ¹/₁,₀₀₀ second plus B. Other features include flash synchronization, swing-open rapid-winding crank, lens lock, focal length indication for distance scales, interchangeable film magazines, 12/24 exposure counter, and much more. Prices: $1,795 (SL66 w/80mm f/2.8 HFT Planar lens), $1,210 (body w/120-220 magazine only), $799.95 (body only).

Rolleiflex SLX—Here is a system SLR 6×6 centimeters (2¼×2¼ inches) with electronic control of all camera functions. Features include interchangeable lenses with "linear motors" for shutter and aperture selection; interchangeable hoods and focusing screens; preloaded rapid-change film cassettes; automatic selection after presetting shutter speed; selected aperture visible on the lens; electronically controlled exposure time with between-the-lens light metering by silicon photo elements; center-weighted light reading over the image area behind the

Sun 80–240mm Macro Focusing Zoom
Sun 38–90mm Macro Focusing Zoom
Sun 24–40mm Macro Focusing Zoom

Sharpshooter "400"

500mm f/8 Mirror Telephoto

Sharpshooter "400" —This is the famous lens that *Modern Photography* called "a fantastic buy!" It's a relatively fast (f/6.3) and incredibly light-weight (22 ounces), well-corrected, four-element design, coated, precision-constructed lens that yields needle-sharp results—even wide open. Now, with Spiratone's Telegrip you zero in as with a rifle for nature photos, sports action, and other photographic excitement. This 400mm lens compresses distance by 87 percent. It has a free rotating collar for vertical or horizontal positioning of camera on tripod or grip. It stops down to f/32 for extra depth of field and takes all 72mm accessories and filters, including FocusXtenders (for exciting telephoto closeups). This is a preset lens. Price: $44.95.

500mm f/8 Mirror Telephoto —This is an economically priced, top-quality mirror lens, featuring catadioptric design with all-spherical sur-faces. It covers a 5-degree angle and accepts standard 77mm filters. Length: 8½ inches. Weight: 2 pounds 6 ounces. Focus range: 12½ feet to infinity; extended to 7 feet with extension tube set (included) to cover a field size of only 3½×5 inches. Price: $149.95.

Aqua Housing —This housing folds so flat, weighs so little, is so simple to load, unload, and use that you'll always want to keep it in your gadget bag to be ready for every picture-taking opportunity. It is safe down to 35 feet, isn't affected by salt water, and should it by accident get out of hand, with the normal air trapped inside, it will float for easy retrieval. No maintenance. No special gaskets. No assembly or disassembly tools.

After use, simply wash with fresh water and wipe it dry. Divers will ap-preciate the simplicity of its assembly and use, and its almost universal adaptability to just about any 35mm SLR. It is ideal for most underwater use, and will afford your gear maximum protection above water for rainy-weather photography, whitewater canoe trips, and the like. Three models are available to accommodate most cameras and cameras with strobes attached. Prices: $29.95 (Model 35 for most SLR cameras), $39.95 (Model 35F will accommodate SLR and small strobe), $44.95 (Model 35L similar to 35F but larger to comfortably hold larger 35mm SLRs).

Aqua Housing

ST. LAWRENCE TRADING CO., INC.

Oberrecht's first law of outdoor photography: On any given photographic expedition (from day hike to extended trip) the item most needed is the one left at home. From observing fellow outdoor photographers lugging all manner of photographic gadgets and gizmos into the boondocks, it would seem that most of them have learned that it is important to go as completely prepared as possible. But heavy gadget bags and dangling cameras are not only nuisances, they're downright fatiguing.

At last, someone has designed a line of photographer's backpacks that can be found in "The Goody Book" that St. Lawrence Trading Company will send you for $1.

Windago Shutterpack Case—This is the largest of the Shutterpack line and it can store all 35mm and 2¼ systems. Pack and dividers are padded for maximum protection of equipment. It features two double-zippered main sections: lower for camera, lenses, meter, etc.; upper for personal gear and accessories. Four exterior side pockets are divided for film, filters, cleaning materials, and cable releases. All have weatherproof vertical zippers. Tripod fits snugly on front for easy access to inside and no damage to other equipment. Padded webbed shoulder straps and nylon webbed waistband with adjustable lock are also featured. The pack has an outside notebook pocket. Top padding is shaped for easy drawstring closure. Weight: 28 ounces. Suggested capacity: 30 pounds. Color: beige. Prices: $59.95 (Windago Shutterpack Case), $2.50 (Aluminum A-frame for additional support).

Albatross Shutterpack Case—This is a spacious, rounded variation of the Windago. It features protective padding and two-part main section, two exterior vertical-zippered pockets, and other features of the Windago. Prices: $55.95 (case), $2.50 (A-frame).

Sundawn Shutterpack Case—This is the smallest, most economical of the backpack designs and is perfect for the day hiker/photographer. It holds all 35mm and most 2¼ systems. Stovepipe design is protectively padded. Top and bottom sections are divided with room for two cameras, three or four lenses, and accessories. Other features include exterior flat pocket (for notebook or filter wallet), padded shoulder straps, webbed waistbelt, easy access lock, and carrying loop. Weight: 14 ounces. Suggested capacity: 23 pounds. Color: beige. Price: $32.95.

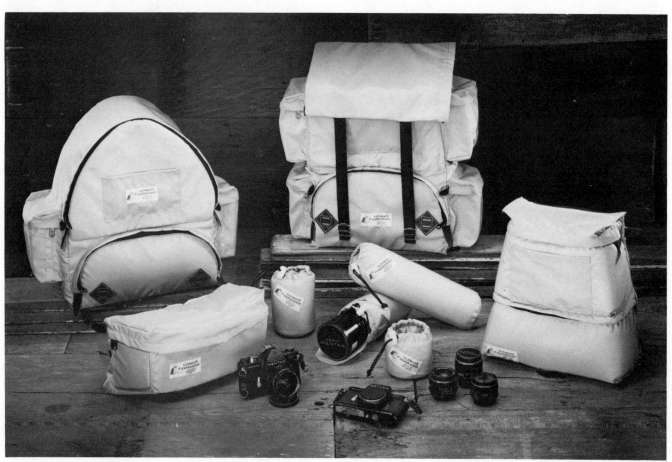

Shutterpack Cases and Pic Pouches

Snowbreeze Shutterpack Case—This is a fanny pack, perfect for skiing, backpacking, climbing, fishing, and hunting. It is fully padded throughout and has three dividers spaced for camera, two lenses, and accessories. It features a comfortable hip fit with adjustable, locking waistbelt. Weight: 8 ounces. Suggested capacity: 15 pounds. Color: beige. Price: $24.95.

Pic Pouches—These are fully padded lens cases that attach to belt packs. They're constructed of fully waterproof materials and have drawstring and lock closure with an interior flap for additional weather and shock protection. Sizes: 4, 6, 8½, and 12½ inches. Prices: $6, $7, $7.95, $9.95.

SUPER-8 STUDIOS

This company specializes in motion picture cameras, films, and accessories. President Garo Alexanian told us that many of the company's customers are nature cinematographers, one of whom produced a film on canoeing that recently won a prize in a film festival.

The experts at Super-8 will offer aid and assistance to anyone interested in producing a film, and they'll send you their big 70-page catalog free.

Bauer S108 Sound Camera—This is the largest ratio single system sound zoom camera from Bauer. It contains an f/1.7, 7.5 to 60mm (8 to 1), variable speed, power or manual, macro zoom lens. It focuses from 1 inch. Super-8 price: $341.90.

Braun Editor/Viewer—This is an excellent editor/viewer with a very bright 10W halogen lamp for illumination, built-in film cleaner, built-in film notcher, 400-foot capacity and dual voltage. Super-8 price: $87.90.

Braun Editor/Viewer

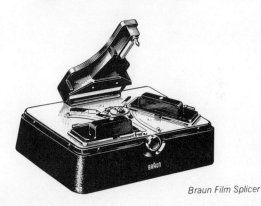
Braun Film Splicer

Bauer S108 Sound Camera

Braun Film Splicer — This is a truly fine Super-8mm film splicer that contains an automatic sapphire grinding disk. With both edges of the film ground, a beveled-edge splice is formed that does not result in overlapping splices. As a result, there is no "tick" heard on the sound track at splice points. A must for sound film editing. Super-8 price: $39.90.

ECCO 202 System — This film-cleaning machine lets you clean Super-8 film, filmstrips, and tapes yourself—instantly, economically, and efficiently. Fingertip adjusting micrometer sight-feed valve lets you see and control flow of solution. Solutions are applied smoothly, evenly, without streaks, smudges, and smears. A must for anyone working with movie films. Super-8 price: $43.90.

ECCO 202 System Film Cleaning Machine

CHAPTER ELEVEN

GENERAL, MISCELLANEOUS, AND SPECIALTY ITEMS

Broadly general products defy classification, and, consequently, can't be worked into any particular chapter. Binoculars, for example, are considered indispensable by countless hunters, but are equally valuable to fishermen, boaters, backpackers, campers, and outdoor photographers. So, you will find binoculars in this chapter. Other items in the following pages include products that might be of interest to all outdoors people, as well as those that are highly specialized and of interest to only a portion of our readers. Our final chapter, then, is somewhat of a potpourri of outdoor gear. We hope you will enjoy browsing through it.

ALLADIN LABORATORIES, INC.

Among Alladin's products for outdoors people are the popular Jon-e Warmers that are favored by cold-weather sports enthusiasts everywhere.

For other Alladin products, see Chapter 2.

Jon-e Warmer and Fluid

Standard Size Jon-e Warmer—This warmer gives comforting heat all day on one filling (1 ounce) of Jon-e Fluid. Wick at side of the new improved burner makes it fast and easy to start. Made of chrome-plated steel and highly polished. Will light cigarettes, too. Comes with drawstring carrying bag.

Giant Size Jon-e Warmer—This model gives heat for two full days on one filling of fluid. It was designed for ice fishermen, hunters, and others exposed to extreme cold for long periods. Other features are the same as the Standard Jon-e Warmer.

AMERICAN HONDA MOTOR CORP.

For extended trips into the boondocks, for a remote hunting or fishing cabin, for running appliances in a motor home, for charging batteries away from electrical power sources, or for any other electrical power need Honda offers a line of portable generators.

EM-400 Portable Generator

EM-400 Portable Generator—Compact size and portability make the EM-400 particularly suitable for outdoor recreation power needs. It has an AC power output of 400 watts maximum and 300 rated watts continuous, and a DC output to charge 12V batteries. Capable of generating power to operate small appliances, such as a barbeque motor and most

camping accessories, the EM-400 weighs less than 40 pounds. It has a four-stroke, single-cylinder, side-valve, forced air-cooled engine, and can run for up to four hours on a full tank of gas, depending on the load. Price: $299.

E-1500 K2 Generator—Owners of recreational vehicles frequently call on the E-1500 as their power source for appliances, tools, and battery-charging needs. It has AC power of 1,500 watts maximum and DC power output to charge 12V and 24V batteries. It weighs less than 123 pounds and has a continuous operational capacity of up to four hours on a full tank of gas. It has a current transformer and centrifugal governor to help assure stable power output. Moving parts are covered for added safety, and a T-joint fuel valve provides auxiliary gas tank capability. This generator can provide power for medium to large appliances, ranging up to freezers, broilers, and air conditioners of 10,000 BTU or less. Price: $453.

EM-1500 K2 Generator

E-2500 K3 Generator—Here's the perfect generator for that remote hunting or fishing cabin, or it can run your power tools while you build your cabin, boat dock, or out-buildings. It weighs just 161 pounds and has an AC maximum output of 2,500 watts and DC power output to charge 12V or 24V batteries. Dual delivery of AC and DC power makes it possible to operate tools, lights, or appliances while simultaneously charging batteries. It can operate several power tools at one time and can run for up to six hours on a tankful of fuel. Price: $649.

ANGLER'S & SHOOTER'S BOOKSHELF

More than 4,000 books covering all aspects of outdoor sports are on hand at any given time at this company, including many collector's books, first editions and others you aren't likely to find at your local bookstore.

Catalogs are issued in two parts—*A* to *K* in the spring, and *L* to *Z* in the fall. Price is $2 for the two-volume catalog and is refundable on the first order. Customers continue to receive catalogs for at least five years after their first order.

Here is just a tiny sample of what you can expect to find in these great catalogs.

#1414 Grey, Zane—Tales of the Angler's El Dorado, New Zealand, Harpers. Illustrated, 228 pages, 1926. Contains rainbow trout fishing in addition to his normal deep sea. One-inch tear top of spine, otherwise fine. Price: $25.

#1794 Hoover, Helen—The Gift of the Deer. New York. Illustrated by Adrian Hoover, 210 pages, 1969. Tale of a deer, his mate, their offspring, and two human friends. Cataloger got ill. Another damned "Bambi." Mint. Price: $5.

#2897 Phillips & Lincoln—American Waterfowl. Boston and New York. Illustrated by Allan Brooks and A. L. Ripley, 312 pages, 1930. First edition. Dust jacket. Mint. Price: $75.

#3100 Robinson, Jimmy—Forty Years of Hunting. Minnesota. Photos, 159 pages, 1947. Much on duck, goose, trap, and skeet. A chapter each on Fred Kimble and Annie Oakley. Presentation copy. Scarce. Very fine. Price: $25.

BLACK AND DECKER MANUFACTURING CO.

Of course, Black & Decker offers a complete line of power tools for the handyman, but their new MOD 4 Cordless Tools should be of particular interest to outdoorsmen.

MOD 4 Cordless Tools—Cordless convenience and interchangeable tool heads let you save money without sacrificing power. You buy one complete MOD 4 tool; the rechargeable Energy Pak works with any of the other MOD 4 precise-engineered tool heads. You just slip on the head you want. Black & Decker's Energy Pak provides enough power for each tool to work at maximum efficiency and, since new tools are being added each year, you'll be able to continue to capitalize on savings. The Spot Vac tool head will prove extremely handy for cleaning out any vehicle, but should be of particular value to the RV owner. The handy ¼-inch Drill Head is just the tool for working on the wilderness cabin or boat. There are one-quart and one-gallon Sprayer heads for use away from electric sources. And the Sealed Beam Lantern Head should prove useful to any outdoors person. There are accessories available to make your MOD 4 system even more convenient, such as Tool and Accessory Holders for mounting tools on a wall, and a Vacuum Cleaner Accessory Assortment for those cleaning chores. Prices: $9.99 (Energy Pak), $6.99 (Recharger), $12.99 (¼-inch Drill Head), $9.99 (Spot Vacuum Head), $9.99 (Sealed Beam Lantern Head), $4.99 (Vacuum Cleaner Accessory Assortment), 69¢ (Tool Hanger).

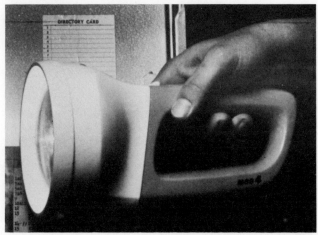

MOD 4 Cordless Rechargeable Lantern

BLACK FOREST ENTERPRISES

If you live or travel in the North Country, you need snowshoes to get the most out of your outdoor sports. This company offers tough, durable, and lightweight snowshoes with frames of aircraft-quality aluminum, coated with a special epoxy resin to protect and unitize the lacing, and to eliminate snow-sticking problems while preventing corrosion.

MOD 4 Drill

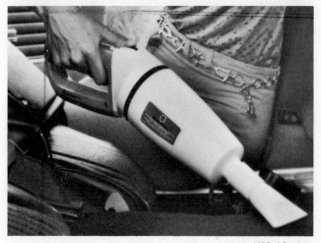

MOD 4 Spot Vac

Their snowshoes are also available in kit form for a bit of a savings. Kits come with everything required, including step-by-step instructions.

Cross-Country Snowshoe—This little snowshoe was made to fill the needs of those who leave the trails and travel cross-country. Their short design allows for effortless movement through thickly forested or brushy areas. It is also a working snowshoe, providing a short but stable base for absolute maneuverability. These shoes can be carried on a backpack or rucksack without projecting out where they will snag branches or brush. A substantial surface area and 4-inch front upturn give them the same

Cross-Country and Trail Snowshoes

deep powder capabilities as the Travel-Light Trail Snowshoe. Length: 32 inches. Width: 10½ inches. Weight: 3.6 pounds/pair. Carrying capacity: 80 to 250 pounds. Prices: $48/pair, $41/pair (kit).

Trail Snowshoe—Only slightly modified from the original snowshoe that Black Forest began making in 1962, this model has proven itself many times as being a fine all-around snowshoe. Its lightweight design and effortless maneuverability allow one to cover great distances with minimal fatigue. The sleek, narrow frame makes for an easy, natural walk. And the 46-inch length is sufficient to support a heavily laden packer, even in the softest powder snow. Also, the 5-inch front upturn reduces the probability of catching the toe in deep powder snow. Its balance is superb. Width: 9 inches. Weight: 4 pounds. Carrying capacity: 80 to 250 pounds. Prices: $48/pair, $41/pair (kit).

BUSHNELL OPTICAL CORP.

Nearly two dozen different models of binoculars are available from this well-known optical firm.

For other Bushnell products, see Chapter 4.

Custom Compact 6 × 25 Binoculars

Custom 7 × 35 Binoculars

Custom Compact 6×25 Binoculars—These binoculars are a startling achievement in miniaturization, with the power and clarity of large, conventional binoculars. Here is pocket-sized convenience with light-gathering capacity well within the requirements of the mature adult's eye pupil at the point of maximum expansion. For eyeglass and sunglass wearers, a unique high eye-point optical system combines with rubber roll-down eyecups to provide a full field of view. Light transmission is increased with magnesium fluoride coatings on all air-to-glass surfaces.

Built-in "Squint-Pruf" filters block reflected glare from water, sand, snow, and haze. Adjustable eyepiece compensates for difference in eye strength. Body is lightweight aluminum covered with nonslip gutta-percha. Comes complete with neck cord and deluxe soft zippered carrying case. Field: 420 feet. Exit pupil: 4.2mm. Height: 3 inches. Weight: 11 ounces. Price: $119.50.

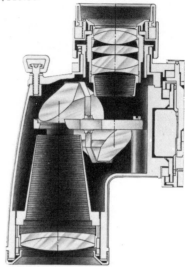

Cutaway of Bushnell Custom Binoculars

Custom 7×35 Binoculars—Top rated by Consumer Test Groups, the superb 7×35 Custom is the established favorite for general use. It's ideal for travel, spectator sports, hunting, birding, and nature study, and it focuses down to 14 feet for close-up study. Special optical elements combine with nonmarring nylon retractable eyecups to provide full wide-field viewing with or without eyeglasses. Now with the revolutionary Insta-Focus, these binoculars focus almost as fast as the human eye. Field at 1,000 yards: 420 feet. Exit pupil: 5mm. Height: 5 inches. Weight: 29 ounces. Prices: $169.50 (center focus), $179.50 (Insta-Focus).

DUNN'S SUPPLY STORE

This company offers a variety of products for outdoors people. One of their specialties is equipment for the care and training of dogs. So every dog owner will want to send for their free 65-page catalog.

Standard Tattoo with Positive Ear Release—This popular tattoo, used by leading breeders and associations, is made of a special aluminum alloy. It is very light, making it exceptionally easy to handle, yet is quite sturdy. It holds up to four digits with each inserted individually from the front. No blank digits necessary, and special design keeps digits from being placed in upside down. The positive ear release prevents the points of the digits from scratching the ear or blurring the tattoo mark. Complete outfit consists of pliers, set of 5/16- or ⅜-inch 0-9 digits, and 2-ounce jar of ink. Price: $15.

Dunn's Dog Houses—These fine dog houses are made of ⅝-inch AC exterior plywood and are easily assembled with 16¼-inch bolts. They're wide across the front with door to side for better dog protection from weather. Door is raised 4 inches to keep bedding in house. Model #1 weighs 65 pounds and is 27 inches wide by 22 inches deep by 22¾ inches high. Model #2 weighs 85 pounds and is 35 inches wide by 26 inches deep by 25 inches high. Shipped unpainted. Prices: $35 (#1), $45 (#2), F.O.B. Grand Junction, Tennessee.

Retriev-R-Trainer—For the amateur dog trainer, this item must rate at the very top in importance. It combines the sound of a shot with the shooting of the dummy at various distances, so that much time is saved

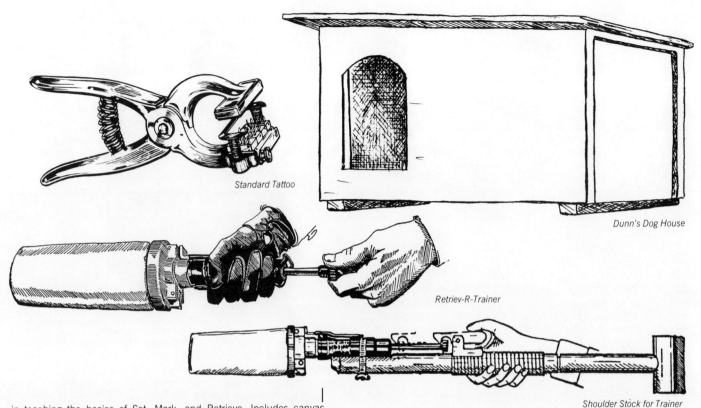

Standard Tattoo

Dunn's Dog House

Retriev-R-Trainer

Shoulder Stock for Trainer

in teaching the basics of Set, Mark, and Retrieve. Includes canvas dummy and sample charges. Prices: $45 (complete set), $8.50 (extra canvas dummy), $9.50 (red canvas dummy or PVC white foam dummy), $5.50 (100 rounds light load or heavy load charges).

Shoulder Stock for Trainer—This handy device allows cocking and firing with one hand, cuts recoil, and can be mounted or removed without tools. Price: $29.95.

EARLY WINTERS, LTD.

In addition to their fine camping and backpacking gear and outdoor clothing, Early Winters offers two sizes of lightweight snowshoes that should interest you North Country folks. Their Northern Lights snowshoes are available completely assembled or in kit form.

For other Early Winters products, see Chapters 7 and 8.

Northern Lights Snowshoes—Ten pounds of snowshoes on your feet equals 50 pounds of extra load on your back. Little wonder, then, why travel on Northern Lights seems so nearly effortless. A pair of Northern Lights 75s, complete with traction claws and bindings, weighs only 3 pounds 11 ounces. The 90-centimeter length weighs only 4 pounds 2 ounces per pair. These snowshoes feature custom-engineered high-strength nylon reinforced neoprene (not vinyl) decking. It is attached to the 6063-T832 aircraft-aluminum frame with carbon-filled nylon ties. What this means is that you cannot experience a catastrophic lacing failure. Though very strong, the ties are designed with a breaking strength just less than the tear strength of the expensive neoprene decking. If one of the unipoint ties breaks, the action of your snowshoes will remain unchanged. By carrying a couple of extra ties with you, you can quickly replace a lost tie while you're still out on the trip. Extra ties are included with each pair of Northern Lights. These snowshoes come equipped with a 1¼-inch deep, full-width claw for unexcelled climbing on icy or crusted snow. And they feature sure-fit, easy-to-use bindings that are true tracking and self-aligning and can be adjusted to fit any boot from 3½ to 5¼ inches wide. Two lengths are available: 75 centimeters (9×29½ inches) for heavy snows and hills and 90 centimeters (9×35½ inches) for lighter snow or heavier loads. Both sizes are avail-

Northern Lights Snowshoes

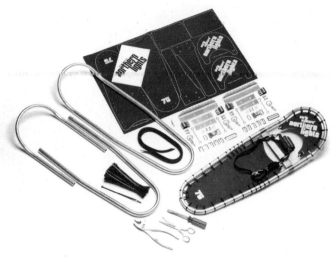

Northern Lights Kit

able in easy-to-make kits that require only a pair of pliers, screwdriver, and scissors for assembly. A pair of Northern Lights can be assembled from a kit in about two hours. Prices: $64.95 (75 centimeters), $75.95 (90 centimeters), $49.95 (75-centimeter kit), $59.95 (90-centimeter kit), all postpaid.

EDMUND SCIENTIFIC CO.

We could probably fill this chapter with Edmund's general interest and specialty items, but we only have room for a few representative products. To see what else they have to offer, mail them 50¢ for their catalog.

For other Edmund Scientific products in this book, check Chapters 2, 3, 4, 5, 7, and 10.

Home Weather Station

Pocket Lensatic Compass—Look through magnifying lens to find the direction in which you're heading. Hairline guide for sighting on distant objects while reading position in degrees or mils. Luminous four points of compass and reference marks on revolving dial for night use. Folds for compact carrying. Dial diameter: 1½ inches. Price: $7 postpaid.

Home Weather Station—This useful set includes a thermometer, hygrometer, and barometer all mounted in a deluxe, ebony grained, hand-rubbed case. Etched aluminum 5-inch dials rotate 90 degrees. Stands 21 inches tall. Price: $24.95 postpaid.

Weather Computer—This professional time-tested instrument is no gimmick. Use it with a barometer to forecast the weather. Predict wind speed and direction, temperature, cloud conditions, and precipitation within a 30-mile radius, twenty-four hours in advance. Great for hunters, fishermen, boaters, and other outdoorspeople. You get a 28-page book that includes a circular plastic slide rule computer (programmed for over 5,000 variations of input data), 13 pages of coded tables for interpreting data, and complete instructions. Can be effectively used in the United States, Canada, Europe, and Asia in all locations north of 25 degrees latitude. Price:N$10.25 postpaid.

8×20 Binoculars—These lightweight binoculars go anywhere and fit into a pocket or purse. They're great for any outdoor activity, and they

Pocket Lensatic Compass

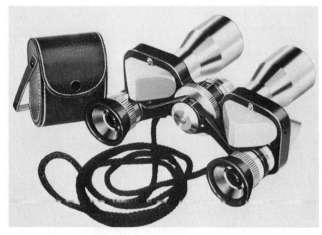

8 × 20 Binoculars

7 × 50 Binoculars

feature fully coated lenses and a brushed metal finish. Field of view at 1,000 yards: 262 feet. Weight: 7 ounces. Carrying case and straps included. Price: $49 postpaid.

8×30 Binoculars—These are great all-around binoculars to take on any outing. They are lightweight, ruggedly constructed, and easy to use. They feature fully coated optics with 8X Kellner-type eye lenses, European styling, fold-down rubber eyecups, and case. Dimensions: 4½ inches high by 6¼ inches wide. Weight: 19 ounces. Price: $39.50 postpaid.

7×50 Binoculars—At noon or dusk, these binoculars give you a bright clear image. A full 50mm lens and the versatility of viewing night or day makes it ideal for hunting, fishing, boating, and other outdoor sports. Fully coated optics with 7X Kellner-type eye lenses, European styling, fold-down rubber eyecups, and case are features of these bargain-priced binoculars. Dimensions: 7 inches high by 8 inches wide. Weight: 36 ounces. Price: $47.50 postpaid.

E-Z BIRD DOG TRAINING EQUIPMENT CO.

This company specializes in products for training hunting dogs. Their pens, carrying cages, and release traps are used by thousands of professional trainers and bird hunters throughout the country. If you have a pup to train, you will want to send for their free catalog.

Pigeon Capture Pen—If you know where pigeons are in great numbers (barns, houses, and other buildings), they can be trapped easily with this pen. And since pigeons are a nuisance wherever they congregate, you'll experience no difficulty obtaining permission to trap them. Pigeons are used by many professional trainers for training bird dogs, and this capture pen can be useful to you if you have a dog to train. It is constructed of sixteen-gauge 1×½-inch galvanized mesh. Size: 30× 16×8 inches. Prices: $19.95, $17.95 (when ordered with any three release traps).

Model 711 E-Z Launch Release Trap—This trap was designed for a trainer who was having difficulty getting his birds to fly. Birds have to fly when they're used in this trap, because when the release is tripped, the birds are tossed up to 5 feet into the air. It is constructed of twenty- to twenty-two-gauge cold rolled steel, plated to blend with cover and give

Pigeon Capture Pen

Launch Release Trap

longer life. An 8×21-inch Nylonnet launch pad launches birds on release. Prices: $19.95, $18.95 (if purchased by the pair), $17.95 (three or more).

E-Z MOUNT, INC.

This company produces do-it-yourself kits for mounting fish and birds. By the time this book rolls off the press, new E-Z Mount kits for mounting mammals, bird heads, and antlers, as well as a tanning kit should be available.

Bird Mounting Kit—Here's everything you need to prepare a professional mount in only a few hours of your time and with no special training or skills required. Kit includes all necessary tools, preservatives, setting agents, and complete step-by-step instructions. Price: $19.95.

Fish Mounting Kit—Now you can mount your own fish in about three hours of working time, plus drying time. Kit comes complete with preservative, expandable foam, setting agents, universal fish eye (others

225

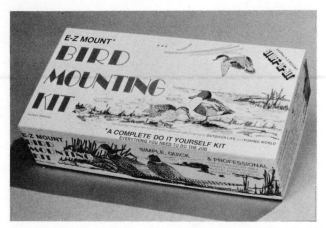

Bird Mounting Kit

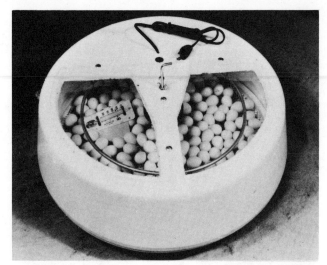

Hova-Bator Incubator

available), inflation bladder, plastic fin backing, primary oil paints, tools required and complete instructions. Price: $19.95.

FATSCO MANUFACTURING AND JOBBERS

This company offers a line of small cooking and heating stoves that are ideally suited for use in a hunting or fishing cabin. They're shipped in kit form and all are economically priced. One model that we think you will find particularly interesting incorporates an oil drum in its design.

They have no catalog, but will send their brochure on request.

Woodsman Stove

Water-All

Woodsman Stove Kit—This kit comes with everything you need, except the drum, cooking top, and elbow. Castings come with all holes necessary for proper assembly. Doors are surface ground and fitted to the frame. All parts can be attached to a 30- to 55-gallon drum (steel barrel) in a very short time. The resulting stove is ideal for camps, cabins, or shops. Doors are deep and will not warp. Those who wish to add a cooking top can order a drawing and six metal bolt-tabs. The top can then be made at your local sheet-metal shop. Prices: $52 (Woodsman Kit), 95¢ (cooking top drawing and bolt-tabs).

G. Q. F. MANUFACTURING CO.

A complete line of equipment for game-bird breeding comes from this company. So if you have plans for raising your own game birds for dog training or stocking purposes, be sure to send 50¢ for their catalog.

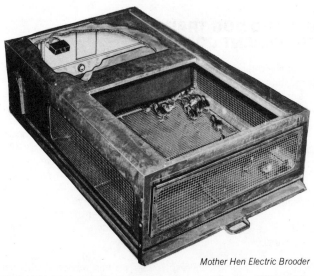

Mother Hen Electric Brooder

Model 501-W Hova-Bator Incubator—Like a mother hen, it "hovas" the eggs, gently warming them until they hatch. This is a scientifically designed incubator of new thermal plastic that will hold a constant temperature. With a built-in Magic Moisture Circle, it maintains constant humidity for setting and hatching of eggs. This new concept in low-cost still air incubators approaches the reliability of circulated air incubators. This model has a double-plate clear plastic picture window, ideal for observation. Weight: 4 pounds. Price: $22.95, plus $1.70 postage and handling.

Model 328 Water-All—This is a complete, self-contained, automatic waterer equipped with 3 feet of hose. Just connect it to any water spigot and your watering problems are over. Adjust for the depth desired, turn water on, and forget it. Made of durable plastic and brass—no more rusting out. Wide base gives adequate support to prevent larger birds from upsetting it. It is 9 inches in diameter, with 3-inch overall height and 2-inch bowl height, providing 28 inches of watering space. Price: $6.98.

Model G-401-N Mother Hen Electric Brooder—This new brooder has such time-tested features as two-section removable top, automatic heat control, removable wire floor and dropping pan, recessed sides for floor, and larger nichrome wire heating element (now 200 watts). Assembly is easy with panels sliding together without use of nuts and bolts. Dimensions: 36 inches long by 28 inches wide by 11 inches high. Approximate capacity through fourth week: 100 quail, 50 chukar or pheasants. Uses 110V AC. Price: $39.98. Add $8.50 for 220V.

IMPACT INDUSTRIES

A portable tree stand that can be used effortlessly by anybody is available from Impact. This sturdy stand should prove useful for observing and photographing game as well as for hunting with rifle or bow.

Other impact products can be found in Chapter 6.

Crow's Nest is ideal for hunting with rifle or bow

Crow's Nest is easy to pack

Crow's Nest—This new tree stand provides a safe, easy means of bow or rifle deer hunting from an elevated position, increasing the odds of seeing more deer at close range. The compact, portable ladder allows you to select the tree in the best spot for seeing and shooting. You are not restricted to easy-to-climb trees. If you hunt different areas during a season, this light and durable stand is ideal for you. The entire unit breaks down to fit into 27×16×9-inch pack. Five 27-inch sections easily slip into each other to make a 10-foot ladder. Nonslip rungs are 12 inches

wide and 12 inches apart. Hinged 15×22-inch platform has heavy-duty slip-hinge connection that automatically locks into the proper angle with the top ladder section. Constructed of high-strength, noncorrosive aluminum alloy for strength and long life, the Crow's Nest weighs only 22 pounds. A chain with locking device secures the platform to the tree to eliminate sway. Price: $65.

JET-AER CORP.

Among the many products for outdoors people that carry the G-96 brand are some that have been developed for the hunting dog owner. Additionally, Jet-Aer makes several different insect repellents that should be of interest to all outdoors people.

Other G-96 products can be found in Chapters 2, 4, 5, 8, and 9.

G-96 Hunting Dog Spray Bandage
G-96 Hunting Dog Odor Destroyer
G-96 Hunting Dog Dry Bath
G-96 Hunting Dog Flea and Tick Killer

G-96 Hunting Dog Flea, Tick, and Fly Repellent
G-96 Ticks Away
G-96 Insect Repellent

G-96 Hunting Dog Spray Bandage—This product is designed to be used as an in-the-field first-aid treatment until the animal can be given veterinarian care. It is ideal for use in the treatment of cuts, minor abrasions, skin irritations, and burns. It helps prevent infection and aids healing, and it soothes itching. It contains an effective blend of antiseptics and pain relievers and "artificial skin." Should be carried by everyone who hunts with dogs. Price: $1.69/6-ounce can.

G-96 Hunting Dog Odor Destroyer—This aerosol spray neutralizes offensive odors from dogs and their surroundings. It is safe and nontoxic to all animals. It will deodorize dog body odors, odors surrounding dog houses, or entire kennels. This newly developed formulation is extremely effective and long lasting. Price: $1.69/7-ounce can.

G-96 Hunting Dog Dry Bath with Flea and Tick Killer—Here's a product that enables you to wash your dog without water in all types of weather. Simply spray on and wipe dry. It will leave his coat clean and shiny. It will also kill fleas, lice, and ticks. Ideal for cold- or warm-weather application. Price: $1.39/7-ounce can.

G-96 Hunting Dog Flea and Tick Killer—This aerosol spray will kill fleas, ticks, and lice and will repel flies, mosquitoes, and gnats. It conditions the coat and checks scratching. It should be applied before Flea and Tick Repellent to kill any existing fleas and ticks hidden in dog's hair. Price: $1.29/6-ounce can.

G-96 Hunting Dog Flea, Tick and Fly Repellent—This product contains a unique blend of repellents combined with special coat conditioners. One easy application will keep your dog free from annoying insects while he is hunting, training, or playing. It will also condition his coat and keep it bright. Price: $1.49/7-ounce can.

G-96 Ticks Away—Here's a repellent for all outdoors people. It contains a unique blend of insect repellent ingredients guaranteed to repel ticks, chiggers, and biting flies. For fishermen, hunters, and campers. Price: $1.49/6-ounce can.

G-96 Insect Repellent—This insect repellent keeps outdoors people free from mosquitoes, biting flies, ticks, chiggers, and other small flying insects. It is pleasantly scented and nongreasy. Spray lasts a long time. Available in pocket aerosol or camp-size can. Prices: $1.25/3-ounce can, $1.49/5-ounce can.

MASTER LOCK CO.

Master, of course, makes all sorts of locks, but their new Armorlock is perfect for the outdoorsman who needs to lock up a boat, trailer, shed full of gear, or the hunting and fishing cabin.

Other Master lock information can be found in Chapter 4.

Master Armorlock

Master Armorlock defies bolt cutters

Master Armorlock No. 37-D—Master's newest high-powered answer to rip-off artists equipped with bolt cutters and hacksaws, Armorlock protects with brains as well as brawn. It provides far more protection against prying and cutting than other locks. Roller bearing shackle guard frustrates sawing attempts—blade slips without cutting. Heavy shackle armor is so thick it won't fit the jaws of most bolt cutters. A super lock for guarding trailers on or off vehicles. Or combine Armorlock with a sturdy Master Crimefighter cable, chain, or hasp to get extra protection when locking up boats, bikes, sheds, etc. It's a terrific security buy at a low price everyone can afford. Also available in keyed-alike models. Fits openings ½ inch in diameter or larger. Shackle guard is removable to accommodate trailer hitch openings to ¼-inch diameter. Master quality features throughout. Price: $5.95.

McCULLOCH CORP.

It's a real pleasure to include in our coverage of products for the outdoorsman a company that is bold enough to say that it is going to "ignore inflation and lower its prices." That's precisely what McCulloch did on February 1, 1977. And we're not talking about token price reductions. Prices were rolled back on all their chain saws, the greatest reduction being on their popular Mini Mac 25. The suggested retail price on that saw was $114.95, but the company lopped off a whopping 21 percent for a new price of $89.95. The price on the Mini Mac 30 was reduced from $129.95 to $109.95.

Here's a sampling of the high quality you are going to get for those low prices.

Mini Mac 25—Here's the perfect tote-along chain saw that can pull rugged duty around camp or cabin. It features a 1.8 cubic inch engine, automatic plus manual chain oiling, and Chain Brake—the safety feature that helps protect the operator from kickback. It has a 10-inch bar that will handle most cutting jobs for the outdoorsman. Price: $89.95.

Mini Mac 25

Mini Mac 35AS—This new Mini Mac makes quick work of transforming a fallen tree into firewood. The saw features a unique semiautomatic chain sharpening system, 2 cubic inch engine, and a 14-inch bar. And, as with all McCullochs, it has Chain Brake to help protect the operator from kickback. Price: $169.95.

Chain Saw Carrying Case—Protection and convenience are offered McCulloch chain saw users with this new carrying case featuring a separating bar guard that stays with the saw when it is removed from the case. Room is provided for tools and accessories. Two new cases are available to accommodate light to medium McCulloch saws. The Mini Mac Carrying Case will carry any Mini Mac chain saw with a choice of 12- or 14-inch bar guards. The Mac 10 Carrying Case is designed for McCulloch's SP 40, Pro 10-10, Pro Mac 55, or 7-10A chain saws, with a choice of either 14- or 16-inch bar guards. Prices: $21.95 (Mini Mac Case), $24.95 (Mac 10 Case).

G. J. MILLER MANUFACTURING CO.

From this company comes the familiar E-Z-Matic Pet Doors that are advertised in the major outdoor magazines. Information on these Pet Doors is mailed free to anyone who writes, but Mrs. Miller asks that you please send a large (No. 10) self-addressed and stamped envelope with

E-Z-Matic Pet Door

your inquiry. And she'll see to it that all inquiries are answered within twenty-four hours.

E-Z-Matic Pet Doors—Any size dog can use an E-Z-Matic door with ease, and there's practically no training time. Pets love it and take to it on their own almost instantly. You can install the E-Z-Matic Pet door over any opening. It takes just minutes with nothing more than a screwdriver. And the installation looks professional—it actually adds to the appearance of your home or kennel. The tough, long-lasting rubber is a special chemical compound designed for E-Z-Matic Pet Doors. Completely weather resistant, it will operate equally well in either extremely hot or extremely cold temperatures. Model A is for small and medium-size dogs (beagles, spaniels, etc.) and is 13×21¾ inches overall with a 10×18½-inch opening. Model M is for large dogs (Labrador retrievers, setters, etc.) and is 14¾×24 inches overall with a 12×21½-inch opening. Two other models are available for larger or smaller animals. Prices: $24.90 postpaid (Model A), $29.90 postpaid (Model M).

NETCRAFT CO.

Netcraft is predominantly a mail-order supplier of fine fishing tackle, kits, and tools for fishermen. But there is one little item in their catalog that you don't have to be a fisherman to use and enjoy—the Luhr Jensen "Little Chief" Smoker.

If you've seen these electric smokers and have been skeptical about them—wondering if they really are all they're cracked up to be—you aren't alone. We had the same misgivings until about five years ago when we were living in Alaska and our fishing partner and next door neighbor, Jim Martin, bought one and started smoking salmon on the back deck that we shared. The unbelievable aroma of smoking salmon was almost reason enough for us to buy our own smoker, and when we tasted the finished product that's exactly what we did. And that Little Chief has paid for itself many times over.

For other Netcraft products, check Chapter 2.

Electric Smoker—This useful appliance uses hickory chips that are furnished with it and it imparts delicious flavor to fish and game. It operates in a garage, fireplace, or outdoors and will smoke up to 20 pounds of meat at a time for less than a penny an hour. It has an all-aluminum exterior with a chrome-plated interior rack that is removable through the

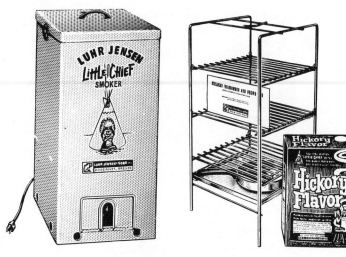

Electric Smoker

top. Chip pan inserts through a side opening to rest atop the heating element. Comes with a great little book of recipes and hints on smoking your catch. Netcraft price: $25.95.

ORVIS

In addition to a fine selection of hunting and fishing gear and top-quality outdoor clothing, Orvis offers binoculars and a variety of gift items. Their best-selling gift items are their beautiful handmade Loop Optic Glasses. We have two sets of these glasses and plan to gradually complete the entire collection.

Orvis Binoculars

Orvis Binoculars—These binoculars are just nothing to carry. So, as a result, you *do* carry them. You can always have them with you, because they slip into an ordinary shirt pocket. Of the finest traditional quality German optics, Orvis arranged for their exclusive importation from West Germany. They are available with either a soft or hard leather case and with flat eyecups for use over eyeglasses. Magnification: 8X. Front lens diameter: 25mm. Field of vision at 1,000 yards: 354 feet. Weight: 7 ounces. Prices: $172.50 (soft case), $177.75 (hard case), $174.50 (flat eyecups and soft case), $179.95 (flat eyecups and hard case).

Loop Optic Glasses—Individually hand-blown quartz glass in the delightful nubbly "loop optic" surface so comfortable to hold, with authentic full color paintings fired on permanently, these glasses are available in sets of eight game birds, or eight ducks, or eight big-game fish, or eight trout, or eight game animals, or eight songbirds. Game sets are by wildlife artist Ned Smith; songbirds are by Mary Sargeant. A set of seven

Orvis pet trout flies and a "garden hackle" (total eight) is available in all except the 15-ounce Roly Poly and 11-ounce Straight Sided. Artwork on these is by fly-tyer Dave Whitlock. The new Iced Tea glasses are available only in sets of game birds, ducks, songbirds, or trout flies. Sizes/styles: 12-ounce Highball; 15-ounce Roly Poly; 10-ounce Roly Poly; 11-ounce Straight Sided; 18-ounce Iced Tea. Price: $29.50/set of 8.

RANGING, INC.

Ranging offers a complete line of rangefinders that are useful to hunters—bow and rifle—as well as to boaters, hikers, and handymen. With a good rangefinder you can determine how far, how high, or how wide.

Ranging 610 Rangematic

Ranging 610 Rangematic—This new rangefinder tells your exact distance to target and game, to every trail, tree, and bush near your stand. No guessing, no pacing off, no sound, scent, or movement to spook your quarry. Just sight through the 3X eyepiece, focus your target, and read the exact yardage on the indicator. Guaranteed more accurate than you can hold, 16 through 200 yards. The compact Ranging 610 weighs 16 ounces and comes with a two-year limited warranty. Padded vinyl carrying case is optional. Prices: $39.95 (Ranging 610), $8.95 (carrying case).

Ranging 1000 Rangematic

Ranging 1000 Rangematic MK 5—The Ranging 1000 is the new name for the "Mark V" that hunters have used for years. It has dramatically increased the number of first-shot hits for long-range shooters and has helped to provide success on many big-game hunts. Just sight your target through the viewfinder, focus until the double image becomes one, and read the scale. It is accurate to within 1 yard at 100 yards, 25 yards at 500 yards. At 22 ounces, it is lightweight but rugged. It is thermally stable and shock resistant. It comes with a two-year limited warranty. Padded vinyl case is optional. Prices: $52.95 (Ranging 1000), $8.95 (carrying case).

REDFIELD

Besides the top-quality rifle scopes and spotting scopes known to hunters and target shooters throughout the country, Redfield also offers binoculars and monoculars.

For other Redfield optical instruments, see Chapter 4.

8-Power Binoculars—Ideal for hunters, backpackers, fishermen, and boaters, these binoculars feature roof prism optics that make them ex-

8-Power Binoculars
8-Power Widefield Monocular

ceptionally lightweight. They offer brilliant clarity and sharp resolution, as well as individual eye focus. Neoprene eyepiece cup shields out random sun rays. Comes with carrying case and lanyard. Objective diameter: 20mm. Dimensions folded: 1⁷/₃₂ inches high by 2⁷/₃₂ inches wide by 3⅝ inches long. Weight: 5.4 ounces. Price: $97.50.

Widefield 8-Power Monocular—For the sportsman who desires a wide-range field of view, Redfield has introduced the unique 8×24 Widefield monocular. With the Widefield you actually see 20 percent wider field of view than with a standard round eyepiece monocular. Comes with case and lanyard. Weight: 3 ounces. Price: $64.

SPORTING BOOK SERVICE

Here's another company offering books on just about any outdoor subject you can think of. Some are rare collector's items, and others are just outdoor books that might be hard to locate elsewhere.

The company has been in business for thirty years and maintains a stock of some 7,000 volumes. Catalogs are issued annually in two volumes: *A to K* in the fall and *L to Z* in the spring.

Following is a small sampling of what you can expect to find.

#3 Ackley, Parker 0.—Handbook for Shooters and Reloaders, Vol. II. Inscribed. Salt Lake City, 1966. Dust jacket. Price: $6.

#480 Freemantle, T. F.—The Book of the Rifle. Illustrated. Inner hinge weak. 8vo. London, 1901. Scarce. Price: $20.

#823 Koch, Ed.—Fishing the Midge. Illustrated. New. Dust jacket. Rockville Centre, N.Y., 1972. Price: $7.95.

#863 Elliot, Bob—Bass Fishing in New England. Illustrated. 8vo. cloth. Dust jacket. New. Lexington, Massachusetts 1973. Price: $6.50.

TASCO SALES, INC.

The Tasco line of binoculars is an extensive one, with models designed to fit any sportsman's needs.

For a description of Tasco's hunting and shooting optics, see Chapter 4.

#108 Executive Electric Zoom 7–15×35mm—Battery-powered convenience opens up new vistas of viewing pleasure. Zoom from 7 to 15 power at the touch of a switch. These binoculars feature fully coated optics, specially designed battery-powered zoom eye lenses, and coated BK-7 Porro prisms. The lightweight, American-style body is black with bright trim on focus wheels and diopters. Penlite batteries are included. Other features include power indicator window, fold-down rubber eyecups, rubber objective rims, battery test light, and camera tripod adapter. Comes with case. Dimensions: 5½ inches high by 7 inches wide. Weight: 38 ounces. Price: $199.95.

#306 Sea Dog 7×50mm—At high noon or eventide, an eyeful of pleasure is yours. Whether you are boating, hunting, or just scanning the beach, the Sea Dog gives you added clarity of vision with a full 50mm lens

and the versatility of excellent viewing night or day. Features include fully coated optics, 7-power Kellner-type eye lenses, coated BK-7 Porro prisms, European style, black finish with fold-down rubber eyecups. Dimensions: 7 inches high by 8 inches wide. Weight: 36 ounces. Comes with case. Price: $69.95.

CARL ZEISS, INC.

If you're looking for superior optical and physical qualities in binoculars, you shouldn't overlook what Zeiss has to offer. Their binoculars are among the finest available anywhere in the world. In addition to a wide selection of binoculars for every outdoor need, Zeiss has plenty of helpful literature to aid you in your selection and a catalog that details all specifications of the Zeiss line.

Dialyt 8 × 30B

Dialyt 8×30B/GA I.F.—Hunting is often at its best at the two extremes of the day—dawn and dusk. Light is limited then. And the hunter needs binoculars designed to make the most of whatever little there is. Zeiss Dialyt 8×30B binoculars take full advantage of the most negligible scintilla of light, revealing the object bright and clear. This is sure proof of the flawless quality that has made Zeiss optics famous. For the hunter whose first rule is "don't violate the silence," Zeiss has the rubber armored binoculars, which not only eliminate the sound of metal, but are shockproof and totally waterproof. Field of view at 1,000 yards: 360 feet. Dimensions: 5¼ inches high by 4½ inches wide. Weight: 20.1 ounces. Price: $419.

Porro 7×50B/GA I.F.—The ever-present motion on waterways makes your hands unsteady on small craft, and even on large ones. So the boating person must allow for shifting movements of the body. Here is a pair of binoculars especially suited for use on the water. They're shockproof, waterproof, and corrosionproof. And they're guaranteed to stay that way for life. Rubber armor protects them against damage. Field of view at

Porro 7 × 50B

Dialyt 10 × 40B

Mini 8 × 20B

1,000 yards: 390 feet. Dimensions: 5 inches high by 8½ inches wide. Weight: 41.3 ounces. Price: $675.

Dialyt 10×40B/GA C.F.—The naturalist wants to see every detail of what he's looking at. He needs binoculars that not only enlarge, but give a clear, undistorted image, its colors faithful to the slightest nuance. This is the image Zeiss assures him. With Zeiss, quality is more than a word. It's a historic achievement, culminating 130 years of scientific effort. The animal world comes into full view at the seeing end of these binoculars. Field of view at 1,000 yards: 330 feet. Dimensions: 5¾ inches high by 4½ inches wide. Weight: 24 ounces. Price: $629.

Mini 8×20B C.F.—This incredible Zeiss Mini sees everything yet weighs nothing. It has become a favorite with outdoors people who regard as little as an extra ounce a burden. Miniature in everything but perform-ance, it delivers all the brilliance, contrast, image quality, and resolution you expect and get from its big brothers. Field of view at 1,000 yards: 345 feet. Dimensions: 3½ inches high by 3¾ inches wide. Weight: 6 ounces. Price: $249.

INDEX OF COMPANIES

Following is a list of addresses for all the companies described in the previous chapters. If there is a charge for a company's literature, we have put that amount in parenthesis after the zip code. If SASE appears after the zip, send a large (No. 10) self-addressed and stamped envelope. If nothing appears after the zip, you can assume that the material is free, although that is subject to change at any time.

AMF Crestliner
609 N.E. 13th Ave.
Little Falls, MN 56435

Action Lures
P.O. Box 10529
Jackson, MS 30209

S.S. Adams Co.
P.O. Box 369
Neptune, NJ 07753

Albright Products Co.
P.O. Box 1144
Portola, CA 96122

Alexandria Drafting Co.
417 Clifford Ave.
Alexandria, VA 22305

Alladin Laboratories, Inc.
620 S. 8th St.
Minneapolis, MN 55404

Allen Archery
200 Washington St.
Billings, MO 65610

The Allen Co., Inc.
2330 Midway Blvd.
Broomfield, CO 80020

Don Allen
Rt. #1
Northfield, MN 55057 ($1.00)

Allied Sports Co.
P.O. Box 251
Eufaula, AL 36027

Al's Goldfish Lure Co.
P.O. Box 13
Indian Orchard, MA 01151

Altra, Inc.
5441 Western Ave.
Boulder, CO 80301

Alumacraft Boat Co.
315 W. St. Julien St.
St. Peter, MN 56082

American Honda Motor Corp.
100 W. Alondra Blvd.
Gardena, CA 90247

American Import Co.
1167 Mission St.
San Francisco, CA 94103

American Sales & Mfg. Co.
P.O. Box 677
Laredo, TX 78040 ($1.00)

America's Cup
1443 So. Potrero Ave.
So. El Monte, CA 91733

Ande, Inc.
P.O. Box 8366
West Palm Beach, FL 33407

Anderson Archery Corp.
Grand Ledge, MI 48837

Andy's Flytying
P.O. Box 30018—Station B
Calgary, Alberta, Canada T2M 4N7

Angler's & Shooter's Bookshelf
Goshen, CT 06756 ($2.00)

Apollo Distributing Co.
245 Park Ave.
Torrington, CT 06790

Applied Oceanographic Tech. Corp.
199 Warfield Way
Southampton, NY 11968

Aquabug International, Inc.
100 Merrick Rd.
Rockville Centre, NY 11570

Aquasonic Lures, Inc.
P.O. Box 118
Cibolo, TX 78108 ($3.00)

The Armoury, Inc.
Rt. #202
New Preston, CT 06777

Arnold Tackle Corp.
100 Commercial Ave.
Paw Paw, MI 49079

Artistic Arms, Inc.
P.O. Box 23
Hoagland, IN 46745

Ashley Products
Box 175
Analachin, NY 13732

Auto-Gaff, Inc.
4 Reynolds St.
East Providence, RI 02914

Balcar Recreational Products
P.O. Box 162
Carrollton, TX 75006

Barnes Bullets
P.O. Box 215
American Fork, UT 84003

Bass Attacker
Box 557
Florissant, MO 63033

Eddie Bauer
P.O. Box 3700
Seattle, WA 98124

Bayliner Marine Corp.
P.O. Box 24467
Seattle, WA 98134

Bead Chain Tackle Co.
Bridgeport, CT 06605

L.L. Bean, Inc.
Freeport, ME 04033

Bear Archery
R.R. #1
Grayling, MI 49738

Beckel Canvas Products
P.O. Box 20491
Portland, OR 97220

Beckson Mfg., Inc.
P.O. Box 3336
Bridgeport, CT 06605 (25¢)

Beeman's, Inc.
47 Paul Dr.
San Rafael, CA 94903 ($1.50)

Berkley & Co.
Spirit Lake, IA 51360

BernzOmatic Corp.
740 Driving Park Ave.
Rochester, NY 14613

Bill's Wholesale Bait
41 Grapevine Rd.
Levittown, PA 19057

Black & Decker Mfg. Co.
Towson, MD 21204

Black Forest Enterprises
Box 1007
Nevada City, CA 95959

Blue and Gray Products, Inc.
817 E. Main St.
Bradford, PA 16701

Blue Hole Canoe Co.
P.O. Box 51
Sunbright, TN 37872

Boatmen's Industries, Inc.
4101 N.W. 37th Ave.
Miami, FL 33142

Bomber Bait Co.
P.O. Box 1058
Gainesville, TX 76240

Bonair Boats, Inc.
15501 W. 109th St.
Lenexa, KS 66219

Bonanza Sports Mfg.
412 Western Ave.
Faribault, MN 55021

Bowen Knife Co.
P.O. Drawer 590
Blackshear, GA 31516

Bowhunter's Discount Warehouse
2285 W. Harrisburg Pike
Middletown, PA 17057 ($1.00)

Braun North America
55 Cambridge Pkwy.
Cambridge, MA 02142

Bremer Mfg. Co., Inc.
Rt. #2, Box 100
Elkhart Lake, WI 53020

Bridgeport Silverware Mfg. Corp.
P.O. Box K
Bridgeport, CT 06605

Brocks Electronics Corp.
12 Blanchard Rd.
Burlington, MA 01803

L. E. "Red" Brown
3203 Del Amo Blvd.
Lakewood, CA 90712 ($2.00)

Browning
Rt. #1
Morgan, UT 84050

B-Square
P.O. Box 11281
Fort Worth, TX 76109

Buck Knives
P.O. Box 1267
El Cajon, CA 92022

Maynard P. Buehler, Inc.
17 Orinda Hwy.
Orinda, CA 94563

Burke Fishing Lures
1969 S. Airport Rd.
Traverse City, MI 49684

Burris Co.
P.O. Box 747
Greeley, CO 80631 (25¢)

Bushnell Optical Corp.
2828 E. Foothill Blvd.
Pasadena, CA 91107

CAF Industries, Inc.
P.O. Box 1625
Rockford, IL 61110

C-H Tool & Die Corp.
P.O. Box "L"
Owen, WI 54460

Camillus Cutlery Co.
Camillus, NY 13031 ($1.00)

Canon USA, Inc.
10 Nevada Dr.
Lake Success, NY 11040

Capitol Plastics of Ohio, Inc.
333 Van Camp Rd.
Bowling Green, OH 43402

Carroll's Archery Products
59½ S. Main
Moab, UT 84532

Century Tool and Mfg. Co.
P.O. Box 188
Cherry Valley, IL 61016

Challenger Mfg. Corp.
118 Pearl St.
Mt. Vernon, NY 10550

Chronograph Specialists
P.O. Box 5005
Santa Ana, CA 92704

Chrysler Corp.
Marine Products Operation
P.O. Box 2641
Detroit, MI 48231

Cisco Kid Tackle, Inc.
2630 N.W. First Ave.
Boca Raton, FL 33432

Clear View Mfg. Co., Inc.
20821 Grand River
Detroit, MI 48219

Dale Clemens Custom Tackle
Rt. #2, Box 850-A
Wescosville, PA 18106

Clinton Engines Corp.
Maquoketa, IA 52060

Coleman Co., Inc.
250 N. St. Francis
Wichita, KA 67201

Colt Industries
Firearms Division
150 Huyshope Ave.
Hartford, CT 06102

Compass Electronics Corp.
P.O. Box 366
Forest Grove, OR 97116

Competitive Camera Corp.
157 W. 30th St.
New York, NY 10001 ($1.00)

Corbin Mfg. & Supply, Inc.
P.O. Box 44
North Bend, OR 97459 ($2.00)

Coren's Rod & Reel Service
6619 N. Clark St.
Chicago, IL 60626

Cortland Line Co.
P.O. Box 1362
Cortland, NY 13045

Cosom
Space Center, Suite 202
7317 Cahill Rd.
Edina, MN 55435

Cossack Caviar, Inc.
101 South Dakota St.
Seattle, WA 98134

Creative Sports Enterprises
2333 Boulevard Circle
Walnut Creek, CA 94595

Creek Chub Baits
Garrett, IN 46738 (35¢)

Creme Lure Co.
P.O. Box 87
Tyler, TX 75710

Cuba Specialty Mfg. Co., Inc.
P.O. Box 38
Houghton, NY 14744

J. Lee Cuddy Associates, Inc.
145 N.E. 79th St.
Miami, FL 33138

Earl T. Cureton
Rt. #2, Box 388
Willoughby Rd.
Bulls Gap, TN 37711

Dan-D Custom Knives
P.O. Box 2F
Del Norte, CO 81132 ($1.00)

Danner Shoe Mfg. Co.
P.O. Box 22204
Portland, OR 97222

Davis Optical Co.
Box 6
Winchester, IN 47394

Dayton Marine Products
7565 E. McNichols Rd.
Detroit, MI 48234

Dayton Traister Co.
P.O. Box 593
Oak Harbor, WA 98277

Decker Shooting Products
1729 Laguna Ave.
Schofield, WI 54476

D'Holder Custom Knives
6808 N. 30th Dr.
Phoenix, AZ 85017

Jack.Dickerson's, Inc.
Lake of the Ozarks
Camdenton, MO 65020

Dickey Tackle Co.
Land O'Lakes, WI 54540 (25¢)

Doll Tackle, Inc.
P.O. Box 2206
Hot Springs, AR 71901

Donzi Marine
2940 N.E. 188th St.
No. Miami Beach, FL 33180

Dunn's Supply Store
Grand Junction, TN 38039

DuPont Explosives Products
Wilmington, DE 19898

Dutton-Lainson Co.
Hastings, NE 68901

J. Dye Enterprises
1707 Childerlee Ln., N.E.
Atlanta, GA 30329

Earlybird Co.
P.O. Box 1485
Boise, ID 83701

Early Winters, Ltd.
110 Prefontaine, So.
Seattle, WA 98104 ($1.00)

Eastman Kodak Co.
343 State St.
Rochester, NY 14650

Edmund Scientific Co.
101 E. Gloucester Pike
Barrington, NJ 08007 (50¢)

Edwards Recoil Reducer
269 Herbert St.
Alton, IL 62002

Lou J. Eppinger Mfg. Co.
6340 Schaefer Hwy.
Dearborn, MI 48126

Evinrude
P.O. Box 663
Milwaukee, WI 53201

E-Z Bird Dog Training
   Equipment Co.
P.O. Box 333
Morganfield, KY 42437

E-Z Mount, Inc.
5050 Excelsior Blvd., Suite 209
Minneapolis, MN 55416

Eze-Lap Diamond Products
Box 2229
Westminster, CA 92683

Factory Distributors
500 S. 7th St.
Ft. Smith, AR 72901

Reinhart Fajen, Inc.
P.O. Box 338
Warsaw, MO 65355 ($3.00)

Falling Block Works, Inc.
P.O. Box 22
Troy, MI 48099

Fatsco Manufacturers & Jobbers
251 Fair Ave.
Benton Harbor, MI 49022

Featherweight Products
3454-58 Ocean View Blvd.
Glendale, CA 91208

Federal Cartridge Corp.
2700 Foshay Tower
Minneapolis, MN 55402

Fenwick
14799 Chestnut St.
Westminster, CA 92683 (25¢)

Fin & Feather Mfg. Co.
P.O. Box 179
Marshall, TX 75670

Fish Hawk Electronics
4220 Waller Dr. (Ridgefield)
Crystal Lake, IL 60014

Fleetwood Enterprises, Inc.
P.O. Box 7638
Riverside, CA 92503

Fly Fisherman's Bookcase & Tackle
  Service
3890 Stewart Rd.
Eugene, OR 97402 ($1.50)

G & H Decoys, Inc.
P.O. Box 937
Henryetta, OK 74437

G.Q.F. Mfg. Co.
P.O. Box 8152
Savannah, GA 31402 (50¢)

GAF Corporation
140 W. 51st St.
New York, NY 10020

A. J. Gallager
319 Delsea Dr.
Westville, NJ 08093

Gander Mountain, Inc.
Box 248
Wilmot, WI 53192

Gapen's World Of Fishin', Inc.
Hwy. 10
Big Lake, MN 55309

The Garcia Corp.
329 Alfred Ave.
Teaneck, NJ 07666 ($1.50)

Gerber Legendary Blades
14200 S.W. 72nd Ave.
Portland, OR 97223

Gerry
5450 No. Valley Hwy.
Denver, CO 80216

Glen-L
9152 Rosecrans
Bellflower, CA 90706 ($1.00 ea.)

Goddards
473 Durham Ave.
Eugene, OR 97404 (50¢)

Golden Key Archery
1851 S. Orange Ave.
Monterey, CA 91754

Graphic Imports
2632 S. King St.
Honolulu, HI 96814

Green River Forge, Ltd.
P.O. Box 885
Springfield, OR 97477 ($1.00)

Grumman Boats
Marathon, NY 13803

Gudebrod Bros. Silk Co., Inc.
12 So. 12th St.
Philadelphia, PA 19107 (50¢)

Hanimex (U.S.A.), Inc.
1801 Touhy Ave.
Elk Grove Village, IL 60007

Harben Mfg. Co.
2101 N. Green Bay Rd.
Racine, WI 53405

Harmony Enterprises, Inc.
704 Main Ave. North
Harmony, MN 55939

Robert W. Hart & Son, Inc.
401 Montgomery St.
Nexcopeck, PA 18635

Heath Co.
Benton Harbor, MI 49022

James Heddon's Sons
Dowagiac, MI 49047

Hefner Plastics, Inc.
P.O. Box 638
Troup, TX 75789

Hensley & Gibbs
P.O. Box 10
Murphy, OR 97533 (SASE)

Hercules, Inc.
910 Market St.
Wilmington, DE 19899

George Herron
920 Murrah Ave.
Aiken, SC 29801

High Standard
31 Prestige Park Circle
East Hartford, CT 06108 ($1.00)

Bob Hinman Outfitters
1217 W. Glen Ave.
Peoria, IL 61614

Hirsch-Weis
5203 S.E. Johnson Cr. Blvd.
Portland, OR 97206

Hodgdon Powder Co., Inc.
P.O. Box 2905
Shawnee Mission, KS 66202

J.B. Holden Co.
Box 393
Plymouth, MI 48170

Holsclaw Bros., Inc.
P.O. Box 4128
Evansville, IN 47711

Hornady Mfg. Co.
P.O. Box 1848
Grand Island, NE 68801

Jack Howard Archery Co.
Washington Star Rt., Box 220
Nevada City, CA 95959 ($1.00)

Don Hume Leather Goods, Inc.
Box 351
Miami, OK 74354

Hypark Specialty Co.
5800 High Park Dr.
Minnetonka, MN 55343

Igloo Corp.
P.O. Box 19322
Houston, TX 77024

Impace Industries
7020 Packer Dr.
Wausau, WI 54401

Imtra Corp.
151 Mistic Ave.
Medford, MA 02155

Indian Ridge Traders Co.
Room 109
22720 Woodward Ave.
Ferndale, MI 48220

Ray Jefferson
Main & Cotton Sts.
Philadelphia, PA 19127 ($1.00)

Jennings Compound Bow, Inc.
28756 North Castaic Canyon Rd.
Valencia, CA 91355

Jet-Aer Corp.
100 Sixth Ave.
Paterson, NJ 07524

Iver Johnson's Arms, Inc.
109 River St.
Fitchburg, MA 01420

Louis Johnson Co.
Box 21
Amsterdam, MO 64723

Johnson Outboards
200 Sea-Horse Dr.
Waukegan, IL 60085

Kelty Pack, Inc.
P.O. Box 639
Sun Valley, CA 91352

Hans Klepper Corp.
35 Union Sq. West
New York, NY 10003

Kolpin Mfg., Inc.
P.O. Box 231
Berlin, WI 54923

Kris Mounts
108 Lehigh St.
Johnstown, PA 15905

Kristal Kraft, Inc.
P.O. Box 787
Palmetto, FL 33561

Lakes Illustrated
Box 4854 GS
Springfield, MO 65804

Land & Sea International
720 Laurelwood Rd.
Santa Clara, CA 95050

George Lawrence Co.
306 S.W. 1st Ave.
Portland, OR 97204

Lazy Daze
4303 E. Mission
Pomona, CA 91766

Lazy Ike Corp.
P.O. Box 1177
Fort Dodge, IA 50501

Leupold & Stevens, Inc.
P.O. Box 688
Beaverton, OR 97005

Jimmy Lile
Rt. #1
Russelville, AR 72801

Limit Mfg. Corp.
Box 369
Richardson, TX 75080 ($1.00)

Lisk-Fly Mfg. Co.
P.O. Box 5126
Greensboro, NC 27403

Loop-A-Line, Inc.
Export Division

P.O. Box 42376
Cincinnati, OH 45242

Lowrance Electronics Mfg. Corp.
12000 E. Skelly Dr.
Tulsa, OK 74128

Lund American, Inc.
New York Mills, MN 56567

Lyman
Rt. #147
Middlefield, CT 06455

M-F Manufacturing Co., Inc.
P.O. Box 13442
Ft. Worth, TX 76118

Magic Worm Bedding Co., Inc.
P.O. Box 38
Amherst Junction, WI 54407

Mallardtone Game Calls
2901 16th St.
Moline, IL 61265

Mann's Bait Co.
P.O. Box 604
Eufaula, AL 36027 ($1.00)

Marble Arms Corp.
Box 111
Gladstone, MI 49837

Mariner Outboards
Division of Brunswick Corp.
Fond Du Lac, WI 54935

Marksman Products
P.O. Box 2983
Torrance, CA 90509

Marlin Firearms Co.
100 Kenna Dr.
North Haven, CT 06473

Martin Reel Co.
P.O. Drawer 8
Mohawk, NY 13407

Martin Tackle & Mfg. Co.
512 Minor Ave. North
Seattle, WA 98109

Master Lock Co.
2600 N. 32nd St.
Milwaukee, WI 53210

Mayville Engineering Co.
P.O. Box 267
Mayville, WI 53050

Harvey McBurnette
Rt. #4, Box 337
Piedmont, AL 36272 ($2.00)

McCulloch Corp.
P.O. Box 92180
Los Angeles, CA 90009

Michaels of Oregon
P.O. Box 13010
Portland, OR 97213

Michi-Craft Corp.
19995 19-Mile Rd.
Big Rapids, MI 49307

Micro Motion
2700 29th St.
Boulder, CO 80301

Mildrum Mfg. Co.
East Berlin, CT 06023

Miller Fishing Tackle
Box 2995
Bell Gardens, CA 90201

G.J. Miller Mfg. Co.
R.R. #3, Box 227, Dept. W
Dubuque, IA 52001 (SASE)

Mill Run Products Co.
1360 W. 9th St.
Cleveland, OH 44113

Minox U.S.A.
Rockleigh, NJ 07647

Mirro Aluminum Co.
P.O. Box 409
Manitowoc, WI 54220

Mirro Marine Division
Oconto, WI 54153

W.F. Moran, Jr.
P.O. Box 68
Braddock Hts., MD 21714

O. Mustad & Son (U.S.A.), Inc.
P.O. Box 838
Auburn, NY 13021

S.D. Myres Saddle Co.
P.O. Box 9776
El Paso, TX 79988

National Archery Co.
Rt. #1, Box 162A
Princeton, MN 55371

National Reloading Manufacturers
   Association
1220 S.W. Morrison
Portland, OR 97205

Navy Arms Co.
689 Bergen Blvd.
Ridgefield, NJ 07657 ($1.00)

Netcraft Co.
3101 Sylvania Ave.
Toledo, OH 43613

Nikko Firearms
714 W. Algonquin Rd.
Arlington Hts., IL 60005

Nikon, Inc.
623 Stewart Ave.
Garden City, NY 11530

Nock-Rite Co.
3720 Crestview Circle
Brookfield, WI 53005

Norma Precision
Division of General Sporting Goods
   Corp.
South Lansing, NY 14882

Norman Camera
56 W. Michigan Mall
Battle Creek, MI 49017

Normark Corp.
1710 E. 78th St.
Minneapolis MN 55423 (50¢)

North American Arms
Freedom, WY 83120

The North Face
1234 5th St.
Berkeley, CA 94710

North Star Devices
P.O. Box 2095
North St. Paul, MN 55109

Nosler Bullets
P.O. Box 688
Beaverton, OR 97005

Numrich Arms Corp.
West Hurley, NY 12491 ($2.00)

Nylon Net Co.
P.O. Box 592
Memphis, TN 38101

Old Town Canoe Co.
35 Middle St.
Old Town, ME 04468

P.S. Olt Co.
Pekin, IL 61554

Omark Industries
Box 856
Lewiston, ID 83501

Oregon Freeze Dry Foods, Inc.
P.O. Box 1048
Albany, OR 97321 (SASE)

Orvis
10 River Rd.
Manchester, VT 05254

P. & S. Sales
P.O. Box 45095
Tulsa, OK 74145

Pacific Tool Co.
P.O. Box 2048
Grand Island, NE 68801

Padre Island Co.
P.O. Box 5310
San Antonio, TX 78201

Ben Pearson Archery
P.O. Box 270
Tulsa, OK 74101

Penguin Industries, Inc.
P.O. Box 97
Parkesburg, PA 19365

Peterson's Labels
P.O. Box 186
Redding Ridge, CT 06876

Plano Molding Co.
Plano, IL 60545

Plas/Steel Products, Inc.
Walkerton, IN 46574

Polar Kraft Mfg. Co.
P.O. Drawer 708
Olive Branch, MS 38654

Poly-Choke Co., Inc.
Box 296
Hartford, CT 06101

Ponder & Best, Inc.
P.O. Box 2105
Santa Monica, CA 90406

Ponsness-Warren, Inc.
P.O. Box 1818
Eugene, OR 97401

Porta-Leggs, Inc.
P.O. Box 1345
La Mesa, CA 92041

Porter's Camera Store, Inc.
Box 628
Cedar Falls, IA 50613

Quick Corporation of America
P.O. Box 938
Costa Mesa, CA 92627

Randall Made Knives
P.O. Box 1988
Orlando, FL 32802

Ranging, Inc.
90 Lincoln Rd. North
East Rochester, NY 14445

Ray-O-Vac Fishing Tackle Division
Box 488
Brainero, MN 56401 ($1.00)

Recreational Equipment, Inc.
P.O. Box 21685
Seattle, WA 98111

Redding Hunter, Inc.
114 Starr Rd.
Cortland, NY 13045

Redfield
5800 E. Jewell Ave.
Denver, CO 80224

Reliance Products, Ltd.
1830 Dublin Ave.
Winnipeg, Manitoba,
Canada R3H 0H3

Remington Arms Co., Inc.
Bridgeport, CT 06602

Republic Tool & Mfg. Co.
P.O. Box 1309
W. Caldwell, NJ 07006

Rigid Archery Products, Inc.
445 Central Ave.
Jersey City, NJ 07307

Rivers & Gilman
P.O. Box 206
Hampden, ME 04444

Hank Roberts
P.O. Box 308
Boulder, CO 80302

Rollei Of America, Inc.
100 Lehigh Dr.
Fairfield, NJ 07006

Rome Industries, Inc.
1703 W. Detweiller Dr.
Peoria, IL 61614

Rorco
Box 350
Alexandria, PA 16611

Rose City Archery, Inc.
Box 342
Powers, OR 97466

H.S. Ross
347 Buchanan St.
Twin Falls, ID 83301

Ross Laboratories, Inc.
3138 Fairview Ave., East
Seattle, WA 98102

Ryobi America Corp.
1555 Carmen Dr.
Elk Grove Village, IL 60007

Safariland, Ltd.
1941 S. Walker Ave.
Monrovia, CA 91016 ($2.00)

Saunders Archery Co.
P.O. Box 476
Columbus, NE 68601

Savage Arms Division
Emhart Industries, Inc.
Westfield, MA 01085

Sawyer Canoe Co.
234 S. State St.
Oscoda, MI 48750

Schwarz's Gun Shop
41 15th St.
Wellsburg, WV 26070

Scottish Pedlar, Ltd.
P.O. Box 314
South Orange, NY 07079

Seaway Importing Co.
7200 N. Oak Park Ave.
Niles, IL 60648

T.R. Seidel Co.
P.O. Box 268
Arvada, CO 80001

Shakespeare
P.O. Box 246
Columbia, SC 29202

Shaw-Leibowitz
Box 421
New Cumberland, WV 26047

Sheldon's, Inc.
P.O. Box 508
Antigo, WI 54409 (50¢)

Sheridan Products, Inc.
3205 Sheridan Rd.
Racine, WI 53403

Ship Shop, Inc.
294 New York Ave.
Huntington, NY 11743

Shurkatch Fishing Tackle Co., Inc.
P.O. Box 850
Richfield Springs, NY 13439

John T. Smith
6048 Cedar Crest Dr.
Southaven, MO 38671 ($1.00)

Smith & Wesson
2100 Roosevelt Ave.
Springfield, MA 01101

Smith's Game Calls
P.O. Box 236
Summerville, PA 15864

Snow Lion
P.O. Box 9056
Berkeley, CA 94701

South Bend Tackle Co., Inc.
P.O. Box 6249
Syracuse, NY 13217

Spiratone, Inc.
135-06 Northern Blvd.
Flushing, NY 11354 (35¢)

Sporting Book Service
Box 177
Rancocas, NJ 08073

Sterno
P.O. Box 540
Jersey City, NJ 07302

St. Lawrence Trading Co., Inc.
7340 Melrose St.
Buena Park, CA 90621 ($1.00)

Storm Mfg. Co.
P.O. Box 265
Norman, OK 73069

Strader Tackle, Inc.
P.O. Box 708
Havana, FL 32333

Sturm, Ruger & Co., Inc.
Southport, CT 06490

Super-8 Studios
220 Pierce St., No. 7
San Francisco, CA 94117

Suzuki International (USA), Inc.
13767 Freeway Dr.
Santa Fe Springs, CA 90670

TMD Knives
139 N.W. St. Helens Place
Bend, OR 97701 ($2.00)

B.D. Talley, Inc.
6110 Shadycliff
Dallas, TX 75240

Tasco Sales, Inc.
Box 380878
Miami, FL 33138

Tempo Products Co.
6200 Cochran Rd.
Cleveland, OH 44139

Ter Mar, Inc.
2300 8th St., S.W.
Lehigh Acres, FL 33936

Thompson/Center Arms
Rochester, NH 03867

Norm Thompson Outfitters
1805 N.W. Thurman St.
Portland, OR 97209

Trailex
120 Industrial Park Dr.
Canfield, OH 44406

Tread Corp.
P.O. Box 5497
Roanoke, VA 24012

Trimarc Corp.
High Point Plaza
Hillside, IL 60162

Triple-S Development Co., Inc.
1450 E. 289th St.
Wickliffe, OH 44092

Anton Udwary, Jr.
1432-B Dover Rd.
Spartanburg, SC 29301

UMCO Corp.
P.O. Box 608
Watertown, MN 55388

Uncle Josh Bait Co.
P.O. Box 130
Ft. Atkinson, WI 53538

Uniroyal Clothing Division
17 N.E. Fourth St.
Washington, IN 47501

Uniroyal Footwear Division
58 Maple St.
Naugatuck, CT 06770

United States Arms Corp.
P.O. Box 1011
Riverhead, NY 11901

Utica Duxbak Corp.
Utica, NY 13502

Val-Craft, Inc.
67 North Worcester St.
Chartley, MA 02712

Varmac Mfg. Co., Inc.
4201 Redwood Ave.
Los Angeles, CA 90066

VIchek Plastics Co.
P.O. Box 97
Middlefield, OH 44062

Weatherby, Inc.
2781 Firestone Blvd.
South Gate, CA 90280

W.R. Weaver Co.
El Paso, TX 79915

Western Cutlery Co.
P.O. Box 391
Boulder, CO 80306

Western Gunstock Mfg. Co.
550 Valencia School Rd.
Aptos, CA 95003 ($1.00)

West Fork, Inc.
Lakefield, MN 56150

W.C. Wilber
400 Lucerne Dr.
Spartanburg, SC 29302 ($2.00)

Wille Products Co.
P.O. Box 532
Brookfield, WI 53005

Williams Gun Sight Co.
7389 Lapeer Rd.
Davison, MI 48423 ($1.00)

Wilson-Allen Corp.
Windsor, MO 65630

Winchester-Western
P.O. Box 906
New Haven, CT 06504

Wood Mfg. Co.
P.O. Box 262
Flippin, AR 72634

Wright & McGill Co.
P.O. Box 16011
Denver, CO 80216

Yellow Birds, Inc.
P.O. Box 664
Sheboygan, WI 53081

York Archery
P.O. Box 110
Independence, MO 64051

Zak Tackle Mfg. Co.
235 South 59th St.
Tacoma, WA 98408

Zebco
P.O. Box 270
Tulsa, OK 74101

Carl Zeiss, Inc.
444 Fifth Ave.
New York, NY 10018

Zenith Enterprises
361 Flagler Rd.
Nordland, WA 98358